Forbes®

GREATEST
TECHNOLOGY
STORIES

Forbes®

GREATEST TECHNOLOGY STORIES

**Inspiring Tales
of the Entrepreneurs
and Inventors
Who Revolutionized
Modern Business**

JEFFREY YOUNG

John Wiley & Sons, Inc.

New York • Chichester • Weinheim • Brisbane • Singapore • Toronto

Copyright © 1998 by Forbes Inc. All rights reserved.
Forbes is a registered trademark. Its use is pursuant to a license agreement
with Forbes Inc.
Published by John Wiley & Sons, Inc.
Published simultaneously in Canada.

This publication is designed to provide accurate and authoritative information in
regard to the subject matter covered. It is sold with the understanding that the
publisher is not engaged in rendering professional services. If professional advice
or other expert assistance is required, the services of a competent professional person should be sought.

PICTURE CREDITS: Page xii: AP/Wide World; Page 32: IBM Archives; Page 62:
AP/Wide World; Page 86: AP/Wide World; Page 114: Intel Corporation, Santa
Clara, California; Page 148: *The Courier Herald*, Dublin, Georgia, and Ziff Davis
Publications, Inc.; Page 176: AP/Wide World; Page 212: IBM Corporation; Page
244: Microsoft Archives; Page 278: © Rex Rystedt Photography; Page 308: © Rich
Frishman

Library of Congress Cataloging-in-Publication Data:
Young, Jeffrey S., 1952–
    Forbes greatest technology stories : inspiring tales of the entrepreneurs and
inventors who revolutionized modern business / Jeffrey Young.
        p.   cm.
    Includes index.
    ISBN 0-471-24374-4 (alk. paper)
    1. Inventions—United States—History.   2. Inventors—United States—
History.   3. High technology—United States—History.   I. Title.
T21.Y68   1998
608.73—dc21   98-30590
                                                                    CIP

Printed in the United States of America.

10 9 8 7 6 5 4 3 2 1

CONTENTS

FOREWORD

So accustomed have we become to change and improvement in our daily lot and in the performance of the myriad tools that make modern life so comfortable, convenient, and relatively secure that we feel it is all somehow inevitable. A cash card from the bank just shows up in the mail, along with instructions on how to use it in ATM machines all over the world. At the grocery store one day, instead of pecking away at the cash register, the clerk simply sweeps the merchandise across a scanner. The largest bookstore in the world isn't to be found at the mall, but on the computer in your study via the Internet. Small wonder that we take progress for granted today. We see it almost as a force of nature, as certain as the wind and gravity.

There has been so much change in just the last 100 years that we can be forgiven this feeling. But it isn't true. Progress is not certain. Inventions don't just happen. Technologies don't simply appear in our lives. People make them happen. And that's what makes this book so fascinating and so important. It restores our sense of reality—and wonder—about the most ubiquitous and far-reaching technology of the last half century: the computer. Behind the screens, the disc drives, the semiconductors, and the software are human faces. Their stories are as exciting as they are extraordinary. Their achievements have transformed the world, but how they went about it, the emotions as well as the ideas that drove them, illuminate the very soul of progress.

Timothy C. Forbes

INTRODUCTION

◈

At the completion of the first half of the nineteenth century, the railraod and the telegraph stood supreme as the two inventions that transformed their era and ushered in a new age of modernity. At the close of our own century, who can argue that commercial jet travel and the digital electronic computer have changed us any less?

Life lived 50 years ago was far different than we experience it today. Command-and-control was the preferred method of organization back then. And why not? Command-and-control won World War II for the Allies; in the high desert plain of northern New Mexico in the summer of 1945, command-and-control produced the weapon that ended the war. It is important to recall that command-and-control was shot through *all* parts of American life, not just the military. In 1956 William Whyte wrote a best-seller called *The Organization Man*. The book preached conformity and obeisance to authority. So did popular movies like *The Man in the Grey Flannel Suit*. Network television attained a 92 percent market share in 1957, meaning we all watched the same shows on TV. It scarcely occurred to anybody that this represented a lack of choice.

In the 1950s, the U.S. Department of Justice successfully prosecuted and bankrupted a small outfit called The Hush-A-Phone Company. Its sin was selling a metal cup that attached to the mouthpiece of a telephone, designed to quiet the chatter in an office crammed with telephones. Illegal! The telephone company had a government-granted monopoly, and that was that.

The worst was yet to come. On October 4, 1957, the former Soviet Union launched a 100-pound metal ball into the earth's orbit. Sputnik I was a shocker. It was worrisome enough that the Soviets had kept pace with the American military's rollout of thermonuclear weapons during the early 1950s; now the Soviets possessed the rocket technology that could rule space and carry nuclear-tipped missiles over the North Pole.

Sputnik caused a national hand-wringing. It struck most intellectuals of the 1950s that the only thing wrong with the American style of command-and-control was too little of it! The Soviets could break a few eggs to make an omelet! James Burnham, a conservative intellectual of the 1950s, confided to *National Review* editor William F. Buckley, Jr., that America and its 181-year experiment in democracy were probably on history's losing side. Far more effective at ordering into existence all the necessary economic goods and military weapons were dictatorships like the former Soviet Union. Or so most intellectuals thought.

It sure looked bleak for the West in the autumn of 1957. But history is replete with irony, too. During the very darkest hours of 1957 came the first sparks of a digital electronic revolution that, like Zeus's lightning bolt, would go forth and slay command-and-control in all its organs and vestiges everywhere on the planet.

The spark jumped to life in July 1957. Eight young physicists in a Palo Alto laboratory staged a revolt against their boss. The boss had discovered that a tiny amount of gold wiring had turned up missing, and his plan was to subject all eight physicists to a lie detector test. The boss was no ordinary boss; it was William Shockley, the coinventor of the transistor and 1956 Nobel Prize winner in physics. He was an autocratic boss, but who wasn't in 1957? However, the eight young physicists were no ordinary young men, either. They included Robert Noyce, Gordon Moore, Eugene Kleiner, and five others, of whom much would be heard in the years ahead.

The eight physicists abruptly quit Shockley Labs, and quickly located a venture capitalist named Arthur Rock in San Francisco, who arranged for some seed capital from a New York financier named Sherman Fairchild. Thus was born, in August 1957, Fairchild Semiconductor. Two years later Noyce etched a transistor's circuitry onto a piece of silicon and called his invention an integrated circuit. Forty-one years later, in our own day, the integrated circuit's celebrated progeny, memory chips and microprocessors, roll off manufacturing floors like candy mints in Silicon Valley and Texas and Korea . . . in the millions per month . . . each tiny silicon mint carrying scores of millions of microscopic transistors. Talk about economies of scale! The price of a transistor has dropped some millionfold since Noyce's invention.

Today's average junior high school math class filled with 20 used PCs costing about $300 apiece contains more computational power than the Pentagon commanded in the days following Sputnik. The West's vastly superior computational power, a lead that started imperceptibly small but grew exponentially larger year by year thanks to the miracles of silicon, eventually grew so large that it brought down the Soviet empire. The symbol was the Afghan tribesman with a Stinger missile launcher resting on his shoulder. Just a tiny bit of silicon that endowed the Stinger missile with its heat-seeking capabilities was enough to turn a small band of Afghan tribesmen into the equal of a powerful invading army. Likewise, Western computational power put American businesses on a far faster trajectory, again, with a lead that grew every year. The results have been happy and thrilling for the West. Nikita Khrushchev's 1956 prediction that his Soviet Union would be around to witness the defeat of capitalism—"We will bury you"—has proven laughably off the mark.

Enjoy Jeffrey Young's romp through the 50-year history of the computer age. Centuries from now, the stories about the rise of the digital electronic revolution, which Mr. Young chronicles both accurately and entertainingly, will be read as fables of daring rebels who sneaked behind enemy lines, ransacked the command-and-control infrastructure, tore it out root and branch, and thus raised the hopes for all humankind that global democratic capitalism might enjoy a long and happy run after all.

Richard P. Karlgaard
Publisher, *Forbes*

J. Presper Eckert, foreground left and John W. Mauchly, leaning against pole, are pictured with the Electronic Numerical Integrator and Computer (ENIAC) in this undated photo.

Pioneers & Pirates

Calculators & Computers

After the Second World War, the American economy went on an explosive spurt. By 1950, median income tripled, rising to $3,000 a year— equal to $20,546 today. Inflation also took off: A pound of hamburger meat cost nearly $1, compared to 36 cents before the war. Cross-country telephone toll rates fell from $6.50 a minute to less than $2.25; call volumes doubled from 150 calls per day per 1,000 people, to 300. More than two-thirds of the nation's homes had telephones, compared to one-third before the war; and television sets were appearing throughout the country. By 1950, nearly twice as many Americans lived in urban areas (96 million) as in rural territories (54 million), a trend that had been accelerating since parity was last recorded in 1920. Even more striking, the number of office workers had grown to nearly 8 million. For the first time, there were more clerks than farm workers. It was a very good time to be selling a new and better office machine—the computer.

A number of technologies emerged from the war effort that would change life in the United States over the coming years—radar, tape recording, nuclear power—but none would have a deeper and more lasting influence than computers. The offspring of a classified project at the University of Pennsylvania called ENIAC (Electronic Numerical Integrator and Computer), by the mid-1950s, computers had entered mainstream American culture to the degree that in the 1957 movie Desk Set, *Spencer Tracy and Katharine Hepburn co-starred with a computer.*

The pair who patented work on the ENIAC, John Mauchly and Presper Eckert, were the first to try and profit from the new-fangled machines. But in the years immediately following the war, computers were of interest to only a specialized group, which included defense con-

tractors like Northrup, various government agencies, a few big commer-
cial companies like Prudential Insurance, or aggressive start-ups such as
A. C. Nielsen. The first machines cost pioneers more to build than
expected, and the engineering problems proved difficult to solve. With-
out many customers, it was hard to succeed.

Then, one entrepreneur appeared on the scene who would make the
fledgling business fly. When the dust settled, his company had captured
the public perception as the preeminent supplier of big machines in the
new field of computing. It was a company with a father-son tradition, a
deep respect for salesmanship, and a brand name known in every Amer-
ican office: Remington Rand.

❖   ❖   ❖

COMPUTERS, AND COMPUTING as we know it today, in a very real sense began one winter evening in December 1937, somewhere out on the flat roads and endless farmlands of the Iowa countryside. On that particular night, John Vincent Atanasoff, 34 years old and an associate professor in the Physics Department at Iowa State, took his new Ford Eight out for a drive after dinner.

It was a crisp, cold, and clear evening as he headed east out of Ames, a tiny college town 50 miles north of Des Moines in the heart of Iowa. He drove aimlessly, first turning left on the Lincoln Highway, then speeding away from the setting sun into the Iowa countryside. He sped past the red gambrel-roofed barns that were every farmer's pride and joy. In square corners and straight lines the road etched the boundaries of the surveyed "sections," each a square mile, 640 acres, in this undulating farmland. Rich, black soil, wheatlands, and cornfields were all covered in a white carpet of snow broken only by a few thin wisps of black smoke from distant farmhouse fireplaces.

As he drove his thoughts leaned toward his latest obsession: building a better calculator. In a high-backed wooden booth, at a run-down roadhouse, where he stopped for a few drinks, Atanasoff caught the seam between the mechanical age, which was just ending, and the digital age that was about to begin. As he made notes, all the pieces of the underlying architecture that we know today as a computer came into play. He jotted these concepts on paper napkins, while in the background billiard balls cracked together. Those primitive notes were to become the first digital electronic calculator, a machine that led directly to the digital age and the first computers.

That winter's evening in 1937 Atanasoff began to invent a new calculator, one that would fulfill his dream to become a successful inventor, get him out of the academic world he was disenchanted with, and most important, let him show up the science faculty, as well as the IBM tabulator salesmen, who continually spurned him.

There had been another rejection from the tabulator salesmen that very afternoon, refusing to make the modifications he wanted to IBM's punch card tabulators. The young professor was angry, angry enough to get into his car and drive a few hundred miles to have a drink in neighboring Illinois, where the teetotalers hadn't closed down the bars the way the religious zealots of Iowa had.

In 1937 America was a land of conformity, where the painful years of the Great Depression had produced fear, deep gut-knotting fear that kept much of the nation paralyzed. An estimated 20 percent of the population was unemployed; hobos rode the rails. That year saw the Flint sit-down strikes at General Motors. Industrial militancy was at its apex as workers tried to protect what little they had. America wanted to be isolated, to be able to lick its wounds and remake itself. Even when the Japanese sank a U.S. patrol boat during their invasion of China, American statesmen thundered, but took no action.

Atanasoff was luckier than most. He owned a small house near the campus, and was the father of two small sons. He had a good job that paid him $1,000 a year, a fortune compared to the average salary in America of $600 a year. And he had a new car. It had all come easily for the bright young professor. As a result, he was insulated from the fear that gripped most Americans. This contributed to his image as a misfit, a square peg in the round hole of Iowa State University, a practical place dedicated to the fields of veterinary medicine, engineering, industrial science, home economics, and most of all, agricultural instruction. It was a school short on theory and long on practice, and a place where conventional wisdom was rarely questioned.

It was also a place populated by farm kids who knew how to fix a tractor when it broke down in the middle of a field far from the nearest farm implement store, a place where the governing principle was "Make it yourself," which suited Atanasoff perfectly. An inveterate tinkerer, he was an inventor with a passion, even a sixth sense for calculating machines. He was a dreamer who was also thin-skinned enough to let the smug faculty and the IBM clowns get to him. His response would be to figure out how to make a calculator that was better than anything else on the market; he would show them just how shortsighted they were, all the way to the bank.

As he schooled his graduate students in the problems of theoretical quantum physics, the lack of an efficient calculating system had become increasingly frustrating. Instead of waiting for a better calculating machine to show up in Ames, Atanasoff decided to build one himself. He believed that somewhere in the nexus of electronics and machinery was an answer, but try as he might, so far he couldn't find it. At the time, the professional literature was filled with descriptions of the Bush Differential Analyzer. This machine, created by Vannevar Bush at the Massachusetts Institute of Technology (MIT), soon to be Roosevelt's chief wartime science advisor, used a number of gears and shafts to increase the slide rule's capabilities. This state-of-the-art machine comprised a 50-foot series of dials and rods with spinning barrels that were set by hand. Essentially, it was an overgrown slide rule, which took several people to operate. Atanasoff, along with a grad student, built a gear-driven machine inspired by the analyzer to calculate simple systems of equations with two variables. But accuracy was only possible to three significant numbers; and the systems of equations Atanasoff was facing involved 30 variables and 30 equations, which were far beyond the scope of these machines.

Atanasoff was one of the few people in the world at that time thinking about manipulating circuit elements—resistors, amplifiers, and capacitors—to create an electronic calculator. He had no literature to consult, no prior work to examine. He would have to invent his own methods.

Eventually, out in central Iowa part of the answer came to him. Binary Numbers. He recalled his mother teaching him binary math. Before marriage, she had been a schoolteacher, and when her precocious son figured out the principles of a slide rule at age 10, in 1915, she started teaching him advanced math. The lessons included binary calculation, for which she had a passion.

All counting systems are based on a recurring pattern of a certain number of digits. American math is called Base 10—1 through 9, then a carry 1 is paired with a 0 to create 10; and so on. Number systems can be any base, say Base 4. In that scheme, 10 would be written as 22. But the number written as 10 would actually be 4. Binary math is significant because each number can be a 0 or a 1. So writing 10 would be 1010. This numbering scheme has some characteristics particularly good for any machine that has to count, because every position in a number is either on or off. Storing a number is also limited only by the number of digits that can be strung together, the number of on/off switches in a row. These are called *registers*, mechanical or electronic places where digits in a calculation or operation can be stored.

Later, Atanasoff couldn't recall why binary suddenly clicked, and gave him the direction he needed. He would convert all numbers to binary digits—strings of ones or zeros. Electronic impulses—the presence or absence of charge, a 1 or a 0—could represent each digit. It was elegant in its simplicity, and the more he examined the idea, the more he liked it.

He had a start, but how could he make it all work? Years earlier, two very important machines had been built that were going to play a role in his solution. Around 1800, a French inventor named Joseph-Marie Jacquard, the son of a weaver, invented the first automatic loom. Working with thick paper cards, he devised a method of punching patterns of holes in the cards. Through each hole a particular wire, controlling a particular thread from the many that made up the warp of the weave, moved up bringing that thread into the next pass of the loom; or if the hole were blocked, down and out of the pass. Single rows of holes represented the threads to be woven in a given pass of the loom; a series of rows of holes punched into the cards could represent complex patterns. Many cards were used to make up intricate drapery and upholstery fabrics, and these could be used repeatedly. It was probably the first machine that could be "programmed" in a binary sense. Each punched hole was the equivalent of either a 1 or a 0 in binary notation, although Jacquard never used it for mathematical purposes. French handweavers of the time saw the Jacquard loom as a threat to their livelihood, and burned a number of them to protect their livelihood; they even attacked Jacquard personally. Nonetheless, the business utility of the cards outweighed the fears of the counterrevolutionaries. By 1812, there were an estimated 11,000 punchcard looms in use in France.

Then, in the 1830s in England, Lord Byron's daughter Ada Lovelace and her associate Charles Babbage conceived of a calculating machine called the Analytical Engine. The machine grew out of Babbage's earlier work, called the Difference Engine, completed in the 1820s. This was a mechanical device for creating logarithmic and astronomical tables. Babbage, a fellow of the Royal Society, was also active in the Astronomical Society. At the time the British government was offering a reward to the person who could find a way to automate the making of astronomical tables. The British Navy was essential to the nation's colonial empire, and all navigation was celestial. Babbage's invention won him acclaim, but very little money because the British government reneged on the deal. Fortunately, he was independently wealthy.

The more elaborate Difference Engine developed by Babbage and Lovelace incorporated the Jacquard concept to read in data from a stack of punched cards. But they intended to do more: They wanted to store data in registers, perform arithmetic operations on these numbers, and eventually print them out. Lovelace conceived of the programming instructions as an element separate from the numbers themselves; these were the underpinnings of today's programming languages. Sadly, they never built the machine. And though it was not electronic in any way, it did have one very intriguing idea: that a complex machine should have both a store and mill, the precursors of memory and a computer. This was the same conclusion that John Vincent Atanasoff came to that wintry evening in 1937, and he had never heard of Babbage or Lovelace. Living in an intellectual vacuum, driven by desire, anger, and a hope for a better economic life, and goaded by his disbelieving peers, he had imagined a new kind of calculating machine that would combine a memory region for storing numbers electronically, connected to a calculation engine that would operate on them entirely electronically.

Atanasoff would use the binary numbering system, though few were familiar with it and fewer still were comfortable with it. Its elegance, as Atanasoff knew from his years of fiddling with analog counting and calculating devices, was that he could make his machine as precise as he wanted. Binary digits don't leave room for interpretation as do a big differential analyzer and calculator shaft. As long as his circuits specifically differentiated between a 1 and a 0, as long as there was a threshold below which everything was 0, above which everything was 1, the eventual calculation would be as precise as the number of binary digits, or "bits," his memory system and registers could handle.

Once he had decided on the numbering system, he needed a way to store those ones and zeroes. At first, he thought he would have to use vacuum tubes, lots of vacuum tubes, because they were the key elements from which his circuits could be built. A tube could either store a charge or control current passing through it. One way or another, he could configure circuits using tubes to represent binary digits.

But this posed a problem. In 1937, vacuum tubes were expensive— a few dollars each at a minimum—and if he wanted fancier ones, he would have to pay $10 apiece. Where was he going to get that kind of money? Even if he limited himself to 266 bits of memory—offered by the best IBM calculators of the day—that would mean an outlay of more than $2,000 for the number registers alone. Then there was the additional circuitry necessary to do anything with the machine. Clearly, he would have to come up with something better. He needed both a program storage station—where he intended to use IBM punch cards to read in numbers for computation—and an interim storage place, or memory bank, for midequation numbers and partial answers.

Punch cards were the world's standard for data storage and recovery, and they had come a long way by 1937. Reinvented by Herman Hollerith in the 1880s, they were used by the U.S. Census Bureau in 1890. Punched holes represented data, and by counting the pattern of electrical contacts, which were made through a punched hole or stopped by an unperforated space, Hollerith designed devices to tabulate, manage, and manipulate data. He patented the devices, and worked hard to maintain his market advantage. However, his company—the Tabulating Machine Company—eventually fell on hard times, only to be rescued by a former National Cash Register salesman, Thomas Watson. Watson promptly renamed the company International Business Machines, organized a paternalistic team of crack salesmen, and stopped selling tabulators. Instead, Watson planned to lease the tabulators, and completely control the market both for punched cards in the format required by IBM machines and for the machines themselves. No modifications could be made to the machines, and no company but IBM could manufacture the punch cards used in IBM machines.

It was a brilliant strategy. By the 1930s, IBM's machines were fixtures in most big offices, where account details and records were keypunched onto cards using special typewriters. Stacks of cards were fed into tabulators, which tallied the numbers on the cards, then spit out an answer to a query or equation on a paper tape printout or on more cards. Initially, the data was not read electrically, but it wasn't long before IBM started producing top-of-the-line calculating machines using a complicated Base 10 system of number storage, assisted by vacuum tubes. These were the most advanced adding machines on the market; they stood about 3 feet and could work on any two numbers—as long as neither was greater than 266. They were also expensive, costing $1,000 at the time, the equivalent of $6,850 in 1998.

This was far outside of Atanasoff's budget. In any case, the punch card calculator systems were too slow for his electronic computation circuits, so he developed a completely different way to store his digits, at a fraction of the cost of IBM's system. He used paper capacitors, an interim method that made it possible to write over numbers with new ones during a calculation. He knew a lot about them; they were part of his Ph.D. dissertation. The capacitors cost only pennies apiece and stored a charge (or the absence of charge) as long as their power was refreshed every second or so. Although they couldn't control and amplify circuits like tubes, Atanasoff didn't need that capability simply for storing charges, and thus the binary digits. He imagined that with capacitors he could build large storage subsystems—repositories for both initial numbers and interim calculations; what today is called memory—at low cost, but only if he could figure out how to keep lots of them refreshed simultaneously. As he doodled on that cold December night, he started to imagine a way to use capacitors. Mount them on a spinning drum, he thought, electrical contacts facing out, and sweep them past charged brushes once a second; as long as the capacitors were electrically refreshed every second, they would store a state—charge, or no charge, 1 or 0—indefinitely.

On a series of napkins, Atanasoff furiously drew the design for a bicycle chain–driven system, attached to a homespun drum of capacitors. He now had two key pieces of a digital calculator: a numerical system based on binary numbers and a possible system for storing a string of digits during a computation, to allow that number to be worked on subsequently by the machine. He needed only one other thing: a method for calculating the numbers, for doing the arithmetic. As he continued scribbling, he had an inspiration that would change the world: to build circuits that could directly handle two binary numbers and calculate their product electronically. He would do mathematics by direct manipulation, not by enumeration.

This was a revolutionary concept. Calculation, computation, had always been done by enumeration; that is, adding 8 to 8 to 8 to 8 to 8, for example, as the analog for multiplying 8 times 5. This was the only way to do this in an analog world, where each 8 clicked through five teeth on a gear, then forward five times on a shaft. Atanasoff saw that, in a binary system, where every digit in a number is represented by a 1 or a 0, he could directly add two numbers electronically. By lining up the binary numbers and combining their charges, representing the answer entirely as a string of charges and noncharges (e.g., 10011), he could perform addition or subtraction without moving out of the electronic realm. Thus was born the first digital addition circuit. This would operate at the speed of electrons, and so could achieve astonishingly fast calculation times compared to an analog calculator. Once he achieved that, all that was left was to convert that binary number back, so that the average person—as opposed to a mathematician—could read the answer easily.

In a flurry of activity on the backs of more napkins, Atanasoff worked out a series of circuits. The basis of his system were circuits known as AND, NOT, and OR gates, which are now the basis of all digital computation. Numbers, represented by a string of ones and zeros, charges or no charges, move through the circuits and line up for addition or subtraction. Binary math has only three possible outcomes at every register place for a pair of numbers: 1, 0, or a carry digit of 1 and a 0. Nothing else fits, and so it is perfectly suited to electronic math using circuits. With this logical underpinning for addition, he could do the same for subtraction. Eventually, with a little more pencil work, Atanasoff created circuits that did math electronically. In these circuits, numbers would be manipulated entirely in the electronic realm, at speeds never before possible. An unimaginably complex number could be multiplied by another equally complex number, and the result, captured in the memory capacitors, could be multiplied again and again, essentially instantaneously.

Needless to say, having the basic insight on the workings of his machine, what he called an "add-subtract mechanism," was entirely different from figuring out how to actually design and build the thing. For a year after Atanasoff returned from his night in Illinois, he refined and redefined his computing machine. Finally he wrote and submitted a proposal to the holders of the research purse strings at the university. In spring 1939, the Iowa State College Research Council granted him $650 to hire a research assistant, buy some materials, and contract with the college machine shop for made-to-order parts.

Atanasoff was a flamboyant thinker, full of emotion and brilliant insight; and he was a captivating lecturer and creative engineer. But he didn't have the methodical nature necessary to, for example, dig through an entire wiring loom to find the one connector that had come unsoldered. He was a kind of wild-eyed inventor and academic—not a great engineer, and certainly not a businessman. To move forward, he needed a highly competent engineer, because there was no precedent for his machine, no other machines to look at, no textbooks to refer to. Atanasoff's schematics were the outpourings of a burst of brilliance, but the machine had to be built to make the genius of his design a reality. Luckily, he found the man who could build it; his name was Cliff Berry.

Berry was a genius—that's what everyone had been saying since he was in grade school. He had graduated from high school at 16 with a straight A average, and was class valedictorian. He was a small, thoughtful, shy kid, who had a twinkle in his eyes barely discernible behind his round eyeglasses; he was delicate and precise, with an almost uncanny ability to make all things electronic work. He was also an early ham radio operator, who had spent hours hunched over his rig talking with fellow enthusiasts. By the mid-1930s, almost everyone had a radio, and Berry was popular for his ability to diagnose and solve every sort of problem in a circuit.

When it came time for college, Berry's mother wanted him to stay near the family, so for an extra year he stayed on at high school taking additional courses. Then it was on to Iowa State, where he studied electrical engineering. He worked his way through college as a technician at Gulliver Electric, a contractor in the Ames area. He graduated in 1939, at the top of his class in the engineering school.

Atanasoff had taught Berry in a couple of physics courses and when Berry needed a job, they struck a deal. When school started again in the fall, Berry would be Atanasoff's paid research assistant while studying for his master's degree. It was the grad student who breathed life into Atanasoff's apparatus. It worked like this: The calculator combined bicycle gears and electronics. Numbers were entered from modified

IBM punch card readers, then stored on a drum, using the capacitors that Atanasoff had imagined a year or more earlier. All their "feet," or terminals, pointed out, where they brushed across metal commutators made of copper brushes; this provided the essential electrical refresh cycle. With its collection of paper capacitors glued together, a cross-section of the drum looked like a honeycomb. It spun via a simple bicycle crank gear and was chain-driven by an electric motor. There were two of these drums, each of which held the numbers for one side of an equation and rotated at exactly one revolution per second. There were 50 rows of 30 capacitors on each, 1,500 digital binary bits in total—1.5 kilobits in modern usage—which could store a large string of binary numbers.

With all the numbers loaded, and both drums spinning to keep the charged drums electrically refreshed, Atanasoff and Berry entered a pair of numbers into the mechanism. Today, this is known as the central processing unit, or CPU. The two engineers kept their fingers crossed. The result—in the form of a string of charges and noncharges—was read into one of the drums while the other retained the operand. The operation could be repeated once every few seconds as long as the two drums stayed synchronized—a big problem that was never satisfactorily solved.

But there was a more immediate problem: recording the answer. The answer to an equation might be in the drum memory while everything was spinning, but there was no way to see it. Handling this many bits at a time, and punching them out instantaneously and simultaneously, was far beyond then current punch card equipment capabilities. Berry devised a modification of an IBM punch card printer that burnt holes in the cards. This "arc method"—whereby a grid of contacts, arranged on either side of a punch card, simultaneously fired (or did not fire) a spark depending on whether a charge was present at that position—was the best Berry could produce. When the system was working, it was as if Rube Goldberg had entered the physics building: The two big drums whirred, bicycle chains clanked, and the smell of burnt paper filled the air; the zap of the high-voltage arcs reverberated down the corridors. Everyone in the building knew when the computing device was in operation.

In spite of the difficulties, by the end of 1940, they had it working well enough to be able to calculate a series of complicated equations for graduate students and professors. One of Atanasoff's faculty colleagues said, "It'll never run a streetcar." Nonetheless, Atanasoff and Berry were already formulating plans to produce small business manufacturing calculating machines. They had exhaustively searched the literature, both patent and technical, and could find no evidence that anyone else was thinking about electronic calculation, let alone doing anything about it. Still, they were dreaming. Neither man was a businessman; both were scientists and academics. So they proceeded in the only way they knew how: by applying for a grant. In the fall of 1940, they wrote a detailed grant proposal, which explained their theoretical underpinnings and carefully enumerated the workings of the prototype; it also pointed out its remaining trouble spots, and laid out a careful and fiscally conservative budget for taking the machine to the next level: a computing machine that could be used by several groups at Iowa State and that could be patented. They estimated their budget at $5,000.

The Iowa Research Council took the proposal under advisement, but truth be told, they didn't see much business future for the idea. They were dissuaded by other professors who thought it was a waste of time and resources. Furthermore, it seemed likely to antagonize IBM, a major supporter of computation classes at the school. Atanasoff was out of luck; no new funding would be forthcoming, although the council did continue to pay for Berry's assistant salary.

In December 1940, Atanasoff went to Philadelphia for the annual meeting of the American Association for the Advancement of Science, AAAS. In the era before instantaneous communications connected the globe, these meetings were crucial for scientists, allowing them to find out what was going on in hundreds of academic and commercial R&D labs all over the country. Atanasoff was actively looking for any evidence of similar electronic calculation going on elsewhere. In one of the sessions, he heard a talk given by a local Philadelphia area college professor on the subject of using machine computation to compare weather and solar activity.

Meteorology, with its complex mix of statistical data and fluid dynamics, is one of the world's most computationally intensive fields. The best that had been done up to that time, used a big Bush Differential Analyzer at the Moore School of Engineering in the University of Pennsylvania, which calculated the weather two weeks after it had already happened! The speaker, John W. Mauchly, despaired of ever getting through enough data to make much headway, and openly speculated that electronics seemed to offer the possibility of an answer, though no one had yet figured out how. Afterward, Atanasoff approached Mauchly and told him he had already built a machine that used electronics to solve complex sets of equations—and cheaply—less than $2 a digit.

Mauchly, a trim, witty man, who had grown up in the academic world, was incredulous but fascinated. His father was a physicist as well, heading up the Department of Terrestrial Magnetism at the Carnegie Institute in Washington, D.C. The son eventually earned a Ph.D. in physics from Johns Hopkins in 1932, and was hired a year later to teach the subject at a small college, Ursinus, in Philadelphia. There he started investigating the effect of cosmic rays and solar flares on weather patterns on earth. Though most meteorologists dismissed this as a harebrained idea, Mauchly was an academic theorist and an unconventional thinker. In the late thirties he had tried to build a number of calculating machines and had studied the literature on others.

But Mauchly was stymied in these efforts because he wasn't an electrical engineer, and he lacked a practical turn of mind. Furthermore, as he revealed in a letter to a friend, he was much more concerned with the glory of creating an electronic calculating machine than with the intellectual challenge of actually solving the problem. "Keep this dark, since I haven't the equipment this year to carry it out," he wrote around the time he gave the speech Atanasoff heard, referring to some musings he had about an electronic computing machine, "I would like to be the first."

So when Atanasoff told him that he had already built such a device, Mauchly was very interested, enough so that within days following the AAAS meeting, he wrote to Atanasoff asking if he might make a trip to Iowa so he could inspect the machine and have it explained to him in detail. The inventor was only too happy to have someone take an interest in his machine, and invited Mauchly to visit. Atanasoff was not above stretching the truth regarding his operation, referring to the then pending Iowa Research Council grant as "an outside source"; and in another letter writing that "pieces for the computing machine are coming off the production line." In reality, at the height of the project, his entire staff comprised one paid and two volunteer graduate students.

Nevertheless, Mauchly was interested, partially because Atanasoff was not very forthcoming with details, promising to reveal the secrets of his system only when Mauchly visited. The inventor also mentioned that Samuel Caldwell, one of the designers of the Bush Differential Analyzer, had just visited in connection with some top-secret national defense work that Caldwell was then engaged in. In fact, Caldwell wasn't at all interested in the unlikely looking calculator in the Physics Building basement; he had actually asked Atanasoff to take command of a different and critically important area of research: the design of fuses, the acoustic and pressure detonators used in bombs.

To be sure, Atanasoff was intrigued by the opportunity offered by Caldwell, but in the summer of 1941, Atanasoff's calculator machine project was still his top priority, although working in Iowa presented obstacles. "I am somewhat out of the beaten track of computing machine gossip, and so am always interested in any details you can give me," he wrote in one of his letters to Mauchly, who was right in the middle of the buzz about electronic calculation, such as it was then. Not only did the Moore School have one of the few Bush Differential Analyzers, but in nearby New Jersey, Bell Labs' George Stiebitz had built an electromechanical computer that used magnetic relays (a charge magnetizes a pair of contacts, clicking them closed and completing a circuit, while no charge demagnetizes them and forces them apart) to perform its logical functions. It was slow, and a strange hybrid of the mechanical and the electronic; nonetheless, it was a working computing machine.

When Mauchly finally arrived in Ames in June, at the end of the academic year, after days of driving across the flat and rolling midlands of America, he was sure that he had made a mistake. He couldn't believe anything of value was being created in the middle of nowhere. He turned to his 10-year-old son, who had accompanied him and said, "We'll only be here for a day or two, then we'll head back to civilization."

After dropping his son off with Atanasoff's wife for babysitting, the two men headed directly over to the Physics Department basement, to see the machine in its operational glory. For the next five days, they barely surfaced for air while its inventor took the would-be meteorologist through every component of his machine, explaining the logic circuits in excruciating detail, over and over again until his visitor understood them perfectly. He ran equations through the punch card reader, showing Mauchly the secret of the electronically refreshed memory drums. Cliff Berry demonstrated the arc and spark punch card technique for capturing numbers by fire. This was still not working very well, so for a couple of days Mauchly, Atanasoff, and Berry worked on it together, trying to make it more accurate. At night, Mauchly pored over the only copy of a book of documentation that Atanasoff and Berry had compiled for the university patent lawyer. There wasn't a single piece of the machine, its logic, or its operation that the Iowa State team hid from Mauchly. They were the very proud fathers of a new kind of calculating machine, and wanted to share their passion with an obvious enthusiast.

Mauchly, for his part, was fascinated by what he saw, although dismayed by the glue-and-baling wire character of the machine. Amazingly, Atanasoff had been able to perform direct mathematical calculation in an electronic realm, using several circuit boards populated with only the standard components of electronics. Though he couldn't really understand it, Mauchly had to admit that the electronic adder circuitry and the decision to use binary numbers seemed inspired. However, a mathematician, Mauchly would remain mystified by this binary aspect of the machine.

The memory drums, on the other hand, were fairly unsophisticated; they operated at only one revolution per second, and thus were far slower than electric current frequencies, which operated at 60,000 cycles per second. This, Mauchly thought, was a weakness. Still, the low-cost memory refresh scheme was brilliant in its simplicity.

"The construction of a differential analyzer on a dime-store basis," as Atanasoff liked to say, was a revelation. In comparison, the Bush Differential Analyzer at the Moore School had cost more than half a million dollars, and it wasn't as accurate or as fast as Atanasoff's machine. Sure there were lingering problems on Atanasoff's machine, primarily that it was built specifically to solve partial differential equations only, and so couldn't be used for other problems. But the cost of this bicycle gear-driven, electronic-circuit powered, cheap condenser memory device was one five-hundredth as expensive as the Differential Analyzer. This was a stunning realization for Mauchly as he watched it go through 30 calculations per minute, minute after minute—until the drums lost synchronization due to wobble and chain slackness.

Mauchly's visit was cut short five days later when his wife called to tell him that he had been accepted in a special summer National Defense–sponsored electrical engineering program for postgrads at the Moore School. Mauchly leapt at the chance. He had been hoping to get hired at the University of Pennsylvania and thought this program might be a way in. He headed back across the country filled with thoughts of digital calculation.

As patriotism became rampant across the country, Atanasoff turned his attention to the war effort, leaving Cliff Berry to improve the first two full-scale production models of the computer until he could get back to the project. Atanasoff did take the time to write several letters to the university patent attorney, trying to provide the documentation required to proceed, and to fan the fire under the commercial possibilities he foresaw for his invention. But the lawyer took his time; after all, he didn't understand what he had in his files. He couldn't see that computing devices had much future. Furthermore, Atanasoff was not particularly popular among the faculty where the math staff wasn't interested in the device.

But Mauchly continued to be excited by it, and all through the summer he thought about what he had seen in the Iowa laboratory. The National Defense summer program had exactly the effect he had hoped for: the Moore School hired him as an instructor in the fall, and so this ambitious man was able to leave Ursinus and head for the much more prestigious environs of the University of Pennsylvania. That fall, 1941, he started talking about his ideas for a computing device with a bright young grad student at the Moore School by the name of J. Presper Eckert, Jr.

Eckert, the only child of a wealthy real estate developer, had attended the best private school in Philadelphia, and somewhere along the line, had become fascinated with electronics. He spent his adolescence in the garage hunched over a workbench, creating strange electronic devices, such as a crystal radio that fit into the space of an eraser on the end of a pencil. At the Moore School, he graduated at the top of his class in 1941 in electrical engineering; every summer, he did consulting work for the legions of electronics companies that were clustered in the region. Though he could be abrasive and abrupt, qualities that rubbed many the wrong way, his electronics skills were dazzling. He would eventually be awarded more than 85 patents in his career.

Mauchly met Eckert while attending the summer engineering course, where the younger man—Eckert was 12 years his junior—was the lab manager. In him Mauchly found a kindred spirit. They both cared deeply for electronics and calculating machines, and often talked about new circuits and ideas far into the night. When Mauchly was hired at UPenn, they were able to spend even more time together. It wasn't long before Mauchly was bending the younger man's ear about the possibilities of using vacuum tubes as the guts of a better type of differential analyzer. But he never mentioned that he had already seen exactly the kind of computing device that he was describing in Iowa earlier that year, albeit on a smaller scale than the grand machine the two of them were talking about. Eckert, therefore, believed the ideas were Mauchly's.

In their combined vision, they saw tens of thousands of tubes, no money-saving capacitors or bicycle gears. At the time, however, there was one argument against using vacuum tubes—they were unreliable; they got hot, then failed at inopportune times. But Eckert, an amateur organist, had taken apart a Hammond organ that used vacuum tubes to discover the secret to its legendary reliability: Its tubes never ran at full power, which made the tubes last much longer. Eckert couldn't see why they could not do the same thing for a computing machine.

At one point, Mauchly did have a moment of remorse for keeping his plans from Atanasoff. Shortly after he had started working at the Moore School in the fall of 1941, he sent a formal letter to Atanasoff, dated September 30. It started off chatty, mentioning his new job and differential analyzers. Then it got to the point:

> Is there any objection, from your point of view, to my building some sort of computer which incorporates some of the features of your machine? For the time being, of course, I shall be lucky to find time and material to do more than make exploratory tests of some of my different ideas, with the hope of getting something very speedy, not too costly, etc.
>
> Ultimately a second question might come up, of course, and that is, in the event that your present design were to hold the field against all challengers, and I got the Moore School interested in having something of the sort, would the way be open for us to build an "Atanasoff Calculator" (à la Bush analyzer) here?

Mauchly knew that no one else in the world had done anything even remotely as advanced as the Atanasoff-Berry Computer, but now he had found a talented engineer who could help him build one himself. Atanasoff had been the creative genius; he had come up with the binary number scheme, the plan to do direct addition and subtraction by electronic circuits, and to use an electronic memory store that fed numbers into the calculation engine. Charitably, Mauchly was coopting it.

Atanasoff realized what was at stake as soon as he received Mauchly's letter. On October 7, he replied, in a tone that was friendly, but that made clear the restrictions he was imposing on the material Mauchly had been shown. The second paragraph read:

> Our attorney has emphasized the need of being careful about the dissemination of information about our device until a patent application is filed. This should not require too long, and, of course, I have no qualms about having informed you about our device, but it does require that we refrain from making public any details for the time being. It is, as a matter of fact, preventing me from making an invited address to the American Statistical Association. . . .

Later that month, when Atanasoff passed through Philadelphia on his way from Washington to Cambridge, he and Mauchly didn't meet. By 1942, following the attack on Pearl Harbor, every red-blooded American engineer went into national service in some capacity. At the end of the year, Cliff Berry moved to Los Angeles where he joined a defense contractor, Consolidated Engineering. That same summer, Atanasoff went to Washington D.C. to continue his work in a highly classified division of the Naval Ordnance Lab on fuses and bombs. He stayed in touch with Mauchly, but it became clear their paths were going in very different directions.

Following Atanasoff's departure from Iowa State, the patent application that he had worked so hard to keep open became lost in the lawyer's file drawer for more than 20 years. A wartime shortage of components required that the two working models of the Atanasoff-Berry Computer be dismantled, and their parts were put to use in other physics and electrical engineering projects. The memory drums, the only elements that couldn't be torn apart, were stored in a dusty room near the boiler in the Physics Building. The project, never very popular among other faculty, was forgotten.

When President Roosevelt declared war in 1941, the Army's Ballistics Lab team commandeered the Bush Differential Analyzer from the Moore School to create firing tables. These were books of master tables that gunnery officers used to calculate the range of a weapon in varying conditions. The numbers were different for each type of weapon, from mortars to naval 16-inchers, and took into account prevailing winds, the resiliency of the ground underfoot, elevation of the barrel, and size of the shell. Since errors could mean death to servicemen, it was crucial that every number be checked and rechecked. To complete the necessary number of firing tables, they also needed hundreds of college educated female "computers" to do the math calculations by hand. It was one of the better jobs for educated women in those days; and it was generally thought, and accepted, that women were better at doing intricate mathematics than men—certainly they were cheaper. However, by the summer of 1942, six months into it, the project was falling behind. The vast and uncertain terrain where the war was being fought was forcing wholesale recalculation of the firing tables. A single set of trajectories could take as long as five days to compute. The Differential Analyzer could do the same work in one hour, but there was a catch. The machine was accurate only to about 1 percent, a failing caused by the physical limits of gears and dials. For a shell fired 5 miles, this meant an error of 250 feet—which was by no means acceptable. Worse, a single firing table, with between 3,000 and 4,000 trajectories, took a month to produce, even running the machine two shifts a day. (A third shift performed maintenance to keep the analyzer working.) The situation was desperate.

The man in charge of the Moore operation was U.S. Army First Lieutenant Herman Goldstine, who had a Ph.D. in mathematics from the University of Michigan. He arrived in the fall of 1942 and found utter chaos. His first move was to commandeer every mechanical calculator and adding machine he could find in the region. Then he hired 200 more human "computers." Nevertheless, by early 1943, the project was falling further and further behind.

One morning in March of that year, Goldstine was bemoaning the backlog, and was overheard by one of Mauchly's former students. The student told Goldstine that one of his former instructors had an idea to use electronics to speed up computation by at least one thousand times. Goldstine, who by then was willing to grasp at straws, immediately went in search of the instructor. That same morning, in a cramped office at the Moore School of Engineering, Goldstine heard from Mauchly himself about the electronic digital computing machine that he believed in. It was a tube-based version of Atanasoff's and Berry's work, with one critical difference: It didn't use binary numbers, which Mauchly had never understood. (Eckert, too, had missed its significance.) The tube-based version would need thousands of tubes, generate a lot more heat, and in short, be far more complex and take up much more room than its progenitor. But Goldstine told him to write it up.

Mauchly and Eckert spent the next few days writing a detailed memo about their machine. Mauchly, with no more experience in electrical engineering than that single summer course at the Moore School two years earlier, was the visionary. Eckert, with his sixth sense about electronic devices, turned the ideas into a practical proposal. However, there were still a number of points that Mauchly couldn't explain. So a few days later he showed up unannounced in the top-secret lab in Maryland where Atanasoff had been assigned. Atanasoff's surprise turned to pride as Mauchly quizzed him on the trouble spots of his machine. Pleading national security, Mauchly wouldn't reveal what he was working on. Over the next few years, there would be numerous similar, unexpected meetings. Atanasoff wondered what was going on, but his work kept him too busy to find out what. In any case, he had moved on by then.

On April 9, 1943, the brass at the Ballistics Research Lab approved the Mauchly-Eckert project, called the ENIAC, an acronym for Electronic Numerical Integrator and Computer. That day, John Vincent Atanasoff was at work 150 miles to the south at the Naval Ordnance Lab. His name was not mentioned in conjunction with the Mauchly-Eckert project, and it would be years before he realized that not only the fundamental conceptual design, but also each of the addition-subtraction circuits, were direct copies of his and Berry's work. Over the years, Atanasoff was awarded numerous patents—more than 100 in his lifetime—but he never again turned his attention to computers, in part because of his disgust at what he considered piracy on the part of Mauchly, but also because once the computer had been officially invented, it held little interest for him. Eventually, he was identified as the true inventor of the computer but not until a landmark legal decision—*Honeywell vs. Sperry Rand*—in 1973, which invalidated the patents of Eckert and Mauchly. Atanasoff died in 1994.

Clifford Berry stayed in southern California after the war, working for various aerospace contractors. Atanasoff and Berry lost touch, so Berry never knew that the machine he had helped to create—which was named the ABC, for Atanasoff-Berry Computer by his former partner—was directly responsible for the development of computing in the United States. In 1963, he committed suicide, ten years before the legal decision that established his place in the history of computing.

As the ENIAC project was launched, Mauchly was credited with the brilliant concept of using electronic circuits and vacuum tubes to create a computing machine. Making a machine that worked, then selling it, were future obstacles.

By early 1944, the ENIAC design had been set, and machine construction began. Deemed top secret, and engineered by a team of top-flight young electrical engineers, it was an expensive project funded entirely by the war effort. The machine ended up costing $400,000 and succeeded in proving the electronic calculator concept, although it was finished in 1945, too late to do any good for the artillery tables. The machine comprised 19,000 vacuum tubes, weighed more than 30 tons, occupied 1,800 square feet, and consumed 175 kilowatts of power. The ENIAC could perform about 5,000 calculations per second—more than 10,000 times slower than an average personal computer today. It was massive, generated intense heat, and was forever breaking down as the vacuum tubes went out. But in about 20 seconds it could perform calculations that took human computers two days to complete. Though it never really helped the war effort, it set into motion two other computer projects that eventually formed the core of an industry; one was centered in the private sector, the other in the public.

Squabbling both for academic credit and patents, and riven by perceived snubs and slights, the ENIAC team of the original University of Pennsylvania computer solved the biggest problems with the Mauchly-Eckert machine in a new round of innovation, but brought new troubles to a head. The new design, the EDVAC (Electronic Discrete Variable Automatic Computer) used binary numbers, could store interim numbers internally, and could be controlled from within a program stored in the machine's instructions. The stored program idea was debated endlessly among the ENIAC team, but was the primary brainchild of an ambitious mathematician, John Von Neumann, who had secretly hoped to run some of the Manhattan Project equations on ENIAC. The stored program characterizes all software programming to this day. The concept, which was not entirely Von Neumann's, was derived from various academic thinkers of the time. It explained and demonstrated how the programming codes that controlled the computer could be modified while the program ran. On the ENIAC, technicians had to set circuit switches by hand, then run the data from stacks of punch cards. The machine had to be reconfigured for different problems. In the new stored program model, the computer would be a passive but powerful framework of circuits. All the configuration and instructions, as well as data, would come from the punch cards. As the program instructions were read into the machine's memory stores, the computer would be configured to solve the specific problem the program was tackling. This self-referential organization allowed for branches in the logic, an initial set of instructions could specify completely different succeeding operations based on the first result. This reprogramming "on the fly" was the crucial step in formulating modern computer programming. No longer was a computer a deterministic machine; now it could determine the answer to one part of a problem, then, based on that result, reconfigure itself to solve a further problem. This almost human capability was what prompted the lay press to refer to computers as "giant brains."

Von Neumann was one of the most celebrated mathematicians of his day. Born in Hungary, he had developed the branch of mathematics called game theory, a way to analyze conflicts of interest mathematically to elucidate the best course of action in any situation. He also had made major contributions to quantum mechanics, statistics, and numerical analysis, and even wrote the first paper, in 1949, suggesting that computer programs could replicate, thus predicting the appearance of computer software viruses half a century later.

His work as part of the ENIAC team led him to suggest binary math as the basis for future versions, and to adopt some of the theoretical ideas of British mathematician Alan Turing. These ideas—called the "stored program" concept—resulted in a computer that could be controlled from within a program that was being fed into it, instead of requiring an external hand, or punch card, configuration for every operation. As it started to tackle a job, a program was stored in the computer by coding in a series of instructions via binary numbers. The data was put in the same program, and enabled the original program to be modified following the results of the first calculations. All of this is taken for granted today but was a mind-boggling concept for mathematicians and electrical engineers back in the 1940s.

Unfortunately, Von Neumann rubbed a lot of the young scientists at the Moore School the wrong way. He was pushy, and had friends in high places. Whenever accolades were given out, he always seemed to be at the front of the reception line. Then, in what he claimed was an honest mistake, a draft of the EDVAC specification was circulated with only his name attached to it. The grumbling about him increased, especially among the two original "inventors."

Of the Mauchly-Eckert pair, Mauchly was the front man. He was glib, well-spoken, and a good raconteur. Perhaps he was the first of a type born of the electronics age—someone with a vision of what equipment might be able to do, and the verbal skills to express it, even if the engineering skills were suspect. But those characteristics also worked against him in the intense environment at the University of Pennsylvania. Whereas Presper Eckert was widely acknowledged to be a superb electrical engineer, and thus deserving of patents, Mauchly was never respected by his peers.

When Mauchly and Eckert announced they were going to file for patents, all the simmering disputes boiled over. The University of Pennsylvania demanded that the two give up any claims. They refused and then resigned. A few days prior to that, however, Von Neumann applied for an Army patent for the design of the vastly improved EDVAC machine. Eckert and Mauchly were furious. They regarded the machine as theirs, even though it was Von Neumann who had initiated the concept of the stored program and promoted binary logic, the only real advances in the new machine.

The émigré mathematician had another motive for applying for a patent: He wanted the computer to be in the public domain; he thought it unconscionable that Mauchly and Eckert would try to own it. On

March 22, 1946, after Eckert and Mauchly had resigned, they filed for a series of patents on circuits and refresh memory technology, a move that forever engendered ill will among the original ENIAC team members. Immediately thereafter, they founded their first company, called the Electronic Controls Corporation. But it wasn't long before the name changed to The Eckert-Mauchly Computer Corporation. Now they had a business, but still lacked business sense.

Bad luck seemed to dog John Mauchly in the first years of the company. The partners were unable to win any crucial government contracts because Mauchly had attended some left-wing meetings in the thirties. In the fevered House Un-American Activities era of the late forties, this made him suspect in the government—especially the defense establishment, which would soon be awarding some very large computing contracts.

By the summer of 1946, Mauchly was irritable and angry. An opportunity to work for IBM dissolved when IBM refused to buy their patents. And Mauchly's security clearance problems continued. And their most promising lead—the chance to run statistical analysis for the National Bureau of Standards (NBS)—was held up by delay. The Census Bureau had also asked for an evaluation of the Eckert-Mauchly machine. (By now they had packaged the pieces of their commercial calculator and come up with a catchy acronym to call it: UNIVAC, for Universal Automatic Computer.) The Census Bureau was planning to use the machine to tabulate 1950 census numbers. Though money had been earmarked in April 1946, the contracts weren't signed until years later. For Mauchly and Eckert, cash flow was a constant problem; they were heavily undercapitalized and overworked. For the NBS and the Census Bureau, they would build UNIVACs. These were classic U.S. Government deals, meaning that the pair didn't see significant revenue until the contract was finally signed three years later. Priced at $150,000 each, UNIVAC development costs would escalate to nearly $1 million per machine. To make matters worse, Northrup Corporation offered them a contract to develop an airborne missile navigation system for the secret guided missile called "Snark." For Northrup, they built a smaller Binary Automatic Computer, or BINAC. The BINAC was also ridiculously underpriced at $100,000 in total, while it cost $300,000 to build. Essentially, the computers the company contracted to build were driving it into bankruptcy, fast.

Then late one night in September 1946, Mauchly went for a moonlit swim with his wife Mary in the surf of a beach town along the Jersey shore where they were spending the summer. Two hours later, Mary's body washed up down the beach. Mauchly claimed that they had been frolicking in the water and she had swum away. The local authorities, however, suspected foul play. Mauchly was never charged, and the verdict was death by misadventure/accidental drowning.

The incident eventually blew over but Mauchly was left to care for two pre-adolescents—a boy 11, and a girl 7, just when Eckert-Mauchly Computer Corporation was in its start-up phase and 20-hour days weren't uncommon. His parents took over raising the kids.

By 1948, still in financial straits, Eckert and Mauchly turned to Eckert's family, who put up money to keep the company going; and a team of young and enthusiastic college grad engineers had been hired to help. But there was still no income. To date, the Eckert-Mauchly Computer Corporation was the only one in the United States with contracts to deliver computing machines; but it had seriously underbid on all its jobs. Prudential, for example, the giant insurance company and long a prime IBM customer, was willing to contract with the young firm because it had to comply with a new governmental regulation that greatly increased its computational requirements for actuarial tables, and no other commercial computer was available. Another client, A. C. Nielsen, was positioning itself as the key independent market research company for the emerging television advertising age, and needed computers to conduct sophisticated demographic research.

So Eckert-Mauchly had the work; what they badly needed was cash to cover the salaries of the engineers necessary to build all these machines. The pair went looking for money—there was no venture capital in those days—and loans were not forthcoming from bankers, who were reluctant to finance an unknown computer business. With 40 people on the payroll, and numerous contracts, Eckert and Mauchly had to come up with $500,000 to complete the machines.

The BINAC was already overdue by the summer of 1948, when they found their first benefactor—Henry Strauss, of American Totalisator. This company ran its American racetrack pari-mutuel betting using an adding machine Strauss had invented in 1925.

Strauss realized the need for a machine that could track betting, and display updated odds before a race was run. American Totalisator essentially had a monopoly on tote boards through the 1940s. It wasn't a great leap from an adding machine to computers that could do hundreds of calculations per second, to a better electronic tote machine. In 1947, Strauss heard through the business grapevine that a would-be competitor had talked with Eckert and Mauchly about building it a computer. He contacted the pair, and when they said they needed money, he decided it would be better to coopt the technology himself. He convinced the dubious financiers who owned his company to take a flyer and invest.

The deal was signed in summer 1948. American Totalisator would eventually own 40 percent of Eckert-Mauchly Computer in exchange for about half a million dollars paid over the course of two years. The up-front cash gave the fledgling computer company breathing room, especially since Strauss let them operate without much interference. By fall 1949, Eckert-Mauchly Computer had 134 employees and another bigger office building. But the firm still had major engineering and production problems. The BINAC project fell further behind schedule, while the big UNIVAC project grew more ambitious and expensive and was thus still incomplete as well.

When Henry Strauss died in a private plane crash in October 1949, within days American Totalisator pulled out of the investment agreement. Mauchly and Eckert went to IBM, National Cash Register, and Remington Rand for help. Straitlaced Thomas Watson, still firmly in control at IBM, refused to meet with them. He was skeptical of computers.

There was also the matter of Mauchly's dossier: questionable patents; a wife who had died mysteriously; a company financed by horse racing and gambling money, and was now essentially bankrupt. Not the kind of person old man Watson wanted to associate with.

Remington Rand at the time had no such qualms. President James H. Rand stepped in as angel to Mauchly and Eckert. Remington Rand, makers of the first typewriters, had a long and interesting history in the office equipment market. By the 1940s, the firm was run by Rand, who would become the first successful computer-age entrepreneur. He was an opportunist, something of an inventor, a man with a business in office machines and a deep fascination for managing information. Starting in the 1930s, cobbling together dozens of small office equipment and supply businesses into a vertically integrated office equipment company, he had created a significant industrial conglomerate that stretched from electric shavers to filing systems. Rand was a visionary. He saw a way to build a business out of the computer even if the inventors themselves couldn't figure it out. He improved the engineering of the product, took the computer into commercial accounts, popularized it on television, and profited from it. In short, he fixed the shambles Eckert and Mauchly had made trying to commercialize the computer. Rand bought the firm out of insolvency in 1950. Remington Rand grew, eventually merging with Sperry Gyroscope Company to become Sperry Rand.

James Rand was the first businessman who built a successful commercial computer. Called the Universal Automatic Computer, or UNIVAC, it made Sperry Rand synonymous with computers in the mind of the public. Probably, it should have ruled the computing world, but it didn't work out the way Rand had imagined when he seized the opportunity to dive headfirst into the computer age ahead of his arch-rival IBM.

Rand, who had battled with IBM for the office equipment market throughout the 1930s and 1940s, had been watching carefully as the fledgling computer business developed. He was looking for an acquisition that could jump-start his entry to the field. Rand, who already had more than 100 patents registered in his name, got his toehold by buying Eckert-Mauchly Computer Corporation on February 1, 1950. The price: $437,000 to American Totalisator; to Mauchly and Eckert: $18,000 a year employment contracts, and a guaranteed patent royalty stream of at least $5,000 a year until expiration.

Rand was familiar with such acquisitions; he had created one of the first electronic age conglomerates by buying up distressed companies, integrating them into his company, and marketing their products. By 1948, as detailed in a *Forbes* profile "Men of Achievement," Remington Rand had produced "more than 1,000 products, including every kind of office record-keeping and record-making equipment, from tabulating cards and filing cabinets to television cameras, transmitting tubes, and photographic machines. The company manufactures all its own plastics and rubber products, and markets these to others. It also manufactures fractional horsepower electric motors, and is the largest producer in the world of electric shavers."

Rand came from Connecticut Yankee stock, the son of the owner of a small manufacturing company that made bank ledger books (the Rand

Ledger Company). After college Rand worked as a salesman for various office equipment manufacturers. A few years later, back in the family business, he invented a record-making and -keeping system called Kardex. In the age before all data would be electronic it was the equivalent to a computer database, but on cards. He filed the patent for Kardex jointly with his father; but when he thought the old man wasn't promoting it sufficiently, he went into business for himself, competing with his father.

A few years later, his company—American Kardex—was publicly traded and very successful. In time, he used his high-flying company stock to begin to build his conglomerate. Eventually, he bought out his dad for $3 million; it was the first of dozens of acquisitions. Rand started to dream of consolidating a number of smaller manufacturers into a single large organization, which was capable of supplying everything for "the business that serves business" as he described his enterprise. Fueled by the run in the market in the mid-1920s, by 1927, he bought typewriters (Remington), tabulators (Powers Tabulating), adding machines (Dalton Adding Machine Co.), loose-leaf binders (Kalamazoo Loose-Leaf Binder Co.), even office cabinets (Safe Cabinet Co.).

Unlike many, he stayed solvent during the market crash of 1929, though he did miss the two most important business trends of the 1930s in American offices: the growth of the electronic punch card tabulator business and the advent of office equipment leasing. For far too long Remington Rand sold typewriters and mechanical adding machines, which used gears and cams to poke the holes in punch cards, instead of using electrical contacts as IBM did. Remington Rand tried to diversify into tabulators, but it couldn't crack the IBM monopoly.

Nonetheless, Remington Rand was powerful enough to negotiate a noncompete deal with IBM in the late twenties which said that Rand agreed to stay out of the electronic tabulator business, and IBM agreed to stay out of the mechanical tabulator business. However, this agreement drew the attention of the Justice Department's trustbusters, and by the mid-1930s the two companies were back in full competition. Then World War II intervened.

With the economy booming, IBM's electronic tabulators, linked to counting and storage circuits based on vacuum tubes, moved far ahead of the mechanical units Remington Rand continued to sell. The advances made in electronics during the war years gave IBM a cadre of young ambitious electrical engineers, who started to rewrite the standard for office calculators. By the late 1940s, Remington Rand was losing the battle with IBM. By 1949, Remington Rand's revenues were better than $148 million, but net margins were less than 7 percent. At the same time, electronic tabulators provided the best profits in the office market, and Remington Rand was a distant second to IBM. Without competition, IBM's profits rose, and the company poured more and more money into R&D—$7.6 million by 1951. This made it even more difficult for anyone else to mount a credible challenge. The value of IBM's stock had grown an astonishing 14,780 percent since 1917, making it the first of the high-flyer technology stocks and a darling among investors. Remington Rand wasn't in the same category; its growth in the same period was a comparatively small 300 percent.

Thus, Rand turned his seasoned entrepreneurial eye to computers, which promised to be a level playing field. Perhaps, he thought, Remington Rand could get traction before the IBM monopoly shut him out. In many ways, Rand's company was both a reflection of his old-world attitudes and one of the first of the great information-age companies. With his feet planted firmly in the principles of the first half of the century, Rand was also an information-age inventor—most of his patents were for variations of information organization and storage, such as those for the Kardex "visible file system." Notecards and filing systems, the operating systems of the business world of that era, were his forte. Also an inventor, he was willing to indulge, support, and insulate his creative engineering teams. His director of research in the postwar years was General Leslie Groves, the man who had administered the Manhattan Project. Groves was a keen student of computing, who had become familiar with the first big computer, the ENIAC, when it was used to solve some of the crucial equations in the development of the first nuclear bombs in 1945. When he and Rand heard that Eckert-Mauchly needed financial support, they were quick to move.

Once Rand took over Eckert-Mauchly, he and General Groves poured money into the technology, and renegotiated all their commercial contracts. The operation had to be profitable and for the customers that made sense. At that point in the early 1950s, no one else was making computers for business purposes—although there were several high-powered scientific machines starting to be delivered. Burroughs,

Underwood, NCR, even IBM were all talking about building their own "electronic brains," but none actually existed outside of test labs.

Remington Rand and its UNIVAC were finally put on the map after a 1952 publicity stunt, which came in the form of a barter deal between Remington Rand and CBS. The network wanted several hundred tabulators and counting machines in place for election night in 1952. The network believed that having dozens of clerks punching and pulling tabulators in the background would add an aura of high-tech credibility to the newscasters. It was to be the dawn of exit-poll election analysis; and CBS, the country's preeminent TV news operation, wanted to be first.

James Rand agreed, but on one condition. He'd supply the calculators to CBS, but the network had to at least once show Remington Rand's new UNIVAC computer and report its predictions on the air. The network agreed. This would put Rand's computer in every American living room, something IBM couldn't even begin to counter. On election night, the CBS political pundits were predicting a close race between Democrat Adlai Stevenson and Republican Dwight Eisenhower. Then it was time to hear UNIVAC's predictions. But then, on live TV, something went wrong. The man on the spot was J. Presper Eckert, and he was refusing to go on the air. It seemed the UNIVAC was predicting a different result! It was predicting that Eisenhower would sweep Stevenson in a landslide, with a lead of nearly 20 percent of the popular vote! Eckert was beside himself; he feared he would be the laughingstock of the country. He refused to go on the air as long as he could. Eventually, Remington Rand's director of advanced research ordered that the computer program be tweaked in such a way that it would agree with the CBS experts. Eckert fudged the numbers.

By midnight, CBS announced that Eisenhower had won, but held the margin to a few percentage points. An hour or so later, more precinct results poured in, proving that Eisenhower was indeed winning by a landslide. Charles Collingsworth, the anchor, went on the air later to admit that the computer had predicted this result hours before, but that no one trusted it. Collingsworth brought Eckert out, and he concurred that the computer had been right all along.

The final victory margin: 20 percent—exactly as UNIVAC had predicted hours before.

When the news got out, the powers of the invincible, omniscient, and mysterious computer reached mythic status. UNIVAC instantly became a household name.

There was only one problem in all the hoopla that UNIVAC created on election night. Tom Watson Jr. watched TV along with the rest of the country, but unlike his father, thought that computers just might make a great business.

Thomas Watson Sr. passes the company on to his son
Thomas Watson Jr., 1955.

>———◈———<

Big Blue
The Mainframe Computer

Before the mainframe computer came of age in the 1950s and 1960s, America had become a country of clerks. After the Second World War, the migration of farm workers to the big cities accelerated. Cavernous rooms were filled with rows of desks and tabulators, as war heroes and their brides were hired to push paper around, to calculate paychecks, to compute bills. Data meant punch cards, and data processing meant feeding them into mechanical and electronic tabulators. In the fastest-growing economy in history, insurance companies, magazine publishers, and market researchers all were building nationwide customer lists, forming a vast sea of punch cards.

It was an America where cars, telephones, and televisions were suddenly affordable within a few years, and a majority of Americans had access to all of them. It was the time of the organization man, when homes in the suburbs were affordable, and when employment promised to be lifelong. Major companies vied for the best and the brightest, and with wages rising meteorically, individuals had little incentive to strike out on their own.

It was during this period of satisfaction that the single most potent product of the late twentieth century—the mainframe computer—was born. By the late forties, the technological underpinnings for the development of powerful computing devices were in place. Technologists, engineers, and scientists all had grasped the revolutionary nature of electronic calculation—its speed, precision, elegance, and potential scope. Remington Rand had launched a credible effort and produced a business-oriented machine, and at least a dozen small engineering efforts were under way to produce variations on the original Eckert-

Mauchly computers for different government agencies. What was missing was a bridge between state-of-the-art engineering and the heart of mainstream business.

✧   ✧   ✧

THERE WAS ONE COMPANY in the postwar American landscape that understood the true nature of business machinery and the marketing necessary to make it a success: IBM. In the postwar boom, its tabulators were more profitable than ever. But led by an autocratic, 70-year-old man, an icon of American success, it was a company mired in its past, hamstrung by a dependence on punch cards, and caught up in the tension between present-day sales and the need to move forward. In spite of, or perhaps thanks to, its heritage, it did move forward, and took the world into the information age. A prodigal son, with little to lose, bet the company on the untried and untested computer. By 1952, when Thomas Watson, Jr. took over as president, IBM was already one of the most fabled companies of the twentieth century. He would turn it into the most famous and profitable computer company in the world.

There may never have been a more unlikely technology and business leader than Thomas J. Watson, Jr., the eldest son of the man who made IBM one of the most powerful companies in America during the twenties and thirties. Born when Watson, Sr. was 40, and raised in a world of wealth and privilege, he was a poor student, a cut-up, and a "predetermined failure," as a dean at Princeton called him when refusing him admission. He was accepted into Brown University only after his father interceded; he barely graduated. A playboy, with a penchant for gorgeous girls, fast cars, and the Stork Club, he was a fixture in the New York and Hollywood club and débutante scene of the late 1930s. Unburdened either by ambition or self-respect, in 1939, he took a job at daddy's company, was given a sales territory where he made his yearly quota on the first day of every year, and spent the next 364 drinking and partying.

Watson, Jr. had one interest where his father had no influence and no prior reputation: flying airplanes. The old man was afraid of flying, and refused to travel by plane. His son, who had a monthly allowance greater than the average family income took to the air. As America readied itself for war in the early forties, Watson, Jr.'s eyesight was diagnosed as too poor to qualify for the fledgling American Air Corps. But he was determined to fly during the war, and joined the National Guard. When

America entered the fray in late 1941, he was called up in spite of his eyesight.

Just before he went overseas, he married the girl he had been dating, a model at the John Robert Powers agency, Olive Cawley. As a teenager she had been a fixture at the Kennedy compound and was a close friend of Jean Kennedy's, the future president's sister. Before the war was over, the first of their five children was born; he was named and numbered Thomas Watson III.

War changes young men into wiser older men overnight. Watson was no different. His goal was to fly over Europe, but again his powerful father intervened. He was reassigned as an air "chauffeur," charged with flying notables and generals to different theaters of action. One of his assignments was to fly Major General Follett Bradley into Moscow, on a mission to arrange the delivery of a number of American P-39 fighter planes to the beleaguered Russian forces, then under siege by the Nazis outside of Moscow. For the first time, the superficial and callow Watson was given real authority as head of the flight crew, and it was a responsibility that hadn't been thrust upon him by his father; it was a job that he had earned. Bradley, a career army officer, took a liking to the young Watson, and in their months of enforced proximity made him believe in himself for the first time.

After the war, when he returned to IBM on January 1, 1946, Tom Watson Jr. was a different man, ready to take his place in the business his father had built. The war had matured him, made him grow up. His father was 72 years old; he was 32. He was given the title of assistant to the executive vice president; his job was to help Charles Kirk, a burly 41-year-old salesman who had risen to the top of the company by hard work and talent. The two clashed from the start. Kirk was supposed to groom the young Watson for the presidency, but it was a no-win situation for him: the better a job he did, the sooner he would be relieved. It wasn't long before the heir apparent went to his father and said that it was either him or Kirk; they couldn't both work at the firm.

In retrospect, it is incredible that such an important company with an unblemished record of economic success could have been handed to a young, untested man like Tom Watson Jr. But the elder Watson's power was almost absolute. From songs of praise that phalanxes of salesmen sang to him to the handpicked board that rubber-stamped his every decision, IBM was his private fiefdom. He was the highest paid executive in America, and had been for many years ("thousand dollar a day" Watson was the tag the press had given him when he reached that salary level in the early 1930s).

Watson Sr. never owned more than 5 percent of the stock in the company—although this certainly was enough to make him and his family extremely wealthy. This stake had a value of about $25 million in the late 1940s—the company had 2.7 million shares outstanding, priced at around $200 a share. The key to his autocracy was the growth in shareholder value that he had created. By 1947, IBM's revenues were $144 million, and its earnings were $24 million—a return of over 17 percent. That meant that $1,000 invested in the stock in 1918 was worth $148,000 in 1947. In contrast, Remington Rand, its major competitor in office equipment in the same year, posted revenues that were almost the same at $143 million, but its income was a measly $8 million, for a return of less than 6 percent. Thus IBM shareholders had no complaints, so if Watson Sr. wanted to promote his eldest son, Wall Street wasn't about to interfere.

So, when Watson Jr. demanded Kirk's removal, the old man acquiesced, but not before sending the two of them on a European sales trip. Along the way, antagonism between the two men rose to fever pitch. Cooped up together for several weeks, they came to loathe each other. Kirk was a coarse man, the kind of salesman who told bawdy jokes and put on few airs. Watson Jr. was a smooth-skinned young man, with an upper-class attitude. They could not have been more different. One day in the south of France, they nearly came to blows; the 33-year-old Watson was barely able to hold himself back from punching the 42-year-old Kirk. The cause? Watson's wife wanted to spend half a day driving out of their way to see a family friend. For Kirk, it was the last straw, another example of how cavalier the rich boy and his family were. That night, Charles Kirk had a massive heart attack and died, almost certainly as a result of the argument earlier in the day.

This opened the way for Watson Jr. But his father wasn't quite ready to hand the entire business all to him, so for a few more years he functioned as executive vice president; an old crony of his dad's was the titular president. There was no doubt, however, as to who was going to take over eventually. The only potential rival was Junior's younger brother, Arthur K. Watson. For him, the old man created a separate, but equal, organization for overseas sales, called IBM Worldwide. There he installed Arthur

COMPAQ

Windows 98 Second Edition

Microsoft Windows 98 Second Edition is available for your Presario.
This CD contains Internet Explorer 5.0, the easiest and fastest way to
explore the Internet, plus some of the latest upgrades for Windows 98.
If you did not receive your Windows 98 Second Edition CD, please call
us at 1-888-202-4598.

NOTICE

First Edition, April 1999

144599-001

as its president, and worked hard to make his second son a success. Watson Jr. was inordinately jealous of his younger brother, and Watson Junior and Senior fought furiously over Arthur's position for several years, until in 1952, the succession issue was settled once and for all. Tom Watson Jr. was made president; his father became chairman of the board. Arthur would turn IBM Worldwide into a significant, but never explosive, arm of the business.

By the time he took the company reins, Tom Watson Jr. had already started to move IBM from a punch card company to a computer business. Though he didn't have the business or financial acumen to appreciate the forces that were coming together in the postwar years, he nonetheless made the right decisions, if for all the wrong reasons.

But still standing in his way was his father, the king of punch cards, and he was supported by a lot of successful and satisfied salesmen who were easily making their yearly quotas every year and didn't want anyone rocking the boat. Shortly after Kirk died, Tom Jr. realized that if he was going to put his mark on IBM, he would have to do it in a new field, or by adopting a new technology, to show the world and his dad that he was master of his own destiny.

That opportunity was the computer, which made obsolete the entire basis of IBM's original business: the punch card. Ironically, although IBM entered the computer field belatedly, it became dominant *because* of all those punch card salesmen and the nature of the business model it had followed so successfully for so long.

IBM's foundation was laid on the reinvention of the punch card, originally developed to control looms in Napoleonic France. An American inventor, Herman Hollerith, had devised a way to use the oblong cards perforated with holes to represent numbers. By combining these cards with a mechanical tabulator that could add or subtract (and hence multiply or divide as well) stacks of them, the new tabulator was first put to work by the U.S. Census in 1890. The machine formed the basis of Hollerith's company, Computing-Tabulating-Recording Inc. (C-T-R). However, Hollerith was a better inventor than he was a businessman, and by the First World War, his company was on the skids.

Its savior was Tom Watson, Sr., then a top salesman for the National Cash Register Company. NCR was widely known as "the Cash," and generally considered the first company to modernize sales. At "the Cash," salesmen were given territories, and received commissions for exceeding quotas. The operation was so successful that it became a monopoly in sales of cash registers—until it ran afoul of the government trustbusters. In the early 1900s, Watson Jr. had been involved in a scheme to put second-hand cash register dealers out of business. They had been taking advantage of the quality of "the Cash" equipment by reselling used machines. By the turn of the century, there was a lively market for secondhand cash registers in most major cities; a number of firms bought up older models, then resold them. This put pressure on the Cash, and forced it to cut prices. To counter this, bankrolled by NCR, secretly Tom Watson Sr. began to buy and sell secondhand machines. He would enter a town, bid up the prices of secondhand equipment, thus driving the other resellers out of the market. Controlling both the new and used equipment markets in this way enabled National Cash Register to set prices without interference. When the government brought an antitrust case against the Cash, Watson was convicted, although he denied culpability. Sentenced to a year in prison, he never served time because the ruling was overturned on a technicality. The government settled with all the other defendants, but Watson Sr. refused to admit any wrongdoing and demanded a new trial. The government never bothered to retry Watson, but he carried an animosity for the Justice Department for the rest of his life.

Watson also felt that he had been set up by NCR as the fall guy, and when the board of directors at C-T-R began interviewing for a new president, he took the opportunity and left NCR. From the beginning of his tenure at C-T-R, Watson Sr. created a sales-oriented company in the mold of NCR, but he made a major change in the way the company operated. Renamed International Business Machines, the company would no longer sell tabulators; it would retain ownership and lease machines. That required lots of handholding and support for the machinery. Watson Sr. realized that all that aftermarket customer service strengthened the sales relationship. He emphasized over and over to the sales force that the key ingredient to IBM's success was understanding the customers' needs, and then selling them the equipment that would meet those needs. To achieve this goal, cadres of service personnel were hired to keep the equipment running; large groups of sales engineers configured the punch cards and tabulators to solve particular problems for customers. This service was the heart of IBM's success.

As the forties drew to a close, however, more than a third of IBM's revenues still came from punch card systems. Since the thirties the company had all but abandoned manual, mechanical punch card tabulators, in favor of a patented electronic system that used contacts on either side of a punch card to generate a current spike wherever there was a hole in the card.

By keeping a tight rein on its patents and building expertise in electronics, IBM grew fast and made itself ready for the next stage in the electronics revolution: electric typewriters and electronic calculators. These businesses continued to develop after the war, but Watson Jr. wanted to find a new and more radical use for electronics. He began to regard the tabulator salesmen, and their determination to maintain the status quo, as a weight around his neck. That attitude was reinforced when, in 1949, he asked some of the firm's top salesmen to look into the future of magnetic tape. He had been alerted by a crony at Time-Life, a long-time IBM punch card customer, that his company was seriously contemplating moving its subscription management to one of the new UNIVAC machines. At the time, three cards were necessary to handle a single subscription, and with *Time* magazine's weekly circulation in the millions, the company was drowning in punch cards. Watson heard the same from Metropolitan Life Insurance, which had three floors of its building devoted to storing the cards. Magnetic tape reportedly was able to store thousands of records on a single tape spool. Staff there wondered, was IBM going to have a similar machine anytime soon?

Magnetic tape was a wartime development from Nazi Germany, whose propaganda machine wanted a way for Hitler to be able to pre-record speeches. Their solution was a kind of plastic-backed tape, coated with magnetic particles of iron oxide. Audio was passed to a "head" that converted the sound waves into magnetic fluctuations, which were imprinted onto the tape. Playback involved picking up the fluctuations from the tape and converting them to sound waves. Shortly after the technology made its way to the United States, engineers began to consider it as a way to store data. A string of digital bits could be represented by clicks, recorded on the tape, then reproduced by playback and reconverted into electronic pulses.

Three months after Watson Jr.'s inquiry, his salesmen told him simply that punch card tabulators would never be replaced by the new computer machines. The reason? With punch cards, a businessman could see and touch his data; using magnetic tape, the data was invisible. No one would trust his business to an invisible medium. Case closed.

Watson Jr. had first seen the ENIAC early in 1946, when he and Charles Kirk had taken a trip to Philadelphia. There they were taken on a tour by the two men who hoped to profit from it—John Mauchly and Presper Eckert. Watson Jr. admitted that, "I had no idea what I was looking at." He and Kirk returned to IBM headquarters, dismissive of the effort and unconcerned with its impact on their core business; they were also contemptuous of Mauchly's and Eckert's intention to file for patents and to compete with IBM.

A year later, Watson Sr. heard about the U.S. Census Bureau's contract for the UNIVAC for the first time. Fury erupted in the executive suite. The Census Bureau had always been IBM territory. The U.S. Census had always been conducted using punch cards. The elder Watson demanded to know how IBM had lost out to a handful of academics and tinkerers without an ounce of business savvy between them.

It wasn't that IBM had ignored or overlooked electronic calculation; rather, it had been burned by its only experience in the field. The firm had funded one of the more visible early projects before the war—Harvard's Mark 1—and yet never received any public recognition for it. IBM had also built a massive machine at Columbia called the SSEC (Selective Sequence Electronic Calculator). This machine was 120 feet long, was composed of 12,000 tubes and 21,400 mechanical relays, and used a programming scheme that made it more flexible than the ENIAC. It was essentially electromechanical in nature, relying on relays, and was much slower than the first big computer. Nevertheless, the gargantuan device was installed in the IBM showroom on 57th Street in Manhattan, and was equipped with dozens of dials, switches, meters, and flashing neon lights. It had been designed by the same team of inventors who built the company's generations of adding machines and tabulators. Impressive looking, it was a dinosaur before it was complete.

Now Watson Sr. gathered the same crew of engineers and demanded that they create a machine to compete with the UNIVAC. A few weeks later, they returned with a proposal that astonished the executives assembled for the presentation. The team had included both punch card data storage and magnetic tape, and had created a calculating engine out of electronics. The price tag? $750,000. In comparison, the company's most expensive tabulator to date had cost $20,000 to build. Watson Sr. rejected the proposal. Who could possibly afford to rent a machine that would cost $15,000 a month? Luckily for IBM, Tom Jr. didn't give up on computers.

About the same time, Watson and his father had wandered into one of the various labs around the Endicott, New York, research facility, and saw a small test calculator that worked with vacuum tubes to perform multiplications and additions. At Junior's urging, the company developed the machine into a marketable product, called the 603 Electronic Multiplier. Even though it was hamstrung by using punch cards for input and output, it did perform mathematics by electronics. To improve on it, the younger Watson set up a new lab in a country mansion in Poughkeepsie, far enough away from Endicott to be free of the stultifying influence of the old engineering guard, yet close enough to New York City to enable him to spend time with the new team. When they introduced an enhanced version of the electronic multiplier in 1948, called the 604, and rented some 300 of them within 18 months at a price of $1,000 per month, Junior decided it was time to get serious about electronics.

Frustratingly, he still couldn't make headway with his father. Then, finally, in 1950, Watson Jr. made his move; he appointed a new vice president of engineering and embarked on a hiring binge that swelled the IBM electrical engineering ranks from 500 to 4,000 over the next few years. Most of them were electronics engineers—much to the dismay of the old line, who couldn't understand why the company was chasing the electronics grail when punch card tabulators were selling better than ever. Watson Junior pushed on.

Missing, however, was a big computer to build, a project the company could really sink its teeth into. That opportunity came with the Korean War. In Cambridge, Massachusetts, a government-funded project called Whirlwind was underway that involved an interactive, real-time computer behemoth originally built as an airplane flight simulator. In the wake of the Russians testing an atomic bomb in 1949, the machine was commandeered and rebuilt to be the center of a massive air defense system. Integrating radar operators and a string of air bases deployed along the country's northern perimeter, the project was seen as crucial to the nation's security. As it had in the past, IBM offered its services to the government. When the project was put out to bid—the government planned to build two of the massive specialized computers, for redundancy, in a half-dozen sites around the country—IBM priced its services on a straight cost basis. As an ex-fighter pilot, Watson Jr. was well positioned and IBM, although it had no experience in computers, got the contract. Eventually, the project would generate half a billion dollars in sales, and provide invaluable early experience in computer manufacturing, which would later help the company distance itself from all its competitors.

Watson Jr. knew this was the chance he had been looking for. Not only would he build the air defense machine to the specifications designed by the Project Whirlwind team, but he would assign a skunkworks group of top IBM electrical engineers to work on the company's own big computer, one that could be sold to other government agencies or commercial accounts. By cloaking his ambition in the guise of his concern for national security, he intended to hide from his father that he was building a full-scale computer—what would be called the Defense Calculator. (The word "computer" was never used at IBM until after Watson Sr. died.)

IBM had never created anything remotely like this, and no one in the company knew much about magnetic tape, memory, binary circuits, or any of the key issues in computing. At an estimated cost of $3 million, this machine would be more expensive than IBM's entire R&D budget two years earlier. Once again, the IBM reputation made it happen. Although Remington Rand had signed contracts with several agencies for its UNIVAC, IBM's federal government salesmen were able to get half a dozen firm orders within months.

They were off and running. The hiring frenzy continued, and Poughkeepsie became the center of a concentrated effort, the scope of which IBM had never seen. And because only the youngest of engineers knew anything about electronics and computers, essentially it became the domain of the new generation. Watson Jr. took to spending days at a time in the facility, and soon he believed that he and the company were doing something as important as the Wright Brothers had when they built their airplane. There was the sense that they were on the verge of a brave new world.

Paying for all this expansion was also a new experience, especially for Watson Sr. Never before had he borrowed much money. He didn't believe in debt, and by 1950, IBM's long-term debt stood at $85 million, paltry for a company with $15 million in cash and current assets totaling almost $70 million. But financing the hiring binge and the development of the Defense Computer required lots of money, and, unlike his father, Watson Jr. wasn't intimidated by spending the enormous sums necessary. His closest associate was Al Williams, an excellent chief financial officer. Williams, handpicked by Watson Sr., played a key role in the expansion by convincing the old man that spending heavily, and borrowing the money to do so, was the prudent financial move. By 1955, company debt had risen to $255 million. In the same period, revenues more than tripled, from $215 million to $734 million. IBM was making a massive investment in a brand new field.

The Defense Calculator, renamed model 701, finally came off the assembly line in late 1952. Designed for scientific calculations, it was a modest success, with a dozen delivered to various military agencies. It hardly mattered, though, because work had already begun on its successor, the 702, a similar big machine, but designed for commercial computing. This machine, which rented for $16,000 a month—an unprecedented amount in those days—along with the air defense computer built for Project Whirlwind, finally gave IBM the know-how to go head to head with Remington Rand. However, in the public's mind, the UNIVAC was synonymous with computing, and that stuck in both Watsons' craws.

But it wasn't the public that was buying computers in those days; it was big businesses, and they were much more comfortable with the IBM sales effort than with the Remington Rand operation. After all, Rand was known as an electric shaver company, whereas IBM's sales force combined service and sales engineering to ensure that IBM equipment solved business problems. Remington Rand, on the other hand, had a sales force that sold a wide variety of equipment via old-line tabulator and adding machine salesmen, who never felt comfortable with the young computer geniuses.

All that emphasis on the customer proved to be exactly what was needed for a generation of businessmen who had started to believe that they needed to buy computers, but didn't feel confident about using them. With IBM they could be sure of having business-oriented sales and support personnel to help them out. Ironically, the punch card tradition was a major competitive advantage for IBM as the world moved into the computer age.

The downside was that some very influential and powerful characters were watching the punch card monopoly carefully. The Truman Administration's Department of Justice was headed by Attorney General

Thomas Clark, who had cut his political teeth by breaking Alcoa's hold over the aluminum market in 1951. The activist Truman White House seized control of the steel industry to stop a planned strike, and made forays into various industries. Attorney General Clark launched antitrust investigations of AT&T, United Shoe, and, finally, IBM.

The IBM investigation in the early 1950s centered on the punch card business. IBM had a better than 90 percent market share. Simply put, IBM didn't have enough competition. The Department of Justice opened the investigation to find out why, and to try to rectify the situation.

Watson Sr. was beside himself. He took out full-page ads in newspapers, claiming the company would cooperate fully because it believed in free enterprise and had nothing to hide. But inside he seethed, remembering his earlier run-in with the trustbusters. In the course of the investigation, IBM turned over thousands of documents, and Cravath Swain and Moore (IBM's law firm) was fully occupied for years trying to satisfy Justice Department fishing expeditions. The government was determined to find something, and went so far as to send in investigators posing as antiespionage agents to pore over the company's foreign sales records.

Finally, on January 21, 1952, the Truman administration filed suit. As the investigation dragged on, Watson Sr. refused to settle, claiming it would be an admission of guilt. Conversely, the younger Watson realized that settling was the best alternative. First, he argued, doing so would provide a clear set of ground rules under which the company could operate. Second, and vastly more important, it would once and for all prove the punch card business was a dinosaur, doomed to die. Furthermore, IBM's lawyers assured the Watsons that any decree they signed would affect only the punch card business, and would have no impact on the new computer business. (On this point, they were very wrong.) Third, fighting the case was distracting the company's focus. It took four years, but Watson Jr. finally convinced his father.

The decree, signed in 1956, called for IBM to make a series of changes: The company had to sell, as well as lease, its equipment; within seven years, IBM had to divest itself of the capability to produce more than half of the nation's punch cards; it had to grant patent licenses to any firm that wanted to compete with it; finally, the firm had to agree to create a wholly owned but arms-length subsidiary—Service Bureau Corporation—to offer aftermarket services and support of various kinds.

Signing the decree didn't seriously harm IBM at that time, but it did change the nature of the computer business. With the advent of computer sales, the leasing market could develop. Companies could acquire IBM machines, then lease them to customers at better rates than IBM's monthly leases. Also, and ultimately more important, by agreeing to grant licenses for all its equipment, IBM couldn't protect its own innovations after bringing them to market. It would have to face competition whenever it introduced a successful product. This only affected products that had been already introduced, but the lawyers were wrong about the scope of the agreement. It would open the door for two crucial developments in the years to come: the appearance of so-called plug-compatible mainframes and, eventually, the IBM PC clone market.

Of course, none of this was apparent then, and to the young Watson opportunity to get out from under the cloud of the investigation was well worth the concessions. By then he was on the way to remaking the company into a computer enterprise, and was poised to dominate this new field as his father had dominated the previous era.

Over the next five years, IBM invested more than $500 million in the computer business. Watson Jr. had no vested interest in maintaining the status quo. And his father, though still autocratic, loved his child, and so was willing to give him the means to either fail or succeed. As it turned out, he made the right move. Certainly no one else could have made the old man agree. But while it brought IBM into the computer age, the company still lagged far behind more innovative competitors including RCA and GE.

A few months after signing the consent decree, Thomas Watson Sr. died, at the age of 82, leaving Tom Watson Jr. in complete control of IBM. Coincidentally, the office equipment market was changing. There was a stampede to the market, as a *Forbes* story on the first day of 1957 pointed out:

> . . . Stampeded is perhaps too mild a word. Last year, to judge by the press releases, pronouncements by top brass, and Wall Street market letters, the electronic computer must have been the main product of the multibillion dollar U.S. office equipment industry. Needless to say, it was not. Computer sales and rentals totaled $125 million, perhaps 6 percent of sales. Royal McBee, Underwood, Remington Rand, IBM, and their minor competitors continued to grind out typewriters by the

millions. National Cash's 500 kinds of cash registers still accounted for a bread-and-butter 37 percent of its business. Burroughs had come a long way in ten years, but still counted on the ordinary adding and accounting machines for the bulk of its sales.

Actually, 1956 was a year in which the office equipment people had no reason to be ashamed of their run-of-the-mill typewriters, cash registers, accounting machines, and punch card equipment. With the exception of IBM and possibly Sperry Rand, every one of the companies was losing money on its computer projects. . . .

The article was illustrated with a chart of computer units ordered or delivered as of September 1, 1956. IBM was far in the lead, having delivered 449 big and midsized computers and with 1,121 more on order. Sperry Rand came next, with 314 delivered, but only 113 on order. Burroughs (which sold only midsized units) had 40 installed, 40 on order; and National Cash Register had 25 installed with 5 on order. But this list of the key office equipment makers did not take into account a pair of formidable competitors just entering the market: General Electric, which had sold 30 giant data processing machines, and RCA, which had delivered two BIZMACs. All of these companies were chasing after a very lucrative market, as identified in the *Forbes'* article: "Arthur D. Little, Inc. spelled it out in dollars and cents. The research outfit figured that there are some 3,000 U.S. companies as potential customers for some $2.5 billion worth of electronic computers." This would prove to be an understatement by at least an order of magnitude.

By the following year, 1957, IBM's sales force had started to pull away from its only real competitor in the computer market, Remington Rand's UNIVAC. That year, IBM's total revenues were $734 million, which included $193 million in computer-related income, 25 percent of the firm's revenues. SAGE, the Whirlwind Project air defense system, accounted for the largest part at $93 million; other military income was $28 million; electronic calculators contributed $23 million; and other commercial stored-program computers, the company's bread and butter, brought in $49 million. This was estimated at about three-quarters of the total computer revenues in the United States. That year was also when IBM introduced its only technological innovation of the era: the model 350 RAMAC (Random Access Memory Accounting Machine) disk memory system. Developed at a new research facility in San Jose, California, it was the beginning of the hard drive industry.

The critical capability of the hard disk drive, with its magnetic platters for recording data, was that it was possible to go to any portion of the stored material at any time, whereas a magnetic tape drive or a stack of punch cards were sequential memory storage repositories requiring users to wind past irrelevant data to find a specific piece of information. The hard disk contained heads that floated over the surface of the spinning platter and could reach any bit of data within seconds. This made computing much more powerful and faster. With IBM in control of the innovation, the company was able to drive its profits forward. The RAMAC had 50 memory disks, or platters, stored about 40 megabits of data (5 million alphanumeric characters, each of which required 1 byte, equaling 5 megabytes of storage), and rented for $3,200 a month, or cost $189,950. Compare this to today's hard drives, which store billions of bytes (gigabytes) and cost merely hundreds of dollars.

Remington Rand also had introduced a new memory system the same year, based on a spinning drum coated with magnetic material, but it was IBM's memory concept that carried the day. And Remington Rand had other, graver, problems. The former undisputed leader by 1957 had only some 19 percent of the nation's computing revenues, and it couldn't hold onto that for long.

In short, IBM had outsold and outmaneuvered it. Nothing the firm did worked. Two years earlier Remington Rand merged with the Sperry Corporation to create Sperry Rand, in hopes of becoming a worthy competitor for IBM. James Rand took over the computer business himself, which consisted of two independent divisions: the remnants of the Eckert-Mauchly Computer Corporation and a scientific computing operation based in Minneapolis called Engineering Science Associates, or ESA. Harry Vickers of Sperry was named president, and World War II General Douglas MacArthur was named chairman of the new corporation. The new company had revenues of $700 million, far greater than IBM's $484 million for that year. But the profit picture was far more troubling: IBM made more money at $46.5 million than Sperry Rand did ($44.6 million), on two-thirds the revenues. It was the revenue from the leasing contracts—long-term predictable income streams, coupled with strong depreciation write-offs—that kept IBM's balance sheet golden and its margins high.

Before the merger, Sperry had forged strong relationships with the military, and boasted a series of industrial operations that produced high-quality equipment, including gyroscopes, hydraulic systems, electronic tubes, computer-directed machine tools, even tractors. Remington Rand's line was primarily made up of office equipment that ranged from typewriters to computers but it also included consumer products such as shavers. But its best asset was its field sales force, second only to IBM's. However, the two were not exactly compatible. The office tabulator and card systems salesmen were very different from the young and ambitious computer proponents—especially the scientific computing geniuses at ESA, where the country's first supercomputers were being designed. Thus, on paper the merger looked like a good one, but because the two companies shared no common ground, it proved to be a difficult marriage. By then Rand was in his sixties, and though enthusiastic about computers, he was out of his depth. He became seriously ill within a year of the merger and retired.

Sperry Rand continued to invest in computers, releasing the UNIVAC II in 1957, with which it pushed the technological envelope by introducing extensive use of new, cheaper, and more reliable transistors. But the division continued to be a major drain on the corporation's finances, and it wasn't until 1965 that the computing operation at Sperry turned a tiny profit.

Meanwhile IBM's enormous, highly disciplined sales force controlled the market, weaning its customers off tabulators and onto computers. And the nature of the computers of the day certainly enhanced IBM's reputation for 365-days-a-year service. Inside the machines of that generation were miles of wiring and hundreds of vacuum tubes that generated lots of heat, so they were often in need of tuning and repair, and who could do that better than IBM?

Ironically, better technology was available. Sperry's machines, as well as those designed by Sylvania, Philco (the S-2000), General Electric, and even RCA, all incorporated transistors more widely than the IBM machines, which stuck with the vacuum tube long after it was necessary. Throughout the late fifties, IBM introduced relatively pedestrian computers in various models: the 7000 series, a line of monster computers, the first (called the Stretch) designed for the military as a supercomputer; subsequent models 7070 and 7090 configured for commercial work; the 1401, a low-priced but powerful office computer, and its scientific counterpart the 1620. Cutting-edge just wasn't the goal of businessmen, who were not big fans of computing anyway; they opted for the safe harbor of IBM, which kept that company on top of the booming market segment. By 1960, IBM's revenues had doubled again, to $1.4 billion, but now the percentage of computer-related sales came to 40 percent, or $559 million. And except for the disk storage system, none of it was very technologically advanced. What was forming was a portrait of an aggressive, but uncreative competitor. It was a picture that would be repeated time and again in the digital age: Great engineering would be copied sooner or later; it was sales and marketing that made the difference to most of the companies that ultimately succeeded.

By 1957 the mantle of advanced computing research was being carried by a strange hermit genius named Seymour Cray, who worked in isolation in Chippewa Falls, Wisconsin, for the company that was formerly the Engineers Research Associates group at Remington Rand. Angered by numerous slights from head office after the 1952 acquisition, and certain that the Sperry Rand executives would never understand the new world of computing, a large group of key employees had left in 1957 to found a competitor company, Control Data Corporation (CDC). Headed by gruff and unpleasant William Norris, CDC's 1604 computer, released in 1957, was indisputably the fastest and most powerful computer available on earth.

Although headquartered in Minnesota, CDC's story was the first in a series that would become famous in California's not yet nicknamed Silicon Valley. The company's stock was offered to early believers at 35 cents a share. By 1964, a single share was worth more than $100. A *Forbes* article from the early 1960s described the keys to Control Data Corporation's success.

> For very specific reasons, [William] Norris displays no fear of his giant competitors, except perhaps IBM. He is almost contemptuous of them. "Control Data and IBM are the only two companies in the computer field making money because they're the only two just in that business," says Norris.
>
> He argues: "In computers, decisions are pretty big and must be made promptly. In big multidivisional companies like RCA, Sperry

Rand, Honeywell or GE, top management is engrossed in many things and is not knowledgeable about the problems in the computer division."

Such absentee management, Norris claims, causes some of his famous rivals to hesitate so long before approving a new computer that they reach the market a little late. And in computers a little late is too late.

Norris also says that rival outfits too often refuse to commit enough funds to produce and push the new product, trying to limit any potential losses by playing it safe.

From the first, since he backed Cray's 1604, Norris, by contrast, has made quick decisions and set a bold course. He has constantly gambled. He has insisted that Control Data must grow into a bigger company, one able to sell and service not just computers, but total systems.

There is no turning back from this necessity to grow. Control Data must be a big successful company or a flop. "As a matter of fact," smiles Bill Norris, "a well thought out, bold course, is least risky. In computers, it is those who play it safe who are in danger."

It was that passion for risk that encouraged Norris to follow the ideas of his brilliant and inspired computer designer, Seymour Cray. Cray believed he could build a computer entirely out of transistors, and thereby change the speed equation of computing. He was right.

The market the company decided to go after was one that IBM and all its competitors were avoiding like the plague: scientific computing. In this small, unaddressed arena, the quality of the equipment meant much more than any other factor. Eschewing sales niceties, the company offered no aftermarket support and precious little salesmanship, the thinking being that its customers were the most technically literate in any company, and so didn't need hand-holding. And as long as the firm kept turning out spectacular computers, that was the case.

In this niche market, where bragging rights were more important than gross sales revenues, IBM ran a distant second to start-up CDC, especially when its much-vaunted Stretch computer turned out to be only half as powerful as promised. The episode so unnerved Tom Watson Jr. that he reduced their machine's price by half—a move unprecedented in IBM's history—then stopped all IBM's work on supercomputers for a number of years. With mainstream customers clamoring for more of

IBM's commercial computers, and with the sales and support staffs focusing on their customers, not the technology, Watson could afford to ignore niches like supercomputing—which is not to say that the success of others in the field stopped bothering him.

What Watson Jr. could not afford to ignore was the two companies that looked as if they would be able to give IBM serious competition: General Electric and RCA. But the RCA tale turned out to be one of misguided market strategy. In the mid-1950s, the company was run by David Sarnoff, a Russian émigré who had made television a household appliance. He was looking for new fields in which to extend his influence. Computers seemed like a good bet, where money and might could make the company a force to be reckoned with. Unfortunately, Sarnoff focused on the business end, and never built a technology base. RCA managers realized that the key to IBM's success was in its sales and marketing power, so instead of emphasizing engineering, it produced copycat computer models and attempted to place them by slashing prices. Lacking a corporate sales force, it tried to hire away IBM's top guns, without success. The division was never profitable, although over the years the giant company sank nearly a billion dollars in its attempt to make it so.

In many ways, the GE story is sadder. Run by a chairman of the old order—Philip Reed—since 1939, GE was one of the first American corporations to buy and install computers. In the early 1950s, the company bought both IBM and UNIVAC models, and used them extensively for payroll and manufacturing. By 1958, the firm had 11 big machines and 32 midsized systems in-house. GE, more than any other industrial enterprise, knew the strengths and weaknesses of using computers for data processing and business operations. But, Reed was cautious. He was convinced that another stock market crash was about to occur in the mid-1950s and so instead of taking on debt and investing in computers, he retired the company's senior notes. By 1954, GE's debt had dropped from over $200 million after the war to only $1.7 million. This was good for the balance sheet, but bad for the future of the business.

By the time Reed retired in 1958, GE was far behind all the other major computer manufacturers. However, the new president, Ralph Cordiner, was a believer in the future of computing. He put the corporation onto a quick turnaround development schedule; and a couple of years later, the firm introduced models that included a striking innovation: the Datanet communications processor, which enabled multiple GE computers to communicate with each other. This was essentially the first modem—modulator/demodulator—a device that made it possible to convert data into a form that could be sent over standard telephone wires. As a result of this innovation, GE also pioneered the concept of time-sharing—whereby multiple users, using terminals linked by the communications processors, could share the power of a single large computer. Unfortunately for GE, it was too little too late. By the late 1960s, GE was losing more than $100 million a year on its computer operations, with no end to the downturn in sight. Early in the next decade, it abandoned the effort.

Other companies that made a run at computer success included National Cash Register, Burroughs, Underwood, and Philco, as well as large number of smaller firms including North American Aviation, Bunker-Ramo, Addressograph-Multigraph, International Telephone and Telegraph, the Monroe Calculating division of Litton Industries, Raytheon, Varian, even General Mills. Each tried to carve out niches, but none made much impact. IBM kept rolling up the sales, even though its equipment was demonstrably less powerful and more expensive than most of its competitors.

By the early 1960s, the stage was set for a competitor that would threaten IBM's dominance. Honeywell, a missile contractor and industrial controls company, had entered the computer field by buying a small early computer start-up called Datamatic in 1955. Much smaller—the total revenues were $500 million in 1961—than any of the other major IBM competitors, Honeywell's management was convinced it could capture a segment of IBM's core business. Walter Finke, head of the firm's information systems group, planned to underprice and outperform IBM's most profitable computer lines, the 7000 and 1400 series machines, especially the latter. He also counted on the government keeping up the antitrust pressure on Big Blue, which would open the door to a strong competitor.

The cornerstone of Honeywell's efforts, however, was in something called "plug compatibility." Because tape sizes for the Honeywell line were the same as for the IBM 1400s—and the formats were deliberately kept the same—the same tapes and programming could work on

both machines. This meant that a customer could buy the more powerful—and readily available (IBM machines were so popular they were
constantly back-ordered)—Honeywell H-200 for less money and be
able to use the same data on both machines. Furthermore, by using a
relatively inexpensive add-on software program called the Liberator,
programs created for the IBM 1400s would run on the Honeywell
machines.

Not surprisingly, the H-200 machines were an enormous success.
Customers loved being able to buy a compatible machine to IBM's at
two-thirds the price. By 1967 new orders had fallen off at IBM, whereas
Honeywell was announcing that its computer division was very profitable. It shipped $300 million worth of computers that year. For the
first time, IBM was being attacked at the core of its business by an
upstart. Honeywell's success in part opened the market for clones and
compatibles in later years.

Suddenly it became clear to Watson and his colleagues in the executive suite that IBM had to regroup. Delivering pedestrian computers
that could be copied by competitors was not the way to ensure a long-
term success. Fortunately, they had something else in the works. By the
early 1960s, IBM was making most of its money from computers—three
out of every four dollars by 1961. The company was also funding two
parallel research and development operations for next-generation versions of its two primary computer lines—the 7000s, and the smaller
commercial 1400 line—along with separate sales forces to market them.
But as the cheaper machines (1400s) went up-market and the bigger
ones (7000s) expanded downward, the two lines collided, causing internal dissension.

By 1960, it had become commonplace in the business world to use
big calculation machines to track data, to calculate payroll and billing
information, to keep tabs on sales and transactions, and to run many
businesses and manufacturing operations. The first programming languages had appeared, with which cadres of software programmers were
creating programs. Every mainframe was different, but there were
enough of them, and the principles were similar enough, that a new job
category emerged to manage and maintain them: systems analyst, a
computer specialist who knew how to apply technology to business. This
was IBM's forte, of course.

Watson also acknowledged that a third generation of computers would be needed to stave off competition. Belatedly in the late 1950s, IBM had created a transistor-based big computer, the 7090. But by then the integrated circuit (IC) was already the talk of the electronics industry, with both Texas Instruments and a division of Fairchild Camera claiming competing versions. The IC combined multiple transistors and components in one package, a development that promised to solve the tyranny of size that threatened to limit the usefulness of transistors. Though transistors were smaller and less intrusive than vacuum tubes, they still had to be connected and wired individually into circuits. Integrated circuits promised an even more efficient compact design size.

The manifesto at IBM was to create a machine to compete with the plug-compatibles. One camp inside the company argued for an interim machine. To be called the 8000 series, it would offer backward compatibility for data and programs with the existing two product lines, while using transistors more extensively. This cautious approach was in direct opposition to the ideas of the man assigned to create a new product line, Vincent Learson, the group vice president for data processing, and a board member. A few years older than Watson, he was ambitious and intended to leave his mark on the firm. He made a crucial decision: His new line would encompass a wide range of machines from low to high end; but it would *not* be compatible with the 1400 and 7000 series.

Taking this step was a big gamble. By doing so, essentially, IBM would obsolete its own machines, which were still fantastically successful. But in that way it would pull the rug out from under Honeywell. More amazing was that the company planned to manufacture most of the components for the new line—called the System 360—internally. This meant developing semiconductor production lines, in addition to computer assembly plants. The scope of the plan was gigantic; it would become the largest single privately funded project in U.S. history, costing more than the Manhattan Project. The only engineering program of comparable magnitude was the space program. Six large new plants were built; 50,000 new employees were hired; R&D costs alone were more than $1 billion a year. In total, the System 360 cost more than $5 billion to develop.

No other company in the United States could have managed such an undertaking. By 1960, IBM had passed the billion-dollar mark—sales for that year were $1.4 billion, and earnings were more than keeping pace; in the first six months of 1961, revenues climbed another 17 percent (to $811 million) and net jumped 32 percent to $101 million. And though the company had taken on debt, it had nearly $300 million in available cash—15 times more than when it started its expansion into computers at the start of the decade, and 4 times more than it had in 1956. Furthermore, for the first time since the war, IBM's cash flow (net income plus depreciation) exceeded its capital outlays by $34 million. The company was self-financing even as it remained one of the most profitable companies on the stock exchange.

At the heart of the 360 project, Watson, his legal advisors, and the ruling junta at the corporation, came up with another scheme they thought would give them a marketplace edge for the long term. Watson had studied the emerging computer industry and had come to the conclusion that the point of differentiation among competitors was software. Thus, the company decided to bundle software with hardware as a package. Watson's attorneys assured him that software, being subject to copyright not patents, was more easily defensible than hardware; better yet, it was not covered by the 1956 antitrust decree. But most compelling was that they could design software that would run on IBM machines only. Invoking copyright law and hiring thousands of programmers would enable the company to tie the sale of programs to IBM hardware. Customers who wanted IBM software would have to buy IBM machines.

This move harkened back to the days of the punch cards. IBM had always made more money by carefully controlling the manufacture and sale of punch cards for its leased machines than on the machines themselves. Software seemed likely to follow the same pattern. And though antitrust issues were still a concern, John F. Kennedy had just been elected president, and because the new First Lady was a long-time family friend, Watson was confident he could fend off legal scrutiny.

Unfortunately, things didn't quite work out the way IBM hoped. First, the company's intrinsic conservatism reared its head: Instead of entrusting the new line of computers to the relatively untested integrated circuit, the IC, the firm's engineers developed a hybrid product they called Solid Logic Technology, SLT. This was a hand-soldered method of arranging a collection of components onto a single module. It was better than discrete transistors, which had to be individually wired onto circuit boards, but it was far less efficient than ICs, which had made their appearance in the first Control Data supercomputers in 1963, a year before the System 360 was announced.

More delays in both the programming and engineering operations followed, and Watson became furious. Still smarting from the failure of his company to make a dent in the supercomputer market, Watson was incensed when CDC introduced a machine. CDC's machine was more powerful than anything on IBM's drawing board, and now the System 360 was delayed again. A memo he wrote after a trip to CDC's headquarters described the competitive operation: "There are only 34 people, including the janitor. Of these, 14 are engineers and 4 are programmers, and only one person has a Ph.D., a relatively junior programmer. To the outsider, the laboratory appeared to be cost-conscious, hard-working, and highly motivated. Contrasting this modest effort with our own vast development activities, I fail to understand why we have lost our industry leadership position by letting someone else offer the world's most powerful computer."

Watson's response was to bring his brother Arthur back from the overseas operation to manage the System 360. This would prove to be a major mistake and was the beginning of the end of the Watson family dynasty at IBM. Arthur Watson was assigned to share responsibility for the System 360 project with its original leader, Learson. To groom his younger brother for the top spot, Watson put him in charge of the R&D effort while Learson handled sales and marketing. It was a disaster. Ill-equipped to manage hundreds of technical details, paralyzed by the engineering decisions he was called on to make, and without a loyal base of cohorts within the U.S. operation to help him, Arthur Watson struggled. The 360 project fell further behind, and all fingers pointed at the younger brother. Learson, who had come up through the ranks of the company on his own talent, resented having to share the spotlight with an "heir" and, he felt, an undeserving, executive. Tensions rose.

By 1964, with the promised delivery date of the new machines rapidly approaching, the reality was that the project was not making progress. All the while, Honeywell was making a big dent in series 1400 bookings, and CDC was successfully selling a more powerful machine than IBM could field. Watson was forced to announce that the 360 line would be at least one year late. At the same time he relieved his brother of responsibility for the new computer, and turned it over to Learson.

Then he authorized the sale of $371 million worth of stock—IBM's first new stock sale in years. The money from the new sale was earmarked for a crash program to fix the System 360.

Learson succeeded in bringing the company together behind the new product, and got it out the door. System 360 would turn out to be a major success. The company leased 1,000 within the first few months at monthly prices that averaged more than $20,000. By the end of the decade, there were some 35,000 IBM computers in customer hands; most were System 360s. This represented monthly income to IBM of more than $500 million, *and* the company owned the underlying machine. It was a worldwide phenomenon, too; international sales accounted for a third of revenues and profits. In the wake of the widespread adoption of the System 360 as the commercial computer standard, IBM shot past stock market stalwarts like U.S. Steel to hit income of $1 billion by 1970. Total revenues were around $7.5 billion, 80 percent of which came from mainframe leasing, service, and support. The marketplace was ripe for a new, powerful, and well-integrated line of computers. Comprising four different, interoperable processors—from simple to complex—the products proved to be just what the market needed. IBM computers met the needs of a wide variety of businesses and negated the necessity of dealing with different manufacturers.

In 1963, there were about 12,000 computers in the United States. By 1965, that number was closer to 25,000; by 1969, the number was 50,000. Most of those machines were from IBM. In 1965, the company's share of the computer industry was 65 percent, its revenues were $2.5 billion, and net earnings totaled $333 million. By the end of the decade its share was closer to 80 percent.

With the System 360, IBM had finally gained technological superiority. The computer was the most advanced full line of machines available anywhere. In addition, the diversity of software offered by IBM was impressive, and could solve an array of business problems. Being able to link software and hardware on a new, and then unique, platform, was an overwhelming advantage. In short, IBM had thrashed the competition.

Ironically, it was the company's famous sales force that would prove to be its Achilles' heel. Stories circulated about how IBM salesmen froze the market in the years before the introduction of the 360; reportedly, they told customers that IBM was about to introduce better machines, and thus were able to stop their defection to Honeywell or one of the other competitors. But that was just the tip of the iceberg. Driven by his hatred of CDC, Tom Watson Jr. set out to crush the smaller company's stronghold in the only niche not dominated by IBM—supercomputing. Even as IBM dominated in commercial computing, Watson became obsessed with winning the supercomputer race.

A few months following the formal announcement of the System 360 line in 1964, IBM unveiled its most powerful computer to date: the System 360/91. As described in glowing marketing terms, the new computer would be more flexible than the CDC machines, would run all the IBM software (Bill Norris at CDC still eschewed software development), and would be less expensive to lease. Not surprisingly, this announcement had a major impact on CDC's sales. By 1966, the small company was in the red; its stock plummeted from $75 a share to less than $30.

By late in the year when the System 360/91 appeared, it was found to be slower, less powerful, and more expensive than the equivalent CDC machines. IBM eventually delivered only 25 of them. For two years, IBM salesmen had been promising customers the phantom computer would solve their problems, and encouraging them not to buy from CDC. When early in 1967 IBM admitted that it would cancel the machine, CDC's Bill Norris was beside himself. As he saw it, IBM always had only one reason for announcing it was in development of the 360/91: to force Control Data out of business.

Norris complained to the Justice Department repeatedly, to no avail. By late 1968, he decided to take matters into his own hands. In December, CDC filed a civil antitrust action against IBM. The first part of the suit alleged violations of the 1956 antitrust decree, implying that the government had been lax in monitoring the company's actions. This threw down the gauntlet to then President Lyndon Johnson's attorney general, Ramsey Clark (son of Tom Clark, who had brought the 1952 action against IBM). The second part of the suit consisted of 34 specific counts. Though there was no smoking gun, the sheer scope of the allegations was impressive. Most centered on the "phantom" computer, citing allegations that IBM froze the market by promising to introduce a "phantom" product solely for the purpose of defeating a competitor.

A month later, on the last day of the Johnson Administration, Ramsey Clark filed a parallel antitrust case, which basically included four charges: First, by bundling service, software and hardware into one price, IBM had "impaired" the ability of independent companies to compete; second, IBM had "used its accumulated software and related support to preclude its competitors from effectively competing for various customer accounts"; third, "by granting exceptional discriminatory allowances in favor of universities and other educational institutions," the company had unfairly influenced academia's decisions on computer purchases; and, finally, by introducing unprofitable models aimed at particular competitors, the company tried to stop its rivals.

This time, Watson was in no mood to settle. He didn't understand that antitrust law didn't require actual intent or overt acts of competitive destructiveness. Once again the company took out newspaper ads: "Has IBM spoiled the computer business for others?" "Of course not!" IBM's defiance was an act of hubris that would practically tear the company apart. Clearly, Watson Jr. had learned nothing from his earlier run-in with his father over the same issue.

Initially, IBM swore it would mount a fearsome defense, but it quickly separated hardware and software and services pricing them each separately. As for the charge regarding the educational discount, IBM didn't understand how that was an antitrust violation. And proving that the company was trying to destroy others by combining software and hardware together would be difficult to prove. Thus the only dangerous charge seemed to be that of announcing phantom computers. And that was the charge on which the investigation focused.

Initially, IBM was faced with two lawsuits: Norris's and the government's. But emboldened by CDC's actions and encouraged by the government antitrust suit, a number of other lawsuits were filed within a year or two by Data Processing Financial and General, Levin Townsend, and Greyhound Computer Leasing, all claiming that IBM's actions hurt them in the services and computer leasing businesses. In addition, leasing firms Itel and Advanced Memory Systems filed suits, as did both Memorex and Telex, two big makers of compatible disk and tape drives. As the cases worked their way through various courts, still more suits were filed. Soon IBM was paying more than 100 lawyers, and much of the Cravath & Swaine law firm was employed full-time on IBM litigation. By the middle of the seventies, a string of suits carried the names of many small companies: Ferro Precision, Symbolic Control, Hudson General, Eaton Allen, Memory Technology, Saunders Associates, Potter Instruments, California Computer Products, Marshall Industries. Big Blue was besieged by lawyers, like Gulliver with the Lilliputians.

The first case to be settled was with CDC. IBM paid Norris and his firm more than $100 million, and sold them its Service Bureau Corporation for the value of its assets. The Telex case was originally won by the plaintiffs—for damages of $350 million—but was then reversed on appeal. Most of the others also were eventually settled. But there was no settlement with the government. The case was kept active until 1982, when it was finally dropped.

Undoubtedly, IBM was damaged by the litigation. At the very least, the company spent enormous effort and money defending itself. Tom Watson Jr. never saw the end of it, either. He had a heart attack in 1970, and retired. The same year his brother was made ambassador to France, and so for the first time since Thomas Watson Sr. had joined the firm in 1915, there was no Watson in the executive suite.

The legacy of the lawsuits changed the way IBM did business. From 1972 on, every decision made was run through the filter of antitrust law. Lawyers drew up codes for what could and could not be discussed inside the firm. From a once aggressive and proud competitor, IBM devolved into a cautious behemoth, afraid of making the wrong move. Sales executives dominated company management; and while the System 370 was a success with its IC-based design, the next-generation product, the FS (Future System) was a disaster and had to be cancelled. By late in the 1970s, IBM was still dependent on its System 360/370 for revenues. Instead of introducing a new line, the company chose to upgrade its existing lines, calling the new mainframes the 3070 family.

Though the company never regained perfect pitch again, what it achieved with the 360 cannot be discounted. The System 360 was the pivotal mainframe computer in leading to the international adoption of data processing. The machines are still deployed around the world today, usually in the newer 3000 series. But their direct ancestor was the System 360.

Tom Watson Jr. had taken on the role his father ordained for him, and made a success of it. When Tom Watson Jr. started guiding the company into the computer age, very few people had any idea what it might mean. He took the kind of gamble small and nimble entrepreneurial companies take all the time. Throwing aside the past and taking enormous risks was the secret to IBM's second generation of success. In the process, Thomas Watson Jr. finally stepped into the limelight in his own right. The son had become greater than the father, and introduced the world to a computer that would change everything.

William Shockley (seated) with John Bardeen, left and Walter H. Brattain, at Bell Labs in July 1948.

>——◉——<

Quantum Leap
Transistors & Semiconductors

It took alchemy, pure alchemy, to create the magical compound of the second half of the twentieth century: the semiconductor. As the 1950s began, a handful of men transmuted a few of the most common chemicals on earth into space-age substances that defied the laws of Newtonian physics, took their early masters into a new realm of quantum mechanics, and made possible previously unimaginable products.

The original semiconductor products were based on a powdery metal-like element called germanium. When melted, then drawn into regular crystalline structures with a miniscule impurity and, finally, sliced into slivers, this new man-made substance exhibited characteristics that baffled scientists. Sometimes it conducted electricity; sometimes it didn't. Hence the name: semiconductor. But there was more: Sometimes it amplified a current; sometimes it blocked it. Sometimes light falling on it set off a current; sometimes it didn't. Sometimes a magnetic field around it created a small current; sometimes it didn't.

After years of fits and starts, endless theories and numerous experiments, these mysterious compounds finally gave up their secrets. When three wires were arranged properly on their surfaces, and the crystals of the semiconducting element were "doped" with just the proper infinitesimal amount of impurity, these lumps of nondescript compounds did exactly what a vacuum tube did: amplified a tiny current running through it.

The transistor—a tiny bit of semiconducting material, with wires attached to both end and the middle, encased in an airtight package— was the only pure science invention of the digital age. Whereas digital calculators, and even computers, were electronic outgrowths of existing *scientific and mathematics thought, this was an utterly new element of the physical universe, a wholly man-made crystal. Its discovery proved to be the dawn of a new age.*

✿   ✿   ✿

PRODUCING SEMICONDUCTORS required a special company—one with massive resources, a penchant for pure research, and a drive to throw over the use of vacuum tubes in favor of something better. All of that came together at AT&T's Bell Laboratories. In the 1940s and 1950s, Bell Labs was one of the most advanced research operations in the world. Housed in a variety of sites, from the largest industrial research complex in the country at Murray Hill, New Jersey, to a warren of labs and offices in Manhattan, the organization employed nearly 10,000 scientists and was the leading commercial producer of scientific papers in the United States for more than 50 years. From 1915 through 1950, the lab spent about half a billion dollars on pure research, representing more than 100,000 man-years of work and more than $140 for every Bell telephone in use in the United States by 1951.

All this work was meant to yield advances that could improve both call fidelity and the switching gear that routed the calls around the nation. Along the way, scientists at the lab were instrumental in the development of a new branch of science called quantum mechanics. They also devised a crucial form of negative feedback control that vastly diminished static and noise on long-distance phone lines. And they formulated the first mathematical theories of communication that calculated the amount of information "bits" in any given message and the capacity of any channel to carry that data. Furthermore, they worked on microwave transmission, high-speed switching, electromechanical computing, radio telescopy, and television. Most notable were the quantum mechanics experiments of Clinton Davisson, which proved the wave-particle duality of matter, and were essential for the atomic energy age. Davisson shared the Nobel Prize in 1937 for his work. But the commercial prize was the discovery and understanding of semiconductors.

In a glorious pure science operation such as this, solving a baffling problem like the behavior of semiconducting substances required someone of prickly brilliance, who could goad and push the work along when everyone else wanted to go on to something new. The man who propelled this effort at Bell Labs was William Shockley. Hired in 1936 right out of MIT, Shockley never really fit in at Bell Labs. He never really fit in anywhere, not at Shockley Semiconductor, a company he started once he left Bell Labs a few years later; not even as an infamous professor at Stanford much later. He just couldn't find an environment that suited his personality.

Shockley was gruff. He had no social graces. There were no "hellos" or "how are yous." At Bell Labs he wasn't afraid to let the rest of the staff know that he was smarter than they were. He would ask what a colleague was working on, and more often than not, as soon as he was told, would make fun of it, then explain the concept using an analogy that was both more plausible and simpler to understand. Then, without any pleasantries he would walk away, leaving the innovator standing speechless.

This was particularly unseemly at the research lab on the western edge of Manhattan, a big cavernous building facing the New Jersey shore. Here modesty was the order of the day, especially among the cadre of young Ph.D.s who were hired in the mid-1930s as part of the first new employee group since the depression had forced a freeze even in AT&T's expansion plans. It was the preeminent commercial research lab in the United States. Although there were many big names from the American scientific community on the payroll, as well as numerous eccentrics, Bill Shockley's behavior raised eyebrows. Eventually it reached the point where people would part as he walked through the corridors, as though an odor preceded him.

Shockley arrived at Bell Labs with a newly minted degree in solid state physics—the behavior of electrons in solids—ready to do breakthrough work. He joined the solid state group who were working on quantum mechanics and developing theories to explain how electrons moved through solids. Even though the rage in the physics labs of MIT had been nuclear power (that magic of fusion and radioactivity), Shockley was interested in something different. Long fascinated with rocks and minerals, he was more excited by challenges of investigating the passage of electricity through various elements: conductors, insulators, and most interesting but puzzling of all, semiconductors.

Both Shockley's parents were geologists. His father, William Hullman Shockley, was a mining engineer and sometime prospector, and was 20 years his wife's senior. Years of living in mining camps and alongside the desolate grubstakes of the mining industry had made him singularly unsuited to the bourgeois life of a father and husband. William

Hullman Shockley was rarely home for more than a few weeks at a time between jobs. His wife ran things when he was gone. May Bradford Shockley was one of the few women to qualify in geology in the early part of the twentieth century. She met her husband in the minefields, but after William was born, at the turn of the century, she settled in Palo Alto, California. As her husband grew more and more distant, disappearing for years on mining jaunts in the Sierra Nevadas and across the far reaches of the Rockies, she concentrated on rearing her son to be the kind of man she thought he should be.

Together they spent weeks exploring geological formations in the western United States. The young Bill learned how to field-test rocks for their composition, how a glance at an escarpment could reveal where fossils were most likely to be found, and which rocks were valuable. Sure of her knowledge of rocks and minerals, May Shockley taught her son an abiding respect, and a deep love, for the chemistry of the earth. He was a good learner and an avid rockhound by the age of 10. Her intellect and drive were instilled in her son. He avoided sports, became the class valedictorian at Palo Alto High, and attended Stanford to stay close to his mother. Later, at MIT, he shone. He was bright, no doubt about that.

Now he was a member of a class of handpicked young Bell Labs scientists, the elite of American students. Besides Shockley, the group included the metallurgist Foster Nix; Dean Wooldridge, a physicist hired from Cal Tech (who went on to be a cofounder of the Ramo-Wooldridge Computer Company); Charles Townes, who was working with high-frequency microwave spectroscopy (and would eventually be one of the creators of the laser); and the crystallographer Alan Holden.

At the time, there were precious few Americans who knew anything about quantum mechanics, so the group started an unofficial study group—they called it a journal club—where each in turn taught a chapter in the only textbook on the subject they could find. Sometimes they invited a distinguished guest lecturer such as I. I. Rabbi of Columbia or John Van Vleck of the University of Wisconsin to help direct them.

Quantum mechanics as a field of study emerged in the mid-1920s when it appeared that atoms—matter itself—could have wave as well as particle aspects. Uncovering all the mathematics of spin, wave-particle duality, and subatomic energy bands took years. Matter waves were conceived of as pilot waves made up of streams of particles that acted in unison—like light wavelengths. The particles each were spinning and could have a particular energy slot, or quantum, depending on the atom each was associated with. Though Davisson and others had confirmed their presence, the mathematics led to several baffling principles at the heart of atomic structure. No two electrons could have precisely the same set of quantum numbers—the exclusion principle—and it was impossible to know exactly where something was at the heart of the atom—the uncertainty principle.

Quantum mechanics turned classic Newtonian physics, with its direct cause-and-effect foundation, on its ear; at its heart, it took a statistical look at the ultimate nature of matter. Atoms were made up of electrons, and different elements had electrons buzzing around in different energy bands, or quanta. But in this new field, actually identifying where an electron was at any moment not only was impossible, but the act of measuring it changed its behavior. Although it was eventually rationalized successfully with relativity, it was a field that drew derision from the greatest scientist of the previous generation, Albert Einstein. "God doesn't throw dice," he pronounced in dismissal. Nevertheless, it made for some lively meetings at Bell Labs in the late 1930s, as an odd conglomeration of theoreticians and experimentalists grappled with the mystifying behavior of electrons in the microcosm.

Shockley's group was formed because Mervin J. Kelly, the general director of research, had made a unilateral decision—one that was applauded in hindsight, but that could just as easily have backfired. He had decided that the future of telephone switching lay in some kind of electronic switch, and he was determined to set these young and ambitious physicists to work on creating it. He brought together physicists, metallurgists, and mathematicians. Shockley's group examined crystalline substances and their conductivity. It was one of many projects launched to help the phone company find an answer to one of its most pressing problems: space—or more accurately, not enough space.

In every town in America, big square block buildings had gone up in the late 1920s and 1930s to house the electromechanical switches that enabled telephone calls to go directly from one telephone to another. Composed of an electromagnet and a spring, each relay switch became magnetized when a current was delivered to the electromagnet. With the current on, one half of the contact became magnetized and attracted the other, closing the contact and making the circuit. When power was shut off to the electromagnet, the magnetism disappeared and the gate swung open under pressure from the spring.

These worked, but they also took up large amounts of space. Furthermore, because the switches were basically mechanical, they wore out. And, finally, they were slow—at least, in an electronic sense. They could open or close in about a tenth of a second, but electricity could be delivered in pulses (or cycles) measured in millionths of a second. For all of these reasons, as well as the high cost of buying new buildings to accommodate more phone lines, one of the charters to Bell Labs was to replace electromechanical switches and vacuum tubes with something better.

The answer, Kelly and other prescient scientific administrators believed, lay somewhere in the quantum physics of solid state compounds; that is, the behavior of electricity as it flows through solid materials. It was into this arena that he sent his bright young team of researchers to investigate. And by the late 1930s, they had narrowed the focus: to the curious behavior of a class of compounds known as semiconductors.

Michael Faraday, the savant of electricity, had discovered these mysterious products in 1826. Certain compounds would change their electrical behavior when heated, when light fell on them, or when they were brought near another current. Falling somewhere between conductors and insulators, this class of crystalline compounds of metals, such as lead sulfide (Galena), exhibited a number of puzzling qualities. In the 100 years since Faraday's experiments with silver sulfide, a number of researchers had delved into the behavior of this class of compounds. They had learned that heat would reduce resistance to current, light would increase conductivity, and a magnetic field could induce an electrical current perpendicular to the main current. By the late 1920s, theories abounded, but none satisfactorily explained these phenomena.

By the time the researchers at Bell Labs turned their attention to the subject in the 1930s, the only working product that used semiconductor technology was the so-called cats whisker radio tuner, comprising a crystal of lead sulfide and a fine wire attached to a radio-tuning circuit. Moving the wire over the crystal let the listener tune in different signals at different places on its surface. But the physics behind this simple phenomenon also remained opaque. Nonetheless, it was clear that there was something important about crystals, and their interaction with electricity, that merited further investigation. A great deal of effort was spent trying to produce pure specimens of various crystalline semiconductor compounds. Scientists generally pursued this by heating compounds to high temperatures, then withdrawing seed crystals out of the mix to form a single perfect crystal. In the process, they realized that one of the keys in transforming an insulating crystal into a semiconductor was to determine how many impurities it contained. Introducing the proper amount of impurity when the crystal was formed could free up electrons inside its carefully controlled molecular structure. As a result, a current could be induced to flow more easily in the material. Conversely, with the wrong amount of impurity, nothing would happen. But how it worked, and just what the relationship was between impurities and crystalline structure remained baffling. Then the second world war intervened.

After the war, Kelly remained convinced that there had to be a better solution to the tyranny of electromechanical relays in switching telephone calls, so he put the ambitious Bill Shockley in the role of project leader. Shockley's two key researchers were John Bardeen, a theorist, and Walter Brattain, an experimentalist extraordinaire. Bardeen had studied at Wisconsin and was known as a top-flight theoretician of the quantum world. True to the academic stereotype, he sported pipe, rumpled clothing, and a brilliantly creative scientific mind. Brattain on the other hand could make almost anything work. He had been at Bell Labs since 1929, after receiving his Ph.D. from Minnesota. He had grown up on a ranch in western Washington, and was the picture of a laconic cowboy. Slow speaking, almost painfully shy, he had slicked-back silver hair and a thin mustache. Add to the mix Shockley to goad the other two on, and the dynamics for success had been set in motion.

As they were working during December 1947, Bardeen kept thinking there was something fundamentally wrong with the entire concept of the quantum mechanics of electron behavior within a semiconductor. He had done a fair amount of work on the surface states of semiconductors before the Second World War, and believed that somehow the electrons were being trapped on the surface of the semiconductor, and thus were not free to help conduct a current. He was convinced that the surface was where the crystal's symmetry was broken and where all those neatly arranged molecules suddenly broke off. The team started to experiment by dropping liquid on top of the semiconductor. Brattain discovered that this changed the surface electrical resistance, but not enough to amplify a current. What they really wanted out of the semiconductor was exactly what a vacuum tube did: to control a large current by varying a much smaller one across the center of it. A vacuum tube accomplished this with a grid set across the main current. Electrodes on the grid, carrying minute voltages, varied a much bigger current flowing through the device in exact rhythm with any variations.

Bardeen's notion got his partner, the farm boy from Washington, thinking. A few days later, he wondered whether placing a flow of electrons from one of the point contacts, near another point that was carrying current might affect the current flow. He tried this and found there was no transistor effect—no matter what he did with the current in the middle, the circuit between the end contacts was unaffected. Then he moved the two fine needle contacts very close to each other. Finally it happened. The one small positive current flowed into the semiconductor at contact point, and increased the current flowing through another pair of contacts on the crystal, by nearly 90 times.

At first, neither Brattain nor Bardeen believed it, so they painstakingly rebuilt their apparatus by evaporating extremely fine gold contacts onto the surface of a big block of germanium. When they touched a low-voltage positive source near one contact, the current flowing through the circuit was 90 times greater. And it duplicated fluctuations in the fainter input. They had created a point-contact device, made entirely from semiconductors, that could conceivably replace the vacuum tube.

The theory was left to Bardeen and Shockley. Essentially, their hypothesis was that the semiconductor substance was a compound that had an unstable outer electron band. They used germanium, because it had a low melting point, was very cheap, and formed crystals in the proper circumstances. With just the right number of impurities introduced into the man-made crystals—doping, it was called—the semiconductor atoms were "fooled" and would hardly pass a current usually. However, when a few electrons were introduced to exactly the right spot between the two main leads, the current would be amplified a great deal. The theorists decided that the low-voltage input was actually shooting holes into the block of semiconductor, holes that opened just enough spaces to facilitate the passage of electricity. Electrons flowed to fill up the holes; and it was these holes that then allowed the electrical current to be amplified.

The notebook entry for the breakthrough was dated December 23, 1947. More important, it was witnessed by several Bell Labs managers, who saw and *heard* the amplification circuit. The inventors set up a microphone for a demonstration. With three wires soldered precariously to its surface the new bizarre-looking hunk of crystal, was switched into a circuit containing a speaker: it amplified their voices; when it was removed, their voices were inaudible. Bardeen and Brattain were given the credit for the device and when it came time to file for the patent they alone were named. Bill Shockley was hurt. After all, it was his persistence, coupled with his knowledge of semiconductor quantum theory, that enabled the two scientists to succeed. He made his dissatisfaction known, but didn't stop there. He decided not only to create his own theory of how to build such a device, now called the transistor, but most of all, to improve on it.

Shockley's new concept was called the *junction transistor*. He believed that instead of injecting electron holes via closely spaced contacts on the surface of the block of semiconductor, the same effect could be achieved by building a block of semiconductor material in a "sandwich." His group had already determined that there were positive and negative semiconductor crystals—called p-type or n-type. Furthermore, by putting the two types back to back, and arranging a current across the junction between them, a semiconductor crystal would either pass a current or block it. This crystal was called a *diode*. But the diode didn't do anything for amplification, which was what this exercise was about.

Shockley aimed for nothing less than replacing the vacuum tube. If he could somehow create the sandwich in which the two ends were of one polarity and a small section in the middle was of the opposite polarity, he reasoned he would be able to use a small charge on the center section to amplify, or block, the current running through the device between the two ends of like material. But no matter how hard he tried, he couldn't get it to work. For the better part of two years he tried desperately to find the answer.

Part of the problem was that no one knew how to make an ingot of material with n-type silicon on either side of a p-type region. The level of impurity required—trace elements of boron, gallium, or indium for positive doping; phosphorous, antimony, or arsenic for negative—was measured in minuscule amounts. (Imagine a pinch of sugar mixed into a railcar of salt.) And the atomic quantity had to be precise. Too much or too little, and it wouldn't work. This was where alchemy came into play. Finally, a Bell Labs expert was able to produce a germanium sandwich. By 1949, the junction transistor was demonstrated. This time Shockley got the credit. With its pair of patents on transistors, Bell Labs was set to completely rewrite the electronics age.

What made Shockley's *grown junction* transistor so much better than the earlier point-contact ones was that it held out the promise that it could be mass-produced. And though the process would take years to perfect, it would prove to be cheaper than building vacuum tubes. And that wasn't its only advantage over the tubes. Since the tiny slivers of semiconducting material had no moving parts, theoretically, they would never wear out. Furthermore, they used very low power—no more glowing red cabinets rippling with heat, as in tube equipment. But there was much work to do to turn this theoretical discovery into a commercial product.

The transistor became one of the most celebrated developments of the century, but only after Bell Labs spent several years trying to figure out how to implement the radical, unproven technology and wondering whether it really could subsume the entire vacuum tube industry. At the time, AT&T was also grappling with a bigger problem; it was under antitrust investigation by the Justice Department to determine whether it held a monopoly on telephone network gear through Western Electric. To deflect criticism in 1952, AT&T decided to license its transistor patents for $25,000—and even offered a royalty-free license to any company willing to use the devices in hearing aids (which was Alexander Graham Bell's original passion; his parents were deaf). At a series of seminars, the Bell Labs staff briefed interested industrial companies on transistor manufacture and use. But attending the seminar didn't give a company the know-how to make the highly finicky new parts. This was still an infant technology, and there were only a handful of scientists who could coax a working ingot of raw doped germanium out of a blast furnace. And most of these alchemists were on staff at Bell Labs.

At the time, AT&T's transistors were made in a small research lab staffed by Gordon Teal and a few other experts. Teal was a young man given the task of duplicating the lab benchwork of the inventors. The germanium transistor he created was a marvel. He started by pulling single crystals, formed around a seed, from a melt of pure mineral in a furnace. To address the critical issue of impurity, Teal figured out a method for adding pellets of impurities to the melt in such a way that they affected the drawn crystals in exactly the proper way. Everything he did was innovative. But it wasn't appreciated, because AT&T wasn't sure it wanted to manufacture transistors anyway. Teal felt that his job was in jeopardy while the company vacillated about what to do with the devices. He was ultimately kept on because no one could duplicate the high yields he produced—but the uncertainty had soured him. The native Texan started thinking about working somewhere else. But where?

In these early years, the early 1950s, other techniques for working with these man-made crystalline semiconductors were perfected. Bill Pfann, another Bell Labs metallurgist, devised a technique for passing a quartz "boat" through the center of a wire loop heating element. The process, known as *zone refining*, made the creation of transistors much more economically feasible. As the boat, with a rod of germanium in it, passed through the heating field, a section of the rod melted. Impurities stayed in the molten section and passed along that region of the rod toward the end. This highly impure region could then be cut off, and the resulting bar could be made as pure as desired. The more times the bar was swept through the field, the further it could be purified. As Pfann developed this technique, he also found a way to add impurities and distribute them evenly throughout the rod. This was called *zone leveling*, and it made it possible to dope germanium perfectly.

Alchemy may have been at the heart of creating the transistor, but it was pure business smarts that made it a success. And that came from the first great business empire of the semiconductor age: Texas Instruments. The chief architect for the operation was a nervy manager who had arrived at the company at the end of the war, Patrick Haggerty. Texas Instruments had an intriguing history. Founded in the 1920s by a pair of geophysical engineers, originally it built equipment that used sound waves to enable engineers to look at subsurface geology—primarily to search for oil. After the war, the firm diversified into defense contracting work. Then Haggerty read about the discovery of the transistor at Bell Labs. The more he read, the more convinced he became that this product had the potential to replace the vacuum tube. He convinced the founders of the firm to get a license to make them. His mission was to get a piece of the enormous business that would ensue if transistors produced even half of what the electronics trade press was claiming they would in the early 1950s.

Raytheon, a big tube maker, was already taking AT&T up on the offer of a royalty-free license, as was Zenith, and RCA, which had a patent cross-licensing deal with AT&T. But the point-contact transistors were very difficult to manufacture, with yield rates of just over 50 percent. The first junction transistors were fabricated in 1951, and the following summer Bell held its first technical seminars on the products. Representatives from Texas Instruments were there.

The jump into transistors was a remarkable move for then tiny Texas Instruments to make. Betting $1.25 million on salaries and development costs, along with $3 million in new plants, manufacturing gear, and fixed assets, was a huge gamble for a firm whose sales in 1952 were $20 million with profits of $900,000. In fact, it took almost a year for Haggerty's boss to convince AT&T to even sell them the $25,000 license to manufacture semiconductors. AT&T thought Texas Instruments was too small, and too inexperienced. But the Texans persevered. By the end of the year, Texas Instruments had an order—for 100 germanium transistors for the Gruen Watch Company—and was in production.

However Haggerty soon realized that germanium wasn't going to get them very far. Too many other companies were working on building transistors, big companies like Sylvania, General Electric, RCA, and Zenith. That didn't leave Texas Instruments with much of a market. Furthermore, germanium had a characteristic that couldn't be engineered out of the equation: its temperature intolerance. The substance had a very low melting point, and therefore wouldn't demonstrate semiconductor capabilities at anything over about 100 degrees Fahrenheit. This severely limited its use and application, especially for military purposes, which was one of the areas where the transistors' ruggedness, and small size, gave them a big advantage over vacuum tubes. A close chemical neighbor—silicon—had been shown to have much better semiconductor features and higher temperature tolerances. But producing properly doped silicon crystals had proved nearly impossible. Germanium was difficult, but silicon was next to impossible, even for Teal and the wizards at Bell Labs. This was due partly to the much higher temperatures needed to refine silicon, but also to the fact that the compound itself was very finicky. At that time around 1953 the conventional wisdom was that silicon transistors were years away from commercial use.

This didn't stop Haggerty, who knew nothing of germanium when he got into the field in the first place. Nine months later, his company was in production on germanium transistors. So he reasoned, how much more difficult could silicon be? They began to search for someone to fill the job of chief researcher. And who should answer their ad in *The New*

York Times but the Bell Labs semiconductor magician, Gordon Teal. When he found out that Texas Instruments planned to make silicon transistors, Teal told the company it would need more money; in response, Haggerty showed him plans to merge with InterContinental Rubber (an old-line tire and rubber company with a waning business) and to get listed on the New York Stock Exchange to access funds. Teal warned Haggerty that he would need men, experienced men; Haggerty pointed out that the company already had on staff transistor manufacturing experts, and then offered to hire anyone else Teal wanted from Bell Labs. Teal said he would need time; on this point Haggerty demurred, saying that he could let him have a year for research, but after that they would have to start building. Teal accepted the challenge.

Although stock options were part of the incentive, the real lure for Teal was the opportunity to perfect the silicon transistor years ahead of everyone else. Teal was one of the few people in the world who really understood how to make Shockley's junction transistors, the sandwich of n- and p-type germanium. Haggerty was one of the few people in the world who saw the potential in them. It was the perfect partnership. Haggerty brought Teal to Texas with a promise of foundries and kilns and assembly lines and all the money he needed. The result was that, by late 1953, they were producing grown junction germanium transistors at high enough volume to supply a segment of the industry. Bigger competitors had even more success though, and by the following year, they would sell just over 1 million transistors, at a total value of $4.8 million.

At the same time things grew tense at Texas Instruments. The company had come to depend on its military business, and when, in mid-1953, the Korean War ended, military spending dried up. TI reported lower revenues and profits for 1954—not an auspicious beginning for its first year as a publicly traded company. Revenues dropped from $27 million in 1953 to $24 million a year later, and earnings fell from $1.27 million to $1.2 million. The stock, which had first been traded in October 1953, fell to single digits.

Facing failure, Haggerty continued to believe it was only a matter of time before Teal perfected his silicon transistor. The manager's faith paid off: by early 1954, Teal had conceived of a way to make silicon-based transistors. His process required much higher temperatures, and a correspondingly complicated doping and zone-refining process. That spring, the scientist was set to give a paper at a conference on airborne aeronautics held in Dayton, Ohio. After listening to hours of speakers who bemoaned the difficulty of silicon semiconductor manufacture, Teal stood up and pulled a handful of them out of his shirt pocket, boasting "We're already in production." On a table nearby he set up a record player that had been carefully modified to allow a transistor to be snapped in and out of the circuits. Then, while a recording of Artie Shaw's band played on a record player, he plunged a germanium transistor into a beaker of hot oil. As the semiconductor reacted to the heat, it shut down the circuit and stopped the music. Then he replaced the germanium with a silicon chip and did the same thing. The song played on.

Pandemonium swept through the auditorium. A Texas Instruments team at the back of the hall was swamped by eager clients. Soon thereafter the news electrified the electronics industry, and the little company was the toast of the business. But the innovation was a long way from reaching the public consciousness. After all, this was an America that still got its news and entertainment from radios that were as big as sideboards. Transistors were an exotic sideshow, a specialty item, of little importance to the common citizen.

Haggerty was determined to change all of that. From the beginning, his interest in semiconductors focused on radios. As a child, he had used a so-called cats whisker crystal radio set. As he led Texas Instruments into the electronic age, he never stopped thinking about radios. He latched onto two things: the transistor's low power; and the fact that this little sliver could replace a vacuum tube. The transistors consumed only one one-hundredth (soon to be one one-thousandth) the amount of power required by a tabletop radio. Instead of running in a vacuum tube environment, which needed the electric current from the wall, transistors were portable; they could be carried by hand, in a car, to a picnic, or out under the stars. Haggerty decided that the ultimate way to show off the new silicon transistor would be in the form of a transistor radio.

To make this product a reality, Haggerty had to do two things. First, Texas Instruments had to be able to make transistors cheaply. This already had been accomplished by early in 1954. Teal and his colleagues had so improved the germanium manufacturing process that they were now confidently pricing their units at $2.50 apiece, down from $16.50 the year before, which made the radio economically feasible. Second, Haggerty had to find a company to market the thing. He chose the I.D.E.A. Corporation, an Indianapolis company that was having great success selling an early consumer electronics device—an antenna signal booster for home television signals.

Using an electronic design supplied by Texas Instruments, the two companies collaborated to produce the Regency radio in time to introduce it to the public for the 1954 Christmas season. Priced at $50, it was an enormous hit. Unfortunately, the price was too low to yield a profit, since every element of the radio had to be created in miniature. Still, the publicity it generated was enormous. TI was on the map as *the* transistor company. Within a year, after RCA and Hoffman had introduced similar radio models, priced closer to $75, TI and I.D.E.A. dropped out of the market because they had lost money on every one of the 100,000 radios they sold. But it didn't matter. Texas Instruments was after a much more lucrative, higher-margin market: the silicon transistor business. And thanks to its radio, the transistor had entered into the collective consciousness of the United States.

It took longer for transistors to be a commercial success, however. Vacuum tube manufacturers continued to hold onto the business; after all, generations of engineers knew how to design electronic equipment using the tubes, so they weren't about to disappear overnight. Between 1954 and 1956, 17 million germanium and 11 million silicon transistors were sold in the United States, for a total value of about $55 million; but in the same period, more than 1.3 billion vacuum tubes of similar performance were sold, with a market value of well over $1 billion. The entire electronics business in the United States for that period was worth about $6.5 billion, so transistors were hardly a blip on the screen—representing less than 1 percent of sales.

Nevertheless, it was obvious that the transistor was going to be a major player in the electronics industry. It was a brand new field, open to new competitors. This was a business of finesse: To succeed required tweaking the mix just so, adding this or that reactant into the brew just as the rod entered the oven. As such, there was no obvious advantage to being a big and well-established firm. In fact, most of the big electronics companies were so busy keeping up with the demand for another new product—the television—that they didn't even bother with transistors and radios.

And so TI came to dominate the field. It had a better man in Gordon Teal, and he could do the best job of growing crystals from silicon. Pat Haggerty could figure out how to sell the things and soon TI earned a three-year monopoly on an extremely profitable segment of the semiconductor business. As late as 1957, silicon transistors were selling for around $18 apiece, whereas germanium transistors were priced under $2 each. Compared to silicon, germanium was easy. Most of the big tube companies had assigned some small group to dabble in germanium; silicon was regarded as far too exotic, and in general, they were content to stay with the status quo—vacuum tubes. Raytheon was probably the most aggressive in making transistors, only for a small market segment. With its royalty-free license from Bell, the big electronics company used its transistors in hearing aids. By the middle of 1953, Raytheon was producing 10,000 germanium transistors for hearing aids alone. It was never able to translate this success into other sectors of the business and it's not clear that its management ever wanted to. Valves, tubes, diodes and all their brethren were doing very well, thank you.

One company that *was* very interested in transistor developments was IBM. By 1955 Thomas Watson Senior had ceded control to his son, and Junior bought 200 of the new transistor radios as soon as he saw them. He distributed them to his top managers, and told them, "If this company's products are good enough for these radios, they are good enough for our computers." IBM became one of TI's earliest and biggest customers as it replaced its tubes and valves with silicon transistors in its largest computers.

All this was very good for Texas Instruments: it became the next big growth company in the digital age (after IBM). By 1956, the company's sales hit $45.7 million, a 59 percent leap from the year before. Though sales of 12.5 million transistors that year still were a drop in the bucket compared to the billion vacuum tube business, clearly, this was a business that was growing. Over the following three years, Texas Instruments continued at this torrid pace, averaging 61 percent growth per year in revenues, and 73 percent in earnings. By 1959, the company posted sales of $193 million (more than double the previous year); and earnings rose 136 percent to $14 million.

While Texas Instruments had focused on government and missile work, and was insulated from the realities of the broad commercial transistor market, the industry overall was going through a steep learning curve. At General Electric, the average price for the company's entire line of 31 transistor types was $2.90 each in 1956; a year later, it was $1.90. In the lower-quality consumer market, transistors suitable for radios had plunged in price from $3.00 each to under $1.25 in the same period—a fall of nearly two-thirds. Assembly-line yields were improving thanks to the refinement in the gear necessary to make semiconductor compounds and transistors; prices continued to plummet. At the same time, demand more than doubled from 1957 to 1958, rising from 12 million to 25 million worldwide. The industry as a whole was doing about $228 million in sales by 1958, rising to $400 million-plus in 1960. There was almost no place where transistors couldn't replace vacuum tubes.

Soon, all bets were off. Technology was remaking industry, and two new Bell Labs innovations—diffusion by gas to dope semiconductors and the mesa transistor—obsoleted the earlier processes for creating transistors. Texas Instruments was the first company to perfect these techniques, which forced many of its much bigger competitors to rethink their entire operation. To keep pace with this rate of change company managers needed nerves of steel. The semiconductor had changed the ground rules of competition, and those who could secure a foothold on the train as it pulled out of the station had a chance at prosperity. Those companies that missed it—like Philco—were doomed sooner or later.

In the years after the Second World War, Philco was one of the biggest tube manufacturers in the United States, and tubes were built under a single process that didn't change much year to year. In order to protect its share of the market, the company decided to enter the semiconductor manufacturing business. But just when it had perfected its junction transistor, the tables turned. When Philco introduced samples of a new transistor in 1956, they were priced at $100 apiece. Six months later, the transistors came to market at $50 each; six months after that the price was down to $19; and a year later, those units could be had in lots of 1,000 for $6.75 apiece.

That was intimidating enough for an old-line industrial company used to producing products that had a certain amount of staying power. But the speed of the technological revolution was only intensifying as the understanding of semiconductors, and the ability to create them, leapt ahead. By the late 1950s, holding on in the semiconductor business meant adopting an entirely new manufacturing process based on the latest work every year or so. That meant throwing out all the old equipment and replacing it—with the prospect of having to do it again in another couple of years. Unless a company was completely committed to building semiconductors, it was hardly worth the effort. Philco management decided it wasn't, that it was too risky and expensive, that it would be better to stick with vacuum tubes, a business it had mastered. Big mistake. Within ten years, the vacuum tube business was all but obsolete; the only tube companies still making money were those that had gone whole-heartedly after transistors. Philco never recovered, nor did Sylvania or RCA. Only GE made a successful transition, probably because it had numerous other product lines in which transistors could be absorbed.

Even Texas Instruments would have problems. In January 1959, an article in *Forbes* described the company in glowing terms:

> Bulling its way into electronics it now claims to be the nation's no. one producer of transistors, the tiny electronic devices that do the work of vacuum tubes and currently constitute the fastest mushrooming field in all U.S. industry.
>
> Since 1950, Texin's [Texas Instruments original name] revenues have sprouted 12 times (to an estimated $90 million in 1958), while profits have swelled by more than 1000% to about $5.2 million last year.

The stock market liked what it was seeing, and within 12 months the shares in Texas Instruments had soared from $73 apiece to nearly $250. Less than a year later, in September 1960, *Forbes* published another article about the company that described the perils of the semiconductor business:

> For years, all Patrick Haggerty had to do to keep Wall Street's security analysts enthralled was to recite a little simple arithmetic. Not since Pythagoras had numbers seemed so magical. . . .
>
> When stockholders met in Dallas last April, Haggerty had confidently forecast more of the same in 1960. But by August, he was lowering his goals, and last month he confessed that even his midsummer targets had been set too high. This time he cut his estimates to pedestrian levels, which brought hitherto high-flying Texas Instruments abruptly down out of its accustomed altitudes. The outlook: sales up only 20%, net up a mere 10%."

What went wrong? Ironically, the problem was another leap forward, for which Texas Instruments was partially responsible. It was the introduction of the packaged circuit—a series of components packed on one ceramic square. Single transistors of semiconducting material were being integrated into circuits in such a way that they could perform multiple functions. Instead of hundreds of discrete transistors all wired together, now modules of transistors, rectifiers, and diodes were being packaged together. The result? Fewer individual component sales for the major manufacturers. Texas Instruments' stock plunged nearly in half, to $148. No longer the darling of the transistor age, investors abandoned TI in the fast-changing market.

Still, Texas Instruments was a success, regardless of how the stock market reacted to peaks and valleys. The same could not be said for Shockley Semiconductor, a venture started by William Shockley back in his old hometown of Palo Alto. Having a great mind wasn't enough; Shockley also needed business savvy and marketplace skill to turn alchemy into gold. He had neither. Brilliance alone wasn't enough, unfair as that may have seemed to the creative geniuses who sparked the digital age.

By the early 1950s, it had not escaped the notice of Bill Shockley that a number of Bell Labs employees were leaving and making big money in the new and booming semiconductor market, a market ripe for the skills he possessed. After all, more than 100 years after the mysterious substances had been identified, it was Shockley who led the team that had solved the mystery of semiconductors.

After Teal left Bell Labs for Texas Instruments, Shockley started to think about following suit. Arnold Beckman, the founder of Beckman Instruments, also wanted to start something in the transistor business. When he heard that Shockley was considering leaving Bell, he offered Shockley a deal that was hard to refuse: a research lab of his own, anywhere he wanted it; a large enough staff to run it; and no interference. Beckman, whose fortune had been made in scientific test and measurement equipment, was willing to take a risk, especially if it had to do with science. And Shockley was the marquee name in semiconductors, so it would be a great coup for Beckman—if only for the prestige value to his customers. After hesitating briefly, Shockley was convinced.

The Shockley operation started in 1955 just after Texas Instruments had just introduced the transistor radio, and soon every hotshot semiconductor engineer in the country wanted to join him. Things were literally hot in Bill Shockley's shed. Between the kilns and young materials scientists, physicists, and electrical engineers, intense heat was being generated. The place was filled with people who believed that the future was in these slivers of semiconducting material.

Things got even hotter on November 1, 1956, the day that Shockley was informed that he, along with John Bardeen and William Brattain, had been awarded the Nobel Prize for inventing the transistor. He took everybody in the lab to lunch at Dinah's Shack, the local watering hole.

Shockley's Palo Alto operation became the center of the world's work on germanium diodes. He ran everything like a brilliant and uncompromising professor. But, as always, he was aloof and distant. Worse, he didn't trust the results the "boys"—"Shockley's boys" as they were called throughout the industry—brought to him. These engineers were not yet experts; Shockley, afflicted by "academitis," didn't trust their results, and so continually second-guessed them. In the wake of the Nobel Prize, his behavior grew insufferable. He became convinced that someone was sabotaging his research. That had to be the reason it wasn't working the way he predicted it should. So sure was he that one of his staff was disloyal that he forced members to take lie detector tests. Nothing conclusive was discovered, but the germanium products they produced still didn't yield the quantities necessary for commercial production. Shockley blamed everyone else. He never considered his own shortcomings.

Shockley was in a perfect position to exploit his own discovery, with access to both money and the brightest electrical engineers of the generation. But he poisoned the atmosphere. He was a terrible manager and was overly cautious in a business where only risk takers were rewarded. Staff morale plummeted. To reduce secrecy, Shockley decided to be egalitarian and publish everyone's salaries. The same thing was being done at Lawrence Livermore, the sprawling top-secret lab complex across the Bay where nuclear research was being conducted in a highly secure valley campus. The move backfired, wounding some and embarrassing others. Shockley, an able thinker, never understood why this caused a problem.

But the biggest arguments at the Shockley operation had to do with germanium. Shockley felt certain of germanium; he understood germanium; and he could work with it. The younger guys, those who had flocked to his shed, wanted to go with silicon, which TI had pioneered nearly two years earlier and which seemed to have much better electrical characteristics. Shockley, they thought, was reacting too slowly, doing too much research, worrying too much about what to produce, instead of just getting a good enough product out the door. One young Turk, Bob Noyce, was especially vocal. He thought that silicon transistors were the answer; Shockley was adamant that they stick with germanium diodes.

Robert Noyce had been one of the first people outside of Bell Labs to get his hands on a transistor. His professor at Grinnell College, in Iowa, Grant Gale, knew John Bardeen from the Ph.D. program at Wisconsin. The two grew up together as faculty brats in Madison, where their fathers worked for the university. Now Gale was a professor of physics at a small private school in central Iowa. When he read the announcement of the transistor, he asked Bardeen for one. A few weeks later, a small cardboard box, roughly the size of a jewelry box, arrived. In it was one of the first hand-wired Bell Labs point-contact transistors soldered onto a germanium crystal.

Noyce had always been a very good mechanic. His dad was a minister, but his mother, Harriet, was the driving force in the family. She had pushed him to get his hands on some of the electronic gear in the Physics building, where vacuum tubes were the key to life. Noyce had been taking the college physics course and had been doing brilliantly, especially in the hands-on work where he could make machines and apparatus work. But Noyce also had some growing up to do.

Noyce had a radiant smile, a winning personality, and a mischievous sense of humor and his hi-jinks got him into real trouble as he neared graduation. Noyce stole a pig from a local farmer to use at a fraternity party. The dean of men, a retired Army colonel and a strict disciplinarian, recommended expulsion. Fortunately, Noyce's parents had plenty of friends, the college attorney among them. They settled on a semester's suspension if Noyce would leave town. So he went to New York where his brother Don was at Columbia graduate school. Bob's math skills were prodigious, and in New York he was hired by Equitable Life in the actuarial department as a "computer." It convinced him of one thing: he never wanted to work in a big cavernous room filled with rows and rows of desks, each one with a clerk calculating rows of numbers. For a free-spirited boy from a small town in Iowa, this was not a world he wanted to inhabit.

He went home for Christmas in 1948, and rejoined his class for the second semester. He had accumulated enough extra credits to graduate on time, even with the lost semester. But what really excited him was the point-contact transistor that Professor Gale had just received. Noyce spent weeks working with it and investigating the phenomena of surface state activity and amplification. By the time he graduated that summer, he was certain about his next step: he was going to study the so-called solid state devices at MIT.

Two years later, armed with a Ph.D., Noyce took a job at Philco creating transistors for televisions. But the old-line electronics company was the country's largest manufacturer of vacuum tubes. The entrenched interests within the company that ran its vacuum tube manufacturing operation weren't about to let their duchy be destroyed by the new-fangled transistors that young engineers were touting. (Being a leader in an outdated technology would destroy the company.) Noyce soon felt stymied and started looking around for a more interesting place to work.

Shockley Semiconductor was his first choice. Noyce called the great man a couple of times, then flew out to meet him. The morning before the meeting, he precipitously rented a house, and then turned up ready and determined to work for the great man of junction transistors. He wasn't going to take an answer other than yes—which is what he got.

But a year or so later, in 1957, the shed team was growing increasingly frustrated by their boss, now the Nobel Prize-winning genius Bill Shockley. A couple of the more ambitious and dissatisfied among them decided to start working on a business plan on their own time. The idea was simple: adopt the latest Bell Labs method for making transistors, and launch into production with a silicon-based part as fast as possible.

But with Texas Instruments way out in front on silicon transistors, and a mature business in germanium dominated by big suppliers, it was a very risky plan. The circle of bright Shockley disciples didn't know anyone who might finance such an audacious and expensive undertaking. Bankers didn't want to back their plans, and there was no coterie of investment bankers and well-heeled acquaintances willing to throw money at such a risky venture.

The next quantum leap taken in the digital age wouldn't be in electrons and the behavior of semiconductors; it would be in financing such a seemingly mad venture. The leap was taken by a tall, taciturn patrician investment banker by the name of Arthur Rock. Rock was working for the New York investment-banking firm Hayden Stone, which was interested in making investments in the electronics arena. Basically, the firm was a funnel: they would package a deal and bring rich investors into contact with promising young firms. For the high-class sales agents, this was investment banking of the day. Of course, it took someone unique to invest in something as new and seemingly impenetrable as semiconductor electronics. At first, Rock had little luck selling the Shockley renegades to his wealthy clients. But eventually, he found them a part-ner—an "angel"—with deep pockets: Sherman Fairchild.

Fairchild Camera and Equipment was a major American defense contractor that produced military surveillance gear. The company had a long history in business and technology—in fact, the founder George Fairchild had been chairman of the board at the Computing-Tabulating-Recording Company (C-T-R Inc.) when Thomas Watson Senior (later, of IBM) was offered its presidency in 1915.

Sherman had ambitions in his own right, and Rock knew it. He had watched as both Remington Rand and IBM made major moves into the digital age, and as Texas Instruments captured the higher ground with its pocket radio and the silicon transistor. He also saw Arnold Beckman taking chances out in California—his company was one of Fairchild's toughest competitors in the marketplace for scientific gear. Rock con-vinced Fairchild that making an investment in this team of young guys, right out of the great Shockley's own lab, was a good thing. Not coinci-dentally, it would hurt Beckman, too.

So Sherman put up the seed money for the young team, and took an option to buy them all out for $4 million anytime within the next eight years—$500,000 apiece with no stock options and thus no dilution of his ownership. It sounded like a good deal; and it was. Within the option period, Fairchild Semiconductor would be contributing more than 80 percent of the profits to the parent company.

Before the deal was finalized, Rock and Fairchild demanded that the group find a manager, someone who could keep all the research going, run the administrative side of things, and be the figurehead, the investors' front man. The team of seven defectors went straight to the guy with the dazzling smile, the handsome fellow people naturally looked up to: Bob Noyce. Noyce didn't think long before he accepted. Now there were eight defectors; more important, the practice of form-ing companies out of the best and brightest from the last skyrocketing enterprise had begun. Shockley called them the "traitorous eight."

Others simply called them smart. Bob Noyce was so smart that he led the industry out of the transistor age, and America into the space age, by pioneering the next great era in electronics. To do so, a few years later, he co-founded a company called Intel.

Jay Forrester, who invented the modern memory system for the Whirlwind computer, August 1964.

>—◆—<

CHAPTER 4

Bits

Memory, Minicomputers & the Mouse

From the end of the Second World War until the early 1990s, one issue influenced every aspect of U.S. government policy: the Cold War. For years, American presidents, policymakers and the public were obsessed with defense and military readiness. From 1945 to 1985, an estimated $2.4 trillion was spent on bombs, missiles, satellites, and monitoring systems. The country turned from a prewar isolationist to a postwar interventionist, fighting the communist menace everywhere; and the "military industrial complex" grew to have extraordinary power and influence.

In all this spending a fair amount was earmarked for the computer field. In fact, the single most influential source of funding during the digital revolution was the Defense Advanced Research Projects Agency, DARPA, and its computer arm, the Information Processing Technology Office, IPTO. Much of their work involved command-and-control systems for battlefield soldiers and mapping and reconnaissance systems for intelligence gathering and analysis. But the agencies also funded a series of highly academic research projects that not only crossed into the supercomputer realm, but also created drawing programs and high-resolution graphics for computers, launched the first networking systems, and made possible the world of time-sharing. The most important innovation it funded was a small project that, for the first time, demonstrated that a computer could be "humanized," and in the process invented hypertext, the concept of windowing, cut-and-paste editing, and the mouse.

When DARPA was founded, in 1960, it was staffed by veterans of another government project: Project Whirlwind. That effort not only spawned the world's first interactive computer, but it also led directly to the development of one of the most significant components of modern computing—dynamic random access memory, or DRAM. Furthermore, it created a new nexus between government and commerce when a team of refugees from the project started a company that would challenge IBM's big-computer hegemony by introducing the world's first small computers. This firm also received some of the first venture capital in the electronics industry. The company was the Digital Equipment Corporation (DEC).

❖   ❖   ❖

SINCE IT HAD DROPPED THE ATOM BOMBS on Hiroshima and Nagasaki, the United States government believed it held the ultimate weapon in the brinksmanship of the Cold War era; the atom bomb shifted the balance of power. Then one August day in 1949, President Truman was given a report by an atomic radiation monitoring station in the Bikini Atoll stating that it had recorded a cloud of radiation moving with a weather pattern from the Far East. It was alarming, because there hadn't been an American test in recent weeks, and certainly nothing on that side of the Pacific since the bombs had been dropped on Japan. It could only mean one thing: The Soviets had detonated a nuclear bomb.

This set off a panic in the highest levels of the U.S. government. Large Soviet bombers had been paraded during the May Day celebration of 1949 followed by news of the A-bomb explosion. For the Joint Chiefs of Staff and others at the highest echelons of the Cabinet, the conclusion was inescapable: The Russians had stolen our nuclear secrets (the Rosenbergs were arrested early in 1950), and now had the capability to send bombers over the North Pole to drop atomic bombs onto American cities.

The decision was made: The nation needed a perimeter defense, a radar and early warning system that would prevent Stalin from launching a sneak attack. The man given the job of determining a course of action was George Valley, an associate professor in the Physics Department at MIT. While researching the advanced projects in progress at MIT, he came upon one very interesting computer project. Called Project Whirlwind, it was being run by a tall and gangly Nebraskan engineer named Jay Forrester. Austere and rigid, with a superb intellect, Forrester was a formidable character.

By 1949, Whirlwind was an astronomically expensive (over $4 million had been spent to that point) and ambitious project whose goal was to build a full-flight simulator. The simulator was being designed around a new kind of "interactive" computer—created completely from scratch—which was the pet project of a colorful MIT graduate, Captain Luis de Florez who was head of training at the Air Force Bureau of Aeronautics. He enjoyed flying into MIT convocations, landing his seaplane on the Charles River and then motoring up and down to the cheers of onlookers. He conceived the idea of a new-fangled flight simulator in the waning days of the Second World War, and had enough influence in Washington—where he was a close associate of John Towers, a powerful senator from Mississippi—to get it funded at a first-class level. Initially, the simulator was intended to be hydraulic, but once Forrester and his band of young turks from MIT were briefed on the ENIAC computer, they changed direction, to create a massive real-time programmable computer to power the plane's cockpit and all its controls entirely electronically.

Every computer built in the first ten years of the field was a batch-processing machine. This meant that data and instructions were fed into the computer in a "batch." The machine would churn and gurgle and compute, then spit out answers to equations or compilations of orders and accounts. Except for limited self-modifying programming—where interim results could invoke different branches of instructions in a computer program—it was not possible to vary the operation of the computer once it was started up. In contrast, a flight simulator would need to operate in real time, an entirely different mode of operation. Moving the joystick had to instantly affect the behavior of the equipment, which would then change the next response. A flight simulator had to react as it was being manipulated. Much later such a process would come to be called interactive, meaning that a would-be pilot could interact with the machine.

It was an extraordinarily ambitious idea in 1945. The Project Whirlwind team commandeered a building in Cambridge, the Barta Building, that formerly had been a printing plant. At the time, no one thought of miniaturizing anything, so everything would have to be built out of circuits made up of vacuum tubes. The completed computer would fill a room 100 feet long and 50 feet wide. Like the ENIAC that inspired it, this machine used enough power to run a small city. And because of its association with the Massachusetts Institute of Technology, it never lacked for phalanxes of bright young engineers to work on it.

For a variety of reasons, including Forrester's over-arching intelligence and MIT's determination to keep hold of a lucrative government contract, the project received $1 million a year from 1946 through 1949. That money paid for numerous young engineers, a brick building filled with custom equipment, and a computer that could react instantaneously to operator input. Unfortunately, it hardly ever worked. This was mainly due to problems with memory—which remained finicky and difficult to synchronize ten years after John Vincent Atanasoff had first struggled with the idea of rewriteable storage. But it was also a remarkably ambitious goal, given the state of the art in electronics at the time.

Forrester had received a master's degree from MIT in 1941, and for a boy raised in the wilds of Nebraska, Cambridge was definitely the big city. In the 1930s, he had built an entirely wind-powered electrical system for the ranch where he grew up, from the windmill to the generator to the lights and switches. He also had created a telephone system using the barbed-wire fences to connect isolated homesteads on the Nebraska frontier. His experiences gave him a different view from most of his contemporaries—a systems view. He thought about engineered machines as complete entities, and liked to sketch them in their entirety, not as assemblages of individual gears and components. He had the laconic character of a ranch hand, and when someone would ask him how something worked, he was always willing to draw the entire system on paper before launching into an explanation. He was not a man who rushed into things, even as a 25-year-old grad student at MIT. He was methodical and precise, kept to himself, didn't volunteer much, and provided reasoned and complete answers to questions he was asked.

He was also, ineffably, a leader. Perhaps it was his height—he was 6'5"—or his ramrod bearing. Jay Forrester wasn't the kind of guy who went out for a beer with the boys at the tavern. When he had a drink, it was in the more rarefied environs of the faculty club. He wasn't one of the guys; he was a leader, and few who met him doubted he could do anything he set out to accomplish.

When asked to take on the flight simulator project, it didn't take Forrester long to realize that a computer was essential to its design. An airplane reacted constantly to the physical universe, changing and responding immediately and sometimes violently; there was no dead time between input and reaction. In a fraction of a second, 92 separate variables had to be sampled. Each one might be the same as in the fraction of a second before, or it could have changed dramatically, in which case the portion of the platform and simulator device that was affected would also have to change instantly in response. Without this instant cause-and-effect response, the simulator wouldn't work as a real plane. The analog computers of the day—especially MIT's own Vannevar Bush–designed Differential Analyzer—were far too slow to provide anything like this kind of swift response. Computers such as the ENIAC and EDVAC were designed to operate on well-defined equations, problems that could be punched onto stacks of cards and run sequentially. Forrester's machine had to be able to provide instantaneous feedback and response.

Thanks to its powerful friends in Washington, the project continued to be funded, but it never came close to fulfilling its goal of a programmable flight trainer. Part of the reason was that, along the way, the team of young MIT engineers shifted their focus, training their sights instead on building a programmable computer that could respond to input from an operator as he or she typed or entered information. To do this, though, Whirlwind had to solve one enormous and intractable problem: memory.

The great advantage of the early computers was that in batch-processing mode, memory could be slow, and results, even interim results, could be printed out onto punch cards or a paper tape. In that era, time and timing weren't crucial, and memory was only one of several issues that early computer designers were grappling with. However, to perform electronic calculations, interactively, a computer had to store interim answers and inputs accurately and swiftly. It had to be able to write over the interim numbers with new ones almost immediately, and for as long as the gear remained in operation. So from the very beginning, the Whirlwind team had to struggle with the fledgling systems available to them for storing interim numbers.

The state of the art in memory was either mercury delay lines or a modified cathode ray tube known as a Williams tube. The former was based on the fact that mercury at room temperature was both a liquid and a conductor of electricity. Individual bits of data were represented as either crests (1), or lulls (0) in a mechanical wave that was started at one end of a column of mercury. The thick molten metal transmitted the wave slowly along its length introduced at one end via a diaphragm—hence the name "mercury delay line." At the other end of the tube, a sensor picked up each bit and fed it back to the starting point. The idea was for the mercury to capture and "delay" the bits so they could be stored. This process was a strange hybrid of the mechanical and the electronic. The Williams tube was a specially designed cathode ray tube—like a black-and-white television tube—that stored strings of bits as spots of dark or light onscreen. Both concepts were hopelessly imprecise as well as subject to all sorts of fluctuations due to environmental conditions. Using either method, the massive new computer refused to work correctly for more than a few seconds at a time.

By the time George Valley, an MIT professor, came around in 1949 looking for a way to build a defense perimeter system, Project Whirlwind was in jeopardy. The flight simulator idea had been replaced by a giant computer that rarely worked—which did not please the bureaucrats who thought that for a million dollars a year they should be getting several computers, at least. Supervision for the project was now relegated to the Office of Naval Research (ONR), whose mathematicians couldn't understand why the government was spending so much on an interactive machine; after all, batch cards worked just fine for them.

When Forrester heard about the U.S. Air Force's need for a system to track radar signals, he believed he could remaster Project Whirlwind, use it as the basis of a radar operator-type screen, and make it the heart of a national defense early warning system. He convinced George Valley to let him try and make Whirlwind work. Forrester's team used a radar set left over from World War II that had a one-mile resolution, and with this primitive equipment they found Whirlwind could track a bomber from strategic air command, and a fighter, and issue computer instructions to the fighter's pilot to route an interception and fire missiles. In summer 1950, they mounted their most elaborate demonstration, using live radar data from the Air Force field at Hanscom Field, an isolated and secure base in the woods north of Boston. They showed that they could track a bomber for miles and issue instantaneous instructions on how to intercept it as well.

President Truman and his defense advisors from the scientific community grabbed hold of the promise inherent in Whirlwind, and ran with it. It was the only interactive computer in America, probably the world. More important, the armed forces basically didn't have an alternative. MIT's academic managers, determined to keep the project on campus, lobbied to convert Whirlwind into a top-secret air defense network. A band of government naysayers thought the air-defense project would be better off with John Von Neumann and a computer that he was building at the Center for Advanced Studies at Princeton (home to Albert Einstein). They regarded the work of the inexperienced boys in a secret building in Cambridge, with disdain, and were sure the machine couldn't work.

The Whirlwind team had been laboring for five years, and the project had grown and grown. It became known uncharitably as Forrester's Folly, or his private pyramid. There was still precious little to show for all the millions of dollars that had been spent since 1945: a single radar terminal, a light pen, and a keyboard, all backed up by walls of electronic gear. It may not have looked like much but it was still the only computer in the world that could handle data in real time and allow a human operator to interact with it.

In the face of the opposition, the Air Force nevertheless decided to support it. This led to the formation of the Lincoln Laboratories, a joint military academic operation. Shortly thereafter, the Digital Computer Laboratory (where Whirlwind had been built), headed by Forrester became Division Six of these laboratories. Just in time too, because Mina Rees, a Navy mathematician in charge of funding, came to a meeting at MIT in March 1950, and reported that ONR was reducing Whirlwind's budget from over $1 million to $200,000. Luckily the university group had George Valley, who that same afternoon agreed to make up the shortfall and carry the economic burden for Whirlwind. Forrester was made head of the project. It was the largest division of Lincoln Labs for quite some time.

Still there was one thing wrong with the picture. While the Whirlwind team could put on a good demonstration, they had no real working model. And the machine's storage memory tubes were becoming less and less reliable. This frustrated the whole team. Here they were, cocky young engineers, students of the technological prowess that had contributed to the defeat of Hitler working on a project of major national security proportions, unable to solve reliability and engineering problems.

Memory was the overriding problem. Until Forrester's team could depend on interim storage of calculations and positions, all their carefully crafted logical circuits wouldn't do much good. The entire computer depended on its capability to continually write and overwrite numbers into registers. Forrester had to admit to the assembled brass in that summer of 1950 that even if they could track a few planes, they had no memory solution yet. That failing would make the project a nonstarter. Therefore, late that summer, Forrester cleared everything else off his calender and took it upon himself to solve the memory problem.

What he needed was a way to store and read digits, zeros, and ones, that is, a charge and not a charge. Forrester searched every piece of literature he could think of. It occurred to him that he might be able to use magnetism in some way to store digits. Because an electric current produced a magnetic field, Forrester thought that he might be able to create magnetism when he had a binary 1. But he needed a substance that had a very clear threshold for becoming magnetic. Eventually, he found an old German ceramacist in New Jersey who was making ferrite transformers for television by fusing iron ore and oxides to obtain certain magnetic properties. The German's ferrites had a square magnetic profile: he could induce a magnetic field in the substance only at a very distinct level of current. For the ceramacist, who wanted a regular ramp of magnetism with increasing current, this was a big problem.

Conversely, it was exactly what the Whirlwind project director was looking for. Forrester had been thinking about storing memory in a grid of wires. Perhaps he could create a mesh of wire, with a ring, or loop, of this magnetic substance at every intersection. By threading a common wire through all the loops and attaching a unique wire directly to each loop, he could magnetize each of the rings individually. Half the necessary charge would be supplied to every ring, the other half only to those specific locations where he wanted to record a 1. That magnetic charge, or noncharge, on each ring represented either a 1 or a 0. After much tinkering and furnace work, the ceramacist and Forrester formulated the perfect magnetic substance, cores shaped like little doughnuts, with a specific threshold for magnetization. This was to be the heart of Forrester's new memory scheme.

That distinctive threshold for magnetization was crucial to the design. The wire grid, nets of cores sewn onto looms of wire, became known as *core memory,* and the patents to it were essential to the development of computing. This scheme was reliable and stable; magnetism was relatively permanent, so the storage of the bits was "saved" after the power to the system was shut off—and for military work, this was key. Since the magnetism could be read at electronic speeds, it made interactive computing possible. Furthermore, because of the wire grid, any portion of the memory array could be queried, eliminating the need for sequential access—different numbers could be stored at different locations in the wiring loom and instantly accessed simply by reading out the string of bits at any particular address in the loom. This became known as Random Access Memory (RAM), and it was the liberating concept for interactive computing. Forrester assigned the patents to MIT, and the school eventually received $15 to $20 million from them.

The primary licensee of the patents was IBM, which eventually won the contract for commercial installations of Project Whirlwind at NORAD (North American Defense) military sites. More important, every big and midsized computer also adopted the system late in the 1950s, and core memory remained the standard way to provide temporary storage through the 1960s and well into the 1970s.

Once the core molecular structure was defined, and a memory array was produced and installed, Whirlwind's performance was astonishing, and its reliability improved by many times. This made it viable in a defense project. Furthermore the memory was permanent; if the power was shut off, the memory remained. This was another critical component for a defense establishment that was dubious about digital systems, but without an alternative. Essentially, they were entrusting the nation's defense to a group of untried engineers at MIT.

The first installed memory bank contained just 2,000 words, each one of 16 bits, for 32,000 bits of storage data in all. Most memory devices represent data using the binary number system, whereby numbers are represented by sequences of the digits 0 and 1. In a computer, these numbers correspond to the on and off states of the computer's electronic circuitry. Each binary digit is called a bit, which is the basic unit of memory in a computer. A group of 8 bits is called a byte, and can represent decimal numbers ranging from 0 to 255. When these numbers are each assigned to a letter, digit, or symbol, in what is known as *a character code*, a byte can also represent a single character.

Memory capacity is usually quantified in terms of kilobytes, megabytes, and gigabytes. The prefixes kilo-, mega-, and giga-, are taken from the metric system and representing 1,000, 1 million, and 1 billion, respectively. Thus, a kilobyte is approximately 1,000 bytes, a megabyte is approximately 1 million bytes, and a gigabyte is approximately 1 billion bytes. The actual numerical values of these units are slightly different because they are derived from the binary number system. The precise number of bytes in a kilobyte is 2 raised to the tenth power, or 1,024; the precise number of bytes in a megabyte is 2 raised to the twentieth power; and the precise number of bits in a gigabyte is 2 raised to the thirtieth power.

In modern terms, a byte has 8 bits. The memory array in the early Whirlwind machines represented 4,000 bytes or 4 kilobytes—not much, considering that the average personal computer today comes with 16 megabytes—16 million bytes, or 4,000 times as much. Still, it proved enough to enable radar operators to sit at display consoles and scan the northern perimeter for unfriendly intruders. It let Americans sleep better at night.

To test the core memory, the MIT team had to build a separate machine. This was the Memory Test Computer (MTC), and its sole function was to randomly read and test memory arrays in all dimensions. The machine was built by a couple of grad students, MIT go-getters who were willing to stay up all night to wire the loom maze and debug the machine's thousands of memory cores, hundreds of vacuum tubes and relays, and miles of wire. Their names were Ken Olsen and Harlan Anderson, and they went on to start the Digital Equipment Company with a computer design based directly on the MTC.

The trial defense system was called the Cape Cod, because the radar feeds came into the building in Cambridge from a series of monitoring sites out on the Cape. Light pens, monitors, people interacting with computers in real time—all of it was running in downtown Cambridge by 1953. The lights in the room were red in order to make the radar images more visually sharp, and there were eventually dozens of 16-inch oscilloscope tubes with airmen peering into them. The programming of the system was done with big paper tapes, which were prepared at a special workstation, then loaded onto the latest and most evolved version of Whirlwind. Cadres of young airmen tracked live data; they were testing components, doing dry runs, and interacting with the consoles. Soon it would be for real, and they would be hooked directly into the airfield scramble system for the East Coast.

The Cape Cod was in place, but programming was still primitive. While spending an allotted quarter hour stint on the computer, a programmer was fully and totally in control of the entire machine, a behemoth as big as a train. Everything was controlled by a programmer working at the only console, which was a maze of toggles, pushbuttons, indicator lights, and arcane labels. There was even a pair of spigots—for hot and cold running water, supposedly—and a shrunken head to provide some good karma.

Whirlwind also had an audio capability that read every thirteenth bit, and clicked. This let the guys running their input tapes hear exactly how efficiently and smoothly their programs were running, because the clicks would either move at a steady rhythm or stumble and stall. It wasn't long before they wrote another program that allowed them to write across the screen, not with a pen, but with a finger; the first touch screen. It was quite a multimedia experience for the early 1950s: light pens, finger writing, a loudspeaker giving audio feedback, all working with the computer in real time. For the first time, there were several elements working interactively. Whirlwind also had the first keyboard that worked with the computer directly, which allowed an operator to create code and input it to the computer while everything was running. The keyboard also produced letters directly onto the cathode ray tube screens a kind of primitive word processing program.

Access to the Whirlwind room required top-secret clearance. Whirlwind was at the heart of SAGE system, the acronym for the computer that ran the Strategic Air Command System until the 1970s. When IBM was chosen as the contractor for it in 1953, it immediately became a competitor for Sperry Rand. It was Big Blue's first major computer installation, and it spelled the end of UNIVAC's reign. IBM did the work for cost, as part of its commitment to help the government during the Korean War. But the value of the core memory know-how alone was worth the price of admission. By the time IBM's System 360 was introduced ten years later, IBM had more experience with big, interactive mainframe computers than any other company on earth.

In the mid-1950s, when the Whirlwind/SAGE system was nearing completion and the machines were starting to be manufactured, MIT was where the most advanced work in computing was being done. The interactive components of SAGE were kept secret, since the last thing the Air Force wanted was to let the Soviets know its capabilities. But word leaked out, and soon every computer company was pursuing it in one form or another. But, the real innovation was in the programming. It was what made this massive machine work. The best and the brightest of this hodgepodge of scientists and fledgling computer scientists gravitated to the Digital Computing Lab where the Whirlwind project had been born. A motley crew, the team included a native Californian who had studied physics at Berkeley under J. Robert Oppenheimer, the physicist who created the first atomic bomb. Wes Clark was a young man fleeing the nuclear age. He had been living in Hanford, Washington, during the postwar enthusiasm for nuclear power. The Department of Energy's Hanford site produced weapons-grade plutonium, and that wasn't what Clark wanted to do for the rest of his life. Having read an account of early computers that included a mention of the Whirlwind project, he decided he wanted to learn more about them.

For the lonely young man stuck in the wheat fields of eastern Washington and scared of the deadly radiation all around him, the Cambridge computer sounded very interesting. Then he read in *Scientific American* about a simple computer, Edmund Berkeley's Simon, a calculator that used magnetic relays to create limited binary additions. This motivated Clark to think about building his own machine and culminated with his arrival in Cambridge in 1951 as a programmer for Whirlwind.

All the Whirlwind components were at his disposal. For Clark, it was tantamount to a religious experience. When he was sitting in front of the machine, taking charge of that building's equipment, he felt a power and thrill he had never experienced in Hanford, where operating the nuclear reactor controls had been more frightening than anything else.

By the mid-1950s, Clark had helped a team of fellow Whirlwind engineers debug the small test computer they had built to run the core memory tests. The Memory Test Computer was very easy to use and incorporated a number of new ideas, most of which were Ken Olsen's. The machine was similar to Whirlwind in character, but smaller. The processor was on boards, many boards, each of which could be removed and fiddled with; the guts were mounted on racks of equipment. Ken's idea for the MTC was to put all the major circuits or circuit families that had to work together onto one plug-in unit, all of which could be moved in and out of the frame that defined the computer. Each module was about the size of an $8\frac{1}{2} \times 11''$ piece of paper, but thicker.

While spending hours talking about the computers and imagining how they might develop, Clark and Olsen found a common ground. By then Clark was one of Whirlwind's key systems architects, and Olsen a key hardware builder. Neither thought there was anything very mysterious about computers. So they went after a way to make one more cheaply and thus give more people access to computers. They focused on using transistors, rather than vacuum tubes.

In 1953, transistors weren't very reliable yet; and at around $80 apiece, they were also very expensive. Clark explained, "We proposed the machine to Forrester, the manager of the Digital Computer Lab. We proposed that the transistor work was promising enough that we thought we could build a computer out of them. It [would] incorporate a big memory. Ken [Olsen] wanted to do some serious production wiring, and I had worked out some very interesting architectural ideas to be used as the basis of the design. We were turned down. The machine we proposed was huge. By comparison, it would have been roughly the size of a full-blown SAGE system. Nobody had built anything like this out of transistors. They were the hottest and fastest things going. Nobody had worked with magnetic core memory of any consequence—the MTC machine was only just being deployed. I sulked for a while, then built a very simple design, a primitively simple design based on a much smaller number of transistors."

To be accurate, his design was deceptively simple. The machine they had proposed to Forrester had been called the TX-1, and since this was a logical precursor, they called it the TX-0. It was simple in every way, whereas the TX-1 was the most complex design anybody had ever proposed up to that time. When it was up and running, Clark had a satori. "I decided that we were all wrong building gigantic expensive computers," he says. "The future was in creating small ones, individual computers, that any one person could use."

His insight was more notable because Clark was one of the top programmers and designers working on the SAGE systems, one of the only people in the world with the knowledge and the skills to actually create a smaller computer. He had proven it was possible with the TX-0. Now he was after a small computer that could be interactive. To date, Whirlwind (now evolving into SAGE) was the only computer in the world that allowed a person to work with it individually. Clark completely changed his focus. He thought computers had to be built for individuals.

The new transistorized design reflected this. Ken Olsen designed removable logic modules that made it relatively easy to upgrade or change elements of the new transistor computer while Wes Clark figured out the logical and command structure. It was the beginning of modularity. Though IBM had won the contract to build the massive SAGE machines it was watching as the transistorized machine was being developed by some of SAGE's key computer designers as a follow-on, so Big Blue began to plan its own machine with transistor elements.

By 1956, Jay Forrester was tiring of the big management game. He had masterminded Whirlwind and supervised and driven two major electrical engineering breakthroughs: an interactive computer and the first Random Access Memory. He had grown Whirlwind into Cape Cod, then into SAGE, and had supervised the Memory Test Computer, as well as TX-0 and the newest model, the TX-2, the world's first transistor-based computers. It was enough for him. He was 38 years old, and spending time with his small children was more important to him than spending interminable hours at Lincoln Labs.

About that time, an MIT provost told him about a new school of management being set up—the Sloan School of Management. He asked Forrester if he was interested in joining the faculty as a professor. He accepted and became one of the founding staff members of the school, then went to work refining his ideas on the ways that systems interact, a field he called system dynamics.

Ken Olsen, too, set out in a new direction. A quiet, thoughtful, and unpretentious man, he drove a Ford Pinto long after he could have afforded something more prestigious. Raised in Bridgeport, Connecticut, the son of a self-educated engineer and small-time inventor, he grew up in a puritanlike environment with a strict disciplinarian for a father. He believed in hard work, and found little time for socializing or social causes. The company (Digital Equipment Corporation) that he created operated the same way, always looking to reduce expenses, simplify its products, and build great equipment, while it left the marketing—determining what the machines were suited for—to its customers.

He took the ideas for the small computer that he and Wes Clark had debated and the design that Clark had worked out with the TX series and ran with them. Olsen believed there was a major business opportunity in selling simpler, but still powerful, computers to scientists and engineers, eschewing the commercial market completely. But when he made the rounds of investment banks and other traditional lenders he couldn't get anyone to take him seriously. After all, he had gone straight from the Navy to MIT, then worked for ten years on Project Whirlwind and its successors. He had never held a commercial job in his life.

Then Olsen approached a small investment firm in Boston, American Research and Development (ARD). Run by an imposing former brigadier general, George Doriot, the firm was one of the few willing to put risk capital into the electronics industry in the late 1950s, and the only one located in the Boston area. Rarely had a publicly traded company been willing to put up risk capital. In describing Doriot's activity, someone coined the phrase "venture capital," and the phrase stuck. Doriot taught a popular course in manufacturing at Harvard Business

School, and in time funded more than 150 companies. A story in *Forbes* a few years later described his approach.

> Doriot spends most of his time talking to people who bring him prospective investments. He says he has considered no less than 5,000 of them since 1946. He is considered by friends and critics alike as a brilliant judge of character. But he has to be, he explains. "When someone comes in with an idea that's never been tried, the only way you can judge is by the kind of man you're dealing with."
>
> Until recently Doriot also taught at Harvard Business School. He says that what he looks for in comparison are the same characteristics he tried for years to teach students: "resourcefulness, perception, courage, mental honesty with yourself, and a complete dedication to the business." Doriot doesn't hesitate to answer "yes," when you wonder aloud whether these are things that can be taught. At the very least, his string of investment successes prove they can be recognized.

Olsen and his new company, which he called the Digital Equipment Company, DEC, turned out to be Doriot's most lucrative deal by far. In exchange for a $70,000 investment ARD received 80 percent of the company stock, leaving the rest to Olsen and his partner, Harlan Anderson. Ten years later, that block of shares would be worth $400 million. By 1958 DEC was in business. The original idea for DEC was to produce small and interactive computers, machines based on Whirlwind, but on a much smaller scale. The ARD investors thought this was a bad idea—going against IBM seemed like a foolhardy strategy for such a small company. So, instead of initially building small computers that would compete with IBM and RCA, DEC made modular printed circuit boards.

These modules tested memory cores on big mainframe computers— exactly what Olsen had done for Whirlwind with the MTC. The timing was perfect. After pricing the modules, they were able to replace some of the circuit components with transistors—whose price had just started to fall. The core memory business was booming, and there was widespread need for small test equipment that could delve into the core memory looms to identify good, and bad, memory cells. DEC's revenues soon were greater than they had anticipated; almost immediately the company was profitable. With confidence, then, they approached the ARD board of directors and requested backing for the business they had wanted to pursue in the first place: small computers. By 1959, they were working on the machine they named PDP-1.

The idea behind the PDP computers was simple. For a price that began at around $120,000, DEC would sell a full-blown computer suitable for engineers and scientists. It wasn't as powerful as a full mainframe, but it was $900,000 cheaper than the least expensive IBM mainframe. Better yet, because the intended users were more sophisticated and therefore interested in doing their own programming, the support costs were much lower. The machine's design was greatly influenced by Wes Clark's work. It came with a cathode ray tube screen, very similar to those on the Whirlwind, and had a keyboard. This was a spectacular leap forward. On the DEC computers, a single user was given complete control and could interactively query the computer, change the programming, and see results.

Wes Clark, however, continued to work on his own big idea. He had already designed two transistorized computers. Once he realized how cheaply he could build a computer this way, he started to imagine a new concept, one that flew in the face of all the computer experts' opinions and attitudes. This concept was heretical to big companies like Sperry Rand and IBM, an idea that ran counter to even small companies like DEC that were making relatively inexpensive machines with hopes of big profits. Clark was going to make small cheap "kit" computers.

In 1963, under a grant from the National Institutes of Health, he created a series of computers for biologists and psychologists called the LINC (for Laboratory Instrumentation Computer). The computers had to be assembled by the scientists themselves—which was part of Clark's vision. He believed that by assembling and really understanding the computer, the user would get much more value from it. But, the project was ahead of its time, and by the late 1960s Clark had retreated to an academic appointment.

In contrast, DEC's machines changed the face of the computer industry. Mainframe computers continued to be the choice for companies that had to track millions of customers and their bills but the small, flexible machines that DEC introduced caught on like wildfire in academic institutions and among engineers. By the end of 1962, DEC recorded revenues of $6.5 million and profits of $807,000.

But DEC wasn't home free. The PDP-1 had its foundations in work conducted outside the company. When it came time for DEC to create totally new machines, it struggled. The PDP-4 was a marketplace failure. The next design, another large computer, was also a disaster. On the third try, they hit success. The PDP-8, a transistor-based small computer was priced at the extraordinarily low cost of $18,000. This computer was a turning point. By cramming a remarkable amount of power into a low-priced box, DEC changed the equation of computing. Companies that provided scientific instruments and typesetting equipment could now afford to integrate the DEC computer into their own systems, then resell them to customers. Sales rose 50 percent in one year—from $15 million in 1965 to $23 million in 1966. Profits rose six times, from 1965 to 1967, reaching $4.5 million.

DEC went on a growth spurt. By 1967, the company boasted revenues of $39 million. The company's signature machine by then was the PDP-8, and it had spawned a new word to describe it: minicomputer. The company's success also spawned a number of competitors who were trying to grow the market. The most significant start-up company was called Data General, formed by a trio of disgruntled DEC engineers.

Olsen was not the easiest man to get along with. A rough, Navy-trained engineer, for long periods he behaved as a hands-off manager, letting everyone work to their own pace, in a style he called matrix management. This involved a separation between functional roles and product line responsibilities. The idea was that the functional groups within the company—finance, marketing, manufacturing, and sales—would in effect contract with the product line managers to provide services to their individual products. It created the illusion of entrepreneurialism inside the company. An illusion because in reality, Olsen was a classic micromanager, determined to have a part in every decision made regarding the company.

This rubbed many of his best engineers the wrong way, especially Edwin de Castro who had created the PDP-8; and when the machine became an enormous success, de Castro was golden. But he had had a run-in with Olsen during the PDP-8 days when the company president wanted to use a new type of circuit that combined multiple components on a ceramic plate. De Castro didn't think they would work; he was right, and luckily he had hedged his bets. Ultimately he was able to solve the problem caused by Olsen's insistence, and ship the computer on time. But Olsen never appreciated it.

De Castro's next project—the PDP-X—took the opposite tack from the stripped-down PDP-8. The new project was too ambitious; its architectural scope required DEC to obsolete most of its existing computers by moving to a whole new series of machines. It had worked for IBM, but DEC was in another league. The plan was to upgrade the PDPs to 16-bit computers (a measure of the size of the internal data path in a computer) and to architect the line so that customers could eventually upgrade to 32-bit machines on the same chassis. This would both provide better return on customer investment and at the same time create an ongoing relationship with DEC in the future. These ideas were at least a decade ahead of the marketplace, and would eventually be adopted by DEC in the 1970s for its VAX line, but in 1967 the project was regarded as too advanced and so was rejected.

De Castro was upset; in the aftermath, he opted to start his own company so he could build a simpler, cheaper minicomputer that would serve the middle market, where DEC had few customers. Although DEC had 85 percent of the minicomputer business at the time, all of its machines either cost more than $100,000 apiece or were stripped-down PDP-8s that cost about $20,000. There was little in between, and de Castro was sure he could come in a bit above the PDP-8 with power and functions reserved for the top-of-the-line machines—and still make a profit. His new company, Data General, set out to create a lower-cost minicomputer. It was called the Nova, and turned out to be a smash success. The new company sold more than 200 in 1969, the first year the computer was on the market. In its second fiscal year, the company reported revenues of $7 million and earnings of $536,000.

By 1970, the minicomputer business had grown from the $25 million charted by DEC when it was alone in the field five years earlier to $250 million. DEC still had about half the market with sales of $135 million, but now there was plenty of competition from companies such as Varian and Hewlett-Packard, Honeywell, and even IBM, which had belatedly introduced a minicomputer.

Another trend was emerging in computing at the same time. Starting around 1960, a great deal of effort had gone into developing the concept of time-sharing whereby a number of terminal-based users shared a big computer's power. Originally devised by GE years before, it had been expanded by a group of computer scientists at MIT. In effect they sliced up the processing power of a mainframe and apportioned it to multiple terminal users. This made the service bureau concept popular; companies would buy a big mainframe, and then sell "time" on it to customers who needed it only for a portion of a day. In this way, expensive computer time became available to smaller companies.

As a result, the computer leasing business, which thrived under IBM's pricing umbrella, was booming, too. It had come about following the consent decree IBM had signed with the Department of Justice in 1956, forcing Big Blue to make its equipment available to anyone, and to separate hardware sales from service and support. This enabled competitors to buy mainframe computers for cash discounts, then lease them back to customers at lower prices. The practice looked particularly good on the balance sheets because most of the leasing firms depreciated their computers over longer time periods than IBM. For instance, Randolph Computer was a red-hot stock in 1968, posting revenues of $18.7 million and earnings per share of $1.55. It also owned about $50 million worth of IBM computers that it leased to customers. It wrote them off over a ten-year period on a straight-line basis—or almost $5 million a year. Had Randolph been forced to use IBM's own four-year depreciation schedule, it would have posted a loss of over $4 million.

These companies became the latest in a long string of stock market darlings that included uranium, bowling, and small electronics companies in the postwar years. Price-earnings ratios for the most popular were astronomical. Data Processing Financial and General, for example, had a price-earnings ratio of 59; Leasco's was 72. Stocks of the five biggest leasing companies sold for a combined market capitalization of $736.8 million, five times book value, 44 times earnings, and 8 times combined sales. It was this wild market that prompted *Forbes* to publish an article in 1968, questioning the practices of the day.

> Earnings after all are what generate action in today's stock market. And action is what these companies have gotten. Data Processing Financial and General currently has a total market value of $181 million. By contrast, Bausch & Lomb, a scientific instrument company that has been around for 115 years and has double DPF&G's profits, sells for only $150 million. These high stock prices are good for more than the egos of the leasing companies' top stockholders. They make it easy to sell convertible debentures to bring in the funds to buy more computers. Which in turn generates more profits. . . . So far the boom

has been good for everybody involved. But what happens when the music stops?

It would be several years before the end of the boom came and it was propelled by the recession of the mid-1970s, when IBM cut prices to lower the umbrella under which they all operated. Time-sharing, so popular in the 1960s and 1970s, suddenly became irrelevant as the prices of minicomputers tumbled. By the early 1970s, a stripped-down minicomputer could be bought for as little as $3,500. At those prices—and driven by advances in electronics and fierce competition—most of the engineers who wanted to use a small computer could afford to do so.

By then, DEC, too, had stumbled, by underestimating the explosive growth of its competitors and dismissing the development of integrated circuits, transistor-based memory, and finally the microprocessor. The company continued to sell its PDP machines with core memory until the end of the 1970s, long after IBM had dropped it. DEC had become complacent, convinced that the market it had created with the first inexpensive machines wasn't changing all that much.

But it was. The most important single change was in the nature of computing itself. When DEC was founded, only engineers and other specialists wanted to use computers, so selling powerful but hard-to-use machines to them was a good business strategy. Those customers were capable of figuring out how to make things work, deciphering the arcane commands, and delving into the innards of the hardware to make it all work. But ten years later, a wider audience had been exposed to computers, for commercial and industrial purposes, as well as in the scientific and engineering arenas. A small group had even started to explore the changes that would be necessary to bring computing power to the mainstream public.

The impetus was a number of experimental projects funded by DARPA's IPTO group, many attempting to build networking systems—modular computer projects that aimed to design machines that could be "snapped" together. And one program was intended to augment human intelligence via the computer. This project was being run out of the Stanford Research Institute, a think tank located near the university. It made use of some advanced minicomputer equipment produced by a tiny Berkeley, California, start-up, Berkeley Computer Systems. The project was run by a man with a clear and unique vision for what computers could do. His name was Douglas Engelbart.

Engelbart was raised in Oregon, and came to the San Francisco Bay Area in 1948 to work in an aeronautical research lab for a division of the government agency that would later become NASA. By the early 1950s, he was an electrical engineering graduate student at Berkeley, working on a general-purpose digital computer. Along the way, he came across some of the ideas of Vannevar Bush, especially a conception of a way to organize much of the information in the Library of Congress using microfilm. This gave Engelbart the idea to arrange information in multiple dimensions, not just hierarchically. Funding for his project had been sporadic since 1953, when he started formulating his ideas—ideas that were widely regarded as crazy. These included the plans to harness the computational capability of a computer, then make it work to an individual's requirements, rather than the other way around. He also planned new ways of ordering, arranging, and viewing information; for creating links between elements; and for hiding complexity. It was the man-computer interface, as he called it.

Over the years Engelbart's funding had been handed off from one defense agency to another. Some called him a crackpot, so he had to struggle to make himself understood, to make his proposals resonate. He finally found a home 40 miles south of San Francisco, in Menlo Park, California. There, the Stanford Research Institute (SRI), spun off from the university, had become a major defense department think tank. To help the generals and State, Defense, and CIA analysts make sense of the possibilities inherent in the microcosmic world of transistors and integrated circuits, the military needed thinkers with unconventional ideas. Where better than the West Coast?

There, deep in the bowels of the web of buildings comprising SRI's campus, Engelbart pieced together equipment and talent, then wrote and rewrote and cajoled others to rewrite the programming code that made his man-computer interface work.

Finally, on December 8, 1968, he stood in front of several hundred of his peers, ready to show them what he had been working on. He was sure they would finally understand just how important his ideas were. To date all computers were based around programming, lines of codes and cryptic commands. Precious little thought had been given to the issues of man-machine interfaces since the earliest days of Whirlwind, when a handful of social scientists had tried to help make the system easier for human operators to use.

With Engelbart's presentation, two remarkable currents in American life came flowing together in a setting that was perfectly suited to it. San Francisco was the center of "flower power." But the Bay Area, with its concentration of academia at Berkeley and Stanford and electronics at Lockheed and Fairchild (what would later be called the Silicon Valley), was also the heart of the digital revolution that was pumping money into the American economy.

That December 8, the computing fraternity was holding the Association for Computer Machinery Winter Conference at Brooks Hall in San Francisco. The attendees represented the top of the heap in the new engineering discipline led by Americans: electrical engineering. And at the forefront of this field was computing. It was in computing that America's power was concentrated, and these were the people who held the keys.

The auditorium at Brooks Hall looked more like the old surgical operating theaters of nineteenth century London than a convention center. At the center, a court was surrounded by steeply banked rows of seats. A one-time home to the local professional basketball team, the place was far too small for a major convention, but it was appropriate for a conference. Folding chairs had been set out in rows along the floor. A dais stretched across the front of the place and off to one side was a lectern, in front of which was an overhead projector. Behind this was a large movie screen.

When the buttoned-down, intellectual audience took their seats that morning, they were confronted with a scene out of place in a computer conference. A couple of video cameras had been set up on tripods in front, and were focused on an odd-looking desk that had been placed below and to the right of the screen. On stage, Douglas Engelbart scurried around, arranging the last of the elements in his presentation. He was patrician looking, tall and well groomed; a man of few words. He wore a headset, an ear-piece, and a microphone, one with a tiny tube for a speaker. As he settled into a desk chair, one of the many technicians plugged him into the PA system, and he pulled a swing-away table toward him. The equipment resembled a kind of lounge chair cum TV tray.

On the left side of the tray was a strange device, with five individual keys, each shaped like a tongue depressor and hinged separately. A wire ran from it to a typewriter style keyboard on the center of the tabletop. To the right was a small block of wood, also connected to the central keyboard with wire. This palm-sized rectangle had three round buttons that poked out of its top, like lobster eyes. This seeing-eye block moved on wheels.

With Engelbart in place behind the contraption, the movie screen above him flickered to life, and an image of a computer monitor appeared. It looked like many of the computer monitors the audience had seen to date: On it, a line of typewriter style letters ran from left to right, filling out the top left quadrant. It was in black and white—or really, dirty light and dark gray, because the video projection equipment was none too sharp. This was 1968, after all.

The lights were dimmed; a spotlight picked out the unlikely speaker. His voice was quiet, relaxed. He almost whispered. The audience was on the edge of their seats. "My name is Douglas Engelbart," he began, "and the research project I'm going to describe has been going on down the road at the Stanford Research Institute. While I'm the only person you'll see up here today, I'm actually backed up by a staff working not just back stage, but also in Menlo Park, where all the computing you'll see is actually occurring."

This got the audience's attention. Engelbart was actually 40 miles away from his computer. What was he doing? They were witnessing the first public demonstration of remote computing. Engelbart continued: "I'd like you to fantasize with me for a moment, to come and share the experience I'm going to describe for you. If in your office, you were supplied with a computer display that was alive for you all day, that was responsive to you without having to wait in turn, intimately responsive to you and only you, how much value could you derive from that?"

It was a revolutionary idea. Computers were giant machines; people didn't have them in their offices. Few employees even got near one. Most handed their cards to attendants who then disappeared and ran their jobs overnight, returning the results in a day if everything went right. Sure, there were minicomputers that brought computing down to the workgroup, or lab level, but these machines still cost tens of thousands of dollars; and they needed dedicated technicians to program and keep them running. No one had an individual computer in his office.

Now the audience was buzzing. Engelbart was hitting something fundamental: It was the intimacy of the computer that was the real draw for the attendees—who as kids had asked for electronics and soldering kits under their Christmas trees in the late fifties. They had been at the forefront of the binary math, Venn diagrams, and Base 2 mathematics that swept through American education in the sixties. It was the potential of making a machine do exactly what they wanted it to do that fascinated and thrilled the thousand technicians sitting in the former basketball court. When Engelbart talked about responsive intimacy, they knew exactly what he meant.

Engelbart had his audience in the palm of his hand. He continued: "This basically describes what we've been pursuing for many years; we call it the Augmented Human Intellect Research Project at SRI. We're trying to augment man's intellect with the machine, with the computer. We're going to show you, rather than tell you all about it. Hopefully, it will all work, but bear with me if we have a few rough spots. . . . In my office I have a terminal like this. There are 12 of these in our operation. What we're really working on is the 'man-computer interface'—how you could arrange and manipulate information if you had a computer you could call your own; and the kind of tools you might need to do so . . ."

This was definitely something new and interesting. Everyone in the room had been intrigued by the notion of humanizing the computer, of creating a giant brain, artificial intelligence. If machines could do such activities as accounting, order entry, mailing list generation, and typesetting, then was it so far-fetched to make a machine that was more human, rather than make humans more like machines?

Douglas Engelbart was presenting the first glimmerings of a machine with "soul." It was the first time anyone had taken the capabilities of the equipment and brought them to the human level. This machine, which evolved out of the behemoths of the mainframe, could become personal, intimate, responsive to a human.

It was an idea that was as essentially American as the mass production of the motor car had been at the beginning of the century, which had touched on the American need for individualism, the ability to drive anywhere, without having to depend upon railroad schedules or the location of the tracks. This shot straight to the heart of the American spirit. When Engelbart presented his ideas on how the man-machine interface might be structured, he was soaring into an uncharted universe.

Engelbart went on: "We've been working on redefining the ways that you might work with information. For instance, here's a very important file for me; it's my shopping list, created by my wife." Up above his head on the movie screen, a list of items appeared: apples, bananas, carrots, lettuce, bread, bean soup, tomato soup, paper towels, aspirin, noodles, Chapstick, milk and much more. "One of the most important things we've been working on is views," he explained, "how you want to see information. So, for instance, I've also organized this list by the stores where I can buy these items." With a series of clicks and chords on the five-key pad, the list was rearranged by store names: grocery, shoe repair, hardware, art supply, drug, and so on.

Engelbart wasn't finished. He said, "Now, I can either expand or contract my lists." Another set of commands caused a list of items to appear under each store. Engelbart explained: "The idea is to present as much, or as little, detail as the viewer needs—and to do so instantly. You'll notice that as I present commands, a series of codes appears then disappears. These are only present because I thought you as an audience would find them interesting. For a naive user they could be completely hidden." With that, he set a small pointer skidding across the screen, generated by the block of wood in his right hand.

"One of the most important aspects of information, when linked to a computer, is the ability to jump from view to view, to investigate new relationships between facts and ideas," added Engelbart. With another couple of taps on the pad, the screen was redrawn into a crude map, with the names of the stores arrayed on the screen, with a line linking them. He said, "I'm a bit absent-minded, so we created a route map for me showing me how I should come home. Under each of the locations is a list of the items I need to get or take care of. For instance, let's look at the library entry." A few more clicks, and a list of items appeared on the map under the word *library*.

The audience was rapt. Engelbart wasn't just presenting collapsible outlines with embedded information; he had now linked a graphical representation of information—a map—with embedded information. Still he wasn't done. "What if I suddenly get a craving for a new fruit that I'll make up—say, a skinless banana. Can I add it to my shopping list?" Within seconds the produce list expanded and a skinless banana was inserted. Then he said, "I think I want the list to be ordered alphabetically." A flash on-screen and the list reappeared, ordered alphabetically.

There was silence in the hall. It was almost too much to grasp—views, links, a map. For engineers, programmers and designers whose worlds were defined by punch cards, the idea of sitting at a console and manipulating data in real time could scarcely be imagined. It promised a world where the user, the person operating the machine, was in control. It flew in the face of the mainframe operating concept where the machine, and those who attended it, worked in almost ritualistic languages.

Engelbart had, in essence, presented an alternate view of computing reality. He had presented concepts that were human in spirit, and computer-enabled in every way. They were also revolutionary, and they attacked the status quo every bit as much as the protestors in the streets in 1968.

But Engelbart knew he hadn't wholly convinced his audience yet, so he hurried on. "To be able to make the changing of views, and the jumps, effective, we had to change the way you maneuver around the screen. Typing a line of coded commands may be okay for those of us in this room, but the world at large, all those millions of people we'd like to bring into our world, will never stand for that.

"So we came up with something very different. You'll see that as I move [this block of wood] here, a pointer or bug moves correspondingly on-screen. We wanted to be able to navigate around the screen without using letters or arrows. This device is the best solution we can come up with. We've started calling it a mouse. We find it pretty indispensable."

As he moved the pointer back and forth across the screen, he explained: "If I position this pointer here, on this line of text, then tell the system to copy the text . . . another line of identical text will appear." The buzz in the room escalated. Still there was more: "I can select a block of text . . . and copy it." A copy appeared, an exact duplicate. It was all done without using the traditional keyboard; the pointer was positioned and a chord played on the five-key pad.

Some members of the audience could no longer contain themselves. They went up to the front of the auditorium and clambered onstage, staring over Engelbart's console at what he was doing with the instruments on his desk.

"As I said at the beginning of the presentation, though," Engelbart continued, "there is a large team of folks behind me making this possible. The computers are in Menlo Park, and I'm connected by phone lines to that machine. As I move things here, the signals are transferred to the monitor I'm operating with down there, which has a television camera trained on it. What we're seeing up here above me is that monitor screen. [At Menlo Park,] one of my colleagues is sitting at another terminal. Can we bring up Bill in a window?" There was a pause. The screen was filled with the lines of copied type that looked like teletype-writer letters. Then, all of a sudden, in the upper left quadrant of the image of the monitor, another image appeared. It was of a man in traditional engineer garb—white shirt, no tie—sitting at another monitor.

"That's Bill English," said Engelbart, "one of the key guys helping me put this together. This is obviously a live television image, but we imagine that you [will be able to] have a number of different views of your data, or even completely different data from different operations you were performing, and each could be in its own space: We call them windows."

It was the first on-screen "window" most of the audience had ever seen. By now the spectators were on complete overload. Sure, there had been primitive on-screen drawing programs, but they were nothing like this. This was an integrated series of ideas that all worked together as an intelligent whole. It all made sense. And it was, well, so human; there wasn't a gulf between the machine and the user. It was completely compelling.

"Now that we've taken you through all of these stages," said Engelbart, "we can finally demonstrate what the project is all about. Our efforts have been focused on augmenting man's intellect, making us better able to work on problems, and to better work together. So what we've created is a way that we can work collectively, from different terminals, on the same problem." First he had described computers as individual tools, and showed how they could be intimately responsive to their users. Then he demonstrated pointers and keypads and a mouse that made it relatively easy to move around the screens. Then he opened windows of different data and pictures onscreen. Now he was talking about linking terminals and having people miles apart from each other collaborate in real time. And they did. For a few minutes Doug Engelbart and Bill English chased each other around the screen, one following the other's pointer. One wrote a few words, and the other finished the sentence. There were a few gasps in the audience. Then there was silence.

Finally, slowly, from the corners of the cavernous space came the applause—decibels of applause.

The spark had been lit. Now the technology itself had to catch up, and someone had to figure out how to make a business out of all of this.

Bob Noyce, Andy Grove and Gordon Moore, founders of Intel (from left to right).

CHAPTER 5

>———◇———<

Chips
Integrated Circuits & Microprocessors

As the presidential election approached in 1956, America was still bask-ing in the glory of its victory in the Second World War. The economy was booming, fueled by more disposable income than any nation on earth had ever enjoyed. Computers and transistors were the rage—the "giant brains" were becoming fixtures in both the business world and in pop-ular culture, while "portable radios" were already a hot consumer item. Cars, telephones, and even houses were affordable to more and more Americans. In November, Dwight D. Eisenhower was reelected in a landslide.

Much of the rest of the world, however, was in turmoil. Soviet troops moved into Hungary, and the Cold War was heating up. Most Americans felt they could prevail over the Communist menace with their country's superiority in science and technology. The turning point came on the evening of Friday, October 4, 1957, when American ham radio operators began picking up signals they couldn't identify. The country was stunned to learn that those signals were coming from an unmanned Russian satel-lite—named Sputnik—which was streaking around the planet at 18,000 miles per hour. It was more than a year ahead of the American space agency's plans to launch its first satellite. Less than a month later, a sec-ond Russian satellite was launched, this one with a passenger, a dog named Laika.

Suddenly, America's faith in its scientific prowess was shaken. Early in December, hurrying to close the gap, U.S. scientists launched a Van-guard rocket carrying a tiny satellite. It blew up two seconds off the launch pad in Cape Canaveral. Soon headlines in the business press were asking: "What Keeps the U.S. in Second Place?" The American *school curriculum was quickly changed to include more science and concepts like binary math. A shortage of scientists was proclaimed as America scrambled to regain its preeminent position in technology. By the end of the 1950s, the nation was in need of some breakthroughs to restore its pride.*

❖   ❖   ❖

IF ONE HAD TO CHOOSE ONE PERSON as king of the digital age, that title would go to Bob Noyce, the personable, incandescent son of a preacher from Iowa. For one thing, he had been working with transistors—those new little replacements for vacuum tubes—as long as anyone in the field. But he matched his experience level with a powerful charisma. He was the kind of guy people wanted to follow, the kind of guy people trusted. By 1957 he was working with the best engineers of the day including William Shockley at Shockley Semiconductor. So when a number of his leading scientists started plans to split off and form their own company to create newer, better silicon transistors, not stick with germanium as Shockley insisted, Noyce was the obvious choice to become the group's general manager.

With his big grin, firm handshake, and thorough knowledge of semiconductor technology, Noyce was the perfect front man: He could explain the company's transistor business to potential investors, who couldn't understand the physics of the tiny devices. On a superficial level, the idea was simple. Properly created and manipulated—"doped" in the chipmaking slang—semiconductor crystals like germanium or silicon could replace the vacuum tube amplifier. The result was called a transistor. Here, a tiny current pulsing across a particular junction of man-made semiconducting crystal, could in turn affect a much larger current passing beneath it. There were two key uses for this. The first was to replace the vacuum tube amplifier, which had allowed very weak radio waves to control much more powerful speakers, and thus produce working radios, by direct amplification. Since the transistor had no moving parts, it would never wear out; and it was much cheaper to make than tubes once its manufacturing process was refined. This was a big economic opportunity in an era when vacuum tubes were a hundred million dollar business.

But that was only the start. The other essential use for semiconductor products based on transistors was as a key building block for most electronic circuits, a business that was only just getting started by the late 1950s. Because of the physics of semiconducting materials, transistors could also be designed with very specific threshold—or "breakdown"—voltages, which is the point where the transistor allows current to flow. This characteristic enabled transistors to create what came to be called *gates* because, just like vacuum tubes, they could stay closed until a particular voltage was reached, when they would open and allow the underlying current to pass. In this way, tiny changes in the current at the transistor "gate" could open or close a particular part of a circuit. So long as the electricity remained on to refresh the devices and keep the transistor's "state" the same, these gates could in effect "store" information. This would become essential to creating the modern digital age—the idea soon to be at the heart of modern memories, all circuit components, and microprocessors. Transistors did the same things as hot glass vacuum tubes, only much more efficiently, and better—and they could be miniaturized.

Noyce knew that the potential market for transistors was huge. But he also sensed that the potential for circuit design using transistors as gates was even greater. While the business was rooted in space-age science and technology, it was going to be driven by economics. Noyce also understood the importance of markets. And, of course, that was something that made sense to the investors.

Noyce believed deeply in the transistors' potential. He felt they would be used to replace vacuum tubes in every industry, all over the world, thanks to their diminutive size, low power requirements, cost-effectiveness, and durability. They would make new applications possible. He loved to talk about how the transistors could make medical equipment portable, and even allow electronic devices to be embedded in the human body—one of his favorite examples was a pacemaker that could be built into a small, reliable product using transistors and that could potentially stimulate a heart regularly.

Noyce was also quick to point out that though transistors initially would be difficult to produce, once the process was perfected, yields would rise and rise. Yield is the essential number in the semiconductor business. It is a measure of how many working end-products are created out of every batch of transistors. Most semiconductors are created in bulk, then sawed apart. (In the early days these were usually long crystals, but since the mid-1960s almost all production has been on flat "wafers" with dozens of individual devices created side by side). Since the raw materials for even the most advanced transistor at the time—silicon-based units—consisted of sand and a few fine wires, all the costs were in the manufacturing process. Once that was worked out, profits could be found at almost any price. Thus, a type of transistor that cost $20 at first, might cost a dollar or less once the plant could stamp them out quickly. Transistor prices fell an average of 30 percent a year starting in the mid-1950s and continuing through the 1960s.

Noyce's most astonishing claim, however, had to do with the transistor's ability to change all consumers' buying habits. If electronic parts could be manufactured from cheap, disposable components, Noyce would ask, why not just throw them out when they wore down? Who needed to repair or rebuild a product like a radio? In the near future, it would make sense to simply buy a new one—one that was cheaper, better, and had more features. In his impassioned presentations, Bob Noyce made it all seem exciting and plausible—if not necessarily inevitable.

According to Sherman Fairchild, Noyce was the reason he agreed to create a new division in his company for Shockley's ex-employees. He trusted the 32-year-old Noyce, and believed in his vision—so much so that at age 62, he decided to bet heavily on a group of young engineers with no business experience at all. His instincts were good. When his company, Fairchild Camera & Instrument, invested in Noyce's operation in 1957, the parent company had total sales of $32 million. By 1959, revenues for the new Fairchild Semiconductor division alone represented $9 million. The division's sales doubled every year thereafter, so that by the mid-1960s the semiconductor group was producing $140 million in sales, representing two-thirds of Fairchild's total revenues—and *all* the profits for the company. In 1966, Fairchild's semiconductor sales were second only to those of Texas Instruments, which had started building transistors five years earlier than Noyce's group. In third place was Motorola, which had set up a semiconductor operation in the Arizona desert, run by Lester Hogan, a former physics professor at Harvard.

But other new companies were quickly getting in on the business. It was the Wild West in the semiconductor industry. The only way to find experts was to hire them away from other companies. Fairchild, of course, had helped start the trend, by hiring the key eight-man team that had decided to defect from William Shockley (who labeled them the "Traitorous Eight"). Alliances and defections became the norm in semiconductor companies. The Fairchild Eight would later be joined by a team from the semiconductor division of Hughes Aircraft, who later, led by Ewart Baldwin, would form the Rheem Semiconductor Division of Rheem Manufacturing. Another group from Hughes left that company to start Pacific Semiconductors, a division of Thomas Ramo Wooldrige (later TRW). A team from an early transistor manufacturer, Radio Receptor Corporation, split off to form General Transistor Corporation, an independent firm posting $11 million in transistor sales by 1959. Alumni from that firm established two more companies, Industro Transistor Corporation and Silicon Transistor Corporation in 1960. Two brothers—Leo and David Balakar—launched Transitron, one of the first transistor companies in 1952. By the end of that decade, it boasted annual sales of $30.9 million, and profits of $6.5 million—a net margin of better than 20 percent. (It later had production and management problems, and by the late 1960s, it had disappeared.)

All of this activity in transistor and semiconductor companies was just setting the stage for the Fairchild company, where technological innovation led to the second great empire of the semiconductor age. The first had been Texas Instruments, an aggressive upstart that took out an early license on transistors from Bell Labs, then proceeded to both introduce the first transistor radio that captured the public's attention, and solve the problems with silicon that had bedeviled the rest of the industry, in the process capturing the electronics industry's notice. The members of Fairchild's new division came up with a mission that sounded simple, but was actually quite complex. Noyce's group was going to create discrete silicon transistors—as opposed to the simpler, less expensive germanium-based transistors that were generally being manufactured then. Silicon was a much more difficult material to work with, but the former Shockley engineers—the best in their field—felt confident that they were up to the challenge. Besides, silicon transistors had some key applications: they could be used in the temperature-sensitive missiles of the space race—and in the aftermath of Sputnik, that was where the action was.

The surprise of Sputnik ignited a race to miniaturize all electronic devices. America's main problem in getting a rocket and satellite airborne was simple: weight. Pulling away from the Earth's atmosphere took an enormous amount of thrust. A single pound of weight required $100,000 worth of rocket fuel. The Russians' first Sputniks, with 200-

pound satellites, were eight times heavier than those of America's heaviest design: 22 pounds. The Russians opted for a brute force approach, creating massive lift-off rockets that were developed in complete secrecy. American engineers, lulled into a false sense of security by the absence of even an inkling of the USSR's plans, focused on intercontinental defense missiles that didn't need to break out of the earth's atmosphere. When the news of Sputnik broke, the U.S. government found that it didn't have anything even on the drawing board that could lift a satellite into orbit. The answer was either to start a launch missile program lickety-split, or to reduce the size of American satellites so that they could be carried on a hastily modified version of the military's defense missiles. Even so, it was clear that for America to get ahead in the space race, they had to reduce the size of the electronics carried onboard any satellite while increasing the components' capabilities.

The trouble was that transistors, for all their proven utility in replacing vacuum tubes, still had to be individually wired, component to component. So, though complicated circuits could be built using many components, they still had significant mass because of the sheer quantity of parts required to build them. The dilemma was called the tyranny of numbers in the electronics trade press of the day. As the designers of electronic circuitry produced more sophisticated designs, they were running into a wall: There were limits to the numbers of discrete components that could be wired together. And there were limits, too, to what a team of workers, hunched over benches with tweezers and soldering guns, could achieve during one eight-hour shift. And finally, there was a limit to how small a soldering gun could get.

The industry needed a way to compress a number of components—transistors, diodes, resistors, and capacitors—into a single device. In 1958, the state-of-the-art computer was Control Data's 1604. It contained 25,000 transistors, 100,000 diodes, and hundreds of thousands of resistors and capacitors. It was the kind of machine that the military was counting on for its most advanced battlefield command stations or missiles. But its complex construction meant its reliability was dubious.

In an effort to simplify the components, the U.S. Army Signal Corps designed something called the "microminiature module," which consisted of one-inch ceramic wafers that each contained several components. The wafers were then stacked in a small wire cage and encased in plastic. Bell Labs came up with its own version of this concept that used larger ceramic disks, in which a number of transistor parts could be wired together. IBM, too, was adopting a similar packaging concept for its next generation of computers. All these devices could be used to build such complicated apparatuses as a mainframe computer, where space wasn't at a premium. But they weren't small enough to be integrated into a guidance and navigation system for an airborne missile or spacecraft. And these modules still required lots of human handwork for assembly.

Fairchild made the first real steps toward solving this critical problem. Up to that point, transistors were being produced with what was called the mesa method. In it, successive layers of doped semiconducting material (negative-positive-negative, or n-p-n), were diffused onto an inert wafer. Each layer was coated with a photosensitive chemical called a photo-mask as it was laid down. The layers were then exposed to light directed through a translucent blueprint: The opaque lines of the blueprint blocked the light and thus left an imprint of that pattern on the surface of the semiconducting material. The photo layers were then "developed," just as photographic film would be, so that portions of the chips that had been exposed to the light were covered with an impermeable thin layer of a chemical that was resistant to the action of an etching compound, while the other portions were not protected. The result, after a series of acid "baths," was alternating "mesas" of semiconductor mounds of n- and p-type crystals on the surface of the wafer. In the "valleys" between the mesas, the transistors could be separated using the same precision tools used to cut diamonds. Contacts—usually copper wires that could carry current—were then attached to the top, bottom, and middle of the assemblage, and a fully operational transistor was born.

With the mesa method, human handwork was still a significant part of the process, in cutting apart the semiconductor mountains and attaching the electrode contacts. To overcome these obstacles, Noyce's Fairchild team developed what came to be called the planar process, whereby the metal electrode contacts were evaporated, a process using extraordinary heat to vaporize the copper metal, and then a few tricks to get the molecules to adhere *directly* to the surface of the transistor as it was being produced. These transistors were still composed of alternating layers of semiconducting material, but instead of featuring mesas, the surface of the finished wafer (which might hold dozens of transistors) was flat and smooth. This made it much easier to handle, and better yet, because of the uniformity, allowed the finished wafers with dozens of transistors to be sawn apart by machine. Because the metal contacts didn't have to be attached by hand, but were already integral to the transistors themselves, the risk of human error was further reduced. Ultimately, because the fine wires deposited by evaporation could be much smaller than human fingers could ever manipulate, it would allow the transistors to be much more tightly packed and much smaller. In this way, the transistors would be uniform in size and already had their metal connections, so they were much easier to cut apart. The planar process was a major step forward. It made the transistor much easier to manufacture and thus accelerated the rush into the electronics age. But it didn't address the biggest problem of all: space and the tyranny of numbers.

The planar process though gave Bob Noyce an idea—a breakthrough idea that created a billion-dollar semiconductor industry in a couple of years, and one that eventually put an American on the moon. The idea came to Noyce while he was writing a series of lab journal entries, culminating on January 23, 1959. It was a year after the founding of Fairchild Semiconductor, when the group was struggling to get its first planar-based product out the door. His notion was to create all the elements in a traditional electronic circuit—resistors, capacitators, transistors, and diodes—out of silicon. He could then interconnect them all under a blanket of a protective surface of silicon oxide. Better still, by creating everything out of different arrangements of silicon, everything was vastly simplified. Complicated combinations of circuit elements could be created side-by-side in the tiny spaces of a few transistors, on a single wafer. In this way, he could create what he called an integrated circuit. What Noyce didn't know is that this idea had already been thought of by someone else—someone who worked for Texas Instruments.

At Texas Instruments, all the employees went on vacation at the same time each year, in July. In 1958, there was a new hire, named Jack Kilby, who hadn't been there long enough to qualify for vacation time, and so he stayed at work. Kilby had just come to TI from Centralab, a military contractor based in Wisconsin. After ten years there, Kilby was a bona fide inventor. He had a dozen patents in his name; he liked to take ideas and turn them into electrical products. But he was no manufacturing specialist—he could dream up a concept and build a prototype, but he wasn't the man to get it into production.

For one month, while the rest of the company was on holiday, Kilby had virtually the huge TI plant to himself. And in the silence, out in the empty labs, wandering past the kilns, he got an idea. Kilby started wondering whether all the devices in a standard electronic circuit—transistors, diodes, resistors, and capacitors—could be made of the same material as the transistor itself, meaning prepared silicon. This wasn't as obvious as it sounds today. At the time, making resistors out of silicon was an expensive, multi-step, high-temperature process, whereas a better-quality carbon resistor could be had easily, for less than a penny apiece. Furthermore, silicon capacitators didn't work as well as the metal-and-porcelain capacitators generally in use then. But by making all the parts of a circuit out of one material, TI could manufacture them all together, out of a single block of material and thereby achieve great economies of scale. Kilby's concept came to be called the Monolithic Idea.

The inventor started drawing primitive but comprehensible sketches of all the key circuit components in various arrangements of semiconducting material. Since the mesa process was TI's forte, his design featured numerous "mountains" and "canyons." To interconnect the components, he proposed stringing tiny wires between the mesas, like telephone poles across a desert.

When his boss, Willis Adcock, returned from vacation, Kilby showed him his design, which he eventually wired up. Unfortunately, Adcock didn't share Kilby's enthusiasm. The primitive model was unimpressive: With its maze of wires between the elements, clearly this design could never be mass-manufactured. The wires were far too delicate for the new world of the electron. The real elegance of Kilby's work was in the basic concept. He knew that what he had done could be greatly improved. As he saw it, dozens of discrete components could be set side-by-side on a single bit of wafer. But Adcock only gave him limited support, so it was Kilby's job to make the vision a reality. He wasn't up to the job. His capabilities didn't extend beyond those of the inventor/architect.

Out in California, Bob Noyce had a remarkably similar idea—but his design included a way to get the product made. Noyce's advantage was the planar process. He talked about it with Gordon Moore, one of the chief scientists at Fairchild. A tall, slow, and soft-spoken engineer, Moore had been a professor of solid-state electronics at Cal-Tech and a consultant to Shockley Semiconductor before agreeing to join Noyce in the Fairchild start-up. The two realized that using wires to connect mesas of components was unworkable. So Noyce sketched out an idea that incorporated the planar process and had the circuit components underneath the flat surface of the semiconductor oxide. Then he took it one step further: He decided to forego independent wires all together, and simply etch tiny lines of metal directly into the uniform surface of the silicon oxide insulation blanket. This enabled the creation of integrated circuits: Each silicon-based component was made from the same steps that produced the silicon transistors, they were all given the same clean surface, and the metal lines that connected them could be laid down directly on that surface.

While the idea of using silicon for all the components made it possible to create integrated circuits, it was the planar diffusion of the silicon oxide insulator and the Fairchild method of etching tiny wires directly into the surface of those wafers that made it possible to manufacture them. Previously, circuit components had to be interconnected by hand; now they could be churned out by machines. It was a new era.

Eventually, both Texas Instruments and Fairchild received partial patent protection for the integrated circuit, and both thrived over time as they produced ICs of increasing complexity. The integrated circuit itself and the planar process, for both transistors and ICs, made Fairchild Semiconductor one of the most profitable companies of its time. As more and more circuits could be crammed onto wafer space, Gordon Moore predicted that transistor capacity—the number of transistors on a chip—would double every 24 months. The prediction became known as Moore's Law, but it soon proved too conservative: A few years later, Moore had to revise his projection to every 18 months. As manufacturing processes greatly improved, so did the manufacturing facilities that housed them. With higher-resolution lenses and better blueprint films, the internal paths and byways of the chip itself were soon reduced to much less than the thickness of a strand of human hair, eventually reaching geometries that were thousands of times smaller.

The new economies of the integrated circuit essentially ended the transistor age. The first integrated circuits were comprised of a handful of transistors, logic gates (electronic switches), and circuit elements. They were square, clunky things, with metal sawtooth contacts along the sides. By 1965 a batch of 200 transistors, priced at 75 cents each, cost about $150. But an integrated circuit that contained 200 transistors was priced at only $15. These economies made it crucial for forward-thinking companies to start manufacturing the new integrated chips, even as sales of discrete transistor products were at an all-time high. In 1966, they peaked at $829 million, while an estimated $150 million worth of integrated circuits were sold. But only five years later, the integrated circuit market was bigger than that for discrete products, at about $1 billion, growing at 50 percent a year in dollar value, already larger than the discrete market had been a few years earlier. The reason was simple price/performance. By then, the average price of a discrete transistor was down to 22 cents (or $44 for 200 of them), while an integrated circuit with 200 transistors cost only $2.

The 1960s were an extraordinarily good time for the electronics industry in general, in spite of the highs and lows caused by sequences of overoptimistic manufacturing when supply was scarce, followed by a glut that drove down prices. That, in turn, instigated a boom as demand roared back greater than before. To ride out the cycles, a company had to expand even when demand was down, to prevent being caught short when it suddenly turned up again.

This strategy wasn't immediately apparent, of course. Many of the biggest companies pulled up stakes following the semiconductor recession of 1961-1962, leaving the field wide open for TI, Fairchild, and Motorola. By the second half of the decade, though, things started to get tough for that trio, too, as the cycle started down again during 1967. By then, the full impact of the integrated circuit was evident on the balance sheets of the industry's leaders. In March 1968, Forbes ran a story about Texas Instruments and the semiconductor industry:

> Texas Instruments leads the semiconductor market along with Fairchild Camera and Motorola. Nearly two-thirds of TI's sales come from electronics, semiconductors (transistors, diodes, resistors, integrated circuits, and the like). The market is one of the biggest and fastest growing in the U.S., where semiconductors have almost doubled since 1963.
>
> At the same time it is a risky market. Technological changes in semiconductors have been bewilderingly swift as transistors have become smaller and smaller and have finally given way to integrated circuits. Also, the average price of a transistor has dropped 50% annually in recent years. Several years ago a small semiconductor producer could

sell a circuit containing, say, four transistors for $120. Today he might find himself selling a tiny integrated circuit with 40 transistors for only $4. TI and the others must sell twice as many transistors every year just to stay even in dollar sales. Thus, despite tremendous year-to-year gains in the volume of integrated circuits, the industry's total sales dollars leveled off at just over $1 billion last year.

The industry is accustomed to this pace but can't always stay ahead of it. "The changeover to integrated circuits from discrete components like transistors and resistors sneaked up on us faster than we had ever expected," said Mark Shepherd, president of Texas Instruments. For 1967, TI's sales slipped from $580 million to $569 million, while earnings slumped from $3.30 to $2.11 per share. Fairchild and Motorola felt the pinch too, with earnings declines of 48% and 55% respectively.

But Fairchild's 1967 drop in earnings was only the tip of the iceberg. The company had internal troubles as well. The semiconductor division was still being run by a group of button-down executives from the headquarters in Syossett, New York, who disdained their Western colleagues, even though the California operation earned the company all its profits. All the operational decisions had to be made by those executives: Every budget, every expenditure, every hiring and firing decision had to have their stamp of approval.

Once a year the representatives from headquarters would visit the Fairchild plant in Mountain View, California, or the research facility just off the Stanford campus and grill the teams there. Though they were impressed by the profits generated by those sites, they were concerned about how to drive the business forward. It was imperative that they maintain this crucial source of income because John Carter, Fairchild's president, had used the profits earned by the semiconductor division to purchase nearly a dozen businesses (Curtis Laboratories, Waste King, DuMont Labs, Cosmic Corp., White Avionics, Mergenthaler Linotype, and others). They were all doing poorly.

Noyce, meanwhile, had been rewarded for his breakthrough work by being promoted to corporate vice president, and he now had responsibility for the four plants that comprised the entire semiconducting division. His general manager was a manufacturing specialist, Charlie Sporck, who was a master of the assembly line. He was a tough, no-nonsense manager who had overseen the building of the four plants, and was reputed to be able to run the tightest semiconductor manufacturing plant in the world. But Sporck became increasingly upset by the attention management lavished on unprofitable operations, while his division essentially kept Fairchild Camera afloat.

Unfortunately, Noyce's seat on the executive committee didn't translate into real control; cronies of Sherman Fairchild constantly voted against him. In March 1967 he lost Sporck, who took four others from Fairchild, as well as men from TI, Perkin Elmer, and Hewlett-Packard to form a new 8-man team at National Semiconductor. They were financed by Peter Sprague, of Sprague Electric, a company that made its mark and money in vacuum tubes. Starting in 1965 Sprague, at age 27 and a few years out of Yale, had used some of the family company's funds (Sprague Electric's revenues were $107 million in 1966) to buy 150,000 shares of National Semiconductor's common stock, then priced at around $25. National Semiconductor had been formed as a spin-off from Sperry Rand's transistor manufacturing operations in 1959, and six years later it was doing $5.3 million in sales, though profits ebbed from $362,000 in 1965 to $238,000 the following year. At that point, Sprague stepped in and took control as Chairman, backed by a pair of West Coast investment firms and a New York underwriter.

It was the beginning of the world of venture capitalists. Around the same time, Thomas Hambrecht and George Quist, a pair of stockbrokers in San Francisco, started bringing together wealthy businesspeople to pool their money and invest in what many considered to be high-risk enterprises, among which were a growing number of electronics firms. Two of the first investors that joined were the Hale Brothers, department store heirs and owners of an emporium chain headquartered in San Francisco. Soon, a loose affiliation of like-minded investors communicated via a grapevine that told them where the best talents were being nurtured and which companies had the most potential. Arthur Rock, a former investment advisor to the Rockefellers and other wealthy New York families, is generally recognized as the first venture capitalist. He moved to San Francisco, accumulated a venture fund—a pool of capital, initially several million dollars—and started accepting business proposals. Together with Hambrecht and Quist, they formed the equivalent of a syndicate. It was called The Group and included an ever-changing band of private individuals and investment funds like Data Science Ventures, Bessemer Securities, Sutter Hill Capital Corporation, Midland Capital Corporation, and the Bank of America's Small Business Enterprise Corporation. Among their deals were investments in Teledyne, Memorex, Scientific Data Systems (SDS), and Measurex. The only common ground? All the investments were in electronics or technology companies, and all were highly speculative. Sprague wasn't directly involved, but the milieu of risk and venture capital was all around him.

Charlie Sporck was one of the first to take advantage of the new availability of venture capital. He put together a proposal, outlining his group's plan to copy a new type of semiconductor that Sylvania had introduced. When he met Peter Sprague, it was a perfect match. The young heir was willing to offer the kind of lucrative stock deal that Sporck wanted: He agreed to a 50 percent pay cut in exchange for options to buy 45,000 shares of National Semiconductor at $13.30, and another 30,000 shares at $11. Finally, if his team could make the firm a success, he would be further rewarded in kind. He did it: In the next three years National Semiconductor's sales rose from $7 million to $42 million, and the company became the toast of the industry. Though profits remained slim—reaching only $1.6 million in 1970, when the semiconductor's cyclical demand bottomed out—his tight-fisted control of manufacturing gave National Semiconductor the lowest costs for semiconductors in years.

Noyce meanwhile, was not faring as well at Fairchild. By the middle of 1967, the company started warning that profits wouldn't be as high as they had been the previous year. In the fall, the company announced write-offs to excess capacity that cost $4 million, or $1 a share. Profits fell to 50 cents a share from $3 a year earlier. The stock dropped into the $70s from its high of $135. In December, Carter abruptly resigned when Fairchild's board ordered him to sell his unprofitable acquisitions. Initially, Noyce was considered as his replacement. After all, he was running the flagship semiconductor division that was suddenly having troubles. But the division had faltered as demand had dropped with the inevitable cycle in semiconductors. The board members voted against the promotion.

Noyce had mixed feelings about being in the world of management anyway. As his responsibilities grew with Fairchild's expansion, he became increasingly frustrated and unhappy. The semiconductor technology continued to improve: more circuits could be integrated onto increasingly complex wedges of silicon, and hundreds of circuits could now be imprinted onto a single chip, allowing electronics designers to build sophisticated equipment in a fraction of the space. But rather than reveling in their role in this burgeoning business, Noyce and his team felt taken advantage of. Fairchild had a big-company mentality, and there was no equity stake for the best and brightest of the engineers. At best, they would get an additional week or two of salary as bonus, followed by a half-hearted pat on the back from the New York managers.

Ever since the Securities and Exchange Commission had changed its rules in 1950, allowing the granting of stock options to executives, companies had started giving them out. The explosion of growth in semiconductor companies in the early 1960s meant that stock options had started to become a big attraction for top-flight talent. When he bought out the original Traitorous Eight in 1958, Fairchild had offered stock options. Sherman Fairchild believed he had been sufficiently generous with the founders of his semiconductor division when he paid them each a couple hundred thousand dollars. He was wrong.

It took Peter Sprague and Arthur Rock to make the addition of stock options—in a quantity that held out the possibility for geometric expansions of wealth—a standard perk in the industry. When the news of Sporck's terms at National Semiconductor made the rounds in the Sunnyvale, California bar where the Fairchild engineers hung out, the Fairchild group's dissatisfaction got worse. Within a year, another 35 Fairchildren (as they were called) also jumped ship, setting up half a dozen new companies, including Advanced Micro Devices (AMD) and Intersil.

As Fairchild continued to struggle, a creeping conservatism became pervasive there. As a result, Noyce was forced to reject a promising new technology for creating silicon-based transistors and circuits when management feared it was too unreliable. Unlike the division's early days, when they were free—even encouraged—to experiment with new ways of insulating and connecting circuits, Noyce's group was now considered a dinosaur that couldn't afford to take chances. This went against Bob Noyce's natural tendency as a risk-taker. In his role as a manager, answerable to other managers, he was hamstrung from betting on a new development.

When he had conceived of the first integrated circuits under their layer of oxide insulation, Bob Noyce had been building on work done by others first at Shockley Semiconductor and later at Fairchild. And while that idea would eventually triumph, right now, in 1966, there was nothing particularly new in the way Noyce formulated transistors. Fairchild continued to produce bipolar integrated circuits using the standard negative-positive-negative arrangement, and forged into the much more profitable integrated circuits. The new integrated chip market was doubling every year, and fueled Fairchild's growth through the 1960s. But by the mid-1960s, if anything could be called "old hat" in the new world of semiconductors, it was bipolar transistors. While the industry struggled to improve on the design of the basic building block of electronic circuitry, especially in light of the manufacturing efficiencies that would ensue if a more elegant formulation could be devised, nothing proved workable.

From the earliest days of William Shockley's musing about transistors, his dream was to formulate a field effect transistor, a single block of semiconducting material that could be controlled by a simple metal gate positioned above it. No negative-positive-negative combinations, no layer after layer of semiconductor diffused onto etched surfaces, this field effect transistor would only need one polarity for its semiconductor block, and current flow would be entirely controlled by applying a voltage across the metal gate. It would be much easier to manufacture because it only needed one polarity of semiconductor, and it could be packed tightly onto a wafer or chip. But unraveling the mysteries of making it remained elusive. By the middle of the 1960s the idea was called MOS, for metal-oxide-semiconductor, since that was the arrangement of the three key levels. (The oxide was the insulating layer between the metal gate and the semiconductor material.)

But MOS resisted a practical expression. For years, researchers had struggled to make an MOS device work. By the early 1960s, all that researchers at both Bell Labs and RCA had succeeded in accomplishing was the construction of some prototype that barely worked. What seemed elegant on paper was proving impossible to implement in reality. Texas Instruments even declared it was impossible. Fairchild, too, gave the project its best effort, before giving up in 1965. Is wasn't surprising, then, when Bob Noyce, weighed down with management decisions and tired of seeing millions of dollars of R&D go up in smoke, declared in 1966 that Fairchild would stick with bipolar integrated circuits for the foreseeable future.

Coincidentally, however, Fairchild had hired a new Ph.D. from Berkeley in 1963. Andrew Grove, born Andras Grof, was a Hungarian émigré who had fled the 1956 uprising in his country at the age of 19. He had crawled across the border while more than a thousand Hungarian partisans were being shot on the streets of Budapest. He eventually made it to America. Barely able to speak English, he had enrolled in City College of New York, graduated at the top of his engineering class, and went on to earn his doctorate in fluid dynamics at the University of California. Hired by Gordon Moore to work in the research lab at Fairchild, Grove was soon assigned to solve the persistent problem of why MOS devices could not be made to work. It was not considered a plum assignment, since Noyce had just declared that MOS was a dead end at Fairchild. But Moore was primarily a researcher, and Grove had proved himself an exceptionally meticulous investigator. Solving the MOS problem was a worthwhile project, so Moore simply overrode his boss.

But Grove was a perfectionist, a man of obsessive neatness with a remarkably analytic mind. He was the kind of person who believes there is a rational explanation for any problem. While pursuing what came to be known as MOSFET—metal oxide silicon field effect transistor—Grove and a couple of his colleagues abandoned exotic theories and went back to basics. They scrupulously cleaned the equipment used to process the silicon wafers, and found that sodium contaminants left by chemicals used to clean the gear were interfering with the development of the new transistors. Astonishingly, with that taken care of, the new MOS products started to work as originally predicted!

Unfortunately, the breakthrough couldn't stop Fairchild's freefall. More talented engineers left. By the end of 1970, 26 different electronics companies had been formed by the various refugees from Fairchild. The company's manufacturing plant was in chaos as engineer after engineer left for greener pastures. Fairchild management in New York didn't seem to notice that its greatest assets—its people—were slipping away.

Noyce did pay attention to his people, and he was impressed with Grove, whose ability to troubleshoot the semiconductor assembly process made him particularly valuable. He had, after all, debugged the MOS technology, which if perfected, promised to revolutionize the manufacturing of semiconductors. Noyce was a smart engineer, with a businessman's head for exploitable opportunities. When he saw that

Grove had solved the MOS problems, he switched gears and tried to convince Fairchild management that this was the next big break-through. By simplifying the manufacturing process once again, and enabling thousands, if not millions, of transistors to be crammed into the space of a single chip, he realized that Fairchild could revolutionize the electronics business again. Talking it over with his colleague Gordon Moore, they thought they ought to be able to create a simple, geomet-ric pattern of MOS transistors that could store binary data. It would be the first memory chip, and could replace the core memory looms—fish-nets of tiny ceramic magnets—that were being used in every computer of the time. Since the key to memory access for a computer was random access—the ability to get at any portion of the stored data instantly—the cells would have to be arranged in a matrix, with an addressing scheme that would allow the contents of any memory cell to be read at any time. But that played right into the strengths of MOS—because the transis-tors could be packed densely together in a geometric matrix, they were perfect for this task.

But Fairchild's management refused to consider manufacturing MOS devices. The company was starting to run into its financial prob-lems late in 1967, and MOS manufacturing on a commercial scale was still quite different from proving how to make the devices in the lab. Furthermore, no customers were clamoring for the new units. So the company's executive committee stood firmly behind the existing bipolar transistors and the integrated circuits the company was already making.

This decision finally motivated Noyce, at the age of 46, to think about trying something different. He submitted his resignation in the spring of 1968, but agreed to stay until a new president was found. That summer, Fairchild hired one: Lester Hogan, and he brought with him most of the senior management from Motorola's semiconductor plant. Motorola chief Robert Galvin promptly filed suit.

The move set the business world on its ear. Not only had Fairchild raided a competitor and taken its top tier of managers, but after years of refusing lucrative financial incentives to its original group of semicon-ductor geniuses, Sherman Fairchild offered Hogan a huge base salary and an option for 10,000 shares of restricted stock at $10 a share—at the time, it had a face value of $500,000. Finally, Hogan was guaranteed a personal interest-free loan of up to $5.4 million to buy another 90,000 shares at $60 three years after he was hired. It was an incredible package for the day.

Nevertheless, 15 months later Fairchild was still in the red. Though sales were up 17 percent for the first half of fiscal 1969, to $126 million, the previous year's six-month profits of $2.8 million had become a loss of $300,000. Hogan proved unable to remake Fairchild into a profitable venture. By the second quarter of fiscal 1970, the company reported another loss—of $5 million. Monthly orders fell from approximately $125 million for the industry in February to less than $75 million by the end of the year. Only National Semiconductor, with its penny-pinching Charlie Sporck at the helm, was able to keep things on an even keel. Because National resolutely continued to cut prices in the face of a recession, the company became the target of much ill will in the field. National's marketing chief Don Valentine made no apologies when he succinctly described the company's attitude: "If it weren't for aggressive pricing, this industry would be a lot smaller."

Conversely, at Fairchild, numbers for all of 1970 were a disaster. The company lost almost $20 million as sales slipped from the previous year's $250 million to less than $225 million. Jobs were slashed by 8,000, with 6,500 of them coming from the semiconductor division. With the stock down to $26, Hogan's $60 options became a joke. Unwisely, management offered Hogan another loan, this one for $1 million so he could buy stock on the open market. Then, instead of investing in new innovations that came from their own labs, Hogan spent heavily on new equipment to help the company grow its revenues in its barely profitable bipolar transistors. In doing so, Fairchild missed the next wave: MOS technology. Fairchild wouldn't be profitable again until the late 1970s, five years after Hogan left.

Fortunately for Bob Noyce, he had a broader vision than Hogan. As he was nearing the end of his tenure at Fairchild, just before Hogan was hired, he had started talking with Moore and Grove about launching their own company. Arthur Rock, the venture capitalist, had assured Noyce that money would be no problem, as long as the trio had a business proposal that had merit. Noyce, Moore, and Grove proposed building a business to exploit a device called the silicon gate. This was a crucial breakthrough because it took the advances of MOS design, and did away with its one major drawback: the metal gate. The problem was that metal required much lower temperatures than silicon. This meant that complicated circuits, which might have transistors at many of the layers of the chip, couldn't be created with the MOS process because the metal gates that were set down in earlier stages would melt at the temperatures needed for creating the semiconductor portions of the latter ones. But when the Fairchild semiconductor experts found out that a fellow researcher at the company had perfected a way to get rid of the metal altogether, and could manufacture CMOS transistors entirely out of silicon, they knew that the revolution had come. Removing all metal from the transistor made Gordon Moore's theoretical predictions about the microcosm tangible. Everything inside the chips would be created out of forms of silicon, and the only limitation now was how fine the resolution of the blueprints, and the machines that could transfer them to wafers, were capable of working. Ultimately, with silicon-gate devices, created in the CMOS process, transistors could be created in sizes that were measured in hundreds of molecules. Understanding the implications of this set Noyce, Moore, and Grove off to write a business plan that proposed building memory chips using this new process. That plan would be the beginning of Intel.

The silicon gate—which replaced a transistor's standard aluminum contacts with silicon ones—was widely regarded as the key to the digital age. It was invented and perfected by Federico Faggin, an Italian émigré to the United States, while he was a research associate at Fairchild Semiconductor in 1967 and 1968, on loan from an Italian-French venture run by SGS Thomson. He did it on his own, working outrageous hours, and in direct contravention to the commands of his boss at Fairchild.

It was the knowledge of Faggin's invention of the silicon gate, a semiconductor with both contacts and gates made out of silicon, that gave Bob Noyce a look into the future. He could foresee what this development could mean once it was perfected. Because everything was made out of silicon, there were two key advantages to this process. First, much more complicated circuit designs were possible since there was no need to design both for the circuit itself, and the manufacturing process itself. When metal gates had to go down last, there was a limit to how sophisticated a design could be. Now that was irrelevant. But there was another advantage, hidden deep in the technology. Because the new silicon gate could be set down first, underneath the semiconductor block itself, all the rest of the transistor could be built around it. That meant that as finer and finer technologies emerged, more and more transistors could be packed into a single chip. This packing factor, that grew directly from solving the problem of making an entire transistor out of a single substance, is what really unleashed the electronics age, and occasioned Gordon Moore's famous comment about a doubling of semiconductor density every 18 months. Eventually, the process that used this, CMOS (Complèments Metal Oxide Semi-Conductor), would lead to the manufacture of the microprocessor, the electronic part that transcended transistors, integrated circuits, and memory chips. And that would set the digital age off in a new direction.

Federico Faggin could not have imagined the impact his work would have. He had been born at the very beginning of the Second World War into a prosperous Italian family in the region around Vincenza, a small Italian city about 100 miles from Venice in the north central part of the country. As a teenager during the 1950s, Faggin designed his own rubberband wind-up planes from parts he found around the village. He entered model-flying contests and usually won with his homemade planes.

"My future was obvious," he said. "My older brother went on to become a professor, but I was going to become a pilot."

Practicality intervened, and Faggin entered a vocational high school. When he graduated at the top of his class in 1958, he forever put aside his dream of becoming a pilot. Olivetti, the Italian office equipment manufacturer, hired him as a junior engineer straight out of high school.

Meanwhile, in the early 1960s, Fairchild had opened a lab near Milan, Italy, in partnership with SGS-Thomson. One of Faggin's former bosses from Olivetti was put in charge of the new lab, and when offered the chance, Faggin gladly joined him there. His first assignment was to develop a process for making MOS devices. "For a year I worked on that," he said, "and found that the key element was the cleanliness of the silicon oxide. As we purified it further and further, we finally got circuits that worked." Exactly what Grove had discovered at Fairchild. After Faggin had been at the R&D lab for about nine months, Fairchild offered him an exchange with an employee in the Silicon Valley lab, who wanted to go to Italy for a year. In February 1968, at the age of 26, Faggin made his way to California.

Six months later, when the Italian operation was sold to Olivetti, Faggin was asked to stay at Fairchild. "I definitely wanted to stay; in fact, I would have stayed even if they didn't want me," he remembered. There was good reason for that. During those first six months in California, he had managed to build a couple of working circuits using MOS technology and a technique he worked out for laying down a silicon-based gate. It was a very complicated process involving a rare acid, and a polymerized form of silicon that he had doped to carry a current. He created a "floating" gate, a bit of silicon insulated in its own oxide that hovered above the surface of the semiconductor transistor. To do so, Faggin had spent nights sleeping beside the ovens, finessing the chips as they were baked. The floating gate was such an enormous leap forward because now all the stages necessary to build complicated integrated circuits could be done at the foundry—the name by which semiconductor manufacturing plants came to be known—and at the correct temperatures for working with silicon. And because everything was made out of silicon—although in different electrical forms such as positive or negative doped silicon—masks or blueprints of greater complexity could be used. This paradox of simplicity in manufacturing, combined with complexity of design, made possible the microprocessor, which was much more complicated in its chip-level intricacies than any simple memory chip. Essentially a microprocessor involved not only a series of built-in instructions that manipulated data by adding or subtracting or storing it in a location, but also registers where data and calculations could be stored, as well as circuitry to move data into and out of the chip. By creating it as a general-purpose chip, one which could be tailored by an individual engineer for a particular need, the development changed the ground rules of the electronics age. Previously all transistors and integrated circuits had fixed capabilities that were determined before the chips were actually made. The microprocessor offered a powerful set of capabilities that could be individualized after it was manufactured. This stood traditional electronics on its ear, and would eventually move the center of power from the electronics firms that made the chips, to the engineers and software programmers who learned how to squeeze the performance and features they needed out of the microprocessor's collection of capabilities.

When Bob Noyce and Gordon Moore learned that someone at Fairchild's labs had solved the problem of replacing metal contacts with silicon, they took note. But their business plan was to make and sell MOS-based memory chips. Working with that was finicky enough. Ever since core memory had been created in the early 1950s, transistor makers had been dreaming about working out a way to store strings of bits, collected into eights and called bytes, on transistors. Once the MOS process was formulated, theoretically, there was no reason that thousands of memory cells—arrangements of transistors—couldn't be lined up in straight lines within an integrated circuit. The idea was that each collection of four transistors in a memory cell and its gates was either closed, thus unable to pass current and read as a zero, or open, where it was a one. Because it needed to be constantly refreshed with electric current, it came to be called dynamic. Eventually, this kind of dynamic random access memory, or DRAM, chip would become the key product used to launch their new company: Intel.

Together with Gordon Moore, Noyce approached Arthur Rock, who made a couple of calls to line up the financing they needed. Funded with $2.3 million in a private placement—plus $250,000 each from Moore and Noyce, and $300,000 from Grinnell College (Noyce's alma mater)—Intel was officially born on July 16, 1968. Noyce's reputation as the golden man of semiconductors preceded him. So in addition to start-up funding, Intel had its pick of young scientists from CalTech, Berkeley, and Stanford. Plus, when they left Fairchild, Noyce and Moore had taken with them a number of the company's best semiconductor engineers, including Faggin's former boss, Les Vadesz. Faggin stayed at Fairchild. The reasons were twofold: First, he had only just succeeded in his first efforts to get the silicon gate process working and wasn't about to leave yet; and second, due to the intricacies of American immigration law he had to stay at Fairchild for at least two years in order to get a permanent resident visa for the U.S.

Grove still had his work cut out for him at Intel, whose first actual product was to be a bipolar memory chip for a new Honeywell computer. That chip was intended only as a stopgap, something to get revenues flowing into the company during 1969. The company's first MOS-based memory device, the 1103, was designed that year, but it was problematic. It could store 1,024 bits of information, and required just over 4,000 transistors. But the yields were not acceptable. The chips were simply too expensive to produce. Les Vadesz couldn't seem to get the manufacturing process to work. As the effort started to burn money throughout 1969, when the company had few paying contracts, Grove focused everyone on getting the memory chip problems solved.

Though the memory chip was the original raison d'être for Intel, it proved hard to make the breakthrough they had seen Faggin accomplish at Fairchild's lab. Intel was struggling, and so, Noyce went out in search of custom chip design work to get some revenues flowing. Nonetheless Noyce and Moore knew that it was only a matter of time before they perfected the process, and with the increased circuit and design complexity afforded by the new invention, the two men predicted the development of new and much more complex integrated circuits. With the kind of memory capacity that Intel was struggling to achieve, they began to imagine the possibility of reducing some functions of the computer onto a series of chips. The question was, who was going to turn this possibility into a reality?

By 1968, there was a small fraternity of electronic investors looking for the next best place to make money fast. But they weren't impulsive; they took the time to find knowledgeable professionals with legitimate plans. Noyce and Moore were not only benefactors of the Rock, Hambrecht, and Quist funds. They were also investors. Among the companies they helped finance when they left Fairchild was a small concern called Micro-Computer Inc. Its pioneer was another young engineer, named Gil Hyatt.

Hyatt had worked as a research scientist at Teledyne and had filed his first three patents while he was working there. In 1967 he decided to go the entrepreneurial route: he set up shop in his home to design something he called a microcomputer. What he had in mind was nothing less than revolutionary: a full-functioning digital computer on a single chip with several support chips. It was, in essence, a microprocessor. Hyatt didn't want to build the device to replace microcomputers or mainframes. The market he envisioned for his product was vastly larger. He recalled, "I knew about the work with MOS devices that was being done at Fairchild, and it seemed apparent to me that a complex chip could be built that integrated all the functions of a traditional rack-mounted and hard-wired computer board. Integrated circuits were evolving rapidly. But they were being misused. There was a massive explosion of devices, with more gates and interconnections, each specifically tailored to do only part of some job. A simple programmable processor could replace many different kinds of custom ICs and be more flexible as well."

In 1969, Hyatt built his design on an engineering test bed called a breadboard, and started trying to raise money to manufacture it. This, however, was still the era when computers filled entire rooms and cost millions of dollars to build, so no one believed he could make this microcomputer work. Just as he was running out of savings and wondering whether to apply for another engineering job, a patent attorney he knew took Hyatt's business proposal to the investors at Hambrecht & Quist in San Francisco. Hyatt, by then worn out by rejections, could scarcely believe it when this group took on his proposal. Gil Hyatt was in business. The private placement netted about $90,000 up front, with $300,000 more committed to getting Micro-Computer Inc. to a full product stage. Both Bob Noyce and Gordon Moore were among the original investors.

Over at Intel, in 1969 everyone was busy trying to meet the contract date for the memory chip for Honeywell's newest mainframe computer. Noyce set out to hire the best and brightest. He grabbed Ted Hoff, a tall, gangly engineer with thick glasses and an academic research background from Stanford. Hoff wanted to be a chip architect, not a researcher, and he got his chance when Intel hired him as employee number 12. His claim to fame: he came up with a clever design for a better kind of memory cell, one that was dynamic because it had to be refreshed every second or so with electrical current, but which used only three transistors instead of the four that Moore, Grove and Noyce were basing their designs around. This design eventually became the heart of the Intel 1103 DRAM chip, but that was still a way off. By the end of 1969, Intel was starting to get desperate—that year's revenues were all of $500,000 and the staff was nearing 100. With all the brilliance of the stellar lineup of scientists it had recruited, Intel still couldn't achieve the yields it needed to become profitable off the memory chip.

Noyce sent out word that for the right price, his wizards would accept a few custom fabrication jobs. A Japanese company approached him about a custom chip job—one that came with a $100,000 cash advance. As a result, one of Hoff's first jobs at Intel was to listen while a team of Japanese engineers from Nippon Calculating Machine Company presented him with a design for a new business calculator. As they explained it, they needed 11 custom integrated circuits, a passel of memory chips for storing numbers, and a variety of other circuits to handle the power, keyboard, display, and printer. Their goal was to produce a low-cost ($3,000) desktop calculator, called Busicom, for the business market.

The calculator design called for plug-in "cartridges" of memory, to enable the user to configure it for specific purposes. Hoff found the design was far too complicated. He was an early opponent of what he called "electronic clutter." He received his first (partial) patent at age 17 for a train-signaling innovation that simplified an older system. The proposed Japanese calculator had familiar problems: too many components, too much that could go wrong. But what really caught his attention was the proposed price: $3,000 was almost half the price of the latest small DEC minicomputer, the $8,000 PDP-8, a no-nonsense, full-fledged computer that could be programmed to do any number of things.

After thinking about the project for a while, Hoff came up with a new idea—or at least a new idea to him: make a single central processing unit on a chip. This involved shrinking the basic circuitry for a computer onto a single chip. Essentially, this was what was at the core of an IBM mainframe, only there it was contained on row upon row of printed circuits and complicated machinery and wiring. This was in some ways the logical extension of the integrated circuit, but it was far more complicated than the early bipolar semiconductor manufacturing processes could support. It wasn't until the silicon gate process was perfected that it was even feasible to do this. Of course, the concept wasn't new. In fact, it had already been done in big integrated circuit assemblies at Rockwell Avionics. The electronics magazines were filled with the idea. And Gil Hyatt had already started a company to do the same thing. But for Ted Hoff, it came like a bolt out of the blue.

While on vacation in Tahiti, Hoff thought further about how to build a calculator more simply and more elegantly. His plan was to put the entire central logic and arithmetic processing unit, the heart and soul of any computer from the biggest to the smallest, on a few custom-made, general-purpose chips that were not much bigger than a human thumbnail. If he created a series of instructions (or logic), joined them to circuitry in silicon that could execute them, and had a way for an engineer to program the chip so he could use these instructors in any order or combination, the microprocessor could serve as the engine for a calculator, as well as an elevator controller, or just about anything else that required taking data and manipulating it in some way. What was new about this was doing it in the micro-circuitry of a set of chips, rather than doing the same thing on circuit boards like DEC did in its mini-computers.

In Hoff's design there were four basic components, each represented by a different chip. A stable, read-only memory (ROM) chip that could store data even when the computer was off was the repository for the start-up instructions that woke up the machine when the power was turned on. An input/output (i/o) device handled input from keyboards or paper tapes or eventually floppy drives or cassette tapes, as well as output to a printer or a screen or a paper tape or even punch cards. A scratch pad or random access memory (RAM) chip could be used for interim calculations and data storage during the operations. The central processing unit (CPU) was the heart of the machine, the computational and control unit; it interpreted and executed a set of instructions. The CPU could crunch numbers for an accounting firm with the same ease it could control elevators for the Otis company. Unfortunately, Hoff had no idea how to execute his diagrams, which called for something far more complicated than any single memory chip could accommodate. It was possible in the new silicon gate technology, but no one at Intel could make those chips work.

Hoff's was the same idea as Hyatt's, right down to the arrangement of chips, though there's no evidence that Hoff had seen Hyatt's business plan. Over the next few months, Hoff's silicon gate design, which took what he knew theoretically about Faggin's breakthroughs and applied them to the problem, remained just that: a design, nothing more. But when Bob Noyce saw the diagrams, he agreed to let Intel have a go at building the device. By early 1970, the desktop calculator was off the drawing board and on its way.

At the same time, the funding for Gil Hyatt's company dried up. He was forced into bankruptcy, and the timing couldn't have been worse— it was just as a bust hit the semiconductor market that lasted through 1971. No one was ready to pick up his financing. He was basically out of business, though his patent application would wend its way through the courts for twenty years.

Back at Intel, Hoff's task was to go from a conceptual sketch of the new product to detailed working drawings in time for the scheduled springtime arrival of the Busicom engineers. And if it was tough to take

MOS from paper to product, the new CMOS process, with its mysterious floating silicon gate component, was next to impossible. The chip design continued to languish.

To solve the problems on the Busicom contract chip, there was only one man to call: Federico Faggin. Early in 1970, Intel hired Faggin away from Fairchild, where he was immediately assigned to the microcomputer project, though few at Intel held out much hope for his success. Just days after Faggin was hired at Intel, the Nippon Calculating Machine engineer, Masatoshi Shima, came from Japan to oversee the final designs. When Faggin showed him the primitive state of Intel's chips, Shima erupted in fury. Faggin, however, managed to convince him that the only option they had left was to hammer out a workable design themselves. Together, the two young men redesigned the chips, finished the actual layouts, then took them to prototype form in the new silicon gate process. The two young engineers found they were kindred workaholics, and threw themselves into the project with gusto. Within three months, all four chips were in the first stage of production; with a minimum amount of rework, they were done. One of these was among the first microprocessors in the world, although Texas Instruments, which was working on a similar project for a client that wanted a flexible and powerful computer monitor, would eventually be awarded the patent. But at Intel, Faggin had saved the day.

The bad news was that the Japanese were infuriated by the outrageous cost of the delays. When they demanded a partial refund, Noyce felt he had no choice but to accede. Besides, he was already thinking beyond this particular deal. He knew that Faggin and Shima had accomplished something invaluable, and he was thinking about the implications of the general-purpose microprocessors—implications that Gil Hyatt had articulated in his original business plan, and that now actually seemed imminent. If Intel were to make a central processor—a complete computer on a single complex integrated circuit—Noyce wanted Intel to control it. So Noyce returned to Nippon Calculating Machine $60,000 of its initial $100,000 fee. But in exchange, he demanded the rights to the design. Though NCM had the right to use the new chip in its desktop calculator, a $3,000 desktop machine didn't have much of a future when handheld calculators were right around the corner. NCM went out of business a few years later.

Now Noyce felt free to sell the new chip elsewhere, but initially he wasn't sure where. As implemented, the processing engine Intel produced was a 4-bit chip, which meant it operated on four bits of data at a time. It contained 2,300 individualized transistors and boasted a set of instructions that could be used by either engineers or programmers. Named the 4004, it was announced to the world in November 1971.

By then, Intel was well on its way. The 1103 memory chip was finally in production, and the firm reported revenues of $4.2 million in 1970, $10 million in 1971. The 4004, though regarded as primitive, sold better than anyone at Intel had expected. A blood-monitoring machine was one of the first products to use it, besides the desktop calculator from NCM.

The 4004 was quickly supplanted, however, because Faggin and Shima (who had been hired away by Intel after his yeoman effort in bringing the first microprocessor to completion) had finished a newer, more powerful chip. This one operated on 8 bits of data and was therefore named the 8008. This design had a much bigger address space, the amount of memory that the microprocessor could directly work with: Mathematically, there were 8 to the 8th power address locations for memory, or instructions, or answers—16 million total—or the new chip versus 4^4 (or 256) for the earlier version.

Throughout the 1970s, Intel's memory products were the only source of profits for the company. All sales and marketing efforts were focused on commodity memory chips because that was where the money was— every computer in the world needed memory. The new DRAM chips were crucial. The second memory product was the 4-kilobit DRAM chip, followed by the 16K. Microchip processors were harder to sell. The new chips would need an innovative sales pitch, because they weren't easy to work with and needed a development system that only Intel could supply. Selling these primitive small computers was beyond any business plan Intel had ever contemplated. So, although many customers were intrigued by the new chips, few were buying. That meant no salespeople were interested in pushing them.

As a result, Intel's small team of microprocessor proponents found themselves with fewer and fewer resources. Only the surprisingly strong sales of the new 8008 microprocessor kept the company in the field. Bob Noyce thought the microprocessor had real potential, but he couldn't get much enthusiasm built up for it among the company sales-men who needed to sell lots of chips to make their bonuses. While he kept the project alive, after its introduction, Intel temporarily aban-doned its development efforts in microprocessors. Nine months later, at the beginning of 1973, Faggin convinced his boss, Vadesz, to let him build an improved processor, using all the knowledge he had gained on the first two. He was given the go-ahead.

Faggin's team had gathered momentum and size during 1973. With close to 80 people in the group, he and Shima improved the micro-processor wisely, by incorporating feedback from their customers. Fag-gin had spent months traveling to customer sites and asking questions about his product. Subsequently, he and Shima pored over new circuit designs. Hoff even got back into the process and was instrumental in improving and streamlining the instruction set. By April 1974, they had a product ready for release. Called the 8080, it was another 8-bit micro-processor, but it featured a much better instruction set and was 10 times faster than its predecessor. (In fact, the design and execution of the chip was so elegant that it remains the basic architecture for Intel's family of microprocessors to this day). Finally the engineers had a chip worthy of their efforts.

At about the same time, Vadesz patented the silicon gate. For his part, Faggin was astonished to find that the patent for what he consid-ered his own invention had been granted to Vadesz and assigned to Intel. It was especially galling because Vadesz had ridiculed the concept when Faggin first proposed it back at Fairchild. Faggin's objections were quickly dismissed by his superiors. He began to question why he was pouring his life into building microprocessors when no one in the company seemed to appreciate his efforts.

For Faggin, the final straw came a few weeks later. In 1974, Bob Noyce became chairman of Intel, giving up the day-to-day role of pres-ident, and replacing Arthur Rock. Gordon Moore replaced Noyce as president, and Grove was named executive vice president. At a regular monthly meeting, Gordon Moore, as usual, sat silently in the back of the room, listening to the discussion of the moment. This time it was a debate over the future of the microprocessor group and how much of an effort the company should expend in marketing the new devices.

A year earlier, Bob Noyce had decided to take the company into yet another business: digital watches. To launch a new division, he had bought a local California company, Microma, and poured money and time into the project. Now the big issue in question was whether Intel could successfully market both watches and microprocessors. Remarkably, the sales force thought watches were a much better opportunity. The only microprocessor champions in the room were Faggin and a few of his colleagues. The debate grew heated.

Moore, as the newly appointed president, was determined to make his mark. He finally raised his voice over the din and shouted, "Intel is a memory company! We will never sell microprocessors!"

There was stunned silence. Then Moore repeated his assertion, banging on the conference table with his fist.

Faggin didn't need to hear any more. He soon left the company, taking Shima with him. The investment community noticed his departure. A few weeks later, Faggin had a visit from an executive at Exxon, who asked whether he'd like some venture capital; the giant oil company had decided it was time to get into chips. With Exxon's support, Faggin formed Zilog, and within two years he shook up the small computer market when he introduced the Z-80. Best of all, the Z-80 was priced at just $200 a piece, versus $369 for its Intel counterpart. It became a favorite in the emerging world of hobbyist computers and ran circles around Intel's 8080, with which it was compatible.

In 1977 Intel sold its watch business at a big loss. Prices had plummeted faster than anyone had predicted. Nevertheless, by 1976 Intel's revenues had grown to about $225 million, almost all of it due to the memory chips. Intel was no longer the innovator in the field. Texas Instruments had taken over technological leadership in the 16K DRAM market, and the Japanese weren't far behind. Meanwhile, Faggin demonstrated he had made the right choice by moving on; even though microprocessors weren't yet an overwhelming success, the world's most successful microprocessor firm was being run by none other than Faggin himself.

As for Bob Noyce, Gordon Moore, and Andrew Grove, they were richer than they could ever have imagined. By 1984 Noyce had seen a bitter divorce split his fortune—but he still had $150 million worth of Intel stock. Moore's equal founding stake was valued at $300 million, and even Grove held stock worth around $15 million. But their company, Intel, the site of the creation of both the memory chip and the microprocessor revolution, had lost its way. The DRAM business looked exciting, and sales volumes were rising, but it was a straight commodity play. Soon big Japanese (and then Korean and Taiwanese) electronics companies entered the fray. While the electronics revolution created a soaring demand for memory chips to power everything from videogames to dishwashers, bigger and bigger competitors drove the margins lower and lower. Despite this, by the end of the decade, Intel reported revenues of $800 million, had watched its stock rise in price by about 10,000 percent, and posted earning per share of $4.50. In 1980, Forbes reported on Andy Grove's decision to get out of the cyclical semiconductor business:

> . . . Analysts like Jay W. Cooper of F. Eberstadt & Co. estimate a virtu- ally flat year in earnings for the semiconductor industry. But they are predicting an increase for Intel of around 13% to 18%—as well as an 18% to 20% increase in sales volume, about twice the industry average.
>
> Behind those projections [are] not only Intel's track record but a decision that Grove gingerly talks about: "We've been fabrication- plant limited for the past two years," he says. "So, early in 1979 we had to decide where to best employ finite resources. After a good deal of soul searching we agreed to de-emphasize the nonproprietary mem- ory area so we could devote more capacity to the proprietary micro- processor market."
>
> Soul searching? The semiconductor memory market amounts to about $1.3 billion a year. Last year it grew at a startling 68%, partially, Cooper believes, because IBM started buying 16,000 bit or "16K" chips for some of its equipment instead of making them on their own. Why?
>
> Simple: One striking aspect of last year's capacity crunch, says Grove, was this: "In microprocessors, we were the sole supplier of many of our customers; but in memories there were numerous others." The result was that Intel, the longtime leader in semiconductor memories, wound up handing market share to TI, Motorola and, ominously, the Japanese, who are now major producers of 16K memory.

It was a prescient move. In just a year, the IBM PC would be released, which used an Intel 8080 microprocessor. At that point, 1980, Intel had 30 percent of the memory chip business; but in coming years the business became more cyclical, and tougher.

Bob Noyce went on to become a spokesman for the semiconductor industry, and spent the early 1980s railing against the Japanese for dumping memory chips below cost. Of course, that was exactly how Fairchild and Intel had started their original businesses. In 1989 Noyce died of a heart attack at age 62. By then, Intel was well into its climb to new power and profitability. It got there by jettisoning the memory business and going full steam ahead with the microprocessor—the little device that the company had tried to kill so many years before.

The first microprocessor-based computer, the Altair 8800, was featured on the cover of the January 1975 issue of *Popular Electronics* and proclaimed by the magazine as the "first commercial type of minicomputer project ever published that's priced within reach of many households."

Edward Roberts in his study, in Glenwood, Georgia, 1984.

CHAPTER 6

>———◉———<

Mechanics

Kits & Microcomputers

As the electronics age moved beyond the space race in the late 1960s, and the microprocessor made possible the integration of electronic circuits—a new generation of American boys were coming of age. They would become electronics mechanics, trading in "blown" and "ported" 356-cubic-inch Chevy engines for an electronic hobby they found every bit as captivating.

Transistors and integrated circuits (ICs) were no longer mysterious, magical components that could be manipulated only by technological wizards. As boys, most had built a crystal radio kit, or had experimented with circuit boards and components, and so had learned the principles of electronics. So-called kit electronics had become big business; companies such as Hallicrafters, Radio Shack, Allied/Knight, and HeathKit sold prepackaged baggies filled with parts and poorly mimeographed instructions on how to assemble them. Primitive though these voltmeters, radios, door buzzers, and counting circuits may have been, they were the training for electronically literate kids who would make the digital age soar.

Magazines like Popular Electronics *and* Radio Electronics *chronicled their universe. The trend marked the digital extension of the traditional American mechanic; the farmboy who once had to keep the tractor running now was building gizmos that turned on the lights when a person walked into a room. A few of these mechanics caught another wave in the American experience; they were the ones with entrepreneurial dreams, who saw the potential in packaging together the parts and pieces necessary to build kits. Kits were advertised in the back of the hobbyist maga-*

zines and shipped via the U.S. mail. It was a tough way to make a living, but it did offer a taste of business life. A few had the drive and ingenuity to turn the hobby into a full-fledged business.

❀   ❀   ❀

Edward H. Roberts, Jr. was a big and burly man of powerful intellect with a degree in electrical engineering from Oklahoma State. In the late 1960s, he was assigned to the Air Force Weapons Lab at Kirtland Air Force Base in Albuquerque, New Mexico. Newly promoted to lieutenant, Roberts was a no-nonsense guy with a hearty laugh and almost overpowering opinions. At 6'4", well over 200 pounds, carefully spoken, and forceful, he was not easy to discount.

At heart, though, Roberts was an entrepreneur, determined to find a way to make a buck at his electronics hobby. This set him apart from his peers, the dozens of other bright young engineers who worked in the top-secret laser lab at Kirtland AFB. Ed, the father of a couple of boys with more to come, had to work hard to make ends meet on his lieutenant's salary. He needed additional income to support his family.

Roberts had become an Air Force officer through a military program that paid for promising candidates' education. While still on Uncle Sam's payroll, he was assigned to Kirtland, which was soon combined into a quasi-public agency: Sandia National Labs. Out in the shifting sands of the New Mexico desert, this was where the U.S. government conducted its most secret weapons manufacturing. The bombs may have been designed at nearby Los Alamos, but they were actually built at Sandia. Roberts was assigned to the Laser Lab as a fire-control officer, whose job it was to devise ways to use the concentrated beams of high-intensity light in offensive weapons; that is, to shoot down missiles in space. "I designed the systems to point laser weapons. At that time, it was a highly classified secret that we were doing anything at all along these lines."

To relax, Roberts and the other young engineers at the base built radio-controlled rocket systems to shoot in the New Mexico desert. Pleased with the result, they began to sell their designs to hobbyist magazines including *Model Rocketry, Radio Electronics,* and *Popular Electronics.* They went so far as to form a partnership and call themselves MITS, for Micro Instrumentation and Telemetry Systems.

By 1970, they called it quits when they saw there wasn't much of a market for toy rocket controllers. Only Roberts wanted to go on, so he bought out the others. He already had another idea: to create a digital calculator kit.

As one of the better-trained engineers at the Weapons Lab Roberts had been given a Hewlett-Packard programmable scientific calculator, the 9100, to work with. Then considered state of the art, this electronic unit fascinated him. Shortly after getting his hands on the device, he wrote a program that calculated the costs of the components in a stereo amplifier. This was the first time a desktop machine had a computerlike programmable instruction set. Priced at $1,000, the HP calculator signaled the end of the slide rule of old. The electronic calculators were awe-inspiring, but too expensive for individual engineers, prompting Roberts to wonder if he could create one in kit form, sell it through the hobbyist magazines, and make some money. He hooked up with two other engineers, who also thought such a product was possible, and they set about doing so. "We weren't smart enough to know that we couldn't do this," he later remembered.

By 1970, the integrated circuit was having an impact on the business of electronics. The devices offered significant cost advantages for electronics manufacturers. Instead of having to wire and test and interconnect dozens of individual components, a single chip collected, tested, and integrated the components together. The military designers working on the Apollo lunar missions were the first major users of these chips. Landing a man on the surface of the moon would have been impossible without the miniaturization and integration made possible by these developments.

To build his calculator, Roberts and his colleagues (who resurrected the name MITS) wired together components on a handmade circuit board—which they would continue to do until the price of ICs came down. Roberts drew the circuit schematic, taped it on tracing paper, and printed his own circuit board through a makeshift process, which involved the sun and an aquarium belonging to one of his kids. Roberts' lab was his garage, the manufacturing plant, the backyard. Creating a circuit board involved a process similar to photo developing: Paint a flat board with copper; cover it with a photosensitive wash; lay a grid made of fine-line wires onto it; bake it under the desert sun; then develop it.

The copper was then etched away, except from where the photosensitive material had been developed, where the copper was protected. Next, Roberts pushed a handful of ICs (which by the time he got to this point had already come way down in price) into holes punched in the boards and soldered the connections. That was it, a working board. The calculator's design comprised some 200 discrete electronic components. It was a full-scale four-function calculator that could add, subtract, multiply and divide, packaged in a nice metal box that featured a display with twinkling green numerals. Called the 816, it provided 16-digit output, eight digits at a time; press a key and the second eight digits displayed—hence the name.

The calculator cost Roberts just over $100; he sold it to customers for $179 in kit form. In addition, a pair of special terminals inside the calculator were designed for an add-on-programming unit, which when attached, could hold a complex formula or equation. For an engineer or mathematics buff, this was a breakthrough. The MITS 816 calculator was the cover story of the November 1971 *Popular Electronics*. MITS, without a microprocessor, was selling a digital calculator for a price that was closer to a slide rule.

Still, Roberts didn't know whether it would sell. More to the point, he didn't know how he would fill orders if they did come in. He only knew that he thought it was a great little product and he couldn't wait to have one for himself.

Within days of the kit story appearing in *Popular Electronics* thousands of orders flooded in. Pricing the 816 at $179 when the nearest competitor cost $1,200 made for an irresistible appeal to the hordes of garage and armchair engineers who had cheered America in the space race. Roberts simply couldn't get the calculators out the door fast enough to fill the orders; MITS was inundated.

The company soon expanded out of Roberts' garage and into a neighborhood house. But with thousands of orders coming in monthly, there still wasn't enough room to open the mail, fill the orders, and address the outgoing packages. MITS moved again, this time to space in a strip mall between a laundry and a pizza parlor, near a massage parlor.

It wasn't long before Roberts realized he could sell a lot more calculators if he assembled them himself. Then the finished calculators could be sold at electronics and office stores all over the country, even the world. Roberts set up a manufacturing line, and soon had teams of assemblers stuffing circuit boards with components, then placing them on a conveyor belt that took them first through a resin spray, then over to an automatic soldering machine, which attached all the components to ribbons of metal running over the circuit boards. In Albuquerque, in the early 1970s, this was a relatively advanced operation. By 1973, MITS had more than 100 employees, working in two shifts, churning out digital calculators as fast as they could.

MITS was one of the first "plug-and-screwdriver shops," companies that bought components from various suppliers to plug in and screw together to make working systems. The calculator's case came from one supplier, the display from another, and the keyboard from a third. This kind of assembly was perfectly suited to the consumer electronics business, and would eventually spawn the original equipment manufacturer (OEM) market—selling components to other companies that would in turn use them in their products. Today's examples of screwdriver shops include Dell, Gateway, and other mail order PC makers, which assemble PCs to order from parts supplied by others.

For almost a year, MITS was selling every machine it made. Then, in late 1973, things changed. Competition came at the company from every corner. These new competitors weren't just a few garage guys; they were well-heeled electronics companies that could afford to really manipulate the market, which was exploding from virtually nothing in 1970 to $700 million by 1975. Bowmar, the office machine company, was the first to seize the opportunity, with machines powered by Texas Instruments (TI) chips and priced at $149. Then Texas Instruments itself got into the act. It integrated all the calculation elements of the device onto a single set of silicon components, and sold its calculator for just $119. Not to be outdone, National Semiconductor released a battery-operated unit that cost $40, followed by Rockwell International at $20 in 1974. Even HP, which was still selling the top-of-the-line engineer's desktop calculator for $395, was forced to introduce a model at $125. Soon Commodore and every other office equipment company wanted a piece of the action. Most used TI's chips, and all of them pushed market prices down.

To compete, Roberts needed money, so he took MITS public, floating an offering of 500,000 shares at $1 each. Called a Regulation A offering, it enabled him to raise up to half a million dollars. It looked like it would be heavily subscribed, but right before the offering, the market crashed in the wake of the first oil crisis. MITS ended up selling only 250,000 shares, which retired the debt Roberts had accrued to that point, but left him with no working capital. For a while, however, he was able to keep his manufacturing line running. But only as long as his machine was competitively priced.

The situation got worse when competitors' prices dropped below his cost, and MITS had no leverage to drive good deals with suppliers. In September 1975, *Forbes* described the hand-held calculator market:

> It was like crying "shark" on a crowded beach or "tiger" in a jungle village when Texas Instruments announced that it was entering the hand-held calculator market in June 1972. TI was famous for initiating the jungle tactics that had triggered periodic bloodbaths in the integrated circuits industry. Even giants like General Electric, Raytheon and Philco-Ford had retired from the scene, leaving a trail of red ink.
>
> Attacking as usual with a barrage of new models and aggressive price-cutting, TI has since seized one-third of the $700 million consumer calculator market. In the process Bowmar Instrument—a former TI customer—dropped into Chapter 11 bankruptcy proceedings.
>
> Even with the price-cutting, Texas Instruments managed to make good money in calculators—until last quarter, that is. At that time TI's calculator division lost $16 million. Most of that loss was almost certainly due to inventory write-downs and write-offs. What has happened is this: TI is fighting as hard as ever; but the competitors are fighting back—and hard.

Roberts couldn't figure out what was going on. He continued to run ads in *Scientific American,* looking for aficionados, but he neglected to recognize the opportunity to go for the much larger consumer market. In any case, he probably wouldn't have had the manufacturing sophistication to pursue the option. Meanwhile a number of more nimble companies, run by businessmen, not engineers, did. "It really got grim when [the calculators] started dropping down to the $50 range," Roberts said later. "The American electronics industry took the small-scale integrated circuit technologies of the late sixties and just blew through to large-scale integration, with hundreds of components on a single wafer of silicon, much faster than anyone predicted." The promise of the integrated circuit, with its capacity for hundreds of transistors, resistors, capacitors, and diodes on a single sliver of silicon changed the economics of electronics. Much more complex products could be made at a fraction of the cost, both in labor and components, of even a year or so earlier. In that crunch, Ed Roberts learned his first lesson about the mad economics of the electronics business.

Within a couple of years, a calculator could be built with a handful of standard products, whereas it had taken MITS 100 components to power its first designs. "By 1974, our bill of materials on the last handheld calculator was about $35. And people were selling a similar machine in town for under $20. We were buying parts as cheaply as anybody; I prided myself on that. But everybody with a garage could build them now. There was one chip you needed, and TI supplied it to anyone who wanted it: Buy a package of other components, and plug them into a circuit board, add a keyboard, and poof, you were in the calculator business."

Roberts was still paying 100 employees and was the head of a public company, so he tried to find other projects along the way—a digital clock and an IC tester—but nothing was of any great significance. Bankruptcy was clearly a possibility, and it had Roberts awake at night trying to find a way to save the company. He talked his bank into advancing him more money, but by mid-1974, his outstanding debt was over $300,000, and he had no idea how he was going to repay it. But Roberts was ever the entrepreneur, obsessed with the thrill of having a "hit" product, and he was sure that if he could find the right next thing he could turn the business around. As he put it, "You're doing it for the fun of it; nothing else matters when you get hold of the tail of something as fascinating as this. Give an entrepreneur the choice of going for the gross, or going for profit, and I'll guarantee that he'll choose the gross every time. You do it because you love it."

Love it he did. There had to be a way out, and he was sure he could find it. The market, however, wasn't cooperating. MITS shares dropped from a $1 to as low as 40 cents, when he finally seized on an idea: building a small programmable *computer* out of cheap IC parts. He knew about the new Intel microprocessors; in fact, he had considered using the 4004 in one of his newer calculators. Now he started dreaming about building a computer around one. After all, the microprocessor could be configured as a calculator, a clock, or a circuit tester. Why not package it with memory for storing sets of instructions and interim numbers, and input and output capabilities, so that the buyer could make it do anything he or she wanted?

Burned by his losses with the preassembled machines, he went back to the kit notion, and marketed the new project through *Popular Electronics.* He convinced his editor there to run it on the cover. With creditors hovering, Roberts and a couple of his Air Force engineering buddies worked for several weeks designing the computer. With no model to follow, they copied the front panel of minicomputer that had just been released which featured rows of toggle switches and 30 lights.

The machine was built around the goal of being able to insert programs by hand, by flipping toggle switches; there was no programming language, no keyboard commands—no keyboard even. It was a difficult machine to operate, but Roberts didn't care because his target customer was the kind of guy who thought the words "some assembly required" were a dream come true.

At the time, several people had been experimenting with building a cheap general-purpose computer out of a microprocessor. A primitive machine based on the previous Intel microprocessor, an 8008, showed up in *Radio Electronics* in the summer of 1974. But that processor was limited, and very hard to work with. However, the 8080, the next-generation version from Intel, made the microcomputer possible. "As soon as [the 8080] became available, as soon as I got the specs for that . . . I called up the publisher of *Popular Electronics* and told him what we were going to do. And I told him that this was going to be a no-compromise, full-blown, general-purpose minicomputer, that it would be able to do anything that a minicomputer could do. He said if we could do it for under $400, they would publish [an article about] it."

That $400 was the key. Roberts became obsessed, sure this was the product that could save MITS, that this was a machine that every engineer would covet. He saw dollar signs, and decided to bet heavily on it. "I was either going to sell a lot of them or I was going out of business." He agreed to order 1,000 of the 8080 chips from a local Intel salesman—who was ecstatic; it was the largest single order for microprocessors that Intel had ever received. And by then, Intel had written off the microprocessor, so any sales were gravy.

Intel cut him a deal: Instead of $359 per chip, which was the quoted price for one-offs, he got them for under $100 apiece. Little did they know that their deal was the first shot of the computer revolution.

The spark that ignited the personal computer age occurred when Roberts put a $100 microprocessor into a fancy metal box and priced it all to sell at $399. Making the device cheaply enough and getting it into the hands of thousands of enthusiasts were the keys: Of course, the margin dwindled once that $100 microprocessor was put in a box, with a tiny bit of memory, circuit boards, switches, and lights to make it run, and MITS would never make money on the computers themselves. To make money, Roberts came up with another innovation: the add-on board.

He had promised an add-on system to the staff at *Popular Electronics* even before he had finished tinkering with the design of the computer. They had to figure out a way for the machine to accept additional features. "That's how I came up with the idea of the bus." Roberts said.

The bus was a crucial innovation. It was a way to connect subsystems—such as more memory, or a hard drive, or a floppy disk—to the "motherboard," which contained the CPU. Roberts imagined marketing his own add-on cards for the machine. He planned to sell the computer itself at a loss, or at best break-even, and then make a profit on the add-on cards. It was the classic give-away-the-razor-make-money-on-the-blades concept. One of the first add-on cards that MITS designed was a memory array card, which quadrupled the computer's memory from 256 bytes to 1,000 bytes.

Late in 1974, the editors at *Popular Electronics* were getting nervous. They had planned for Roberts' machine to be the cover story of the January issue, traditionally the best-selling issue of the year. They expected this remarkable and inexpensive machine to captivate their audience. So every month they checked the competition, to be sure no one else had anything like this in the works.

When MITS finally finished the prototype in October 1974, it was in the wee hours of the morning. "It was fantastic," said Roberts. "I flipped a small program into the accumulator. We called it 'jump to zero.' All it did was light up the first two lights—0, 1, 2, in binary notation—then jump back to 0. The machine was going so fast that the lights stayed on continuously. But we knew what it was doing." It worked. The little lights bounced up and back, over and over for an hour. Roberts and his engineers stared at each other, shook hands, and congratulated each other.

Later that month, they shipped the first, and only, prototype to the *Popular Electronics* offices via Railway Express, (these were the days before Federal Express). Roberts flew to New York himself with all the documentation. Though he arrived safely, the machine never did; it was lost in some bus or rail station between New Mexico and New York. In a mad scramble the MITS team created a nonworking model for the magazine's cover photo, and went ahead with the story anyway.

The only thing missing was a name for the machine. One of the *Popular Electronics* editor's daughter had been watching a *Star Trek* episode that involved the star Altair. That was it. They didn't like the number 8080 though. So they decided on the Altair 8800. "I didn't care what they called it as long as it sold," said Roberts.

As soon as the January issue hit the stand (in November), MITS was inundated with orders. It was an even bigger explosion than they experienced with the calculator. In a matter of days, there were a thousand orders for the Altair 8800 overflowing the bins at the MITS offices. And these weren't just requests for more information; they included checks and money orders.

Unfortunately, as he admitted, Roberts was not much of a businessman. While he would spend hours debugging his add-on boards, he paid much less attention to ensuring that the orders were filled. In the first month after the *Popular Electronics* story appeared, no machines shipped. When Roberts finally did hire someone to handle sales, remarkably, months after sending in their money, their customers were there waiting for them. Nobody wanted money back; they just wanted the Altair.

In reality, the basic Altair couldn't actually do much of anything. It needed a paper tape interface card to store information—another of MITS' long overdue add-on options—and a memory card to expand the working memory of the machine. Worse, to enter a program users had to write program code in a binary assembly language, then enter it line by line by flipping each of the row of toggle switches, read it into the microprocessor's registers, and move on to toggle the next line. But no amount of tedious flipping of switches could dampen the enthusiasm of most of the buyers.

Creating the add-on boards however, turned out to be more difficult than constructing the computer. For one reason or another, the memory boards that Roberts designed never worked right. Roberts didn't perfect his memory card until a year after the machine came out. This hurt MITS, and more significantly, it opened the door to a lot of other companies that appeared, like pilot fish, to feed off the MITS minicomputer concept. This angered Roberts, and it wasn't until much later when he could reflect on it all calmly that he understood that it was exactly this robust third-party market that made his computer successful. "I'd have been much better off to support them than to try and stop them," he mused, "but I wasn't much of a businessman, and I didn't see it at the time." The most successful of these competitors was located in the San Francisco Bay Area.

The article in *Popular Electronics* had ignited the interest of thousands of engineers in the city by the bay—which after all was the birthplace of the microprocessor itself. As the magazine hit the stands, the talk at the People's Computer Company (PCC) in Menlo Park, California, centered on the little machine. PCC was an outgrowth of the Whole Earth Catalogue empire, and was founded in 1973 by a former schoolteacher—Bob Albrecht—who came to believe that widespread computer access would solve many of society's problems. The PCC was staffed by engineers who wanted to proselytize for electronics, and by teenagers who just wanted to get their hands on the group's time-sharing terminals. Two years later, it had evolved into a funky place that was part computer café, part storefront schoolroom, and part stoned-out digital outpost.

In 1975 two people from the PCC group—Gordon French and Fred Moore—had a handbill printed and posted it on key bulletin boards in the area. Their intent was to attract a group of like-minded enthusiasts. They were unprepared for the response this little flyer would generate. It read:

AMATEUR COMPUTER USERS GROUP/HOMEBREW COMPUTER CLUB . . . you name it:

Are you building your own computer? Terminal? TV Typewriter? I/O Device? Some other digital black magic box?
Or are you buying time on a time-sharing service?
If so, you might like to come to a gathering of people with like-minded interests. Exchange information, swap ideas, help work on a project, whatever. . . .

The date for the first Homebrew Computer Club meeting was set for March 5, 1975; the location was in French's garage in Menlo Park. That evening, a motley group of computerists sat on a concrete floor and saw the Altair that Bob Albrecht had just received from MITS. The 30 or so attendees were a mix: engineers from Hewlett-Packard, a parts dealer, a freelance software programmer and a born-again Christian, and a mishmash of others, all ready for the computer revolution in varying degrees. They were fascinated by the Altair's flashing lights and steel box containers, which occupied the place of honor on a folding card table at the front of the garage.

One of the group was Steve Dompier, who had read about the meeting at the Lawrence Hall of Science, a futuristic place high in the hills above the University of California campus. He had been to the MITS offices, and he offered a succinct explanation for the MITS delivery slowdown: the company was so inundated by orders that they had no hope of filling them all. This report set another attendee, Bob Marsh to thinking. Marsh had been working sporadically for a local electronics parts store in Berkeley, which was where he heard about the Homebrew meeting. Seeing the Altair, and recognizing how much interest it generated stirred up his capitalist juices. If MITS couldn't even fill its orders for the computers, what hope did it have to supply the add-on boards? Since memory was the critical addition, wasn't there a market for these?

Marsh was quick off the mark. By the time that he was back in Berkeley, he was planning how to launch a business. Together with Gary Ingram they started Processor Technology. A month later, at the second Homebrew meeting, on April 2, 1975, Marsh handed out flyers that described Processor Technology's purpose: to produce add-on memory boards for the Altair.

Marsh desperately needed his business to succeed. His rent was due, and he had no money. He had to start selling the boards or he would be out of business before he even started. Slowly, the orders came in, and money started appearing. Marsh took out a one-sixth-page ad in a new computer magazine called *Byte*. Shortly after the ad appeared, all hell broke loose at Processor Technology.

Now Marsh had to meet the demand. He recognized that he was a good idea man, but not a top-flight engineer. For that he turned to a Berkeley radical named Lee Felsenstein. At the time Felsenstein was in trouble with the hobbyist community because in a review he had written of the Altair for Albrecht's PCC magazine, he had sung its praises and avoided any mention of its myriad flaws. But he later wrote a follow-up article that catalogued every flaw of the machine and offered details on how to fix them. As a result, he was swamped with requests from Altair owners to fix their machines.

When Marsh asked Felsenstein if he wanted to be part of Processor Tech, he refused, citing a disinterest in the American capitalist system and a belief in the purity of engineering. So instead Marsh offered him a consulting gig, which he did accept. By the summer of 1975, Processor Technology was shipping memory upgrade boards for the Altair that actually worked, unlike MITS', whose boards continued to be plagued by flaws and intermittent errors.

In the meantime, Steve Dompier, who had pointed out at the first Homebrew meeting why MITS had shipping delays, had finally received all his parts for the Altair. He had worked for 30 hours straight to get it running. Now he could enter little programs—because that was all the machine's memory space could handle. But he made the most of it.

After switching hundreds of paddles, entering row upon row of instructions, Dompier was ready to face his peers at the next meeting of the Homebrew Club. He requested a moment to show off his newest program. He set a small portable radio on top of the computer, reached over and flipped the power switch. Lights flashed, there was some static, then all of a sudden, a song was heard coming out of the tinny little radio speaker. It was unmistakably the Beatles' "Fool on a Hill." The group was transfixed. The little $397 computer was playing a song!

What Dompier had discovered, quite by accident, was that various memory address locations in the Altair produced different frequencies on his little portable radio. With passion, and perseverance he had spent an entire week determining how to make the Altair play the song. The group was aghast. At the end of the song, there was a moment of silence, and then the computer played another song, "Daisy." Supposedly it was the first song ever played by a computer—at Bell Labs in the late fifties—and was the last thing that HAL, the computer in the movie *2001, A Space Odyssey* played as it was dying. When it finished, the room erupted in applause. Dompier had made it clear why they were there. It was the beginning of a whole new world. This wasn't about money; it was about showing off.

By early 1976, dozens of competitors had entered the market Ed Roberts had uncovered, companies like Cromemco (which made the graphics display cards and computers that would eventually be used in most television weather map displays), Kentucky Fried Computer, the Sphere, North Point Computers, and more. There were board makers and computer kit manufacturers, including a strange design from two kids who had financed their project by selling a Hewlett-Packard calculator and a Volkswagen bus. They called themselves Apple Computer and gave away their Apple I design as a schematic at the Homebrew meetings.

Bob Marsh's Processor Technology now had plenty of money in the bank. ProcTech (as it was nicknamed) sold nearly 1,000 boards before going in a new direction—selling its own computer called the Sol.

The Sol—one of dozens introduced in 1976 and 1977—was named after the editor of *Popular Electronics*, Les Solomon, who was considered the motivator behind the hobbyist computer movement. It was more than a tribute; it was a politic move on Marsh's part, for it helped ensure that the Sol would end up on the cover of the magazine—which it did late in 1976. The Sol proved worthy of the attention. Built around an all-in-one keyboard and monitor design, it was the first self-contained computer on the market. It had add-on card slots in the back, and was sold already assembled and ready to work. It didn't require soldering and wiring, and thus broadened the market.

But there was a missing link: There still was no programming language to enlarge functionality. Flipping toggle switches got tiresome quickly, no matter how enthusiastic the user was. A programming language, which would more effectively harness the machine's power had yet to be developed.

To meet this need, Roberts settled on the simplest language that was available, BASIC, short for Basic All-Purpose Symbolic Instruction Code. BASIC had been developed at Dartmouth University in 1964 by two math professors, a Hungarian émigré, John Kemeny (who had worked with John Von Neumann on the mathematics for the atomic bomb during the Second World War) and Thomas Kurtz. The simple programming language was used to teach undergraduates; and to make it easy for other schools to adopt it, the inventors had put their copyright into the public domain.

Roberts let it be known that he would buy, then supply to customers, the first good BASIC programming language implementation that showed up in Albuquerque. One day in the spring of 1975, a few months after the Altair started to sell, he got a call from a guy in Boston who claimed that he and a friend had designed a version of BASIC to work on the MITS hardware. This would enable an Altair-specific program to be written. Roberts by this time was skeptical; he had heard from plenty of hobbyists who had promised the same thing and never followed through. A couple of days later, though, Paul Allen, a red-haired 23-year-old came into Roberts' office brandishing a paper tape that he had hand carried from Boston. To run, it required a kilobyte memory card (still unfinished), a paper tape reader (still unfinished), and a keyboard and Teletype combination to enter commands and print out results (created by another hobbyist and still incomplete).

Remarkably, when it was run on the almost operational advanced version of an Altair they had in the lab, the program loaded—then quickly died. A day later a roomful of engineers tweaked and finessed the program into working, but it was by no means ready for prime time yet. It was, however, a major step forward. The programming language freed the engineers from having to manipulate the Altair's hardware and the user. Rudimentary programs could be entered as strings of programming code in the form of phrases such as GOTO (for "go to" an address). This was a big step forward from the strings of binary commands used in machine code (known as *assembly* language). Roberts was impressed because Allen had created this version of the BASIC programming language without having seen an Altair.

Allen and his programming partner had simply taken all the commands from the BASIC language that had been developed at Dartmouth, then implemented most of them on a version of the Altair machine running on a mainframe. "It was primitive, but we had a programming language," remembered Roberts.

Roberts hired Allen as his vice president of software at the then princely salary of $30,000 a year. Then he cut a separate deal with him, and his programming partner, an undergraduate at Harvard named Bill Gates. The essence of the agreement was that MITS would sell the language, providing royalty payments up to $180,000, but MITS would own it outright. The pair signed a license agreement with MITS in March 1975. The original deal listed the duo as individuals, but a more formal partnership christened Micro-Soft was formed by the following year. Gates assumed two-thirds ownership because Allen still had a full time job at MITS. As part of the contract, Micro-Soft (later the company would lowercase the s and drop the hyphen) agreed to do additional development on the language, to improve and fine-tune it. However, with Gates still in college and Allen trying to sort through the avalanche of hobbyist software that started appearing at the MITS offices, nothing came of the development effort. Eventually, MITS hired staff—including Gates in the summer of 1975 when he arrived at the end of the school year—and made a DEC machine available for software development to improve the language. "A lot of people on the MITS payroll developed the BASIC. There is no question in my mind that we owned the BASIC," said Roberts, referring to the widely used version running on Altairs.

Not everyone agreed, and the issue would later cause a legal battle. Roberts claimed that he owned it, and wanted to stop Micro-Soft from selling the same language to competitors' machines. Gates and Allen felt they should be able to sell it where they wanted because MITS had abrogated a key clause in the contract—"to make its best efforts to sell the program to other computer manufacturers"—when Roberts acknowledged that the programming language was a key competitive advantage. The dispute caused bitter feelings between Gates and Roberts that persist to this day.

Later, after the dust had settled and Roberts had left the company, he heard from several software developers who had offered the company more advanced programs. Roberts said, "Allen sent one guy over to see Gates; Gates bought the program from him for $5,000, then turned around and sold it to MITS for $15,000 and a royalty. Everybody who came to see us with any language or software had it creamed off the top by those guys. We didn't have any idea they were doing it."

However, that wasn't Roberts' biggest software mistake. What angered the hobbyists at Homebrew, the idealistic engineers who believed they could change the world through computers, was that Roberts wanted to charge for the software, and that he had tied it into the memory cards. If someone bought the 1K memory board, priced at $600, BASIC was included in the price. The stand-alone price for the paper-tape version of the software was $500. This was an affront to the share-the-wealth concept of computing that prevailed in the San Francisco Bay Area at the time—especially since many of these engineers were trying to sell memory cards themselves.

In the summer of 1975, the MITS Blue Goose—a van loaded with Altair equipment—toured the country, stopping at enthusiast clubs everywhere. As Roberts recalled "The reason we used the van was because folks simply didn't believe [what we had accomplished]. So we decided that if we drove a van around the country, with a bunch of working machines, people would be able to see working computers and that would convince them to buy. We would rent a room, almost always at the Holiday Inn, set up the machines, and give a presentation. It was evangelical. These people were so damn excited that they simply couldn't stand it. We knew we were onto something like a cult."

When the Blue Goose showed up, people could see first-hand that these machines were for real and that they worked. More sales ensued. Assembled units ran about $600, though add-ons quickly drove the price above $1,000.

Software was a different story. When the Blue Goose was in the San Francisco area, one of the Homebrew crew took a paper tape with the BASIC code on it. The program began to mysteriously show up on lots of computers. By the end of 1975, the pilfered MITS BASIC was starting to appear all over the country. And while this annoyed Roberts, he had more important things to worry about. But the 19-year-old hacker who had written it grew more and more incensed. Finally, in the MITS company newsletter, Gates published an "Open Letter to Hobbyists," dated February 1976, decrying their piracy of "his" work.

Nothing changed except to further cement the hard feelings many of the hobbyists had toward MITS. One computer client threatened to sue Gates for calling them pirates, and hobbyists in general were furious at the price of the software, and refused to pay it. At Homebrew, Gates was repeatedly castigated. One member, however, decided to stop complaining and create his own competing product (he named it Tiny BASIC). He gave it away.

He wasn't the only one. Around the country, a software development boom was beginning. Bob Marsh's ProcTech was distributing a set of programmer's tools called Software Package One, and one user wrote his own word processing program based on it. He called it Electric Pencil, and it became the first successful and widely used word processor for the Altair, and for dozens of computers to follow.

Retail computer stores also began appearing. The first of these dealers was in Los Angeles. Started by a member of the Southern California Computer Club, SCCC, Dick Heiser had been taking note of how many people had ordered Altairs. He decided to open a small shop to meet the demand. He called it the Arrow Head Computer Company—The Computer Store, and opened for business in 1975 with a stock of Altairs, soldering irons, and lots of peripheral equipment. Heiser quickly learned that sales of computer kits were only the beginning. Most customers also spent thousands of dollars on add-on cards, printers, teletypewriters, and software. The business thrived.

Other enthusiasts started thinking about more complex business applications for software. The country's second retail computer shop opened in Atlanta, another hotbed of technology. IBM had a major presence in the still-dozy Georgia town, and Georgia Tech turned out thousands of electrical engineers each year, some of whom had seen the Altair and went into business selling them. They called their store Computer Systems Center, which opened in the fall of 1975. MITS had the equipment market sown up. There was really no choice in mid-1975: If you wanted to sell small computers, you had to buy all your gear from MITS.

The Atlanta group had bigger plans, however; they wanted to deliver a small business suite of software. Their idea was to use the hobbyist sales to finance the development of a series of business applications— software for accounting and word processing—that they could sell all over the country. But there wasn't much software forthcoming from MITS, so they simply went ahead and created it themselves. Using Altair BASIC, they wrote a word processing program and designed an interface to drive a letter-quality daisy-wheel printer. They also generated a file system so that documents could be filed and manipulated more easily. Then they wrote a hard disk controller to store the material that their applications generated. And most important, they developed an accounting system.

All of this material, along with additional programs provided by independent programmers, stores, sales reps, and others, became the product basis for the Altair Software Distribution Company, which the Georgia-based computer enthusiasts ran out of their store. This company, called Peachtree Software, provided the first widespread access to personal computer software. Peachtree supplied the cassette tapes or disks with manuals and marketing brochures in plastic bags for both their own programs and others they distributed. Included were the accounting programs as the core applications, along with several other programs. (In the late 1990s, two of those products—a form of Microsoft BASIC and Peachtree Software's accounting package—were still being sold for personal computers.)

Other stores opened on the heels of the Atlanta operation. Paul Terrell, an electronics sales rep in Silicon Valley, had seen the *Popular Electronics* cover story and decided that the Altair was just the kind of product that could make a big difference for him. By mid-1975 Terrell had control of MITS sales in the northern California territory, but he had still bigger plans. Ed Roberts offered him a 5 percent commission as a rep; but at a speech, Terrell heard Roberts offer retail Altair stores a discount of 25 percent. That made Terrell rethink his approach. His idea was to open the equivalent of a stereo store, for computers. He would offer all related products, and for a small payment, he would also provide support for customers with problems in assembly or operation. Prompted by the first issue of *Byte* magazine, which appeared a few months later, Terrell named his store The Byte Shop and sold licenses (they weren't actually franchises) in various locations. He made it mandatory that everyone who ran one of the stores attend Homebrew club meetings, or the equivalent in their area; and if there was no club in their area, they were to start one.

In Albuquerque, at MITS, Roberts was beginning to see that he could make more profit producing and selling complete units, rather than kits. At the same time he was busy signing up exclusive sales territories for various states and regions, in an attempt to reduce the complaints about late delivery. At the same time he was juggling the cash that was pouring in with each day's mail delivery. At night he worked on electronic design, trying to find a solution to the continuing problems of the memory boards, while supervising the variety of other add-on boards that MITS had already advertised and taken money for, but had not yet created.

By 1976, MITS had more than 230 employees; its hardware distribution was run out of Austin, Texas; software distribution was handled by the company in Atlanta. MITS also had 40 distributorships. All told, some 10,000 of the early Altairs were sold, generating more than $3 million in sales over a two-year period. For a time, MITS was big time, and it was the only company that could report revenues from small computers in 1975. But it was all cash, no profit. The price of the kits was so low that there was no money in them. The add-on boards that Roberts thought would save him never worked properly.

In March 1976, the first Altair Users Conference was held in Albuquerque. Thousands of enthusiasts came from all over the country to the booths set up at the local Holiday Inn. Bob Marsh of course knew about the conference. His business had expanded manyfold thanks to the constant demand for ProcTech's memory boards. ProcTech had moved out of Marsh's Berkeley house and into an office complex. In spite of his success, Marsh was denied a booth at the conference because his ProcTech memory boards competed with MITS' add-ons. (Because it was an MITS-controlled conference, the company could dictate who bought space.) So Marsh rented the penthouse at the hotel, and set up his display there. When Ed Roberts wandered in, he couldn't help but be impressed. Nonetheless, Roberts' director of communications took down all the signs pointing attendees to ProcTech's suite. It was a futile effort. ProTech's products were in too great a demand to be ignored.

While Processor Tech was already showing off prototypes of its first self-contained computer, the Sol, many small, garage-based companies were springing up all over the country, selling their own kits and strange hybrids of various kinds. By this point, the Intel 8080 was no longer the only microprocessor available. Both Texas Instruments and Motorola had released similar units. And two key designers from Intel had jumped ship to start up Zilog. In fact, the Intel 8080 was considered second rate.

Zilog's Z-80 was considered a better, enhanced and improved version. Within ten years Zilog's would be the most widely used microprocessors in the world, primarily on the strength of its practice of supplying so-called smart processors for elevators, test equipment, even cars.

In contrast, Texas Instruments never was able to get a foothold in the microcomputer market, even though the company managers always claimed that TI was the first to create a working microprocessor (a claim backed up by the courts). TI essentially had a stranglehold on the hand-held calculator market, and the enormous growth of that market kept the company preoccupied.

Motorola was a different story. Burned by the wholesale departure of most of its top integrated circuit managers to Fairchild in the late 1960s, the company set out to completely revamp its semiconductor operations. By the mid-1970s, it had a microprocessor design that was clearly superior to Intel's 8080. To sell it to the legions of hobbyists who hoped to sell their own kits, or assembled microcomputers Motorola launched an aggressive marketing campaign. The 6800 microprocessor was priced lower than Intel's, and had a better instruction set. Machines built around it included the Wave Mate Jupiter II from Gardena, California; the Micro 68 from San Diego-based Electronics Products; Poly-morphic System's Micro Altair, later the Poly-88; the Sphere, another Utah product, which was advertised with a case and keyboard, all in one, but which rarely worked. Even MITS, attempting to cover all the bases, announced its own 6800-based machine.

Competition had to be expected. After all, microprocessors were extremely complicated integrated circuits, and in those days, there was no penalty for having a different operating environment, different tools, or a different way of doing things in general. Every computer was being designed from scratch, and no one knew which would be the best design in the end. No company was spared the onslaught of aggressive direct competition. In Philadelphia, renegades from Motorola's operation started their own microprocessor company, with products aimed squarely at the low end of the market. Their company, MOS (for Metal Oxide Silicon, a form of semi-conductor architecture) Technology built the 6502, a knock-off of the Motorola chip and sold it at a fraction of its predecessor's cost—$65 apiece. To promote the stripped-down proces-sor, MOS sold a kit computer called the KIM-1.

In the face of all that competition, however, there was only one company that really hurt Ed Roberts and MITS, and for one reason: its machine was a direct copy of an Altair, right down to the errors on the circuit boards. The company was called IMSAI.

William Millard was IMSAI's founder. A salesman and struggling software entrepreneur, Millard was about to default on a small engineering contract when his two employees suggested they copy the Altair computer. Millard at the time had a small computing and consulting firm in San Leandro, California, a blue-collar town to the south of Oakland where rents were cheap. Millard and his wife and partner Pat were trying to get back on their feet after a failed attempt to create software for mainframe computers. When offered the opportunity to develop a networked accounting system for auto dealers, Millard was certain he could answer the call by using some of the new microprocessor-based computers he had seen. What mattered was that the client had money—and that Bill had taken EST which he felt gave him the confidence to succeed. Of all the self-realization and self-improvement movements that swept through California in the years between the late sixties and the end of the seventies, EST was the most successful. Devised by a former car and encyclopedia salesman, Jack Rosenberg, who renamed himself Werner Erhard, the movement was centered in Mill Valley, California, a little town 20 miles north of San Francisco in trendy Marin County. At its peak in the late seventies, tens of thousands of followers graduated from EST, whose primary focus was a confidence pyramid game. Participants had to prove their devotion to the charismatic and forceful Erhard by signing up their friends for the various seminars—at $300 apiece.

But EST notwithstanding, the networked accounting system proved impossible to build for the price Millard had quoted. It didn't work right; the software was primitive. Things were looking pretty grim in the summer of 1975, when Joe Killian and Bruce Van Natta stuck their heads in his office one day and suggested a simple solution to the cash flow problems: plagiarize! Their plan was to copy the Altair machine, then use it to create the network. And if they assembled the machine themselves, they could not only deliver on the contract, but maybe sell a few to other people, too. A couple of weeks later, they borrowed an acquaintance's Altair—they were too broke to buy one from the company they intended to rip off—and made a perfect copy of its circuit boards. Taking a page from the Processor Tech casebook, they pooled their money to pay for a small ad in *Popular Electronics,* a one-sixth page announcement offering an Altair-"compatible" computer.

Millard's company, IMSAI, changed the landscape for Ed Roberts. Here was a company that offered nothing new, except a better copy of his products. IMSAI's target market was not engineers, it was business people who cared about being able to print out 100 letters with names and addresses on them.

By the time IMSAI's machine was available, MITS was into its second version of its computer. Roberts was angry about IMSAI, but what could he do? "Sue them? I had so much else to worry about that I just didn't have time or energy to go after them. Sure we should have patented things, not just the original machine design, but the bus as well. But when you're sitting at your desk and you're so far overdrawn that you don't know how you'll get the bank to clear [your checks], spending thousands on a patent attorney is not your highest priority. Maybe I was naive. But I was just trying to keep the company above water; I wasn't worrying about details." As it turned out, Roberts should have found a way to worry about the details.

At IMSAI, the money started coming in. It wasn't a flood as it had been for the Altair, but there were enough orders to compel them to design their own products. To begin, they improved a few elements of the Altair; they gave it a better power supply, added blue and red lights across the front, and designed a slightly different paddle switch. But essentially it was the same machine, so that any board that worked in the Altair worked in the IMSAI 8080, too.

Just before Christmas 1975, the first of 50 "original" IMSAI computers, priced at $1,000 were shipped via UPS. IMSAI became so emboldened by its success that it began to advertise products that didn't exist yet. But those machines that did, worked. In the process of copying the Altair, they had cleaned up some of the problems that had plagued Roberts' company. Also, there were dozens of enthusiasts who wanted to sell computers, and they were finding that Roberts' strictures made it very difficult, if not impossible, for them to make any money. For example, Roberts refused to allow any Altair dealer to sell any other computer or product. This restriction alone drove many ambitious dealers straight into the hands of IMSAI, which didn't care what dealers stocked, as long as its machines were included. Roberts was also still having difficulty filling orders. In 1976, the backlog was a month or more, and many buyers decided they would rather have an IMSAI machine, which they could have right away, than not have one at all. Although Roberts finally caught up with his orders by late in 1976, by then the market was much more competitive, and the memory boards never sold as well as he had hoped. As his high hopes for profits from add-on boards disintegrated, and production problems continued to plague him, MITS failed to exploit the opportunity its leadership position offered.

But the death-knell for MITS sounded not only because of poor management, but also because of compatibility. Software that ran on an Altair could also run on an IMSAI. And though Roberts had paid to develop a working version of BASIC, IMSAI reaped the benefits by licensing the programming language from Gates and Allen. Programs worked on both machines.

The success of IMSAI marked the rise of the businessman in what was formerly the territory of the engineering elite. Although Millard's business practices weren't always the most noble, he did found ComputerLand, a successful chain of stores that catered to selling small computers to big business. ComputerLand turned out to be a very successful business by figuring out how to sell small computers to big businesses.

Selling computers was a specialized business, and as dozens of different machines vied for success, accompanied by myriad software, businesspeople needed a retailer whose staff understood how a computer might fit into their world. Millard was smart enough to recognize that franchising was the best and fastest way for him to build a nationwide chain. By the early 1980s, Paul Terrell's Byte Shops had disappeared, a victim of its founder's inability to finance a nationwide chain of wholly owned stores. Thus, ComputerLand became the first major national franchised chain. By 1983, it had 582 stores and more than $1 billion in sales.

That year *Forbes* described what made the first giant retailer of the personal computer age a success:

ComputerLand's growth has been like nothing seen before in U.S. retailing. Fiscal 1984 store sales will be up 50% at least (to $1.5 billion or so) from 1983's, which in turn were 150% above the previous years.

Today only Tandy's Radio Shack chain, with 1,065 stores handling computers, is larger than ComputerLand. Entre Computer Centers, the second largest franchised chain, has only 75 stores vs. ComputerLand's 474 in the U.S. and 108 in 24 other countries.

What secrets enabled Millard to blitz this fast-growing business? There are no secrets, just good common sense. Millard sells his franchisees inventory at his cost, rather than marking it up a few points the way Byte Shop's Paul Terrell did. ComputerLand's revenues come instead from the 8% of gross sales it collects and from new franchises that run $75,000 apiece. With the growth that he quickly attained, Millard could well afford not to be greedier.

Speed also contributed to Millard's success. He expanded his network of stores quickly—and, of course, with franchisees' money. Consumers came to feel they were not dealing with a fly-by-night but with a strong chain. To the manufacturer, Hayward, California-based ComputerLand was the first to offer truly broad market coverage.

Millard isn't the only one who got rich. The average ComputerLand store grosses at least $2 million; some do much better. Typical pretax margins may run 10% or higher. Some franchisees own as many as six or eight stores, and are themselves becoming rich.

The success of ComputerLand helped drive the enthusiasm for personal computers well into the 1990s. Millard wasn't so lucky. Eventually he was forced to give up a sizeable chunk of his equity when an old promissory note from his IMSAI days—with intervening stops in the hands of several investors—was judged binding. Disgusted, Millard, turned over control of his companies to his daughters, and fled to Saipan in the South Pacific. From an estimated fortune of a billion dollars in the mid-1980s, Millard's ultimate take was less than $200 million when he sold his 96 percent stake in 1986. ComputerLand lost direction, went public in 1987, tried to struggle back, and eventually was subsumed by VanStar Corporation, which is still active today.

But all that was much later. The summer of 1976 saw the first computer show held in Atlantic City. MITS was heavily represented, though unbeknownst to most of the attendees, the company was already over the hill; IMSAI had become predominant. And ProcTech was not to be outshone. Its up-and-coming product, the Sol, was finally ready to be shipped in mass. With its video display and built-in keyboard, it was a much more consumer-oriented computer than either the Altair or the IMSAI. Thousands came to the show. It was a market whose time had come.

By mid-1976, competition was already tightening in the fledgling small computer market. Ed Roberts had decided that he had had enough and started looking around for a bigger company to buy him out. At the time, MITS was the world's largest small computer company, so it wasn't hard for him to set up interviews with most of the semiconductor companies, minicomputer firms, and the various hard and floppy disk manufacturers. The rumor of his desire to sell the company swept across the floor of the National Computer Festival in Atlantic City, and one company in particular was very interested. Pertec, a Canadian hard disk and tape backup manufacturer, with sales of $48 million and profits of $2.5 million in 1976, outbid everyone else to acquire MITS.

MITS had grossed about $13 million, that year, but showed hardly any profit. Roberts, however, predicted the market would double every year and that profits would start rolling in during the next year. His projections convinced the button-down businessmen from Canada that they were on the verge of a massive market. Pertec offered him $6 million. Roberts jumped at it, pocketing nearly $2 million in the process (the other $4 million went to shareholders in the original MITS). Roberts was kept on to manage an R&D lab; the professionals from Pertec would run the day-to-day computer business. Finally, Roberts was rich and able to slow down.

His respite was short-lived, however; by 1977, Roberts and the Pertec managers were butting heads. Pertec had begun pushing for a games division that featured cartridge machines based on the Altair; Roberts in contrast was sure that the future was in business systems. So he retreated into the skunkworks Pertec had set up for him—his research lab—and he began his next project: a laptop computer. His intent was to build a small machine, about the size of an 8½ × 11″ sheet of paper that would run business applications. Though far ahead of its time, Roberts succeeded in creating a prototype many years before Osborne Computer and Compaq trailblazed that market. Pertec wasn't interested, though, and eventually Roberts left. In 1978 he took his millions and went back to Georgia. He bought land in the south of Atlanta, in the country, beyond Macon, in Wheeler County. There he became a gentleman farmer, and watched the computer business develop from a distance. He never went back to Albuquerque. Pertec ran MITS into the ground, then sold it to Adler, a German office equipment company. In the early 1980s, Roberts started another computer manufacturing company in the Georgia pine forests. It failed. That, and a bitter divorce, left him with virtually nothing. At the age of 35, he entered medical school, and is today the only doctor in the small town of Cochran, Georgia, population 2,600.

Steve Jobs on March 31, 1977 as he introduces the new Apple II in
Cupertino, California.

CHAPTER 7

>———◉———<

Wireheads

The Apple Computer

By the mid-1970s in America, good things were coming in small packages. The world of electronics had gone beyond NASA laboratories and into every dorm room across the country. Home stereo systems were in widespread use, spurred by the baby boom generation that had more money than any other young generation in history.

When the gadget and kit electronics geeks teamed up with this new generation, interested in self-fulfillment and money, the result was a revolution that rocked the world. One pair of boys headed to India in search of enlightenment. They gave away everything they owned, visited a guru who had more interest in sex than religion, and finally ended up in a gully during a flash flood, nearly losing their lives. The experience made one of the pair, 19-year-old Steve Jobs, realize that, "Thomas Edison did more for the world than all the Eastern religions combined." Soon after, he returned to his hometown of Cupertino, in the heart of California's Silicon Valley, where his activities started a chain of events that would make the personal computer a part of the consumer landscape forever.

❖ ❖ ❖

THE INVENTOR'S NAME WAS STEVE WOZNIAK, but everyone called him Woz. He had the right stuff: He was part of the new generation, born in the transistor age; he had never known anything different. He was a California kid in an era when that state was known for surfing, hotrods and drive-ins.

Woz had little to do with any of that. He lived in a world of semiconductors and silicon, where Lockheed and NASA, science fairs and high school electronics clubs, and used parts stores dominated the landscape.

His dad was an engineer at the defense contractor Lockheed, the Santa Clara Valley's single largest employer in the days before it was known as Silicon Valley. Woz grew up on a curving subdivision street in Sunnyvale, a white bread community on the western side of the San Francisco Bay, just north of San Jose. His mother was a homemaker.

Woz, the eldest of two brothers, had a peculiar skill for creating working electronic gadgets. By the time he was in junior high school, he had won first prize at a local science fair (which, in Silicon Valley, had an elevated connotation) for a digital calculator design. In high school, he became the star of Cupertino's Homestead High School's electronics club. According to the club's faculty sponsor, John McCollum, "Woz could make the electrons sing. He was forever drawing schematics. He used to get into trouble in classes for daydreaming about his circuit designs. He lived inside those circuits."

In other respects, however, he was a mediocre student. Electronics was all he cared about. Though his father encouraged him, his mother would grow so frustrated at escapes from reality that she took to rapping him on the head to bring him back to attention. Woz was a born circuit designer, but he was also a prankster and practical joker and used his skills in science to engineer exploding lockers or to hoist a Volkswagen onto the roof of the gym. Years later, Woz's broad sense of humor prompted him to run San Jose's "Joke of the Day" phone service from his apartment.

Stocky and of medium height, he had poor eyesight and was always squinting. Girls played almost no part in his high school experience; electronic gadgets and pranks filled the void. Woz was also something of a hero to several younger boys, especially those who were interested in the electronics club. In him they found someone who not only shared their sophomoric sense of humor, but who was willing to spend hours explaining the intricacies of circuit design to them. For Woz, circuits were beautiful things. He filled reams of paper with intricate and carefully drawn designs, and gave heartfelt descriptions of them. Speaking in rapid-fire cadence, he enjoyed guiding his young cohorts through the pathways, bridges, resistors, gates, diodes, and transistors that he instinctively understood.

Woz went to college at the University of Colorado, and his experience there was similar to many American students of that era: He played bridge all day and night; he partied hard; he cut classes; he let his hair grow down to his shoulders. And he came to realize that he didn't have to think like his parents; there was another world out there, and for a kid of the American middle class—who had never wanted for anything—college gave him license to experiment. He flunked out.

In the summer of 1969, he came home. While thousands of his generation were streaming into Woodstock, and antiwar protests were turning violent, Woz was working part-time at the California Department of Motor Vehicles writing programs for their massive batch card mainframe. In his spare time—and he had a lot of it—he enlisted a neighbor kid to help him build his first computer. Bill Fernandez was five years younger and every bit as obsessed by electronics as Woz was. He had grown up across the street from the Wozniaks, and he idolized the older hacker. With painstaking care they went to work on their computer. Everything had to be perfect; instead of wrapping long lengths of wire to make connections, they meticulously cut every wire to size so that the machine looked neat and professional. It featured a row of eight mechanical binary switches, an enter button, and eight red lights. Programs were entered by setting a combination of switches; any of the eight could be set either up or down. The machine allowed two, four-digit binary numbers to be added, subtracted, multiplied, or divided, depending on the way they wired the circuitry.

Later that summer, Fernandez brought a friend over to see the computer. He was another electronics club kid from Fernandez's class, and was four years younger than Woz. His name was Steve Jobs. Woz, who was justifiably excited about his machine, proceeded to explain it to Jobs in intricate detail. Jobs listened attentively, but understood only a fraction of what he said. For the first time in his life, the 14-year-old was awed by someone else's technical brilliance.

Like Woz, Steve Jobs was a loner, but he wasn't an engineering natural like Woz. And though he found electronics interesting, he wasn't obsessed enough to put up with the discipline of the electronics club's faculty sponsor, John McCollum. He hadn't been raised in a household where electronics was an everyday part of life the way that Woz and Fernandez had. To Jobs, electronics was only one of his many passions during high school.

There was one thing that always obsessed Steve Jobs: Steve Jobs. He had been adopted into a blue-collar family; his mom was a school secretary, his father a technician who was forever fixing and selling cars. They lived in a nearby subdivision, in Cupertino, next door to Woz's Sunny-vale. Jobs was an anomaly in the Santa Clara Valley engineering world. His natural mother had been a beatnik artist; his father had been a professor; his natural sister, whom he didn't discover until he was 30 years old, was the novelist Mona Simpson.

Jobs' outstanding characteristics were great intelligence and chutzpah; he was always willing to wade in and go after what he wanted. A few years before he met Woz, he had needed a few electronics parts for one of the club's projects. He called up the founder of Hewlett-Packard, David Packard, whose name was listed in the phone book. He got the parts he needed—and also a summer job. By the time he met Fernandez in high school, he thought he knew everything there was to know about electronics. Meeting Woz cured him of that. Briefly.

They became friends. After school, Jobs and Fernandez would show up at Woz's house, and the three of them would spend hours building electronics projects and talking geek. Better yet, Woz had a car, so they would pile into it and head for the Stanford engineering library where they would while away the hours going through arcane technical references. The two Steves were a study in contrasts. Woz had a twinkle in his eye and a prankster's sense of humor; Jobs was gloomy, almost morose unless ignited by his latest interest, whether it was playing the guitar, listening to the songs of Bob Dylan, coordinating light shows for school dances, or contemplating the big questions of life. But there was one that the three of them shared: love of pranks. Woz would come up with ever more complicated practical jokes, and Jobs and Fernandez would carry them out. Jobs had a brazen disregard for authority, and an almost uncanny ability to talk his way out of any situation, so he became the perfect front man.

However, by his senior year in high school, 1971–72, Jobs had drifted away from the electronics geeks, and even had—horror of horror for true brothers of the engineering crowd—a girlfriend. Woz had by now enrolled at the University of California Berkeley, so the trio didn't have much opportunity to see each other. But one day when Jobs came to see his old pal, he was brandishing a copy of that month's *Esquire*, which featured a detailed story about a new breed of outlaw, called the Phone Phreak. The bandits had discovered that by reproducing the tones the phone company used to rout phone calls, they could circumvent billing systems and thus phone anywhere in the world for free. The devices they used were called blue boxes, and Jobs told Woz he should build one right away.

Woz agreed; it was exactly the kind of challenge that he loved. With his knack for electronic design, he easily figured out a way to cram all of the circuitry into fewer chips than anyone had been able to do previously. As quickly as Woz built the gadgets, his partner made the rounds of the residence halls at Berkeley and sold them for $150 apiece. It was the Steves' first business.

The following autumn, Jobs left for college, and their business quickly fizzled out both from lack of interest and an increasingly aggressive legal stance by the phone companies. (A sales episode in the parking lot of a local restaurant, where they were robbed at gunpoint, might also have dampened their enthusiasm.)

Jobs turned out to be ill-suited to college. He discovered LSD, joined a commune, and lost interest in academia. After an abortive second year crashing at Reed College in Portland, Oregon, he left for India with Dan Kottke, a college buddy. There they had a remarkable, though not entirely positive, experience. The two relatively privileged white American youths came face to face with the relentless poverty and fight for survival that India's poor faced each day. It changed their lives.

Upon returning to his hometown, Jobs applied for a job at Atari, then the world's foremost video game maker. And though he showed up barefoot, malnourished, unwashed, and turning orange from a steady diet of carrots, he somehow talked his way into being hired. The man he convinced, Nolan Bushnell, was another unconventional thinker and self-promoter, a former carnival barker and a glib salesman with a new vision a minute. Bushnell had made his fortune by creating the first video game, Pong, and installing it in bars and taverns. He bought Jobs' impassioned pitch, but put him on the graveyard shift where the Atari plant manager thought the strange-looking fellow would be less of a distraction to the rest of the staff.

Atari was one of the first big consumer electronics successes of the digital age. In 1971, the company had created the first successful arcade games built around integrated circuits. But that wasn't the primary reason the company was successful: It was marketing that drove Atari to sales revenues of $40 million by 1975. Bushnell, in a moment of genius, had acknowledged that the arcade business was too tough to crack, what with big companies like Bally introducing game after game that were also powered by electronics. He had the foresight to put together a sales team to approach a new market: bar, restaurant, and nightclub owners. His pitch was simple: In exchange for a nominal monthly lease for the units, Atari would split revenues from the machines with the owner. Pong, based on Ping-Pong, was a seductive game, and was simple enough for anyone to play immediately. As soon as an Atari machine was installed in a bar, patrons would play it obsessively. In this way, Atari not only promoted itself, but also made bar owners its partners.

But Atari was on a quest to find new games to fill the void when the appeal of Pong started to wane. The company's management was also astute enough to parlay its success in the arcade-style games into a much bigger market. By the late 1970s, Atari introduced the next great step forward in consumer electronics: the video game machine. These were essentially small, single-purpose computers that used cartridges to implement the programming for the game, which was contained within a set of integrated circuits inside the cartridge. In other words, the cartridges were designed so that they couldn't be duplicated. Atari controlled the market: It manufactured the player machines and sold them for a few hundred dollars, and was the only source for Atari compatible cartridges. Most of the games were based on movies that were being released, so they had a ready-made audience. The videogame machine was another phenomenal success thanks to the innumerable teenagers who bought both players and cartridges in quantity.

But the video game market proved as fickle as the movie industry. Last month's hit was next month's forgotten star. This posed a problem, in that the cartridge format required advance manufacturing and a relatively high fixed cost of nearly $10. This meant that guessing wrong on which games would be popular could seriously destroy the financial underpinnings of the company. Clearly, Atari needed deeper pockets, so in 1976, Bushnell sold it to Warner Brothers for $28 million. As the consumer computer and video game markets boomed, the division grew to a $435 million business by 1980, with a net of $65 million, or 29 percent of Warner Brothers' operating income. Then flush with money and run by a new president who had little sense for the interests of teenage boys, the division released a series of games that were marketplace disasters. In early 1984, after a particularly brutal Christmas season, tens of thousands of cartridges had to be destroyed.

At the same time, a small Japanese company, Nintendo, had taken the ideas that Atari had developed, and used a much better set of games to capture the market as Atari faded. In the end, Bushnell's company was sold to the man who had put Commodore on the map in the calculator days—Jack Tramiel. For a while, Tramiel tried to turn the company around, but by the early 1990s, Atari had disappeared. Bushnell went on to launch a series of other consumer products, most notably a teddy bear that had computer chips sewn into its body enabling it to speak. But none of his other products were as successful as the arcade and video game industries that he created almost single-handedly.

In late 1974, the first assignment Jobs was given was to design the circuitry for one of a Bushnell's game ideas. To be called Breakout, the game involved bouncing a moving ball against a brick wall long enough and accurately enough to break down the wall and win the prize. When Jobs had sold himself to Bushnell and to the company's more skeptical chief engineer, Al Alcorn, as a first-class, self-taught electronic engineer, they agreed to remuneration that included a bonus for every integrated circuit *less than* 50 that he used in the design. Alcorn thought it almost impossible to do it with that few circuits, and so assumed the bonus would be a moot point.

Little did they know that Jobs knew just where to go for help and just what to use as bait. Atari had the world's best collection of arcade video games, and Woz was the world's best circuit designer. So Jobs offered him unlimited access to the machines at night, in exchange for help in designing the Breakout circuitry. It was a deal that Woz, by now an apprentice engineer at HP, couldn't possibly turn down. Spending his nights at Atari was a dream come true. Because Jobs didn't know how to design the circuits, Woz did it for him, but it was a small price to pay. In the end, he built the system with fewer than 30 integrated circuits, and Alcorn had to pay a bonus of several thousand dollars. Jobs pocketed most of the money, though he shared a small amount with Woz. He then headed to Oregon for the apple harvest at his old commune. (Years later Woz admitted to being deeply hurt when he learned how unfairly the bonus had been split.) Atari was a loosely run place, so they let Jobs go with a vague promise of more work when he returned. He never did.

In early 1975, Woz happened to see notices for a computer meeting; "Do You Want to Build Your Own Computer?" read the mimeographed sheet for the Homebrew Club. Woz went to that meeting, and thought he had died and gone to heaven. Here was a garage filled with other gadget freaks like him, wireheads who loved circuits and thought that designing schematics was a worthwhile calling. By the second or third meeting, he had drawn his own computer schematic, and had given it away to anyone who was interested. Woz was in his element. He would spend hours designing new machines, then take his plans to the Homebrew meetings and debate their merits. In this way, he learned an enormous amount about computer design that year. It wasn't long before the club's membership numbered several hundred, and the meetings had to be moved to an auditorium just off the Stanford University campus.

Steve Jobs returned from Oregon in the fall of 1975 and accompanied Woz to a Homebrew meeting. Jobs was immediately fascinated by the passion and exuberance of the new movement, as well as the money that everyone thought could be made from selling the machines. He talked to Bob Marsh of Processor Tech and thought that if they could make money, so could he. Marsh, a former Berkeley radical and electronic parts store employee, had started selling add-on memory cards for the first kit computer, the Altair. The company behind the machine—MITS, in Albuquerque, New Mexico—had been unable to keep up with the demand for the kits, let alone the optional memory card, which gave Marsh and a couple of his buddies a ready market for their home-built memory cards. The original Altair was woefully undersupplied with memory, so this was a good business in the early days of the personal computer marketplace.

Jobs listened to the first-hand comments of some of the attendees who had visited MITS and reported seeing mail bags full of orders arriving every day. He decided this was the business he and Woz should pursue. It was just like the blue box phone devices they had sold a few years earlier, but with one big difference: It was legal. It didn't take Jobs long to convince Woz to stop giving away his computer design as a schematic; then he went looking for a store where they could sell kits for the one-board computer. Woz's machine didn't have a power supply or display option; it was really just a central processing unit board, so it was the buyer's job to make it do anything useful. Jobs and Woz called their fledgling business Apple Computer—in honor of both the communal life in Oregon and the Beatles, who had chosen the same name for their recording label—and named their first product the Apple I. To finance

it, Jobs sold his Volkswagen bus for $1,300, and Woz, who was still work-
ing at Hewlett-Packard and could buy company products at wholesale,
sold his HP 35 calculator for $200 (its retail value was $350.) (Unfortunately, the VW Bus had a bad engine and the buyer demanded a refund.
Jobs had to return part of his money.) With less than $1,000 between
them for parts, they brought in hotrod airbrush artist, Ron Wayne from
Atari to design a logo and brochure. In payment, they gave him 10 percent ownership instead of cash. (Wayne would eventually back off from
the risk, and in one of the great missed opportunities of all time, agreed
to be bought out for about $300 when Apple found a former Intel engi-
neer to invest. When Apple went public in 1980, that 10 percent share
of the original company would have been worth about $67 million.)

With no job, little experience, and only a roughly soldered prototype,
Jobs set out to sell the new computers. It didn't take long to find a taker.
Paul Terrell's Byte Shop was booming. From his original store in Cupertino, he was fast on his way to having more than 70 by the end of 1976.
Unfortunately, that would be the extent of his expansion. Ed Roberts,
the former Air-Force weapons engineer who had started MITS, the
company behind the first Altairs, forced Terrell to relinquish his Altair
dealership territory because he was also selling equipment that wasn't
made by MITS. Thus, Terrell was forced to look for other computer
equipment, especially computers, wherever he could find them. He had
taken to driving over to MITS competitor IMSAI's loading dock, with
cash in hand, buying as many computers as he could get. But even this
wasn't enough to meet the demand. Then Steve Jobs walked in to the
flagship Byte Shop one day in the spring of 1976.

Terrell had seen Jobs hanging around Homebrew meetings, but had
steered clear of him. He found Jobs too intense and driven. But when
Jobs came in the store Terrell was desperate. Jobs offered him the
Apple I boards, in kit form, for customers to assemble. At first, Terrell
told Jobs he wasn't interested, saying "That isn't where the market is
anymore Steve. People want to buy complete computers." With that
Jobs' eyes lit up, and on the spot he offered to supply assembled Apple
I computers. "How much will you pay for those?" Terrell took a long
look at him, and decided to be honest. "I'll give you $500 apiece for
complete computers."

It was all Jobs could do not to run out of the store after he said he
would think about it. He called Woz at work from the first phone he could

find. The cautious Woz didn't believe him; no one else in his lab at HP believed it either—$500 each for a computer board designed by Woz, a guy who hadn't even received his BA at Berkeley, and his partner, a long-haired hippie with an attitude problem? There must be some mistake.

It was no mistake. Terrell agreed to buy 50 of them, for $25,000. At the time, that was a lot of money for the duo: Woz was earning about $24,000 at HP, and Jobs was essentially unemployed and living at home. To fill the Terrell order, Jobs turned his house into an assembly line, enlisting the help of his pregnant sister, Kottke, and Fernandez. A woodworker friend agreed to make Koa wood cases to house the computers. Next, Jobs convinced an electronics parts house to extend them credit on the strength of Terrell's order. In Woz's apartment, two teenagers worked on software—a version of BASIC, of course—and a cassette tape interface to be loaded on the machine. While Jobs whirled into action, Woz played it safe and stayed at his nice secure job at HP.

Terrell kept his end of the bargain, and paid for the boards when they were delivered, even though an assembled circuit board wasn't quite his idea of a finished computer. They *did* work, albeit sporadically, and the Apple team was available to get them up and running. At least Terrell had another machine to sell in his stores. Eventually, some 200 Apple I's were sold. But when the country's enthusiasts descended on Atlantic City for a small computer convention in the summer of 1976, Jobs realized that if he was ever going to move up from the bottom rung of the computer business, he was going to have to do something more inventive. Very few people stopped at the booths where the hand-lettered Apple Computer sign beckoned. If they were going to make a go of this business, they would have to crank up, and fast. Money was starting to show up in the kit computer market.

Jobs returned from the Atlantic City show with a fire in his belly. Many people at the age of 21, when confronted with the obvious success of firms like MITS and its competitors, IMSAI and Processor Tech, would have folded their tents and joined one of the better-capitalized firms; or at least built a compatible machine to ride the wave. Not Jobs. He became consumed with building a business around Woz's designs. It didn't matter to him that the Apple I was primitive, simplistic, and uninteresting to many hobbyists who could—and would—choose more advanced systems. He knew that Woz was already developing a new machine, and he was convinced that if all these other companies could succeed, then he and Woz could, too.

And now Woz was convinced as well. He went to his bosses at HP, showed them his designs for the new computer, and asked whether they might be interested in making it. His managers politely told him that they didn't think there was much of a market for baby computers like these, but assured him he could do whatever he wanted with his design.

A few weeks later, a couple of reps from Commodore came by the Jobs family garage, which was doubling as an assembly plant. Commodore, originally an office equipment manufacturer, had been taken over by Jack Tramiel in the 1960s. Tramiel who had had a rocky go of it during the hand-held calculator days, had regrouped. By the late seventies Commodore also owned Mostek, a semiconductor manufacturing operation making one of the few microprocessors in the market, the 6502. Mostek's claim to fame came from the chips that powered the first small hand-held calculator, in 1972. Mostek had fallen on hard times during the price wars of the mid-seventies, and was bought by Commodore. In order to push the Mostek 6502, Commodore sold the KIM-1, the first of the company's many personal computer models.

Apple was the only other company making a computer with the same microprocessor (the 6502 was the cheapest microprocessor on the market at $25, when Woz was designing his machine). When the Commodore reps were at the garage, they asked Jobs how much he thought his little business was worth. Jobs quoted $100,000 cash, plus $36,000 in salaries for himself and Woz. The head of the delegation thought it a good deal, but he couldn't convince his boss, Jack Tramiel.

The prospective offer jeopardized the partnership between the two Steves. Woz's dad, Jerry, thought it was unfair to give Jobs half the value of the company for having nothing more than a ready tongue and an ability to sell. As he saw it, the real value was in the engineering design, which was his son's contribution. It turned out to be a moot point when the deal fell apart, but Jobs was hurt, and even more determined to prove his worth. In fact, Mr. Wozniak was wrong. It's not technical know-how that drives the digital economy; once a technology is invented, it quickly becomes hard to protect. Thus it becomes the ability to sell the technology that makes all the difference. Without Jobs, Woz would have been just another inventive Silicon Valley engineer.

Apple needed three key elements if it was going to succeed: a better computer, publicity, and money. Jobs went after all three with a vengeance. First, he enlisted another engineer, Rod Holt, one of Atari's top wireheads, as a consultant. Holt's job was twofold: to eliminate the noisy fan that all computers had then (it offended Jobs' perfectionist personality and bothered him when he was trying to meditate); and to actually finish the computer that Woz had designed. Jobs had come to realize that while his partner was a great circuit designer, he was also an inveterate nonfinisher. Woz always wanted to add just one more feature, and then one more and one more. They needed someone who could get the machine out the door. Holt was that guy.

To generate publicity for Apple, the kind that IMSAI and MITS had, Jobs went looking for contacts, and learned that Regis McKenna was widely regarded as the best of breed among public relations and marketing wizards in the Silicon Valley. At that point, McKenna was running an image campaign for Intel that revolved around friendly icons—designed variably as poker chips, cleavers, hamburgers, and racecars. The campaign used no technical jargon. This was exactly what Jobs had in mind.

McKenna was the first of the public relations and marketing agency specialists to focus on the electronics business. A small man with a twinkle in his eye, he was remarkably astute at simplifying a company's technological message and framing it in a way that made it understandable and interesting to the general public. He was shrewd and savvy in the ways of the media, and he wanted to build a major agency. His business cards read simply, "Regis McKenna, himself." But in 1976, he was still a local phenomenon, although already too busy to meet with just anyone.

Jobs, though, was persistent. He called McKenna repeatedly, until he convinced one of McKenna's account execs to come see his operation, if for no other reason than to get him off the phone. The agency turned Apple down. Jobs wouldn't give up. Finally, he got McKenna himself on the phone and convinced him to give Jobs 15 minutes of his time to have his mind changed. He did. Regis McKenna was so smitten by the force of the Jobs' sales pitch that he agreed to take Apple as a client—and even suggested that they call a couple of different people to invest.

The first of those investors was Don Valentine, a no-nonsense former employee of Fairchild and National Semiconductor. He agreed to meet the Steves, but turned them down, because he found them too flaky, and there was something he didn't trust about Jobs.

But the next one on the list was the jackpot. Mike Markkula, who had been a marketing executive at Intel in the 1970s had retired on the strength of his stock options. He was searching for his next project, though none too strenuously; he was busy enjoying life. But he had also been following the explosion of interest in the small computer market, and remembered long talks he had had with Federico Faggin, Intel's Italian-born designer, builder, and champion of the microprocessor, years earlier. He remembered the passion that Faggin had shown—passion that had made him wonder whether he was missing something important. By now, he realized that maybe both he and Intel had.

Markkula agreed to come over and meet Jobs and Woz to see what they were up to. Woz wowed him. Markkula knew enough about engineering to recognize that some of the features Woz had designed for the Apple II were pretty spectacular. For this second machine, Woz again had used the MOS 6502 chip, and by now he knew his way around its corridors. Most impressive, he had figured out how to use a standard color television monitor as a display. He had also figured out how to co-opt the circuitry of the television itself, thus precluding the need for much additional video circuitry in the computer. This was a brilliant achievement. It meant that anyone with a spare TV could get color graphics out of an Apple computer, at a time when everyone else was stuck with the ugly terminals with hard-to-read amber or green letters. It was a Woz trademark: do something with fewer chips than anyone believed possible. Woz had honed the design in the company of his buddies at Homebrew. To each meeting he would bring his latest schematics and ask members to critique them. By the time Markkula showed up late in 1976, the Apple II had been thoroughly finessed.

Within 15 minutes, Markkula was deeply involved. Woz gave him a brief course on programming; several hours later, the two were still working at the machine. It was only a matter of days before Markkula agreed to finance the company, partly with his own money—$91,000 in cash—and partly by guaranteeing a bank credit line of $250,000. The three would each have 30 percent of the company, while the final 10 percent went to Rod Holt. They signed the agreement on January 7, 1977, sitting beside the pool at Markkula's house. It was the same day Jimmy Carter was sworn in as the 37th president of the United States.

Now they had money. Markkula's first order of business was to hire a true president; he persuaded Mike Scott—Scotty to all—to come over from National Semiconductor, where he had been running a chip pro-ducton line. As a businessman, Scotty was a no-nonsense, button-down guy, with a firm grip on the bottom line; in private, he was a wild and crazy guy. He and Jobs clashed from day one. But they managed to put aside their differences long enough to finish the Apple II, and to get it ready for the upcoming West Coast Computer Faire. Markkula, a marketing man, went all out; he contracted for a snazzy booth made of smoked plexiglass panels and also upgraded the size and location of the booth.

The Faire was the brainchild, and the outgrowth, of the free-wheeling atmosphere of the People's Computing Club (PCC) and Whole Earth Catalogue group in Menlo Park, California. Jim Warren of the PCC was the publisher of the first computer magazine—*Dr. Dobbs' Journal of Tiny BASIC Calisthenics and Orthodontia*—and had decided that, given the success of the Atlantic City Festival, it was time to do something compa-rable in California. But he wanted to organize something reminiscent of the Renaissance Faires that leant a friendly mercantile angle to the coun-terculture. Warren intended to combine technology with a free spirited atmosphere, and cloak the whole thing in hipness.

It was by no means clear in 1977 what people would do with small computers. For starters, there were only a few application software packages available for the Altair and IMSAI machines, and more often than not, getting them to work involved writing programming language instructions. While BASIC wasn't too difficult for an engineer, most nonprofessionals were stumped by it, especially the rudimentary ver-sion sold by MITS and then Micro-Soft. Furthermore, peripheral devices were in short supply, and those that did exist were flaky. Expen-sive punched paper-tape recording devices had given way to a cassette tape interface, but it didn't work very effectively on any machine. To date, disk drives were still too expensive—in the thousand dollar and up range—and those that were sold required tweaking to enable them to interface with the small machines.

Markkula tried to steer the small computer market. He wrote a for-mal business plan for Apple, describing the benefits of the new machine. But he was shooting in the dark. The document focused on the home market. And Markkula was being overoptimistic when he said the Apple II would be the ideal application for "most middle-class homes that will have a personal computer by 1985." He believed that computers would be used as "protection from fire, theft, personal injury." An excerpt from his business plan explains:

> The Apple II, when equipped with soon-to-be-announced added compo-
> nents, will monitor all the existing systems in the home: heating and cool-
> ing, burglar alarms, fire and smoke detectors, and lighting. When the
> homeowner is out of the house, Apple II can randomly light different
> parts of the house on different days to give the appearance that someone
> is in residence. Outside the home, Apple II can be pressed into service
> watering the lawn at appropriate times in the day, and turning on and off
> security lighting.

Jobs in the meantime had been spending a lot of time wandering through stereo stores, and had decided that the Apple II should be encased in plastic. He wanted a case that looked great, that accessorized a living room or den the way radios and televisions could. He convinced Markkula to hire an industrial designer, who created a wedge-shaped box of beige plastic, with brown keys. They were pleased. However, get-ting the plastic molded cases made was no easy matter, and prototypes were delivered just one day before the Faire. The staff spent the night before the show assembling the machines.

The West Coast Computer Faire was a smash success. Thousands of people were waiting when the doors opened. Jim Warren had optimisti-cally projected attendance at 7,000; it was closer to 15,000. To even the casual observer, it was becoming apparent that the computer business had arrived.

One of the better-attended booths was Apple's, where Woz' newest machine was on display, and promised to be for sale "soon," for the price of $1,500—a figure Markkula had chosen because it was three times Apple's cost. Displayed on a big TV screen, Woz' color graphics were the hit of the show. Spectators who also took the time to "look under the hood" saw a circuit board with an unbelievably small number of compo-nents. Many thought there must be a big computer hidden under the skirts of the demo tables. Steve got very good at whipping them aside to prove there was no hanky-panky. Once again Woz had used his insight, his uncanny feel for the electron, to build a machine in a fraction the components; *and* it worked in color. As a result Apple was always able to manufacture the Apple II for lower costs and keep the margins high.

Surprisingly, immediately following the Faire, it was not Apple that set the computer world on fire. Tandy captured the headlines, with a machine called the TRS-80, powered by another competitive microprocessor, Zilog's Z-80. Tandy's chain of ready-made consumer stores, Radio Shack supported this effort and gave it a big head start. In contrast, Apple had no particular distinguishing feature other than the color TV screen; and on the downside, the television monitor resolution was not very sharp. Worse, text appeared only in uppercase letters, a serious drawback for business use. Therefore, in the spring of 1977, MITS, IMSAI, and Processor Tech were still leading the way; and soon all of them had versions of the first widely adopted operating system, CP/M, as did the TRS-80. This was the first operating system for small computers. It would take several years before CP/M could run on the Apple II.

With the introduction of a new version of BASIC that ran under the CP/M, the commercial small computer market was poised to take off. The new version, called CBASIC (for Compiler BASIC), could translate a program into an intermediate language (in a process called compiling) so that a programmer's work was not visible to the user. This meant that if you had just written a particularly valuable application, you could distribute it without fear of it being pirated.

All the pieces were seemingly in place: There was a standard operating system, CP/M, that could run on a number of machines, thus providing a standard computing platform; there was a programming language, BASIC, that was both powerful enough to use and secure enough to protect the software designer and programmer; and now there were plenty of companies making computers. Commodore produced another model, the PET; Tandy and Radio Shack offered the TRS-80; Atari came on the scene; IBM was rumored to be working on something; Hewlett-Packard had designed a microcomputer for its scientific product line; Digital Equipment Corporation, Data General, Zenith, Nippon Electric (NEC), and Texas Instruments all released first-generation products within a year or so.

In 1977, some 25,000 personal computers were sold; by 1980, the number rose to 600,000; in 1981, retail sales estimates for the computer makers business was $2.2 billion, with approximately 2 million machines sold. Apple, for all its plans for market dominance, initially was popular only with a few game hackers. It simply was not a business-oriented computer. Businesspeople wanted high-quality word processing and accounting machines, supplied by the likes of Wang, NBI, Lanier, and the Radio Shack TRS-80. Apple, with its funky operating system, color monitors, and trendy plastic case, was definitely an also-ran. As 1977 ended, Apple management and owners met to draw up a plan for the second year of the company. At the top of their to-do list was a disk drive. Markkula urged Woz to build a floppy disk drive in time for the Consumer Electronics Show (CES), which would be held in Las Vegas early in January. This was less than a month away, but Markkula had sized up his brilliant engineer perfectly. He knew that impossible challenges were exactly what got Woz's creative juices flowing.

IBM had been selling floppy disk systems for its big machines for years. While at HP, Woz had taken one apart as an exercise and had drawn his own circuit schematic. Now he resurrected it. He also took apart the only disk drive then available in the hobbyist market. With his ability to look at a piece of electronic machinery and figure out the design, he quickly determined that he could do a better job with a fraction of the number of parts, and thus at a fraction of the price. He agreed to have the drive ready in time for the show.

Once he got started, he had the kind of idea that characterized his approach at solving complex problems; it was an insight far in advance of current thought. It revolved around formatting. To date, IBM was using complex circuitry and timing mechanisms to ensure that every floppy disk worked to the same standards and could share data. Woz believed he could circumvent all of that by creating a very simple circuit that effectively wiped each floppy disk clean and then gave it a distinctive Apple II fingerprint or format.

Woz set to work, and on Christmas Eve 1977, he had created drives that could read and write a few snippets of data. Working ungodly hours, the floppy drive was working in time for the show. The disk drive was the turning point for Apple, and it kept the company afloat through 1978 and 1979, because no competitor offered anything nearly as good or simple for storing data—certainly not for the $500 price.

Coincidentally, Apple became the beneficiary of the first great "killer app" of the personal computer age. It came via a new program called Visible Calculator, written by two programming buddies in Cambridge, Massachusetts. One of them, Dan Bricklin, had decided to return to college for his MBA after working for a few years for DEC. In his first year at Harvard, he conceived of a way to bring sophisticated number-crunching capabilities to the microcomputers that were becoming popular. His buddy, a serious programmer by the name of Bob Frankston, helped him with the coding. The computer they used—on loan from a friend—was the new Apple II with a disk drive.

The program, eventually named VisiCalc, was the first electronic spreadsheet, a program that could instantly recalculate rows and columns of numbers as soon as one had changed. But when they traveled to California and showed it to Markkula at Apple, he wasn't impressed. He had put one of Woz's teenagers to work on Apple's own financial program. So Bricklin and Frankston found a business partner, Dan Fylstra, who wanted to try marketing VisiCalc. In the fall of 1979, they released it themselves, and it was an instant hit.

In 1982 *Forbes* recounted VisiCalc's beginnings:

VisiCalc—for visible calculator—has in three years become the infant personal computer software industry's first gorilla hit—over 250,000 copies sold at about $250 a copy. That's $62 million (retail) for a product that a big league Harvard prof said would never fly.

Almost alone, VisiCalc changed the personal computer from a hobbyist toy for computer buffs, into a business tool. In doing so, it helped to propel Apple Computer into the forefront of personal computer makers (since early VisiCalc only ran on the Apple II). And it made Bricklin and Fylstra rich.

Surprisingly, for an engineer, Fylstra recognized that marketing, not gee-whiz engineering, was the key to success. This was back in 1978 when what little software was available was sold by mail order because there weren't many personal computer stores. None of the cottage-industry types turning out games they packaged in plastic baggies with a mimeographed sheet of instructions wanted to share profits with what few dealers there were. Figuring that dealers would one day be important, Fylstra provided his dealers with eye-catching point-of-sale displays, good-looking packages, and printed manuals that told even amateurs how the software should be used. He also tried hard to provide software that really worked. That sounds obvious but, Fylstra points out, "Most firms then were long on programming development and short on things like testing, quality assurance or documentation. That became an opportunity for us."

The real impact of spreadsheets wouldn't be felt for a few more years, when many credited the tool as a significant component in the leveraged-buyout craze of the late 1980s. By then VisiCalc had disappeared, along with the company behind it—VisiCorp. The key reasons: the inability to deliver an ambitious software system—VisiOn—which, along with the Macintosh, was the early inspiration for Windows; too much venture capital money ($8.8 million); and squabbling among the partners.

It was Apple's good fortune that the first spreadsheet was available only on the Apple II. This was the first truly innovative and eminently useful tool to emerge from the microcomputer business. Once the software arrived, Apple dealers couldn't keep the machines on the shelves. Anyone who had to manipulate numbers as part of their work recognized the value of the program. Certainly, word processing had been a big step forward in helping writers, but this was a tool that could not have existed before the advent of the computer.

Apple reached critical mass in 1979, when, fueled by the development of the disk drive, it sold $55 million worth of equipment. In 1980, that number doubled to $117 million. More important, VisiCalc's visibility in the financial community, and Regis McKenna's masterful public relations campaign made the story of Apple and its two youthful founders almost too good to be true. Apple may not have been the largest small computer company—that honor went to Radio Shack and its TRS-80 line—but it was the most talked about.

It seemed Apple could do no wrong. Halfway through the year, with the company set to triple its previous year's stellar performance, Markkula decided it was time to go public. Along the way, the company had raised additional capital and was already a hot topic in the business community. Arthur Rock (of Fairchild and Intel financing fame), along with the new technology brokerage firm of Hambrecht & Quist came in, bringing along a handful of blue-ribbon venture capitalists (as the trade was starting to be called). The buzz started in the fall of 1980, and by the time the company went public in December, the investment community was seized with Apple mania. Massachusetts even barred the sale of the securities, saying that the offering was too risky. The shares were being offered at $22, which was more than 90 times the previous year's earnings of 24 cents a share. (That state's security laws stipulated a maximum of 20 times earnings for new listings.) But 27 other states imposed no such restriction, and ten days later the shares were going for more than $30 apiece.

Suddenly, Woz, Jobs, and Markkula were all worth more than $230 million in stock. Jobs, the photogenic front man, was a handsome bachelor of 25. He had more money than he could ever spend, and his patter revolved around saving the world with small computers. By this time, Apple had elegantly sewn up the educational establishment, with a low-cost seeding program; as a result, the Apple II was regarded as an educational necessity as well as an open-ended consumer product. Jobs was fast becoming the evangelist for a populist vision of computing. But there were cracks in the Apple image. For one, when Apple went public and cashed out, Kottke, Fernandez, and a couple of other early believers were given no shares. Forty other Apple employees became instant millionaires along with Jobs, Wozniak, and Markkula. But the team that had assembled Apple I computer boards in the Jobs garage and the guy who had accompanied Jobs to India (Kottke) were left out. Woz would later give some of his millions to repay those who had sweated on the benches in the early days, but Jobs refused. He had started to see himself as his handlers and the media team at Regis McKenna's PR firm portrayed him, as the true inventor of the personal computer. And for a while, the story of the two American "originators" of the small computer revolution played well in the press.

Early in 1981, Apple faced a series of crises that kept the stock prices in the upper 20s. The firm's first president, Mike Scott, was ousted in mid-1981 after a particularly inept and messy day of firings called Black Wednesday. (Apple had hired a lot of people to manage fast growth, several of whom did not measure up; on that day, 40 were fired.) Mike Markkula took the reins as president. At next year's annual meeting, Scotty, one of the company's largest shareholders, tried to place his own directors on the board, and thus stage a coup. He failed, but in the aftermath, when Jobs, now vice-chairman of the board, made intemperate remarks, Wall Street reacted negatively, relegating Apple to high flyers, but steering widows and orphans away.

Soon Markkula was becoming fed up with the sprawling and squabbling firm, and especially with the escalating internecine warfare among the development groups within the company. Markkula was a quiet and gentle man who had no taste for politicking. From the beginning, he had tried to keep an intermediary between himself and Jobs, whose emotion and passion exhausted him. As president he couldn't do that.

Apple was the most successful personal computer company in early 1982, but there were a number of signs that things were unraveling. Markkula had rejected VisiCalc, but the spreadsheet was what had kept the firm afloat in 1980 and 1981. And in a remarkable example of revisionist hindsight, Apple decided to reposition itself as a business computer company on the strength of its success in delivering machines that could run the remarkably successful spreadsheet. That led to the disastrous introduction of the Apple III. That machine, the first computer system developed as part of the corporate and well-financed Apple, didn't work right. It sported a complicated double-tiered motherboard that presented both connection and heat problems. When the first machines were sold and were found to be plagued by intermittent errors, they had to be recalled. The Apple III never recovered marketplace momentum. Jobs had also alienated the firm behind VisiCalc (VisiCorp) by demanding a $10 per-copy license to put the spreadsheet program on the Apple III. VisiCorp refused, and the Apple III ran without the product that had made the Apple II a success.

By 1982 the company had all but written off the Apple III. This meant that all revenues were still coming from the Apple II line—the company sold $335 million computers in 1981, for $39.4 million income, on 180,000 computers, most of which were by then five-year-old Apple IIs. Apple's next great hope was the Lisa, a computer system scheduled to be released early in 1983, bearing the name of Job's first child. Its concept grew out of an incandescent meeting Jobs and a group of Apple engineers had had at Xerox PARC (for Palo Alto Research Center) one day late in 1979, before the public offering. In Apple's second private investment placement, one of the investors had been the Xerox venture capital arm. When Jobs made the pitch to the group, he told them that he would let them put money into Apple only if "they'd open the kimono a bit at PARC." Up to then the reports coming out of the place were that it was a kind of Land of Oz, with remarkable things going on behind the screen where the wizards worked. Xerox agreed to Job's demands, and a few months later the Apple corps were given a peek "behind the curtain."

Xerox's PARC was already legendary in the brief history of the computer age. Located in a campus of low-slung buildings not far from Stanford University, PARC was funded by the success of Xerox's copier machine. Its charter was to develop the technologies for the office of the future, and it was meeting the challenge. Management had hired brilliant academics, then set them free to do anything they wanted. PARC innovations included creating and refining pull-down menus, on-screen icons, cut-and-paste text editing, laser printers, and typeset quality fonts, Ethernet networking, and more. But remarkably, most of its seminal innovations were never released as commercial products. The company spawned enormous industries and companies, including Adobe and 3Com, but Xerox itself never commercialized on much of this success.

Accompanying Jobs that day at PARC were Apple employees Jef Raskin and Bill Atkinson, among others. Raskin, a disheveled and cherubic professor type, had started at Apple as a manual writer. By 1979, he had convinced Markkula to fund a small R&D project Raskin cared about: He called it the Macintosh, deliberately misspelling the name of his favorite apple. An eclectic genius, Raskin's goal was to develop a low-cost, completely self-contained computer, which he thought of more as a household appliance than a computer. He knew about the work going on at PARC from some colleagues at Stanford and wanted to be part of the tour.

Atkinson had been a student of Raskin's at the University of California San Diego, where he had studied programming. Raskin had brought Atkinson to Apple to create a version of the PASCAL programming language for the Apple II. Atkinson, a soft spoken and affable sandy-haired programming whiz, with passionate eyes and a way of getting tangled up in words when describing his latest project, had been given the task of designing graphics for the Lisa. These graphics were supposed to manage the way that the computer displayed items on-screen. He had studied the few available reports in the trade literature about the work at PARC, especially what was rumored to be an exceptionally crisp display screen. Until then, all computers used what was known as a command-line interface, whereby data and commands were entered from keyboards as cryptic strings of letters and numbers. Graphics were almost nonexistent.

While the Apple group was at PARC, Larry Tessler, who had been a peripheral member of the PCC, demonstrated the Alto, a computer system that Xerox mysteriously had chosen not to release as a commercial product. (Instead, the company was readying a second-generation machine that a few years later would be offered as an $18,000 commercial system called the Xerox Star.) Tessler was the only member of the project's programming language team who had interest in small personal computers. Few of the PARC veterans had even looked at a personal computer much less bought one. Though Tessler agreed to do the demo for the guys from Apple, he felt that "these were going to be a bunch of hackers, and they wouldn't really understand computer science . . . [or] what we were doing."

That attitude was symbolic of the problem at PARC: disdain for the public, and more precisely, for the notion that a cheap microprocessor could be capable of doing the complex work that their hand-tooled and mega-memory machines were capable of performing. The PARC staff knew they were on the cutting edge of computing, that they were ahead of the rest of the world. The hoi polloi couldn't possibly understand what they were up to, so why bother to explain?

Tessler was wrong. The Apple contingent took one look at the Alto and their world changed. They saw for the first time icons, windows, menus, fonts, crisp black text on a white background, a word processing program that enabled cut-and-paste commands, and best of all, a system that made extensive use of the mouse, which meant the entire computer could be controlled without the keyboard. Like Alice in her wonderland, they had fallen down a hole into a new world. "Atkinson was peering very closely at the screen, with his nose about two inches away, looking at everything very carefully," Tessler recalled. "Jobs was pacing around the room acting up the whole time. He was very excited. Then, when he began seeing the things I could do on-screen, he watched in awe for a few minutes, then started jumping up and down shouting, 'Why aren't you doing anything with this? This is the greatest thing! This is revolutionary!' "

For Jobs, it was the Tao of personal computing. He had found enlightenment in a series of dots—called pixels for *picture elements*—in a closed demo room in Palo Alto. The high-resolution bitmapped screen they were looking at allowed them to voyage inside the digital world and swim among the bits. Atkinson stared more closely as Tessler showed him that everything he was seeing on-screen was simply made up of more and more layers of dots. Deeper into the microcosm they went.

Jobs was so thrilled that he immediately wanted to build a machine like this one, only better. But the Lisa project was already underway, and it had no provision for a mouse. And it was too late to revise the design to include on-screen graphics, windows, icons, and menus. An internal battle at Apple ensued. Jobs fought for his view, badmouthing and denigrating anyone who didn't agree with him. Others with more experience but less clout fought for the status quo. In the end Jobs triumphed. The Lisa would be Apple's first visually oriented machine and the first commercial personal computer to sport a graphical user interface, or GUI (pronounced "gooey").

But Steve's behavior left a lingering bitterness and animosity in the Apple offices. By the end of 1980, Markkula removed Jobs from the Lisa Project in hopes of smoothing the waters. But that left Jobs at loose ends. He needed something he could make his own. He focused on the machine that would fill his every waking hour for the next five years: Raskin's Macintosh. Jobs pushed the small team's hardware designer Burrell Smith—a moon-faced young technician with heavy-lidded eyes and a Woz-like skill with circuits—to build a version of the Macintosh using the same microprocessor as the Lisa: the Motorola 6800.

The advantage to upgrading the small appliance Macintosh to a 6800 microprocessor was that the additional computing power would enable it to manipulate and display graphics on-screen—of course, it would have to have a much smaller version of the full screen planned for the Lisa, but then, it could be sold for a quarter the price as well. During the week between Christmas and New Years in 1980, Apple was closed for the holidays, but Burrell Smith was there laboring at his workbench. Steve came marching through one day, having heard that Burrell was close to making the "Baby Lisa" work.

He was indeed. And it was an extraordinary feat of small-scale, personal computing engineering for the time. Whereas the Lisa had been designed over a two-year period, by 24 engineers, required five circuit boards to operate, and was scheduled to cost $10,000. Smith, with the kind of hands-on technician's training that preferred cheap and commodity to expensive and custom had built a little sister to Lisa on one circuit, which could be produced for less than $500. And he had done the hardware design entirely on his own.

Jobs was impressed. And from that moment, the Macintosh was his baby.

By February 1981, Jobs had taken over the Mac group, moved them to bigger and better quarters, and was on his way to making the Macintosh the newest Apple computer. Along the way he organized a young team who bought into his vision. They were going to change the world. This was going to be their chance.

Secrecy played a big part in the excitement. The Mac team occupied its own building, Bandley 3, to which access required a special badge. The ambience was "clubbish": Fresh fruit juices were always stocked in the refrigerator; an endless supply of state-of-the-art video games were on hand; there was even a Bosendorfer $100,000 grand piano. The first time the Lisa group tried to enter the building the security guard stopped them.

As 1981 moved into 1982, the atmosphere grew uglier at Apple as the Lisa, Mac, and Apple II groups came to hate each other. It came to a head when Burrell Smith, Jobs, and Bill Atkinson went one day to try to convince the Lisa team to change the shape of the pixels on their screen. Because the Lisa screen was rectangular, the designers had made their pixels rectangular, too. The result was that elements looked slightly skewed on a Lisa screen. That didn't bother the hard-nosed engineers on the Lisa project. But the Mac staff were into aesthetics; the look of the machine mattered as much as anything else. While developing software for the Macintosh they had to use a development and language system that simulated the smaller computer but ran on the Lisa. So, they had to look at the objectionable screen every day. When they couldn't get the Lisa engineers to change it, the Mac guys did it themselves in another grass roots hack. This further convinced Jobs and his team that the Lisa team was incompetent.

With the Lisa, Apple became its own worst enemy: producing an expensive office system that would cost $10,000 was difficult enough, but to have Jobs telling everyone that within the year Apple would release another machine, that was just like the Lisa but at one quarter the cost, was an insidious form of sabotage. To top it off, Apple announced that only Apple programs would be able to run on the Lisa. But the machine's all encompassing suite of office programs were slow and buggy. There was no alternative—take them or leave them.

The Lisa was not a success when it was released in early 1983. R&D estimates for the machine were in the $50 million range. At the time, a few thousand Apple IIIs a month were selling at $3,000. The Apple II was still the world's best-selling personal computer, selling around 30,000 a month. In contrast, the high-priced Lisa never sold more than

1,000 machines a month, before being discontinued two years after its introduction. This was the second consecutive failure for Apple, and astute observers were wondering whether the company really had the right stuff, or was just a flash in the pan.

Of course, not all of Apple's failures could be laid at the Macintosh door. The Lisa was overpriced, and its software wasn't very good. Also, 1983 was a very tough year for many computer makers; that was the year when the IBM PC finally took off, selling an estimated 20,000 a month. IBM had added a hard disk for more data storage right out of the box, and a bigger power supply. Called the PC-XT, it was a smash from the start. By the next year Big Blue was churning out tens of thousands of PCs *per day* from a series of plants in Boca Raton, Florida, and was still behind in filling the orders. That year, too, Compaq had introduced the first IBM-compatible, helping to define the future shape of the personal computer industry. In the wake of Compaq's success, a number of companies rushed to become PC-compatible and soon the IBM PC compatible market was where most of the action was.

Apple, however, chose not to follow the crowd. Again, it was technological arrogance; Jobs and the Mac team were openly disdainful of the IBM PC, but they were mistaking technical issues for marketplace realities. Gates, six months younger, had known Jobs since 1976, and thought it was naïve that Jobs believed he could prevail. Gates of course had created his own competitor computer with IBM. But he understood that hardware and software could be separated. Why not put Mac software on the PC? Gates' advice to Jobs was to create an Apple product line that was IBM-compatible. But Gates wasn't going to push too hard to convince Jobs since he had the one thing that Jobs needed desperately to make his Macintosh fly: applications.

Jobs was determined not to make the same mistake that he had made with the Lisa—designing it so it only used Apple programs. But to get other software companies to create software for an as-yet unavailable computer, especially one coming after a series of Apple disasters, he either had to pay a lot of money or convince software developers that the Mac was so far advanced technologically that they would be left in the dust if they didn't develop for it.

In a move for which he would be both lionized and vilified in coming years, Jobs sent Mike Boitch, a Stanford MBA who had been an early Apple II hacker, to evangelize in the development community. Jobs' idea was to get programmers so pumped up about the Mac that they would create "insanely great" software programs—even though Apple could produce no evidence that the little Macintosh had any chance of succeeding in a market that was rapidly changing from a hobbyist domain into a booming business and office market.

One of the companies Apple partnered with was Microsoft. Though the relationship between Gates and Jobs was often at odds, the two struck a deal. Microsoft would create a set of three applications for the Mac: Chart (to draw graphs and tables from data), Multiplan (a version of an old copycat spreadsheet that Gates had sold to just about every computer manufacturer), and File (a simple database). Apple would have the right to sell or bundle them with the Mac, along with two applications from Apple: MacWrite (a word processing program that was being written by one of Woz's teenage pals, Randy Wigginton) and Mac-Paint (a drawing program developed by Bill Atkinson of the Mac team).

But even with the deal in hand, Jobs knew that Microsoft was developing two other applications for the Macintosh and the PC: a word processing program called (eventually) Word, and Excel, a much more advanced spreadsheet, designed to go head to head with Lotus 1-2-3. Jobs had not forgotten that to date the two most successful computers both had a spreadsheet program associated with them: the Apple II with VisiCalc and the IBM PC with Lotus 1-2-3. Jobs wanted one of his own for the Mac. And wanted to keep it off the PC.

Lotus 1-2-3 was the brainchild of two Boston friends—Mitch Kapor and Jonathon Sacks—who first collaborated on an add-on program for VisiCalc. When the IBM PC looked like it was going to be a hit, they decided it needed a great spreadsheet, and took a shot at designing one. They wrote the program so that it took advantage of the unique hardware of the IBM-PC. VisiCorp, in contrast, wasn't willing to make a commitment to one computing environment, and hedging their bets, its designers rewrote VisiCalc for several different computing environments, including one version for the IBM PC. The result was that Lotus 1-2-3 had blistering speed on the IBM PC, whereas VisiCalc was slow.

After Lotus 1-2-3 was released in 1982, sales of the IBM PC with the spreadsheet program skyrocketed. Where the Apple II had been designed for the consumer market, and VisiCalc had sold businesspeople on it, the IBM PC had been designed specifically for businesspeople, and Lotus 1-2-3 was a tool perfectly suited to their needs. Without doubt, the business computer market was where the money was to be made, and Apple was without much of a product for that sector. Neither the Apple III nor the Lisa had a "killer app" like 1-2-3, and Jobs was determined to change that.

Jobs proposed to Gates that if he would keep Excel off the PC for at least three years, Jobs would kill the BASIC programming language that had been developed by his Mac team, enabling Gates to maintain control of the Macintosh language market. (At that point, languages had always been the Microsoft cash cow, because Gates was convinced that they were key to success in the personal computer market.)

It wasn't a bad offer, but it wasn't good enough for Gates, who pointed out that the BASIC market was a lot smaller than that for the IBM PC spreadsheet. And besides, Gates noted, the Apple II BASIC license was coming up for renewal (Apple had licensed it in 1977 for a ten-year term), intimating that he might not renew it. This would be a big blow to Apple, which was still generating all its revenues from the venerable old machine. But Gates did have one suggestion: He would agree to Jobs' deal if Jobs would throw in one other provision, something that wasn't worth much anyway because Jobs had taken it from Xerox in the first place: the right to use some elements of the Macintosh interface in his own fledgling graphical user interface, Windows. Jobs scoffed at the very idea. Sure, Apple might have seen what they were doing, but it was the hard work of the Mac team that had created the interface. That belonged to them.

Publicly, Jobs rejected the Gates counteroffer, but, secretly, he kept the discussion alive with Apple's president, John Sculley. Sculley was an East Coast preppie who had risen up the corporate ladder at Pepsi by marrying the boss' daughter, then made his mark by convincing the company to sell the soft drink in a wide variety of bottle and package sizes. Sales shot up, and he became Wall Street's golden boy. Brought into the Apple constellation following a long search for a new CEO, Sculley came onto the "Steve Jobs reality distortion field" and loved it. Looking to prove that his success at Pepsi was not the result of nepotism, he signed up, and became absolutely besotted with Steve Jobs.

At the time, Jobs' goal for the next stage in his life was to turn Apple into a major American corporate giant. Sculley was acceptable to the board and to Wall Street; and Jobs hoped that along the way Sculley could teach him how to be presidential. And because Sculley knew nothing about computers and technology, Jobs would give him that knowledge in return. And then, when he was ready, Jobs' intention was to take over as president of Apple.

Sculley and Jobs talked about the Gates offer. In their analysis, the single most important issue was to get the best software applications running on the Macintosh. Software was the Achilles Heel of the Macintosh. Without good applications, buyers would be loathe to buy the machines.

So they traded their internally developed MacBASIC, in order to ensure renewal of the Apple II BASIC license. And they gave Gates the go-ahead to use some of the features of the Macintosh in the first version of Windows, while he agreed not to include Excel for the PC for a while. It seemed like an incredible deal.

But there was another deal in the offing. One day late in the summer of 1983, just as the Macintosh team was about to launch into full warp speed to meet the Mac introduction date of January 1984, Jobs had another satori. A bearded guru, formerly of Xerox PARC, came to the Apple offices to make a presentation. His name was John Warnock and he had been one of the programmer-designers behind another new technology at Xerox involving laser printers (based on the principles of xerography) and fonts for printing. This technology was another that Xerox never released commercially. Despairing of ever seeing his work reach the marketplace, Warnock and a business partner left Xerox to try to sell a printer description language that would enable computers to produce typeset-quality fonts on laser printers. The product was called PostScript, and when combined with a laser printer like the ones that Canon had perfected (also based on technology developed at Xerox PARC but never released), it enabled a PC user to output typeset-quality text and graphics.

None of the dozens of venture capitalists Warnock approached, however, thought there was any merit to the technology. At that time, 1983, all anyone wanted from their computers was that they be IBM-compatible and that their printers output letter-quality pages.

Warnock's concept for his firm, Adobe, was that the printer generate an entire page at once and transfer it to memory; once in memory, a drum then picked up toner, fused that to the page, and finally spit it out. The idea was similar to the Xerox copy machine, but altered for printers connected to computers.

Warnock's idea may not have been interesting to the venture community, but Jobs loved it for the aesthetics: Typeset letters were better looking than anything else available. Eventually, he convinced Sculley, and the two of them cajoled the board into buying 3.4 million shares, fifteen percent of the fledgling Adobe. The $2.5 million investment saved Adobe; it gave the company enough capital to bring its typesetting system to market as part of a new Apple product, the Apple LaserWriter, which meant Apple had high-quality printing several years before the IBM PC.

In spite of that success, the grumbling among the businessmen on Apple's board was growing louder. They thought Jobs was increasingly out of control, and that Sculley was being led around by him. (The board would later be proven wrong. Desktop publishing, as the process came to be known, grew into an enormous market, and it kept Apple alive. To this day, the company's strongest redoubt is in the publishing world, where the Macintosh is dominant. Adobe is now a $1.6 billion company, with a full line of products from page layout to photo retouching; and the Postscript printing language is ubiquitous in the digital printing industry.) But in late 1983, the Mac was due to be released, and it was no time to make waves, so the board went along with the Adobe investment.

Then in the fall of 1983, Sculley and Jobs really shook things up when they showed the board the ad they planned to run during the Super Bowl. Costing nearly half a million dollars for a one-time airing, the ad was of a beautiful young woman, dressed in colorful running clothes, jogging through a futuristic world of mindless drones who looked like badly fed inmates in a Russian gulag. As the drones shuffled under an oversized face of their leader, who appeared on a gigantic video screen spouting endless and meaningless phrases, the beautiful jogger hurled a sledgehammer at the screen and shattered it. The tag line was: "Find out why 1984 won't be like *1984.*"

It was shocking, bold, and daring. The board hated it. They thought it too controversial, and certainly, too expensive. They demanded that the air time be sold; but Mike Murray, from Mac marketing, didn't try very hard to find a buyer, so the ad ran.

The day after, the entire nation seemed to be talking about the ad. (Later, it won most Ad of the Year awards; and it was voted Best Ad of All Time by *Adweek* magazine.) A few days later the Macintosh was introduced at the annual meeting. Jobs lifted it out of its carrying case, placed it on a table, and, in essence, let the computer speak for itself.

The audience whooped and hollered. As they filed out of the meeting, they were handed copies of a slick new magazine, *MacWorld*, dedicated to the machine. Jobs and his followers had thrown down the gauntlet to IBM.

Jobs talked wildly about selling 750,000 Macintoshes in the first year. To be ready for the anticipated flood of orders, Apple had built a state-of-the-art factory. But, three months into the year, projections had been scaled back to 40,000 a month. And in the summer of 1984, very disquieting news started to make its way through Cupertino's computer duchy. Actual sales of the Macintosh were only 10,000 a month, and dropping. By the fall, Macintosh was selling at the rate of about 60,000 for the year—less than two months' sales for the Apple II. The machine was a failure in the office market—the one place where there was money.

There were a number of reasons for its failure to capture that lucrative market. First, there were too few applications to run on it. Even Microsoft had let Apple down; the MS programmers had found the Mac too hard to program. Upon release, a joke circulated that there were six applications for the Mac: MacPaint, MacWrite, MacPaint, MacWrite, MacPaint, and MacWrite.

The look of the machine hurt it too. Though truly unique in its small upright box (about the size of a telephone book and approximately 18 inches high) it was by far the "friendliest" looking computer on the market. It had a small black-and-white screen built-in, and came with keyboard, mouse, and speaker. But it wasn't businesslike, and for all its charm, it was woefully underpowered.

So, for the fall of 1984, Apple rushed a new "fat Mac," the 512K Mac (referring to the amount of internal random access memory) into production. But memory wasn't the only problem with the machine. Its keyboard had no cursor or movement keys—because Jobs thought everyone should use the mouse. He forced the mouse on even the most proficient keyboard typists. His director of marketing, Mike Murray, once told him during an argument, "The market of 28-year-old multimillionaire isn't exactly our target niche."

But Steve wouldn't listen. Why should he? In his mind, he had invented the personal computer, and believed he knew best what everyone needed. Likewise, the printer Apple offered—a low-quality dot-matrix machine relabeled from a Japanese company—produced amateurish business letters. The Macintosh's small memory space made it ineffective. Everything ran ponderously as programs tried to manipulate all those pixels making up the crisp onscreen graphics.

Still Jobs clung to Raskin's concept of the Mac as an appliance, and he continued to minimize everything he could. Thus, there were no expansion slots, no way for anything to be added to the machine. Initially there was no hard disk, either; a second floppy disk drive had to be added externally. The floppy drives were Sony 3.5-inch, which Jobs had first refused to use. He agreed to use them only after some midnight engineering by the boys in the Mac lab showed him how much better they were than the drives used in the Lisa. From then on, he was hooked on Sony disk drives. But this decision had caused a big problem: The new drives were incompatible with the Apple II drive—the disk drive that had made the company a success. This meant that the million-plus Apple II users were frozen out of the next-generation machine—unless, of course, they bought a Mac.

By the summer of 1984, the Mac was a bomb. For the first two years Apple sold about 500,000, a third of the number IBM had sold three years earlier.

No doubt about it, Apple was in trouble. The company had now delivered three products back to back that had failed, and the only successful computer in the arsenal was still the Apple II, Woz's nearly 10-year-old machine. The Mac sales team tried hard to sell the concept of the Mac, and they did attract some of the best and the brightest. The Mac managed to become something of a cultural phenomenon. The interface, with its cute trash can in the lower right-hand corner, and its patterns of pixels—chevrons, stripes, closely packed cherries—that could be created and manipulated under MacPaint, or the fonts that could be produced under MacWrite, found a contingent of devotees. But for most of the computer-buying public, it seemed like a cute toy. Serious business users chose to stick with the IBM PC or its clones and the Lotus 1-2-3 spreadsheet.

Nevertheless, Apple's dedicated band of users powered Apple into a $6 billion company by 1995. While Apple never took more than 15 percent market share in the personal computer marketplace (the IBM PC compatibles had the rest), for years it was able to stay neck and neck with IBM in unit shipments. It was the market that Jobs had foreseen, and for a time the Macintosh was a viable alternative to the PC-compatible.

But by the fall of 1984, things were getting ugly at Apple. Theories abounded as to why the public wasn't "getting it," but none of them assumed there was anything wrong with the Mac; there was just something wrong with those stupid consumers. Couldn't they see how insanely great the computer was? Once again Apple tried a marketing ploy that had worked before. During the 1985 Super Bowl, Apple ran another ad. This one was even more controversial, a reflection of the prevailing atmosphere at Apple. Called "Lemmings," it showed an endless line of blindfolded businesspeople, trudging forward, whistling, "We're off to work." They were then seen plunging off a cliff, until one free spirit lifts his blindfold and steps out of line. But this ad was too stark. The response to the ad was swift and mostly negative.

At the 1985 annual meeting a few days later, Jobs introduced the Apple LaserWriter; priced at $7,000 it was supposed to compete with $1,000 letter-quality and $500 dot-matrix printers. In an attempt to justify the high price, they added an inexpensive and slow networking system called Appletalk, which enabled up to 32 users to share a printer. They also announced the Macintosh Office strategy, but it was mostly smoke and mirrors aimed squarely at the business user.

By the following month, things were worse. Macintosh sales had dropped even further. In March 1985, forecasts called for 20,000 Macs to be sold per week; the actual number was closer to 2,500. Several key execs resigned. Mike Markkula and Arthur Rock told Sculley to get a grip on Apple no matter what it took. Then, just a couple of days after Ronald Reagan awarded the two Steves the National Medal of Technology, Woz resigned because he felt the Apple II line was being denigrated. Rumors of boardroom fights and troubles started leaking out. They were denied, of course, but tensions were high and the Mac team members were never very good at keeping their mouths closed.

Next, a number of the original Mac team members, burned out by the hard work, started to leave one by one. Sculley felt he couldn't trust Jobs; Jobs thought Sculley was incompetent and tried to use his position as chairman of the board to oust him. In early April, Jobs and Sculley made competing pitches to run the company. The board chose Sculley. Jobs lost.

A Frenchman, Jean Louis Gassée, had been brought in to run the Macintosh division. Not surprisingly, he walked into a great deal of resentment, and total chaos. Gassée thought of himself as a product guru, but his claim to fame was that he understood the French retail computer market, where as head of Apple France, he had successfully sold Le Mac. He immediately went to work fixing the glaring deficiencies of the Mac. A great fan of the Apple II, Gassée opened up the Mac, giving it expansion slots, and adding color. What he did was all pretty obvious, but because of the infighting, the Apple staff never saw how easy it would have been to move forward.

Gassée was also at the heart of the push to finally oust Jobs. A few weeks after Gassée had arrived, when the warfare between Jobs and Sculley was at its height, Jobs took the Frenchman aside privately and said he intended to call an emergency board meeting while Sculley was out of the country and vote him out. Could he count on Gassée as a supporter?

That evening Gassée went to a barbecue at the home of one of the other senior Apple execs. He told Apple's general counsel, Al Eisenstadt, about the developing coup; then he told Sculley. The next day, Jobs and Sculley had a shouting match that culminated in an executive meeting where Sculley demanded that every manager publicly declare fealty to one of them. That was the end of Jobs at Apple. The confrontation was widely reported, and Jobs left a month later for a long bicycle trip through Tuscany. When he returned, he officially resigned and started a new company, called NeXT Inc.

During Jobs' and Sculley's reign, Apple had made a series of disastrous errors over the years that had destroyed its market position. The company remained proprietary about its hardware, refusing to allow any clones until well after its market share had dropped below 10 percent in the early 1990s. (A couple of years later, with Jobs back at the helm, the company would reverse course and put a halt to the clones again.) This meant that Apple's machines were always significantly more expensive than the commodity and multimanufacturer PC-compatibles. Apple also failed to develop a successor to the original Macintosh line. It was eventually forced to join with IBM and Motorola in an ill-fated effort to build a future on a consortium microprocessor. But, because Apple didn't control the consortium, this destroyed the reason for being proprietary in the first place.

And, finally, the company relinquished its position in the educational market, and destroyed the goodwill it had there, by never offering a way for Apple II computers to work with Macintoshes. A couple of years after Jobs left, Sculley finally killed the Apple II line. Somehow Sculley never understood that the reason the PC family was so successful was because, no matter how primitive or advanced they were, they could still share data and disks. This meant that investing in IBM PC-compatibles offered protection in a rapidly changing marketplace that Apple never provided.

Through the late 1980s Gassée proved a formidable product vision-ary. Apple continued to consolidate its product lines, and introduced a series of successful new Macintosh models that pushed the company into desktop publishing and graphics arts dominance. Gassée was behind the Mac II, the portable Mac, and more. Eventually, however, he fell out with Sculley over an unsuccessful pet project—the Newton hand-held computer. When he left, Gassée founded Be Inc, which developed an alternative operating system for the Macintosh. Shrewdly, Gassée tried to sell it to Apple in 1996, when the company was reeling from the success of the PC-compatible market and the failure of its own inept management. But the deal fell through.

In a dramatic twist, it was Steve Jobs who grabbed the big payday—$400 million from the sale of his then failing company, NeXT Inc., to Apple. This was the second fortune he had made from the company. (When he quit and left the company in 1985, he had sold all his stock, netting about $200 million.) (Jobs' third fortune came when a small computer graphics and animation company he had bailed out of trouble while still at Apple—Pixar Inc.—had a smash success in the hot IPO market of the early 1990s. His stake in that company is valued at nearly a billion dollars.) By moving in at the last minute, he cut off Gassée, the man who had spilled the beans about his coup ten years earlier. As part of the deal he took over as interim CEO and finally had the chance he had wanted originally: to run Apple. This time Jobs had the last laugh.

It was the prodigal son come home to his family. Could he save Apple? Does lightning strike twice?

Philip D. (Don) Estridge, head of IBM's Boca Raton PC division, in the early 1980s.

The IBM Personal Computer—developed at the Information Systems Division's Boca Raton, Florida facility—was ready for sale to the public in 1981.

CHAPTER 8

>———◆———<

PCs

The IBM Personal Computer

As the 1980s began, two icons symbolized American technological supremacy: the mainframe computer and the telephone system, both of which were controlled by enormous corporations. Yet within five years, both would be reeling from market forces unleashed by unparalleled levels of competition. Although a few software and hardware companies were doing well enough to go public, they amounted to a trickle, not a roar. Computers remained a mysterious product to much of the public, too expensive and too difficult for many people to master.

IBM changed all that. While West Coast entrepreneurs were busy fighting over a limited microcomputer market, a band of straight-laced, crew-cut middle-aged IBMers introduced the IBM personal computer. Before long, Big Blue was churning out 13,000 PCs from its Boca Raton plant every day. Within a couple of years, the world had adopted and adapted to the IBM standard; the market grew exponentially.

But riding the rocket overwhelmed the boys in Boca, and IBM's corporate leaders proved powerless to control the new market with their stodgy mainframe mentality. That attitude, coupled with a series of business errors, turned IBM's early success against itself.

Lying in wait was Microsoft.

❀   ❀   ❀

THE MAN DESTINED TO BUILD the pivotal personal computer wasn't a veteran of IBM's vaunted research facilities, nor was he a computer scientist; and he didn't have much to do with IBM's storied mainframe past. What Lew Eggebrecht did have was experience working with the inexpensive microprocessors created by Intel. With them he built test equipment, gadgets and gizmos he used to probe the computing equipment IBM sold to its customers. Along the way, he became expert at putting together off-the-shelf electronic parts that made microprocessors work. In fact, they came to obsess him. He would work all night, sleeping in spurts at his desk, until his systems functioned the way that he knew they could.

Eggebrecht was a country boy from Minnesota, born during the Second World War. His family were German immigrants to the Midwest, brought by railroad agents who had canvassed Europe in the late nineteenth century looking for industrious farmers to settle the vast tracts of land that spread out from Chicago. As Lew worked his way through high school, it became obvious that he had a special skill for electronics engineering. Straight from college he went to work at IBM. At the time it was the natural step to take: join a paternalistic company and stay there all your working life.

In the late 1960s Eggebrecht joined an IBM division in Rochester, Minnesota, located 50 miles to the south of Minneapolis. A sleepy Midwestern town of about 60,000, famous for the Mayo Clinic, this was also the site for IBM's center for test engineering, an unglamorous field whose practitioners created test gear for IBM's many electronic products. Management paid little attention to these devices: They weren't sold by the famous IBM sales force, they didn't produce significant revenue, and no one was interested in their architects. Rather, this was a hidden, albeit necessary, part of the giant company's business.

IBM continually created new pieces of equipment that had to be designed, prototyped, tested, refined, and built. As a result, the small teams of test engineers were able to build working equipment and see it through to completion. It was a rare opportunity in the numerous and diverse divisions of IBM, where most employees had to hand off their work to one of a series of committees which would then pass it on to another group, which made further revisions before handing it over to a final group that approved it and put it on the schedule. Finally it would pass through the pricing, marketing, forecasting, finance, and administration groups, all of which made suggestions. It was said that no IBM product could be released sooner than two years after the design had been approved: cynics said it was more like five years.

Shortly after Eggebrecht joined the Rochester group, he began to read about Intel's microprocessor. In the next few years, he and two other test engineers—Roger Kleinschmidt and Dennis Gibbs—started building test gear using these microprocessors. Eggebrecht was so good at designing circuits around the Intel family of microprocessors, that by 1975 he was producing small test computers at IBM. These machines were capable of controlling various peripherals like printers and disk drives, and running them through their paces. Eggebrecht handled the architecture, hardware, and system design; Kleinschmidt and Gibbs designed the software.

Coincidentally, the success of DEC had prompted IBM management to consider offering its own line of smaller computers. A new division in Atlanta, Georgia, called the General Systems Division (GSD), was established for that purpose; the products created there were eventually called midrange computers, which would evolve into the AS400 line. Other IBM engineers at GSD had seen Eggebrecht's work, and they believed that something even smaller could be created.

Eggebrecht, Gibbs, and Kleinschmidt became the nucleus of a GSD lab team in Atlanta, dedicated to investigating a microprocessor-based computer for the low end of the IBM product line. To begin, they studied the competition; they bought a series of personal computers from Altair, IMSAI, Radio Shack, Apple, and Commodore. Eggebrecht ripped them apart, then identified the good and bad points of each. Kleinschmidt took on the task of convincing the IBM administration of the value in such a machine, so that it would be assigned product status, not just research status.

Initially the brass showed very little interest in the machine. One detraction was that Eggebrecht's team claimed that they could make and sell it for under $20,000, a price tag that was not impressive to IBM's commission-driven sales force. (At the time, IBM's least expensive computer—the 4300—sold for between $69,000 and $250,000 without software or support.) Furthermore, it wasn't clear to management what a machine like this could be used for. The microcomputer was then still entirely dependent on the hobbyist market.

Fortunately, Kleinschmidt had become roommates with a fellow GSD staffer who had recently been promoted from Minnesota. A charismatic rising star with a granite jaw, Bill Lowe had been earmarked for a fast ride to the top. He joined the GSD group as Vice President of Manufacturing. He was intrigued by the role he thought electronics—specifically IBM electronics—might play in the future. He listened to

Kleinschmidt and was impressed by Eggebrecht's work. He believed the machine they were talking about might have commercial potential, if only they could find the right applications for it. Lowe was a far thinking manager. He saw a future where computers could be sold directly to consumers. He tried to imagine what the home of the future might look like, so as to plot a course that would give IBM an inside track to this yet untapped market.

The home market offered great potential, but it was one in which IBM had never made any effort. Still, Lowe kept his eye on Apple's progress. In 1978, Apple was a $15 million a year company offering more than 100 software programs. Lowe conducted more research and discovered accounting software that had been written by a local Georgia company, Peachtree, for the other standard for microcomputers, the CP/M market. (At that time, users of the CP/M operating system could purchase software written for other machines to run on their equipment relatively easily.) This information prompted Lowe to change his mind about the consumer market, realizing that business might be the best fit for the GSD machine.

His concept: Build a relatively inexpensive accounting system and tap into the small business market. By mid-1978, management had approved this idea, but did not back it up with much funding. The result was the Datamaster, or System 23, the first personal computer built by IBM.

Designed around the Intel 8080 microprocessor, the project was finished late, never worked well, and never won mainline support within IBM. Worse, while Eggebrecht had created a working design in a matter of months, two years later he was still waiting for software from an army of IBM programmers. Orders backed up, giving Apple's new program, VisiCalc, the first spreadsheet for the microcomputer age, a leg up. Before long, the Apple II was the darling of the small business world. IBM's $20,000 Datamaster had no competitive advantage.

This didn't deter Lowe, who by now was convinced that if he could find the right project, IBM could capture the business users that Apple was currently supplying. As he saw it, the only other major competitor was Radio Shack, and he was sure that, with the IBM name, he could overtake that company as well.

The Datamaster project was moved down to Florida (GSD stayed in Atlanta) to the beach town of Boca Raton, between tony West Palm Beach and blue-collar Fort Lauderdale on Florida's Atlantic coast. A mere blip on IBM's corporate radar screen, it was never intended to be a serious operation. The existing Boca Raton operation was hardly a major division of IBM. It produced small quantities of low-end products such as specialty keyboards, and had meeting facilities for sales convocations. In that sleepy environment, the Datamaster project promptly fell into a black hole. It was one of several projects that failed during this time. In 1980, *Forbes* reported:

> In just three years International Business Machines Corp. ran through some $4 billion in cash and then borrowed $1 billion in the first bond offering of its history. It announced products it couldn't deliver, and delivered products it couldn't support with necessary services and software. IBM is in the midst of an apparently self-inflicted earnings decline from the superaggressive pricing of its medium-size computers, the 4300 series, and a breathtaking 80 percent slash in memory prices.
>
> With all of this, IBM earnings slipped last year to $5.16 a share from $5.32 the year before. Its stock, down 30 percent from last year's high, has shed $15 billion in market value. At its recent price, $55, IBM sells for a lower multiple of earnings and dividends than at any time in recent history. . . .

At one point during this timeframe, IBM had 1,000 programmers assigned to various small computer software projects, but nothing came of their efforts quickly enough. As Apple's VisiCalc earned more attention and business, the former test engineers became disheartened. They knew VisiCalc was a better product than anything the IBM programming minions had produced in three years. All around them they watched as other firms succeeded in the market they had targeted. Wang, NBI, and Lanier were selling word processing and accounting systems, that cost about $20,000 and were directed at the office market. On the consumer end, Radio Shack and Apple saw sales going through the roof. By 1979, Apple, still privately held, was projecting sales of $75 million. Those in the industry began to wonder: What is IBM doing about small computers? For Bill Lowe and the GSD engineers who had built dozens of machines over the years, it was a hard pill to swallow.

To its creators, software design is an art, not conducive to decision by committee. As the personal computer age emerged, another metaphor became popular: it would be said that giving birth to a software program took nine months—regardless whether 2 or 200 programmers were working on it. This was a lesson that IBM would never learn. Mainframes could accommodate plenty of room to accommodate thousands of lines of programming instructions; microcomputers could not. Committees could write convoluted mainframe software; but for microprocessor-based machines, one person, who could see how to reduce dozens of instructions to a few, was much more valuable.

In New York, IBM's president, Frank Cary, was frustrated by the problems the small computer lines were experiencing. Cary was a brilliant man, perhaps IBM's most exceptional president. He had succeeded Tom Watson Jr. as president in 1972, and his term included managing the long-term antitrust actions against the company. Cary had drawn up plans to split IBM into two companies as a potential solution, and it was out of this planning that the General Services Division (GSD) was formed in Atlanta, to provide a place for all of Big Blue's nonmainframe computer businesses should they need it.

Although he was a mainframe man through and through, Cary understood the economics of the electronics business: that ever more powerful microprocessors would be built for lowering costs in the coming years. He could see the fascination that Apple's personal computers held for his best engineers, and he sensed that IBM would have to offer similar machines to stay competitive. Yet he was faced with the fact that all of IBM's small computer projects seemed doomed to failure. But he didn't give up.

It was the age of "intrapreneurship"—encouraging innovation within a big company by supporting small unconventional projects—and Cary thought that might be the way to produce a small computer for IBM to sell. He let it be known that he was looking for a microcomputer project. After he saw VisiCalc for the first time in 1979, at every management committee meeting thereafter Cary would ask the assembled executives: "Where's my Apple?"

Word soon trickled down that one way to get a fast ride to the top was to come up with a viable way for IBM to get to market with a microcomputer. The man with an answer was Bill Lowe. When Lowe heard that IBM's management committee was open to proposals for personal computer projects, he wasted no time. His was a radical idea: He talked with the folks at Atari, now owned by Warner Brothers. At the time Atari, originally an arcade and video game maker, was manufacturing a series of small, inexpensive microcomputers. Lowe struck a tentative deal with the company; IBM would buy Atari's computer motherboards, repackage them in an IBM case, supply them with IBM peripherals, and sell them as the IBM product line. And because Atari had already created an operating system and had designed software he would get around the crippling problem of having to wait for internally developed IBM software. Furthermore, because the boards were already designed and completed, it would take much less time to get a product out.

Lowe was pleased with the plan, and his colleagues in Boca thought it was workable as well. They had listened to Lowe's assertions that IBM could grab the mainstream business market away from Apple and all the other little firms. He was fond of asking: "How many business owners are going to go into a Radio Shack store, stand in line next to some pimply-faced kid buying a power antenna for his hotrod, and order 200 personal computers. Not many!"

For all Lowe's disdain of the Radio Shack line—"Trash 80" as its TRS 80 machine was derisively called—it was vying with Apple for leadership in the marketplace. Apple had a following based on teenage gamers, kids in schools learning BASIC, supplemented by a growing number of business professionals using VisiCalc. It sold 180,000 machines in 1980, for an installed base of 350,000 computers. By then Tandy, Radio Shack's parent company, had sold about 400,000 of its no-nonsense looking computers, more than 170,000 in 1980 alone.

Clearly, there was money to be made in this business, and IBM was getting none of it. So in June 1980, Lowe summoned his courage, flew up to corporate headquarters, and went before the management committee to pitch his Atari/IBM proposal. When he was finished, he was confident he had done pretty well. But Frank Cary had a different opinion. "That's the stupidest idea I've ever heard," Lowe would later recall Cary telling him. "Go back and rethink it. We want a personal computer, but we want an IBM personal computer."

On his way back to Florida, Lowe was disappointed but not derailed; he had already formulated a Plan B, and he knew just the man in Boca who could implement it.

Lew Eggebrecht had designed several different personal computers by 1980. He drew them in his spare time, usually after he had taken a look at one or another of the hobbyist machines on the market. He had worked out a number of issues, and was convinced that the road to success was to follow the open architecture of the original microcomputer—the Altair. The Altair contained a number of add-on boards to expand the computer's capabilities, making customization a big part of its appeal from the start. By incorporating the advances made since the Altair's 1975 introduction, Eggebrecht intended to make his machine much more user-friendly, along the lines of Apple's design. He planned to use only standard components, meaning that everything could be bought from parts suppliers; nothing had to be created at IBM.

Finally, he wanted to use Intel's newest microprocessor, the 8088, which featured a 16-bit data pathway, double the size of its previous top-of-the-line microprocessor chip, the 8080. The new chip's big advantage was memory space. With a 16-bit architecture, the microprocessor could accommodate more than a megabyte (1 million, 8-bit bytes) of software instructions at a time. That enabled it to run much more sophisticated programs than the previous generation of hobbyist machines, all of which were based on 8-bit microprocessors. The biggest single difference would be in graphics. A 16-bit microprocessor promised a much better on-screen display because this was a function of how many pixels (picture elements, the dots, of a monitor screen) could be controlled.

When Lowe told his colleagues that the Atari deal had been rejected, Eggebrecht was nonetheless pleased to hear that at least there was support at the top for the idea of a personal computer. Lowe and Eggebrecht set about finalizing the design for a small microcomputer that could be built entirely by IBM, yet was generic enough to take advantage of the burgeoning collection of software now available on the market. And because it had no custom parts, it would be less expensive to manufacture. Within weeks, they had a workable design, and Eggebrecht had even wired up a prototype for demonstration.

Lowe began working out the business side of the equation. Sales was his most pressing concern: Could they sell something cheaply enough to be competitive in the small computer market? It was obvious to him that if IBM's highly disciplined sales force, trained to generate high profits and do lots of customer hand-holding, couldn't sell a $20,000 system like the Datamaster, they certainly wouldn't be interested in selling one at $2,000 which was Lowe's target price. His conclusion: Sell the machines through retail outlets. That meant a complete turnabout for IBM, which had never sold anything that way. Even its typewriters were sold through office equipment dealers, not retail stores.

The next management committee meeting took place in early July 1980. Lowe was ready, and returned to corporate headquarters to present this new plan. He showed the assembled executives a design spec, and presented some preliminary performance benchmarks. He suggested that they contract with software vendors to move their applications over to the IBM machine. Finally, he proposed that IBM buy an operating system from Digital Research, makers of the popular CP/M (Control Program/Microcomputer). CP/M ran on most of the microcomputers of the day, and software had already been developed for it.

CP/M, the first widely adopted operating system, had been created by Gary Kildall, a civilian mathematics instructor at a Navy officer training college in Monterey, California, where he taught courses in computer programming. In 1972, he was hired as a consultant to Intel to help develop an operating system for a new kind of computer on a chip the company had just produced: the 4004 microprocessor. But the company had little faith in microprocessors so when Intel's marketing managers stopped touting Kildall's CP/M, he decided to sell it himself.

By 1976, he had sold a license to the Altair cloner, IMSAI. Although the software managed the operation of that computer effectively, Kildall knew that with a few modifications he could make the program work with different microprocessors and different machines. Kildall and his wife, Dorothy McEwen, started licensing their updated software operating system to various new microcomputer companies. As a variety of new microcomputers started appearing, most of them adopted CP/M as their operating system.

Money started flowing in as manufacturers of new personal computers bought licenses to use CP/M. By maintaining all the different versions of his operating system himself, Kildall made a lot of money. Privately held, DRI was owned entirely by Kildall and his wife. By 1980, it was estimated that some 600,000 personal computers had been sold and by 1981, company revenues were at $6 million. But he missed the opportunity to build software applications that worked with his operating system. He later said it was because he "didn't want to compete with his best customers."

While creating CP/M, Kildall had made some choices that would have deep implications later on. For one, he didn't want his operating system to be able to run on only one type of machine; so he designed a section of the machine's system, called a BIOS, or Basic Input Output System, where the hardware's "personality" would be stored. This enabled Kildall to reconfigure the program to be compatible with the various microcomputers. All that had to be done was to change the "personality" file. Then software developers could greatly expand their market by selling the same program for a variety of machines. Around this common operating system, a software market grew big enough to support a number of small companies. By the time IBM was ready to make its PC move in 1980, CP/M was the industry standard, running on nearly every microcomputer, with the notable exception of Apple's. This was what made CP/M so attractive to Lowe's team: Software was already available.

When Lowe made his second presentation to the IBM management council, it wasn't Cary who was the naysayer this time; it was the head of Lowe's own division, GSD, who found fault with the plan. He said he had too many projects on his plate, and that he didn't know how he would be able to finance such a project. Another salesman questioned the idea of selling a low-cost machine via retail. What about service and support?

Lowe countered by proposing two key channels: IBM's sales force could sell the new PCs directly to their big company customers; and the PC division would launch consumer distribution by supplying computers to certain of the big computer chains. But no matter how many answers Lowe came up with, he found precious little support in the room.

Then Cary interrupted, asking, "Can you do it in a year?" Lowe assured him that he could. "Then I'll pay for it," said Cary. "Get a dozen guys working on it. Come back in 30 days and show me a working prototype."

A few minutes later Lowe came roaring out of the meeting room with the authorization to put together a team and establish an operational plan for IBM to build a personal computer. The schedule—one year, start to finish—looked impossible to meet, but Eggebrecht thought he might be able to pull it off if they could do an end run on the IBM hardware procurement procedures and bypass Big Blue's inept software teams.

On the Saturday morning after the July 4 holiday in 1980, Lowe started handpicking his team. Naturally, Lew Eggebrecht was the system architect. The dozen engineering and manufacturing execs that would make up the rest of the original team were all battle-scarred veterans of IBM's previous attempts to create small systems. They were men in their forties, who had families, and who had been with IBM an average of 20 years. And they shared one other thing: a desire to prove that IBM could produce a different kind of machine, that IBM was still the greatest computer company on earth. They took over an ugly conference room in the corner of an even uglier IBM manufacturing building. It was a dreary place located down an alley on a side street in the Boca Raton industrial section. They chose it deliberately in hopes of keeping a low profile so they could do their work undisturbed.

Of course, they were quickly found out as the company grapevine began to buzz with word of the new project. With technical leadership by Eggebrecht, who was widely considered one of the finest engineers at IBM, and driven by Lowe, who was thought to have a shot at the top spot at IBM, the project took on an aura of importance from the beginning.

Their plan was brilliant in its simplicity. They would build the computer using off-the-shelf parts and subassemblies (things like keyboards and disk drives) that could be manufactured by several competitive suppliers. They would have them bid against one another, and against the internal IBM operations that manufactured the same items. In essence, they were refusing to pay the standard IBM overhead for the hordes of service, sales, support, and administrative charges that bloated the prices of internally manufactured parts and supplies. Their computer had to compete in a retail marketplace where the most important three selling points were price, price, and price.

As far as software was concerned, Lowe's team knew IBM couldn't possibly produce what they needed in time, so they intended to build prototype machines in a few months, get them into the hands of the best software companies in the world (there weren't many at the time), and somehow convince them to adapt their products to work on the new machine. The obvious choice for an operating system was CP/M. But they also needed a programming language in order to develop any other programs. The obvious choice here was the company with the team who had written BASIC for the first Altairs, then proceeded to license it to all comers: Microsoft. Reps from IBM called Bill Gates and told him they wanted to talk to him about software. He said sure.

A couple of days later Eggebrecht and a handful of other IBM execs showed up at Microsoft's then minimalist offices above a bank, where the company had some 25 programmers working on various programming language projects. Gates and Steve Ballmer, a college buddy he had just hired, sat around a table with the IBM contingent. After Gates and Ballmer had signed the standard IBM nondisclosure forms, the group started talking. They discussed the personal computer market in general, and licensing deals for software in specific; and Gates tried to answer questions like, "If a company like IBM wanted to license a programming language like Microsoft BASIC, how would it go about structuring a deal with you?" Gates was careful not to make a commitment to any hardware. He asked the IBM team which operating system they were going to use. They in turn asked what he recommended, to which Gates replied, "CP/M. Gary Kildall. You gotta go down there to see him." Gates offered to call and set up an appointment—which he did, for the next day.

That night the IBM delegation left for Monterey where Digital Research Intergalactic (DRI), Kildall's firm, was located. When they arrived, they learned that the owner was out flying his plane; and his wife, who was the business manager, refused to sign an IBM nondisclosure form. (By signing, she would be agreeing to keep anything IBM said confidential, while giving IBM a release to use any information the signer shared.) The Kildalls had reason to be dismissive: They virtually owned the market.

When Kildall returned, he brushed aside the confidentiality issue and talked to them without signing any nondisclosure forms. Since the IBM cadre wasn't free to reveal their plans, it was hard for Kildall to figure out just what they were planning to build. After a few nervous go-rounds, Kildall said it sounded like IBM wanted a 16-bit version of CP/M (to be called CP/M 86), and that he was already working on releasing it. He also said that DRI was more than willing to put it on the IBM PC, and would work with them to get it up and running. But if IBM wanted something special, it would have to get in line with all the other computer companies who were already licensees. After haggling over fees (flat rate versus per-unit), the IBM team left unconvinced that Kildall could get the software out on IBM's schedule. They were worried enough to stop at a pay phone and call Gates asking if he would intercede with Kildall. At their earlier meeting, Gates had mentioned a simple operating system that a friend had written. The IBM team asked if he could look into that, to find out what it would take to adopt it for the new IBM machine? Gates agreed to see if he could supply it.

On the plane back to Boca the following day, the IBM contingent made their decision: It was Microsoft over DRI. It was clear Gates wanted to work with IBM; and though Microsoft's BASIC might not be the world's finest software, at least it worked, and the company had a track record of delivering BASIC for a number of computing platforms. That would give the new IBM microcomputer a built-in programming language. Gates also said he could design an operating system (OS) for a computer if IBM decided it needed one. This was crucial to the team, who knew there was no way they could get an operating system out of IBM's bureaucracy in time.

Gates wasted no time. He contacted the proprietors of a local computer shop—Seattle Computer Products—who had written a knock-off of CP/M called Quick and Dirty Operating System, QDOS. Within days Steve Ballmer had negotiated a sweetheart of a deal: Microsoft would pay $10,000 up front for the unlimited right to distribute Seattle Computer's renamed 86-DOS to an unlimited number of end users; for an additional $15,000 per customer, Microsoft could sublicense the system to another company, such as a hardware manufacturer. The deal would close in 60 days; no money was due until then.

A week later, Ballmer presented IBM with the operating system during a series of all-day meetings. Microsoft had paid no money for the OS, but had, in essence, taken out an option on it. When the deal between Microsoft and IBM was finally signed, it called for up-front payments from IBM totaling $1 million, comprising an advance against royalties of $400,000 to Microsoft for the operating system, another $400,000 for four programming language compilers (Pascal, COBOL, FORTRAN, BASIC), and $200,000 for adaptation and programming labor to make the system work within the one-year timetable. In exchange, IBM had limited use of DOS for no further payments, as long as Microsoft BASIC was embedded in the underlying architecture of the machine. This gave Microsoft the inside track for selling programming tools for the new machine. It also joined the two companies at the hip.

In mid-August 1980, Lowe, accompanied by Eggebrecht, and a working prototype of the IBM personal computer, took a flight to company headquarters for the critical demonstration to the management committee. The machine could do just two things: draw a picture of a voluptuous woman, and run a simple animation of a rocket ship launching. This demonstration was known as the "vixen and the rocket," and except for a minor technical glitch caused (Eggebrecht fixed it on the spot) by a loose wire, it worked.

Then Lowe made the formal presentation, after which he underwent intense questioning. The interrogation didn't center on the team's decision to use Microsoft. As luck would have it, John Opel, soon to be Cary's successor as president, sat on the national board of United Way with Mary Gates, Bill's mother. When he asked if Bill was "Mary's boy," Lowe knew their decision in the software arena would present no problems. There wasn't much contention over the recommendation to go outside the company for parts and subassemblies either; the management committee knew all too well there was simply no time in the schedule for IBM's ponderous procurement procedures.

The concerns centered instead on the sales effort. Lowe and his team had suggested that the product be launched with a massive, and expensive, retail advertising campaign, the likes of which IBM had never done before. They were also planning to sell the computers through ComputerLand, which had several hundred stores by then, along with a few other selected outlets such as the Sears Business Centers. The management committee again raised the after-sale support issue. Who was going to uphold IBM's reputation for quality? Would the corporation be expected to fix these tiny machines?

They weren't going to need much fixing, Lowe replied. Look at Apple. Its machines don't need fixing; they're based on semiconductors that don't wear out, he patiently explained. Further, he pointed out, at these prices, no consumer would expect the kind of handholding IBM traditionally had supplied.

Lowe's presentation was a hit, and the project was upgraded to a Product Development Group, which meant the team could have code names and, more important, special funding. Henceforth, the operation was officially called Project Chess, and the machine they were developing—the little computer that would dramatically shift IBM's business future—was called Acorn. Most important, the project came under the direction of IBM's chief executive, Frank Cary. The company's entry into the microcomputer age had the most powerful champion it could have wanted.

Lowe would be denied the glory of ushering the Acorn into the world, however. A few weeks following the presentation, he was offered the job of general manager of the Rochester plant, with 7,000 employees. It was a major step up from his post in Boca Raton, and he had to take it. Upon his departure, many of the guys on the project, especially those in the inner circle, thought they might get the chance to take over. But Lowe had another person in mind: Don Estridge.

IBM's idea of a "wild duck," Estridge, a tall native Floridian, was a veteran of some of IBM's earliest air defense computing systems, where he had cut his teeth as a software systems programmer. Next he took on an abortive minicomputer project called the Series 1. When the software proved to be a failure, much of the blame was directed his way. He eventually bailed out, and moved to Boca, where he took to wearing cowboy boots and generally thumbing his nose at the IBM culture.

Lowe had met him and liked him. Estridge didn't do things by the book, and he didn't care what anyone thought. For an unconventional project like Chess, with its outrageous deadline and "damn the corporation, full steam ahead" attitude, Lowe believed Estridge was the perfect leader. And Lowe was right; Estridge created an us-against-them atmosphere that made his group loyal and totally dedicated. And because he would be reporting directly to Cary, he had clout and was regarded as untouchable.

The hardware was essentially complete by early 1981 (though finetuning would continue until products shipped in August that year). Only the software had to be written. Microsoft's team went to work on the operating system—now called PC-DOS for IBM and MS-DOS if Microsoft could find anyone else to license it—revising and rewriting it. In only a few weeks, Microsoft had a rough version running on the first prototype machine they received from IBM. It was remarkably similar to CP/M. DRI made threatening noises about lawsuits, but Kildall never followed through. He thought there was room in the market for two operating systems. He was wrong, and Gates knew it. His colleague, Ballmer, made sure that PC-DOS was so inexpensive that it could be bundled with the hardware at no extra cost. So when Kildall's new and improved CP/M86, costing $279, arrived on the market about a year after the IBM PC was introduced, it never got off the ground. CP/M never recovered, and within five years it was essentially finished.

The IBM management committee gave the final go-ahead to the product in October 1980. By the end of that year, the Boca team had delivered working prototypes to Microsoft; a few months later they were able to distribute machines to other key software houses. In a flurry of activity, they met the August 1981 deadline with a few days to spare. They named it the IBM Personal Computer, or the IBM PC.

The team had done the impossible. At a company that was hide-bound, resistant to change, and paralyzed by a ten-year antitrust investigation, they had developed an inexpensive computer with software, and were ready to sell it through retail channels, in one year, start to finish. August 12, 1981 was the official release date. The introduction went off without a hitch in New York.

Upon release, the IBM PC's software included a version of VisiCalc; the popular accounting programs from Peachtree Software; BASIC; a game called Microsoft Adventure; and EasyWriter, a word processor that had originally been written for the Apple II. As a bonus, a crude game called Donkey was added; it involved chasing farm animals on-screen and was written by Bill Gates. It would be his last solo effort at commercial software programming. There were also three operating systems available for the machine: PC DOS, was bundled, and free; the other two could be purchased: CP/M at $279, and P-DOS, a PASCAL programming language-based product that had been created at UC San Diego for $299.

IBM's entry into the market had the side effect of legitimizing the world of small computers. Big Blue's costly advertising campaign featured a Charlie Chaplin–like tramp character to demystify the computer for the retail consumer. Until then the consumer microcomputer audience had primarily consisted of engineers and technically skilled hobbyists, who could write their own programs and create games, and who were willing to put up with troubles, inconsistencies, and complexities. The IBM PC made it clear to a new generation of businesspeople that personal computers could be valuable in their work. The IBM name made it credible; it carried with it a reputation of reliability and support.

IBM PC sales gained momentum fast. In a remarkable display of hubris, Apple took out a full-page ad in *The Wall Street Journal* when the PC was announced. Its headline read "Welcome IBM." Computer buyers soon echoed the sentiment. By the end of 1981, IBM had shipped just over 13,000 PCs. But by 1982, the orders poured in and soon backed up. At one point late that year, IBM was turning out 13,000 personal computers per *day,* all from remote Boca Raton, Florida. Production had the whole town jumping. Parts shipments arrived around the clock; as soon as one truck pulled out, another pulled in.

The effect on IBM's finances was profound. Before the IBM PC was introduced the company's share price was 55; in the next two years, it doubled—during a recession in the U.S. economy. With 602 million shares outstanding, the company's market value rose by $36 billion in the first few years after the machine was introduced, totaling $74.25 billion, or one-quarter of the entire market value of all the stocks in the Dow Jones Industrial Average by 1983. Quickly, the company's share of the computer industry's revenues for personal computers grew to 25 percent, equaling about $1 billion, and climbing fast. PC production was ramped up, from about 40,000 in 1981 to more than 400,000 by 1983. Rumors flew that the company had already ordered enough parts to build 2 million machines in 1984.

Not surprisingly, IBM's balance sheet changed. Revenues from mainframe and minicomputer systems dropped to 50 percent by 1984; PCs accounted for another 20 percent; other businesses (office equipment, typewriters, service, etc.) made up the rest. Interestingly, though the PC was great for cash flow, profits were another story: In 1985, fully 75 percent of the company's net income of $6 billion still came from the mainframe—a paradox that led the company to stay focused on the legacy business, with its plush margins, for far too long. The fast-growing small computer market was leading IBM into a new commodity thicket, where competition was fierce, profits were lower, and volumes were enormous. And returns weren't going to be like anything the company was used to.

In all the media hoopla and glory surrounding the IBM PC, one name got lost. Don Estridge had been made company spokesperson for the PC, so he became commonly known as the father of the PC, as the charismatic leader who had been responsible for it all. The corporate PR machine trotted him out. He trimmed his hair. He started acting more straightlaced. He accepted the honors and the kudos

It wasn't long before Lew Eggebrecht began to feel slighted. After all, he had created the machine almost single-handedly. Didn't he deserve some attention?

In the summer of 1982 he had been awarded a $50,000 bonus as the architect of the PC. That constituted only internal recognition, and he wanted his 15 minutes of fame, too. He and another longtime employee started talking about leaving Big Blue and setting up a company to sell peripherals products: boards that would enable the IBM PC to link to IBM's mainframes. This would not be difficult to do, given Eggebrecht's intimate knowledge of the machine. In 1983, while still at IBM, they formed Bridge Technology Inc. Such an undertaking was explicitly prohibited under the terms of the employment agreement all IBMers signed. Everything an employee created while an IBM employee belonged exclusively to IBM, but the two plowed ahead anyway, signing on another partner, a salesman. Their business plan was to create the peripherals products, then supply them to other companies that were already marketing retail products to add on to the IBM PC.

One of these companies was TecMar, based in Cleveland, Ohio. Its founder, Martin Alpert, was a doctor who had been bitten by the PC bug. He had bought two IBM PCs at a Chicago ComputerLand store, then resold them with hard disk systems as add ons. (Those were the days when the only storage was on floppy disks.) He founded TecMar to expand the resale business, and it grew faster than he had expected. So when Eggebrecht and the Bridge Technology group called to offer him their new product that could link PCs with mainframes, he agreed to meet with them. They told him they had more products in the pipeline, and that the "chief architect" of the PC was designing them, which would give them an edge in the marketplace. Was Alpert interested in reselling Bridge products?

Then, before the meeting, Alpert got cold feet. He wondered whether they were offering him trade secrets. Could IBM sue him? Would he lose his valuable but still fledgling business? He agonized over what to do. Finally, he called IBM security and told them about his scheduled meeting with Lew Eggebrecht. IBM's reaction was swift. A group of Big Blue's security agents flew to Cleveland and outfitted Alpert with a tape recorder. On Saturday morning, September 11, 1982, Alpert met with Eggebrecht and his partners, all still employees of IBM. While they were offering him the new communication product, Alpert was taping the conversation.

A few days later Eggebrecht was fired. The rest of the PC division staff, who had no idea of Eggebrecht's sideline, were shocked. At a hastily called division meeting, Estridge wasted no time in letting them know what had transpired. He said, "There was a thief among us. This morning we fired Lew Eggebrecht for trying to sell IBM secrets to a company in Cleveland Ohio."

The engineers, colleagues of Eggebrecht, all with dozens of years at the company were devastated. It was the end of the dream. If Eggebrecht, the finest engineer most of them had ever known, had done this, what did this mean for their future? Although they were on top of the PC industry, with the most successful personal computer of all time, they had just lost the soul of their operation.

To fill the shoes of the legendary Eggebrecht, IBM hired Bill Sydnes, a capable engineering manager, and at first things went well. IBM had another smash success in the spring of 1983, with the next version of the PC, the XT, which had more memory and a hard disk. By 1984, IBM's share of the PC market had risen to what would prove to be its peak—50 percent of worldwide shipments, nearly $5 billion worth of computers sold. The XT cemented IBM's grip on the market. Apple's Lisa computer had just been introduced, but it was regarded as overpriced and underpowered. It was no contest. By the end of the year, IBM was turning out tens of thousands of PC XTs every day in Boca Raton too.

IBM owed its success, in large part, to Don Estridge and his intuitive grasp of the importance of spreadsheets. Estridge, the team's general manager, had bought an Apple II long before he became head of the PC group. Naturally, he kept it at home—no self-respecting IBM employee would be seen with another company's computing machine on his desk. Early on Estridge had become fascinated by the little machine and its spreadsheet software, VisiCalc. The IBM PC version of VisiCalc had never worked as well as it did on the Apple, and so in 1982 Estridge began talking up the idea of a new spreadsheet created specially for the PC. The resulting program was called Lotus 1-2-3, and it helped fuel the IBM PC rocket.

A peculiar kind of investor was drawn to the PC phenomenon in the early 1980s. Encouraged by the seminal electronics investor, Arthur Rock, a new industry had sprung up: venture capital (VC). The idea was to invest early in electronics firms, help build them, and then cash out with spectacular public offerings. A number of these investors were setting up shop along a road that wound alongside the Stanford campus, called Sand Hill Road.

Everyone in the VC community was looking for the next big deal, which presented itself when L.J.Sevin, a former Texas oil wildcatter, and his partner Ben Rosen, a former Wall Street analyst, put up venture capital to fund two products that had been introduced at the 1982 COMDEX show. One was the spreadsheet program Lotus 1-2-3; the other the first IBM PC clone.

Dan Bricklin and Bob Frankston, developers of the first spreadsheet program, VisiCalc, had never patented their work. In fact, they may not have been able to do so in the late seventies, when common wisdom held that software was like a book; that is, copyrightable as to the specific words or instructions, but not as to overall functions.

Dan Fylstra, a friend of the creators of VisiCalc, agreed with them that there was money to be made selling their product. The group decided to keep the programming operation—named Software Arts—separate from the marketing team, called VisiCorp. Fylstra raised about $10 million in venture capital—the most to date for a single project—and had moved VisiCorp's offices to a fancy address in California. He also started buying add-on programs to enhance the features of VisiCalc. One of these enabled rudimentary charts to be created from spreadsheet data, and when Fylstra offered to buy out that company, its founders, businessman Mitch Kapor and programmer Jonathon Sachs, jumped at the chance.

Kapor, a perennial grad student in the academic community of Cambridge and a former transcendental meditation instructor, believed that the only computer platform worth supporting was the new IBM PC. He knew that VisiCalc had been rewritten to run on that system, but was slow. Using the money from the sale of VisiCalc, Kapor and Sachs set about creating a spreadsheet that was even better and that took full advantage of the PC's hardware.

The result was Lotus 1-2-3, the "Lotus" a reference to Kapor's days in the eastern religion subculture, and the "1-2-3" a reference to the three components of the program: spreadsheet, graphics, and database. They designed Lotus 1-2-3 specifically to run only on the IBM PC; then they backed it with a novel marketing plan: target the Forbes 500.

Lotus was released early in 1983 and it stoked the PC fires. The software was originally capable of running only on an actual IBM PC, nothing similar. That dependence on hardware-specific commands meant Kapor and Sachs could produce a very fast operating spreadsheet. But it wasn't long before the program would find a wider base on which to perform.

A trio of Texas Instruments engineers—Rod Canion, Jim Harris, and Bill Murto—had been examining the product specifications for the IBM PC since it first came on the scene, and had realized that only one element of the machine was unique: the BIOS (Basic Input Output System). This was a permanent chip in the circuit that contained the "personality" of the system—essentially the PC's genetic code. It seemed to them that they could devise a way to create another noninfringing version of BIOS by making their chips do exactly what the IBM circuits did, but without using IBM's code.

The procedure they invoked was called reverse engineering, and it entailed viewing the IBM BIOS as a kind of "black box" with commands going in and other commands coming out. They believed that as long as they didn't copy the IBM directions *inside* the box, yet produced the same functions *outside* the box, it would not constitute a breach of intellectual property. In this way, they could manufacture a 100 percent compatible, IBM PC clone. And they were sure they could do it more cheaply, and thus sell the machine for less than IBM's price, thereby grabbing a niche that IBM so far was ignoring: portable PCs.

Sevin-Rosen, the Texas-based venture capital firm, put up the money and was willing to risk litigation. As a result, the first COMPAQ machines were delivered to the same stores where the IBM PCs were sold, in time for the Christmas selling season in 1982. The portable "clones" sold extraordinarily well—though weighing in at about 30 pounds, they were more luggable than portable.

COMPAQ also succeeded in dodging the infringement bullet, which in turn inspired another set of hackers in Boston who also cloned the BIOS. They called their company Phoenix Technology and soon they were selling a version. Suddenly the door was wide open for others to copy the IBM PC. All they had to do was combine the new BIOS, an Intel microprocessor, off-the-shelf drives, and memory, along with a few straightforward engineering components soldered onto a simple PC board, and they had a PC clone!

By 1983, the market had inexorably shifted. The IBM PC platform had indisputably become the standard bearer. COMPAQs were available, followed shortly by cheaper no-name garage clones. All of them were 100 percent compatible with IBM PC software. And Lotus 1-2-3 ran on all of them, and topped the software best-seller charts, where it would stay for years.

But no good deed goes unpunished, especially in a bureaucracy like IBM. In the wake of its success, corporate IBM wanted the PC division's wings clipped. A new division was formed around the PC: Entry Systems Division (ESD). IBM promoted Estridge to run the by-now 10,000-member group. To help manage it, legions of IBM middle managers arrived on the scene. It seems it never occurred to corporate executives that the division was successful precisely because they were separate from the weight of Big Blue's bureaucracy.

Estridge's accomplishments were being noted outside IBM as well. Apple's Steve Jobs tried to seduce him to run his company before he latched onto John Sculley. But Estridge couldn't abide Jobs, and he wanted to stay in Florida where his teenage daughters were attending high school. But things were changing. Estridge's group wasn't the same small team whose members were motivated by a passion for computing. Now it was a big corporate IBM division with Estridge as its rising star. Then the company took some missteps.

Initially, Estridge and his cohorts strongly backed the XT. But then they were distracted in an effort to expand the franchise (After all, if the PC was a great success in the business arena, wouldn't a simpler, stripped-down version be just as likely to succeed in the home market?) So IBM designed the PCjr., a kind of PC-light. Designed by Eggebrecht's successor, Bill Sydnes, the concept sounded reasonable—to create a little brother that had the potential to be upgraded to a full PC, sell it through discount stores like Wal-Mart, and get an IBM product into every home in America.

The PCJunior was a disaster. Delivered in the fall of 1983 it was too expensive (at $1,500 it wasn't much cheaper than a full-size PC-compatible clone), and in its final form, could not be upgraded to a full PC. It also sported a keyboard whose little clicking keypads—called the Chicklet keyboard after the gum—made it impossible for adult hands to use comfortably. IBM only sold an estimated 250,000 units, and PCjr. was discontinued a year or so later, having generated only an estimated $150 million in revenues for the $46 billion company. Estridge was blamed for the failure. Maybe he wasn't presidential material after all.

IBM's response was to send more finance people to install tighter fiscal controls on the ESD operation.

In contrast, the PC and the XT continued to destroy the competition. In 1984, IBM was responsible for nearly 50 percent of personal computer sales in the world. Apple and all the clones carved up the rest of the market. Eventually, Estridge and his team were forgiven for the PCjr—and they had another machine up their sleeve.

The PC AT—for Advanced Technology—was due to be released midway through 1984; it was the next-generation machine for loyal IBM customers. Based on Intel's latest microprocessor—the 16-bit 80286— it was a much more powerful personal computer. A year earlier, in order to ensure a steady supply of the essential microprocessors, IBM had bought 12 percent of Intel's stock, with an option to increase the stake to 20 percent. Big Blue paid $250 million, more than one-quarter of Intel's total revenues—$900 million—for 1982. At that point microprocessors accounted for approximately one-third of $800 million of Intel's revenues. As one of the terms of the arrangement Intel also granted IBM the right to modify the microprocessors in-house. Remarkably IBM, which had the world's most advanced semiconductor plants, never took advantage of this opportunity.

Unfortunately, the first PC AT hard drives IBM shipped turned out to be defective. The result was massive holdups in delivery. So many failed hard disks were sent back that they filled a barge that a local Boca company later sank offshore.

Though it was not one of the PC division's shining moments, the PC AT ultimately became a marketplace success. Faced with competition from COMPAQ and the first of what promised to become a tidal wave of clones, IBM's management searched for a way to differentiate their machines from everyone else's. Estridge's brilliant idea: to buy every 80286 microprocessor Intel could make. His reasoning was that if IBM had them all, no one else could turn out a machine based on the chip. It was a classic IBM solution. But because he was thinking like Big Blue, Estridge didn't think far enough ahead: Once Intel started ramping up production, it would not only be able to drop the price of the 80286, but it would be able to improve the chip's speed. Worse, it turned out that the 80286 microprocessor had been a poorly designed chip to begin with. Even Intel scrapped it and went off in a whole new direction for its next version. So IBM actually paid premium prices and bought hundreds of thousands of relatively slow processors; when the cloners did start introducing knock-offs about a year later, they had faster and cheaper processors, and IBM's machines looked clumsy.

The clones were capturing major market share from IBM by early 1985. From its estimated high of 50 percent the previous year, IBM's share of all PC sales fell to less than 30 percent 18 months later. By then, the PC market was worth $35 billion worldwide, and the cloners were shipping more units—3.6 million machines in 1986 versus IBM's 3 million. Worse, average selling prices had tumbled from around $2,250 when IBM was dominant, to just over $1,500 a year later. This was a massive erosion of base, even as IBM struggled to keep up with demand for the new and more powerful PC ATs. COMPAQ grew exponentially; by 1985 its revenues were $503.9 million. More astonishingly, COMPAQ was able to double its pretax margins from 4.4 percent to 8.7 percent between 1983 and 1985, while IBM was watching its own margins tumble.

But the figures were somewhat misleading; IBM didn't lose its advantage completely on the PC AT. The machines featured an add-on feature, called a bus, that could both accommodate earlier products and provide enough power to expand the computer's capabilities. This feature came to be called the AT bus, and it was a very popular component. Once the kinks were worked out, IBM's PC AT was a success. On the face of it, the Boca Entry Systems Division wasn't doing badly either. In 1984, the group charted sales of more than $4 billion, putting it squarely in the top 100 companies in America. But serious problems remained.

Just before the AT came out, Estridge declared there would be no more 8088 development efforts—effectively IBM was going to migrate its loyal customer base to its 80286 line, and leave the lower-priced PC and XT markets to the cloners. The decision was hotly disputed, but to no avail. As of summer 1984, IBM placed all its bets on the new PC AT architecture. It relinquished a robust market sector for the original cheaper and less powerful PC style computers for the clone makers to exploit.

Another critical development, which took place outside of IBM, would serve to strengthen the clone business. Out in Silicon Valley, an ambitious marketing manager by the name of Gordon Campbell had learned that the venture capitalists who had financed his chipmaking startup had lost their faith in him. He was ousted from his firm, Seeq. But he wasn't down long before he came up with a flash of American entrepreneurial genius: Why not design an IBM PC-AT chip set—clone chips—and have other manufacturers produce it? The chips would be designed to allow any team of engineers to create PC AT-compatible computers for low cost.

The concept—to design a chip, then contract with semiconductor fabrication (fab) plants to make the part—came to be called "fabless." It freed superstar electronics designers from having to work at big manufacturing companies, and would eventually unleash an enormous amount of creative energy in the field.

This was what Gordon Campbell pioneered at his new company, Chips and Technology, which was financed through a consortium of Japanese PC chip makers. The chips were ready for market in 1985, and the company's set of five chips cost $48. They had the capability to replace 63 chips on IBM's PC AT motherboard. A long line of cloners snapped up the product. By combining it with a few other key parts and an 80286 microprocessor from Intel, anyone could now build an IBM AT knock-off for a much lower price than Big Blue's. Taiwan's two biggest contract manufacturers—Multitech and Mitac—shipped more than $700 million worth of PCs to the United States in 1986, and South Korean companies like Leading Edge, GoldStar, and Samsung surged into the business as well. So even as IBM's PC AT sales were skyrocketing, the scene was set for another act.

It opened with the transfer of Don Estridge to corporate headquarters. It was becoming apparent that there were troubles with product development in Boca—both the PCjr and the PC AT had been hampered by mistakes in execution—and the clones were making major inroads into IBM's newest business. The company "promoted" Estridge to vice president of Worldwide Manufacturing, and brought back Bill Lowe to run the Entry Systems Division.

One of Lowe's first moves was to try to renegotiate his original deal with Bill Gates. DOS, the operating system for the PC, was by now sadly underpowered. It was time for a new operating system, and IBM wanted to enter a joint development agreement with Microsoft for it. Lowe was smart. He knew that one reason the market had grown so fast was because of the common operating system that everyone used. As far as DOS was concerned, Gates had the right to sell the program to any other companies he wanted. Lowe intended the new operating system to have two versions: one for IBM and one for everyone else, which

Microsoft could sell. Of course, IBM's would be better; and IBM, not Microsoft, would be in charge of who got what.

It was a tough negotiation. Gates and Ballmer offered Microsoft's about-to-be released overlay for DOS—Windows—as a basis for the new operating system, but IBM rejected it. They also urged IBM to create the new operating system for the next generation of Intel micro-processors, but IBM refused. In 1985, IBM was still fat and arro-gant, believing it owned the PC market, even as that dominance was crumbling.

The two companies battered out an agreement. For Gates, the deal essentially put all the cards in his hands. First, in the terms of the arrangement Microsoft got all revenues from the sales of DOS, so that gave Gates a major incentive to continue to sell DOS to all the clone makers. Second, he had every reason to develop Windows because he would own it entirely. Conversely, he was disinclined to finish the new IBM operating system—soon to be called OS/2, it would work only on IBM machines. Microsoft was paid for its work as it went along, but Microsoft wouldn't make much money from it once IBM started hand-ing out the new operating system with its machines. For Gates, it was a brilliantly negotiated contract but for IBM it was a disaster.

The scene that opened with Don Estridge's transfer ended in tragedy; he and his wife were killed in a plane crash. While the company mourned, IBM became more dependent on Gates than ever.

The future of the PC line was in Bill Lowe's hands. He wasn't up to the test. Through the mid- and late 1980s, IBM, its management and its technical staff, would make a series of poor business decisions that would destroy its powerful market position and, in essence, hand the personal computer business to Microsoft.

Perhaps things would have turned out differently if the Justice Department had gone ahead with its massive antitrust action against the company and split it up, the way AT&T had been divided in 1984. Instead, IBM now had two mutually exclusive businesses to manage: mainframes and PCs. And instead of cutting loose the PC business to compete on its own, IBM management tried to integrate it into the big picture. And part of that picture was an evolving set of software stan-dards that was going to define everything that IBM sold. The concept was called Systems Application Architecture (SAA).

The idea, which came from an IBM manager named Earl Wheeler, didn't look bad on paper: it was an attempt to enable all IBM machines to "talk" to one another, by means of a mainframe-centric software interface that would be common to all of the company's machines. (The concept was later integrated with Windows, where it was called an Applications Programming Interface, API, and made to work, by Microsoft.) To be sure, the plan made sense to an IBM that was finally free from the antitrust strictures that formerly had hobbled it. But in a personal computer universe where every user's needs were different, and where graphical user interfaces (like Microsoft's Windows, Visi-Corp's VisiOn, and Digital Research Intergalactic's GEM) were the up-and-coming feature, it made no sense at all.

The SAA plan was an attempt by Lowe and his boss, Mike Armstrong, to reduce the company's dependence on Microsoft. In 1986, Microsoft had gone public, and Bill Gates, at age 30, was a mega-millionaire. Worse was that many of the legions of young Microsoft programmers had also become paper millionaires. For those in the trenches at IBM, who had given their all for stability and years of regular paychecks, it was almost inconceivable—especially since they believed that Microsoft had succeeded only because of IBM. Bill Gates and Microsoft had become IBM's nemesis, and so Big Blue wanted to cut the apron strings tying it to Microsoft.

OS/2 development went forward in fits and starts, as the relationship between the upstarts from Seattle and the IBMers in Boca went from bad to worse. At the same time, IBM struggled with SAA, trying to figure out a way to integrate the PC machines into the corporation's main lines of business. And to their dismay, they did not have the luxury of time to study the problem. By 1986, the clones were capturing significant market share from Big Blue. Compounding the financial downturn was that IBM had stopped leasing mainframes in 1980, and the last of the four-year contracts were now finished. A new line of mainframe computers—the Sierra—was introduced and promptly rejected as too expensive and not powerful enough. The line never met sales expectations.

A new president, John Akers, took over just as the downturn began. Revenues rose only 1 percent in 1985, and earnings were soft. By the beginning of the next year, when the company was counting on a 15 percent unit rise in PC shipments, Akers had to scale that estimate back, admitting that the dollar value of the PC business would be flat. In the second quarter of 1986, IBM announced an earnings disappointment: income was down 8 percent from the previous year, to $1.3 billion even though revenues rose 12 percent to $12.3 billion.

Akers and the IBM board panicked. To get cash fast, they sold the Intel stock the company had bought three years earlier for $400 million. IBM's stake had been increased to 20 percent, and the stock was now worth $625 million; the sale helped to make 1987 look better on the books. Not only was this a bad investment decision—had IBM held onto its 20 percent share of Intel, it would have been worth about $25 billion ten years later—but it also removed the last opportunity IBM had to control the PC business.

In 1985, Intel was led by Andy Grove, a tough Hungarian émigré. Grove had taken the company out of the memory business, realizing it was a losing battle that would never again feed high margins to the corporate coffers. Microprocessors, he felt, were different. By virtue of IBM's choosing Intel microprocessors in 1980, and the fact that the IBM PC had been so successful, meant that Intel was now in the cat bird seat. The company had a very profitable microprocessor franchise.

More to the point, Grove had not forgotten that previously IBM had forced him to second-source the 8088, 8086, and 80286 microprocessors, thus giving up exclusivity in exchange for IBM's business and investment. Now he had a new idea. Intel's next-generation microprocessor, the 80386, was much better than the previous ones—in fact, it was an entirely new design that could support several later generations of upgrades. Intel had originally provided second-source production agreements to several major competitors, including Advanced Micro Devices (AMD) and Nippon Electric Company (NEC). But with the 80386, Intel decided not to license the chip to anyone.

An enormous legal battle ensued. AMD claimed that its original deal with Intel gave it the rights to all "members of the chip family"; Intel disagreed. The battle raged for years. Eventually, a split decision was handed down: Intel lost on the 80386, but won on subsequent products (such as the 80486 and Pentium class microprocessors). Though AMD and others were eventually able to reverse-engineer the more advanced chips and make clones, Intel had at least a year's head start each time it improved its microprocessors. By the 1990s, the company had increased its share of the worldwide microprocessor market to well over 80 percent and was the dominant company in the PC hardware business. Had IBM not sold its stock in Intel, it would have had a hand in Intel's burgeoning marketshare and its development of the microprocessor.

In the meantime, Lowe and IBM had dug themselves into a hole with the SAA strategy, against a backdrop of worsening fiscal years. When IBM decided in favor of the older 80286 microprocessor over the newer and radically different but improved 80386 family, Grove chose to work with COMPAQ and got the new 80386-based PC to market almost a year before IBM had anything similar on the market. The mantle of technological leadership passed to COMPAQ that day. No longer was IBM in the driver's seat. Between 1985 and 1988, COMPAQ's revenues had quadrupled, from $500 million to $2.1 billion. Better yet, earnings rose sixfold, reaching $249 million.

IBM became obsessed with cutting off the clones. Its PC division came up with a strategy that sounded good in theory. Change the hardware just enough to obsolete the old PCs, yet maintain several features as proprietary to prevent them being copied; supply a new operating system; and, finally, convince the software companies to write new versions of their programs for the new product line. The new hardware, designed by the ESD team, was called the PS/2, and the entire line was based on the 80286, so that existing programs, disks, and files would work. But there would also be a world of new features available only on the new machines.

This plan might have worked if IBM's OS/2 hadn't been so ponderous under the 80286 microprocessor. But the joint development was a disaster. Driven by COMPAQ, the marketplace was already buying up 386 machines and IBM was trying to sell a new series based on a microprocessor that was at least seven years old.

IBM had also made the mistake of radically changing the add-on architecture of its PCs, so that the PS/2 machines were now incompatible with products designed for the previous slots. This angered its numerous corporate customers who had peripheral products that fit into the older buses. Vendors had spent millions in research and development creating add-on boards. Buying an IBM PS/2 meant throwing out all of that money. The resistance started quickly and built.

Timing also played a part in the PS/2's failure. Running OS/2, the IBM/Microsoft-designed operating system, required large quantities of memory. As the PS/2 line with OS/2 was being introduced, the world was in the throes of a memory chip shortage, occasioned in large part by U.S. sanctions against Japanese chipmakers, and in smaller part by Intel pulling out of the chip business. The price of memory chips skyrocketed. Running OS/2 required at least 2 megabytes of memory, at a cost of more than $2,000 in 1987—on top of the price of the computers, which started at $3,000. Compared to the clones, generally priced at around $2,000, OS/2 was prohibitively expensive. Furthermore, to make DOS software work, Microsoft had built a clunky workaround called the "compatibility box," which was unwieldy and never worked properly; there were very few applications for OS/2, and nothing compelling enough to justify the minimum investment of $5,000 when a perfectly good 80386-based clone, running thousands of programs available for DOS, could be had for half of that price.

Still, IBM's PC business might have survived but for one more poor business decision. Lowe announced that upon introduction of the PS/2, IBM would stop making the PC AT. Just as Estridge had done before him, Lowe abandoned a viable market too early. IBM was caught trying to reorient the PC market all by itself. The company's leaders simply didn't understand that IBM could no longer dictate to America's businesses which machines to buy—especially since the benefits it offered were proprietary, in the face of a much bigger, more robust, and cheaper PC-compatible market. By the time the dust cleared a few years later, IBM's market share had plummeted to less than 10 percent of the worldwide PC market. Financially, the company was deeply wounded (some thought, at the time, mortally).

Microsoft and IBM stopped working together on the new operating system in 1991. The divorce led to a marketing war between the two; it was Windows versus OS/2. IBM proved no match for the nimbler, more aggressive Microsoft. Ultimately Gates and company launched a new operating system project—called Windows NT (for New Technology)— that contained many of the features that OS/2 had intended to offer. Freed from IBM, and with more powerful hardware from Intel, Microsoft made it work.

IBM would recover somewhat in the mid-1990s, and be able to vie for second place in PC market share—ironically, by selling PC-compatibles. But before it regained its footing, the company went through some very tough years.

Today, the engineers in Boca are gone. The buildings that once turned out 13,000 PCs a day stand empty, except for the skateboard ramps built by kids on the loading docks. The administrative center has likewise been abandoned; and the swamps, with their kudzu vines and mangroves, are once again taking over.

Paul Allen and Bill Gates, co-founders of Microsoft, in October 1981.

CHAPTER 9

>———◆———<

Hard Core
Windows

Americans knew what the personal computer was by 1983. Time Maga-
zine even made the personal computer the "Man of the Year." It was no
longer regarded as something esoteric that only a handful of electronics
geeks could understand. Many people had seen a personal computer,
even though by that date less than 5 percent of the country used one,
and less than 1 percent owned one. Most of the public agreed that PCs
would play a significant role in business, although in exactly what
capacity few could say.

A new industry had emerged: electronics for the consumer. Rapid
price decreases made products like VHS video, Sony's Walkman, and the
compact disc affordable for most consumers; even the telephone experi-
enced rising popularity, especially in the wake of the AT&T breakup in
1984. For the average Joe, though, computers were far too difficult to
consider using. The electric typewriter was still the country's preferred
business machine. A computer screen flashing its C: prompt was just too
intimidating.

But the widespread availability of software programs would
change the personal computer into a consumer force. Operating sys-
tem standards like CP/M, then DOS, made it possible to sell the same
program to thousands, (and later millions) of users. The software busi-
ness charted incredible margins: 60, 70 percent was not atypical for a
software company with a hit program. Essentially, all the costs of cre-
ating a software program were in the design and in getting the first
copy out the door; after that, it was mostly profit. This generated enor-
mous cash flows, and created a booming market for workers highly
skilled in the new technology.

By the early 1980s at least half a dozen very creative software programs had made it to market, with the promise of many more. Each generation of software was better and easier to use, and most of the original programmer-entrepreneurs became fabulously wealthy. Success, however, tended to dampen their competitive fires, and as the decade continued, the staying power of the early leaders wavered—in everyone, that is, but the kid who was born with a million-dollar trust fund: Bill Gates.

❀   ❀   ❀

BILL GATES WAS 27 YEARS OLD in 1982, and he was scared. As the young president of Microsoft, and the software programmer behind the first widely distributed version of the BASIC programming language for microcomputers, he was scared that he was about to be left behind just as the game was beginning. His concerns were well-founded. Apple was more successful than Microsoft, and had an as yet unreleased graphically oriented duo of machines: the Lisa and Macintosh. Lotus was poised to become the biggest software company thanks to its hit spreadsheet program for the IBM PC: Lotus 1-2-3. COMPAQ had just introduced a 100 percent compatible clone that promised to greatly expand the already fast-growing personal computer business. Of all the companies that were playing in the game, Microsoft seemed to be one of the dullest. It was hamstrung by its ties to the IBM PC, and selling primarily esoteric programming languages.

But that was about to change. Bill Gates' youthful appearance belied the ferocity of his competitive nature. He looked younger than he was. His hair was lank and unkempt; dandruff followed him everywhere. His glasses—framed in plastic—were often smudged. In short, he looked the least likely of the budding tycoons in the computer game. He was a mousy rich kid, a boy who had never had to worry about where the rent was coming from. His grandmother had left him a million-dollar trust fund, and his dad had bought him his first house, a $900,000 mansion-cum-bachelor pad. He was the kind of kid that many people alternately like or loathe. He was smarter than everyone else and, he knew it.

To Gates, business *was* a game, a war of the intellect and the will, one that he was determined to win. In a business that attracted opportunists and wannabes, he played not for fun, but for keeps. His competitors rarely realized, until too late, that Microsoft's copying their innovations wasn't a mark of flattery, but incipient murder.

Gates and the other wunderkind of the personal computer age, Steve Jobs at Apple, shared a penetrating and uncompromising personality. Both were quick to judge; both shot from the hip; both could be insensitive to the feelings of others. Though born the same year, 1955, they came from diametrically opposite backgrounds. Jobs, an orphan, had been raised in a blue-collar machinist's home. Gates was the grandson of the owner of one of Seattle's largest banks. Jobs had charisma, and seduced the media, but ultimately lost the company he cofounded. Gates seemed an also-ran, a laughingstock, socially inept and creatively uninspiring, but he persevered until his company bested both Apple and IBM, and he became the world's richest person.

There were two other differences between Gates and Jobs, differences that would prove crucial in explaining how two young men with such similar personalities could end up with such different fates. Jobs was charismatic and self-assured, he was no programmer. Granted, he knew a lot about the technology and could converse with the most technically literate, but he wasn't an engineer. What he had was style, lots of style. On the flip side, Gates was a true technical geek. He could write code and knew what went on in the heart of the machine. Computers, to Gates, were home turf. He had plenty of substance, no style.

So though both had a passion for computers, they differed widely in their personal approaches to managing programmers. Gates would berate a programmer only to offer constructive criticism. His input addressed only the project at hand; it rarely crossed into the personal. Conversely, Jobs could never hold himself back, and since he really couldn't offer any technical help as to how to make the changes he wanted, more often than not he resorted to emotional tirades, which had the effect of wounding the target rather than encouraging him to improve. In his wake Jobs left dozens of angry and hurt colleagues. For sure, Gates was every bit as intense, but his critiques—filled with words like "random," "nonlinear," and "stupid"—were never taken personally. Gates was uncompromising, but he wasn't unfair.

Because of Jobs' technical incompetence, he believed the computer's hardware to be its crucial component, not understanding that the machine was essentially irrelevant and that it was the content, the software, that really counted. Gates harbored no such misconceptions. As early as 1981, he was talking about software as the reason consumers preferred one machine over another. Jobs' myopia contributed to Apple's downfall. Even though Apple had better software, it ultimately allowed Microsoft to use its ideas on the PC platform without much resistance because Apple believed that the hardware mattered more. This was a crucial mistake.

The other big difference between Jobs and Gates had to do with their respective attitudes toward ownership. Originally, Gates owned 64 percent of Microsoft (which at current valuation would be worth approximately $125 billion). He and his first partner Paul Allen had agreed on a 60–40 split when the company was launched in Albuquerque in 1975; but by the time they actually signed the agreement a year later, Gates had negotiated his stake up a few points, while the softer-spoken, less aggressive Allen had lost some of his. It was one of the first demonstrations of the unremitting and overpowering force of the Gates' negotiating prowess. Whereas for many 21-year-olds, a few percentage points wouldn't make much difference, for Bill Gates every percentage point was worth the effort.

By 1982, when Microsoft had incorporated, Gates' share had diluted to just over 50 percent, but it was still a majority position. Today he owns 25 percent of the company, a stake worth $51 billion. From day one, Microsoft was, and remains, Gates' company in almost every respect. In contrast, Jobs never owned more than 15 percent of Apple, which meant he was unable to control the board; so when things got tough in the mid-80s, it was Jobs who was ousted.

Both rising stars of the personal computer industry had been involved in business from their high school days. But even then their differences were striking. Jobs had established an illegal, door-to-door business selling so-called blue boxes (for circumventing long-distance telephone billing systems) that his friend Steve Wozniak built in his dorm room. At best it was a marginal, countercultural business; at worst, it was fraud. In contrast, Gates—for all his family wealth and privilege, the private school, the trust fund, his parents' position in society— started several computer consulting businesses.

It was at Lakeside High School that Gates and a big bear of a boy named Paul Allen became fast friends. Allen was two years older but always deferred to Gates. From the moment the private school installed a computer terminal, Allen and Gates became inseparable, and most of their time together was spent in front of a computer screen.

Many of the Gates traits that would later be almost legendary first came to light in the ugly little closet that doubled as a computer room at Lakeside. There, Gates would work late into the night, often falling asleep under the desks. When he woke up, he would immediately return to writing programming code. (Even as early as the seventh and eight grades he had exhibited a single-mindedness that was regarded as extraordinary.)

Besides Allen, Gates had another sidekick, Kent Evans, who shared two qualities with Gates that Allen lacked: Evans was fearless, and he was more fascinated by the business possibilities of computers than the technology itself. Evans treated the Lakeside programmers club as a small business, rechristening it the Lakeside Programmers Group, or LPG. He soon brought in programming contracts for the new partnership. (LPG was the only endeavor in which Bill Gates agreed to an equal share in a business with anyone else. When they formed the small company, Gates and Evans each received 4/11ths of the profits; Paul Allen got 1/11th; and another programmer, who later became one of Microsoft's first employees, got the rest.)

Initially, the LPG group was able to get free computer time on a local DEC computer in exchange for ferreting around in the code and finding bugs. Then, when LPG was disbanded, another firm hired the team to create a payroll program. At the time, Gates and Evans were all of 15. The bigger company tried to renege on some of the terms of the deal, figuring they could get away with it because of the programmers' youth. But Gates and Evans promptly headed over to Gates' father's law office and requested that he write a letter demanding that things be put right. For the first time, Bill Gates learned the importance of sweating the details in a contract, and of holding the cosigner to their end of the deal.

Gates and Evans were inseparable. But just before the end of their junior year, Evans was killed in a fall during an outing with a mountaineering class. Gates became distraught. To give him a change of scenery, his parents pulled strings to get him a summer job in Washington D.C. as a congressional page. He was already on the lookout for a way to make a buck. While in D.C., he happened to see the press conference at which Thomas Eagleton, George McGovern's original choice for running mate, admitted he had undergone electroshock therapy. When Eagleton pulled out, the 16-year-old Gates decided to corner the market on McGovern-Eagleton buttons. How much money he made is a matter of debate, but the young gambler was already showing his colors. Someone nicknamed him "Trey," a card shark's term for three of a kind. His extraordinary intellect made it easy for him to calculate the odds and remember the cards already played in a game of poker, or to win the classic Japanese game of strategy, Go. But he had trouble with chess—not because he was unable to anticipate moves, but because his aggressive instincts forced him to attack, attack, and attack. Paul Allen would simply outwait him, and often win.

When Gates returned to Seattle after his stint as page in D.C., he formed another business with Allen and a couple of friends from Lakeside. Called Traf-O-Data, the company used an early Intel microprocessor to analyze traffic flows on Seattle streets. The company's equipment never worked very well however, and it would turn out to be Paul Allen's and Bill Gates' first, and essentially last, effort at creating hardware.

At about the same time, the software for a TRW project to automate and computerize the power grid in the state of Washington ran into trouble. Somehow Allen's and Gates' names came up as the whizkids who had written debugging programs for several local companies. The pair was hired. While at TRW, they used the big computers to simulate the small Traf-O-Data computer, and so learned how to write programs for small computers. At barely 18 and still in school, Gates was making $30,000 a year. He started telling friends that he wanted to be a millionaire by the time he was 25. (And he was, 310 times over.)

The job lasted until Gates went off to Harvard. By that time, the key components that would make up the future software king were already well in place: He was fascinated by computers; he had the makings of a tough and aggressive businessman; he was willing to risk his own money to make a significant profit. Finally, and perhaps most important, there was his competitive streak.

In fact, Gates had been raised on competition. His whole family was competitive. One friend recalls, "They played rochambeau [a game of rock, paper, scissors] to decide who did the dishes every night." His grandmother had been a college basketball star, and was a card game fanatic. Most nights, the family played cards or Hangman after dinner. Today, the Gates family games have evolved into an elaborate Microsoft annual event called the MicroGames. One software entrepreneur recalls beating Gates in a table tennis match. Hours later, after most of the guests had departed, Gates turned to him, genuinely angry that he had lost. "You made me look really bad in front of all those people," he yelled. Bill Gates, the world's wealthiest man, was smarting from the humiliation of losing a ping-pong game in public.

Perhaps Gates' competitive streak grew wider than most to make up for his appearance. He was small and skinny, with a high-pitched voice. A left-hander, he became adept at seemingly inconsequential accomplishments like leaping out of garbage cans in one jump, or over benches from a stationary start. But the size of his intellect was never an issue. He had an exceptional gift for doing math in his head and a near photographic memory. Many years later, he would delight in repeating the license plate numbers of many of Microsoft's hundreds of staffers.

His combination of computer skills and business acumen, plus his ferocious desire to win, might have led many to believe he would excel at Harvard. Instead, college was the first crisis of his life. At Harvard, Gates was just one of many bright kids. For the first time in his life he couldn't ace a class just by showing up for the exam. During his freshman year, Gates managed only a B average, despite having scored a perfect 800 on the math part of his college admissions test.

Desperately unhappy, he nonetheless returned to school for the first semester of his sophomore year. But he began to cut classes regularly and became a fixture in a floating high-stakes poker game in his dorm. Then one night, he met another undergrad who would have as great an impact on him as his old high school friend Paul Allen. Steve Ballmer was the opposite of the introverted and unhappy Gates. Big, loud, and boisterous, Ballmer was a social lion, the manager of the football team, but he was also a math whiz. The friendship was cemented when the two went out to catch a late night showing of *A Clockwork Orange.* From that point, Ballmer took Gates under his wing and introduced him around. As a result, Gates was accepted into a social club at Harvard. But, always awkward and inept, he remained the odd man out. Fortunately for Gates, Paul Allen had dropped out of college and moved to Boston. One day Allen rushed over to show Gates the most recent copy of *Popular Electronics*. On the cover was a picture of the Altair, the first microcomputer. Immediately, the pair decided to write a computer language to work on this new machine. Only one problem: They didn't have a computer.

Somehow they got their hands on a detailed specification sheet for the 8080 microprocessor from Intel, and Allen began to write a software program that would "act" like the microprocessor. Using the equipment at the Harvard computing center, they ran a simulation; Gates cobbled together a rudimentary version of BASIC, a simple programming language that had been created at Dartmouth University to teach students the principles of computer software. Because of its academic roots, BASIC was in the public domain, and was widely known by software engineers.

A few months later, when they had it in working order, Allen flew to Albuquerque to demonstrate the program to MITS, the company behind Altair. MITS accepted the Allen-Gates design. Allen stayed on, to be followed by Gates at the end of the school year, 1975. They served as the independent software arm of MITS, and established themselves as a company called Micro-Soft.

Their royalties from MITS eventually totaled $180,000. Buoyed by their early success, Gates attempted to break the contract he and Allen had with MITS, claiming that Ed Roberts the MITS head hadn't extended his best efforts to license BASIC to other computer makers. That was, in fact, true. Roberts had wanted to make the language proprietary to his machines. But Roberts had his own gripe: he didn't feel that Gates and Allen improved or debugged the language, which he had hired a number of programmers, including Gates, to do. The dispute was eventually arbitrated, and in what would become a trend, Gates won. Thereafter, Micro-Soft (they soon dropped the hyphen) licensed its language to all comers, and began to build its business.

From the start, Microsoft was a programmer's company; its products were primarily programming languages and software programs. Microsoft made a successful stab at the consumer market with Typing Tutor, a keyboard program bought from outside software programmers. It also marketed a program called Adventure, a text-based game originally developed at MIT and then rewritten for Microsoft by Gordon Letwin, a programming whiz who joined Microsoft in 1978. It was possibly the last time in Microsoft's history when a staffer was given a royalty deal, and the last time, too, when an individual programmer would be publicly identified with a Microsoft product. The names of individual programmers don't appear on any MS product.

But it would be a while before the name Microsoft meant anything to most Americans. In 1982, the company wasn't publicly traded; its revenues that year were $32 million. Its products were buried inside a computer's operating system or in its programming languages.

To the casual observer, the business landscape for the personal computer was confusing. While the new IBM-PC was doing well in the market, there were still several other competitive models available. None were fully compatible with each other, and Microsoft was busily selling each hardware maker slightly different versions of its operating system, DOS, and its programming language, BASIC.

Microsoft's contract with IBM to create an operating system had given the small company, now based in Seattle, some legitimacy. However, under the terms of the deal, money didn't come in when IBM gave away DOS. Microsoft's money was made in selling programming languages and tools for other software companies that wanted to create software for the IBM PC. And Microsoft desperately needed the business. Gary Kildall, the man behind the world's most successful software operating system CP/M was making noises about suing Microsoft. There might have been strong grounds to do so: Microsoft had bought the guts of a clone of CP/M from a local Seattle programmer who would later admit that he had always intended to copy the operating system. The commands and structure of the two systems were identical.

A few months earlier in 1982, on the evening after Seattle's SeaFirst day, an annual summer event, Kildall and a couple of his lieutenants met with Gates and Ballmer at a Seattle bar. Though Kildall was furious about what he regarded as Microsoft's plagiarism of CP/M, he couldn't bring himself to broach the subject with Gates. Kildall thought it was ugly to threaten a lawsuit, when his competitors were so young, and he thought Gates was really only interested in programming languages. So instead of threatening, or even discussing his grounds for legal action, the two had a rather noncommittal conversation. Ultimately, Kildall decided that the best way to compete with Gates was to develop a better version of his operating system, along with a better programming language. But his heart was never in it; it was hard to imagine that the kids in Seattle could really compete with him.

At the time, Kildall's Digital Research Incorporated (DRI) was one of the biggest personal computer software companies in the world, reporting $6 million in sales in 1981. Kildall had a personal fortune worth $15 million. Microsoft by contrast at the time was a minnow with no sign it would transform into a shark. Kildall's complacency, however, proved to be his downfall. He refused to play ball with the IBM troops when they came hunting for an operating system. Gates on the other hand wanted to work with IBM and had no compunction about invading Kildall's territory.

For Microsoft, in its early days, winning business with IBM was crucial for its survival. And Gates understood that whoever controlled the dominant operating system would control the future. A computer couldn't start without an operating system, so whichever competitor won the battle to control the dominant system would control the marketplace. To fulfill their end of the IBM deal, Gates and Ballmer licensed a CP/M clone from a local Seattle programmer for $10,000 upfront, with the rights to resell it to other companies (Microsoft paid an additional $15,000 for each sale). They then turned around and licensed the program to IBM for an adaptation fee of $200,000, and an advance of $400,000 against royalties of $1 per machine.

Not bad; but what Gates really wanted to do was tie Microsoft's BASIC programming language—the same product that launched the company years earlier—to the PC. So the agreement was amended to make royalties unnecessary as long as BASIC was inherent to the IBM computer. It was a superb agreement for Gates and Ballmer because it allowed Microsoft to resell DOS (its operating system based on CP/M), while prohibiting IBM from doing so. From 1980 to 1990 Gates made hundreds of millions doing just that. Moreover, when IBM wanted third-party software developed for the machine, Microsoft had the inside track because its BASIC program was on the system. When the PC began to look like a runaway best-seller, Kildall began to rue his intransigence with IBM. Kildall's own operating system became irrelevant. And though DOS looked and acted remarkably similar to Kildall's CP/M, Microsoft had made one key change: it had a different file structure for storing data. That meant that programs that worked under CP/M could be con-

verted to run under DOS, but going the other way was much more difficult. In short, CP/M had been boxed out.

In 1982, not entirely thwarted, Kildall decided that, as a product,
BASIC was a disaster. To a great degree, he was right; it was not an easy
language for beginners to master. Kildall, a master programmer, chose
to fight fire with fire, by designing a programming language that could
be used to teach young users how to program. The result was an academic program called Logo, which was simpler and more visually
appealing than BASIC. He campaigned to have his Digital Research
LOGO (or DR Logo) adopted as the educational programming language of the future.

Sadly, although he had poured his heart, and much of his fortune,
into the project, LOGO never took flight. The world just didn't care that
much about programming languages anymore. Already, applications
were where the action was. And this was where Kildall, the gentle giant
of personal computing's early days, drew the line. He felt he would be
competing with his own customers if he created a group of key productivity applications to run under his own operating system. He chose not
to go one-on-one with software companies that were writing programs
like WordStar or VisiCalc, which depended on his operating system.

Gates never had such qualms. Early on, Microsoft began selling
packaged consumer software titles even as it also supplied programming
languages to others to create similar programs. By the time the deal for
the operating system (DOS) had been struck with IBM, Microsoft was
already laying the groundwork for a series of productivity programs that
would run on a variety of hardware platforms.

By 1982 Microsoft had instituted a new software applications strategy. Gates hired Charles Simonyi, a Hungarian programmer from
Xerox's PARC, a few years earlier. He was the kind of computer scientist whose intellect was far greater than his grasp of the practical world.
Simonyi brought with him from Xerox an intimate knowledge of the
graphical user interface (GUI) that had been pioneered at Xerox's
PARC. He had worked on the first word processing program for the
Xerox Star, that company's visually oriented computer system—which
was the machine that so captivated Steve Jobs when he saw it in 1979.
Once at Microsoft, Simonyi decided that the right way to create a new
family of programs for word processing, spreadsheets, and databases,

was to create one kind of meta-program, or kernel, shared by all of them. This basic clay could then be quickly and easily customized to do different things and to run on different models of PCs.

At Xerox Simonyi had been part of a team, but at Microsoft he was expected to create the visually-oriented family of programs on his own. He failed. Simonyi's Multi-Tool concept, as the system was eventually called, proved exceptionally slow and clunky and even hindered using a mouse.

Multi-Tool's weaknesses became obvious to Gates in late 1981, when Jobs invited him to Cupertino to see the new Macintosh. Gates had heard about these machines, but he was unprepared for the Mac's sophisticated black-and-white graphics. On the screen he saw a realistic bouncing-ball demonstration, evidence of a smooth and elegant program. It was far better than anything Microsoft's programs could do. Jobs' purpose in having Gates visit Cupertino was that he wanted to make a deal with Microsoft. Apple needed software to run on the Mac. In exchange for a confidentiality agreement, Jobs offered to "allow" Microsoft to produce three programs: a spreadsheet, a business graphics program, and a database, while Apple would maintain the right to either bundle the applications with the Mac (and pay $5 per program, up to $1 million per year) or sell them separately. (Microsoft would get $10 a program or 10 percent of the retail price, whichever was greater.) Microsoft also had to agree not to create similar programs utilizing "a mouse or tracking ball" for any computer not manufactured by Apple for 12 months after the shipping date of the Mac or January 1, 1983, whichever came first.

Gates readily agreed. If there was one thing he knew, it was that software and computer projects always took longer to complete than most people anticipated. Furthermore, though "getting into bed" with the mercurial and arrogant Steve Jobs might be unpleasant, it would give Microsoft two key elements it needed: a way to reduce its dependence on IBM, and to be part of what surely would be the next great leap in computing—the graphical user interface, or GUI (gooey). Jobs, too, thought he had made a great deal. He would get more applications for his beloved Mac, and wouldn't have to pay through the nose for them. The problem, of course, although he didn't see it then, was that he had just let the fox into the chicken coop.

Back in Seattle, Microsoft's troops put Macintosh prototypes into a locked room, and a team of young and dedicated programmers were charged with creating spectacular programs for them. Unfortunately, writing programs for the Mac proved much more difficult than for the IBM PC. While Microsoft struggled to solve the mysteries of the system, the company's own software projects fell further and further behind schedule. In the end the Mac would be introduced more than a year later than Jobs had planned, and the software for it would take another two years to start arriving en masse. The delays meant that Microsoft was free to release Mac-like programs by the time that computer was eventually released, in January 1984. By then Microsoft was already close to releasing Word for the Mac.

But even before it became clear how delayed the Mac would be, and notwithstanding the terms of his agreement with Apple, Gates had launched a project to create a graphical interface for the IBM PC, first called a Windows Manager, then Interface Manager, and finally Windows. Gates wanted the Mac on a PC. However, with his hands full with the Macintosh applications, IBM PC applications, and improvements and bug fixes for PC DOS, the Windows project initially didn't get very far.

The Windows concept was really born in the fall of 1982 when Gates went to the computer convention called COMDEX (COMputer DEalers EXposition). Held in Las Vegas, in later years, it would explode into a 100,000-person extravaganza and be sold to SoftBank for $800 million. At the time, though, COMDEX was still a small-gathering; never the less, it was *the* place to see and be seen if you had microcomputer software or hardware to sell.

On the floor of the Las Vegas Convention Center, in the heart of the gambling capital of the world, Microsoft had a large and well-designed booth, befitting its staff of 200 and sales of around $32 million. Microsoft wasn't yet in the same league as Digital Research or VisiCorp (distributors of VisiCalc, the first spreadsheet), but by no means was it insignificant. Gates was in his element; he loved the passionate and sometimes heated exchanges with other programmers. He was prepared to answer any complaints about his products and to challenge hackers to ad hoc contests in any computer language they wanted to pit against his beloved BASIC.

It was ironic that Gates took such pride in BASIC; after all, it had been created by others. In terms of its products in general, though, Microsoft was not an innovator. From its earliest days, Microsoft took its cues from the creativity of others. Throughout the 1980s a joke making the rounds was that you could tell which features would be in the next release of Microsoft Word by looking at the latest version of WordPerfect, then far and away the market leader. Microsoft's skill was in reworking those ideas with superb programming and relentless effort. And Gates ran his business at a pace and with a competitive edge that was a league apart from the other companies in the fledgling personal computer business.

Microsoft also made it a practice to hire only the smartest people it could find: "Smart people can learn to do most things," said Gates' long-time friend and colleague, Steve Ballmer. "Workaholic smart kids is what we're after." Housed in a building complex in a suburb of Seattle, Microsoft nurtured a corporate culture that expected ungodly work hours from its somewhat homogenous group of 20-something graduates recruited from the world's best universities. Attracted by the stock options and the challenge and excitement of working in an entirely new industry, these software and marketing minions came to be called MicroSerfs, while the most obsequious toadies among them were dubbed "little Bills."

But these so-called serfs weren't hired to make some kind of technological breakthrough. Creative engineering is easy enough to find. But translating new products into market successes is a rarer and even more valuable talent. So though the MicroSerfs might have had technical degrees and programming skills, what they were really hired to do was to *sell* Microsoft software. It was the marketing juggernaut Gates generated, using revenues from the DOS licenses as the PC compatible market grew and grew through the mid- and late 1980s, that ultimately made Microsoft so successful.

It is generally agreed that there are three key components to success in a technology market: innovation, execution, and competition. In the American pantheon, the inventor with the innovation, that flash of brilliance, is often admired the most. But that artist rarely succeeds on his own. Success in the marketplace is all about execution and competition. So though Bill Gates wasn't an innovator and his company was rarely the creative spark behind any product development, Microsoft became the best at executing other people's brilliant ideas, and then making the products it adapted (or stole) successful in the marketplace by outcompeting, outselling, and outhustling everyone else.

This signature strategy became apparent for the first time at the 1982 COMDEX show, at which Gates saw a demonstration of a new program from the biggest software company of the era, VisiCorp. On the success of its spreadsheet program, VisiCalc, the company had built an empire, and by 1982 its revenues were in the hundreds of millions of dollars. Flush with success, VisiCorp's managers made the move to design an operating system intended to run on top of the underlying PC hardware. Called VisiOn, it was the equivalent of an overlay to DOS that gave the still-clunky PC mouse and graphical interface capabilities. The goal was to combine a series of applications under one consistent graphical user interface. According to the marketing representatives Gates talked to at the show, VisiOn was an integrated operating environment for the IBM PC, but could in fact, be adapted to any other hardware. If true, that meant it could control the personal computer business: It was graphically oriented, like the Macintosh would be, and it was running on top of *his* DOS. Gates freaked out. This was his vision for Windows.

He had no way of knowing it at the time, but the demo he was watching was the only time the software had actually worked. To be sure, a team of top-flight software engineers might eventually have sorted out its glitches, but VisiCorp was in fact falling apart. Management was at complete loggerheads with the two original programmers who had created VisiCalc and VisiOn. The result was that the company wasn't able to renegotiate the royalty agreement with the program's two authors. Instead of moving forward, the company took its internal battles to court. The fight effectively stopped the company's momentum, and VisiOn never made any headway when it was released in 1985, a few months before Windows 1.0 finally limped into release.

But Gates couldn't have known this, so to him, VisiOn spelled trouble. He already knew the Mac was a better personal computer design, and now he was looking at the same thing available for the PC. He was even more alarmed when, down another aisle he got a look at a new spreadsheet that was about to be introduced for the PC. Lotus 1-2-3 was clearly a better spreadsheet application than Microsoft's Meta-Tool hampered Multiplan. The team behind this new "killer app" for the IBM PC had thumbed their noses at the conventional ploy of supporting various hardware configurations, and instead put all their efforts directly behind the IBM PC. The audacity of this move took Gates by surprise. Even though Microsoft profited significantly from the IBM PC, it was hedging its bets by supporting all the near-compatibles (not the least because Microsoft sold each of them slight variants of DOS and its applications). The handwriting was on the wall. The IBM PC was going to become truly dominant, and Lotus had the hit program.

Gates made sure Ballmer saw the VisiOn demo and Lotus 1-2-3. Then he started scribbling on legal pads. He called Charles Simonyi, his PARC-trained programmer, and instructed him to catch the next flight to Vegas.

Immediately thereafter, Microsoft's equivalent to VisiOn—Windows—was put on an accelerated schedule. Even Gates rolled up his sleeves and toyed with the code. But his most important role had nothing to do with programming. Since he didn't have a demo, let alone a product ready for release, all Gates could do was talk up Windows to every company with a DOS license. In essence, he was attempting to freeze the market, that is, to line up hardware manufacturers to agree to support the independent layer of software that Microsoft would supply "real soon." Windows, Gates promised, would provide a consistent user interface regardless of the underlying hardware. It would include menus and multiple on-screen windows capability, the skeleton of a graphical user interface, and a mouse. Gates' colorful description of Windows compelled many companies to withhold their support from VisiOn, which had made itself vulnerable by demonstrating its operating system too far ahead of its release.

The early Windows announcements (called "vaporware" by industry skeptics) were part of a strategy that Gates would learn to perfect over the years, and it would become even more effective as Microsoft became larger and better established. By announcing a revolutionary new product when it was still very much in the conceptual stage, Gates effectively undermined his competitors. IBM had been forced by the Department of Justice to pay millions in damages to Control Data Corp. in the late 1960s for doing exactly the same thing in the super-computer market. With Windows, however, Gates raised the gambit to a new level and was widely castigated for it in the press.

But Microsoft defended itself well once it found Pam Edstrom, a public relations expert, who by the end of the decade would build a powerful "influence machine" for the growing giant. With her help, Microsoft launched a masterful marketing and trade press assault that deflected criticism and burnished the myth of Bill Gates as Microsoft. Only Gates was available for statements or public appearances. He seemed to relish engaging in badinage with a skeptical journalist, and indefatigably, he made time for most requests. And Gates knew how to take actions that made small but powerful statements, too. Whereas Jobs behaved like an emperor, Gates refused to ride in limousines, and always flew coach class. For all his wealth, he tried to appear down to earth, and that started to pay off.

Part of Microsoft's original deal with IBM involved improving and updating DOS on a regular basis. Since this was a contract programming job, it involved payment for programming time but no royalties. With other opportunities to produce new programs that did generate royalties, for obvious reasons Microsoft didn't assign its best talent to the DOS maintenance work.

All the while, IBM was losing patience with the MicroSerfs, as the revised version of DOS, 2.0, was increasingly delayed and still bug-ridden. In 1983, when Microsoft was lining up a number of hardware manufacturers to support Windows, IBM refused to be one of them. Big Blue explicitly rejected Microsoft's overtures and announced it would support VisiOn instead. If that upset Gates, he didn't show it. A year later, Microsoft was ready to introduce Windows to the world.

On November 10, 1983, Microsoft took over the Plaza Hotel in New York City to present a software extravaganza: the formal introduction of Windows. Twenty-three hardware manufacturers signed up, with IBM conspicuously absent. At that point, Microsoft was promising delivery of the software by the following spring, although it would be two years before it was actually released as Windows 1.0. But timing was everything, and Gates knew that Apple was set to release the Mac two months later, in January 1984. Worse, VisiCorp was due to release VisiOn by the end of November, '83. Gates knew he had to make his move in advance, ready or not.

One week after the Plaza event, at that year's COMDEX, Microsoft PR staff blanketed the attendees with Windows advertising and hype, from packages pushed under hotel room doors to banners and bumper stickers hung everywhere. It was a massive preemptive marketing and publicity campaign. The VisiOn rollout was lost in the shuffle, as Microsoft had hoped, even though VisiOn had a product ready to ship. VisiOn was actually much better than the anemic Windows, as were the Apple products. Those in the know dismissed Microsoft's Windows. But there was one thing they didn't count on: perseverance. Gates didn't care how bad his first efforts were—eventually he would get it right.

Microsoft had positioned itself well on all fronts. Gates had even found a seasoned leader in Jon Shirley, a veteran of Radio Shack's personal computer business. Shirley, 20 years older than both Gates and Ballmer, was good at dealing with all the details the two young Turks had little interest in: profit and loss statements, order entry, inventory management. As Microsoft reached $100 million in sales in 1983, nearly all of it from DOS licenses, the company needed a president who could teach Gates how to run a business.

But in the software trenches, things weren't shaping up very well. Microsoft still had no completed applications for the Macintosh, which was finally introduced in 1984. This so infuriated Steve Jobs that in January 1984 he cancelled the original deal, which meant Microsoft was free to do whatever it wanted with its Macintosh programs, and Apple was free to hire other software companies to write a spreadsheet program. This opened the door for Lotus, which had been shut out under the exclusive terms of the Microsoft-Apple arrangement.

Jobs' withdrawal was a big blow to Gates, who had decided that Lotus was the software company to beat. Not only was Microsoft's slow and ugly Multiplan a weak competitor to 1-2-3, but Lotus was bigger than Microsoft, grossing some $160 million in 1983. For the hypercompetitive Gates, this was worse. In true Gates' style, though, he did not accept defeat and back off. Quite the opposite: he attacked head-on. Microsoft launched another all-or-nothing project: to design a spreadsheet for the Mac that would be better than 1-2-3. He dangled the challenge in front of one of Microsoft's top programmers, Doug Kunder, who bit. The program he came up with, called Excel, was essentially a 1-2-3 clone, but with a better interface, more effective menus, and a smoother presentation. And it offered a key innovation: an intelligent recalculation feature. Instead of having to recalculate an entire spreadsheet and all its cells when even just one number was changed (as was necessary on Lotus 1-2-3), Excel reworked only those cells affected by a change. This made calculations speedier, especially for people who created massive worksheets. This was a huge advantage for the business user who had fueled the personal computer success in the early 1980s. By targeting the business customer Microsoft was countermanding Apple's consumer-oriented marketing.

Gates received an unexpected boost when the Lotus founder, Mitch Kapor, made a disastrous move. In 1983 he decided that the future lay in integrated software, software that could exchange data between different programs. Kapor's goal was an integrated application for the Macintosh that would incorporate a spreadsheet, word processor, and business graphics. The ambitious effort, however took far too long to make it to market, and when it was released in 1987, it was decimated by Excel for the Mac, which had come out a year earlier. Eventually, Kapor's concept would indeed become the industry standard. But in the mid-1980s, the power and performance of personal computers was not up to the task.

But for all of Excel's success, Microsoft's Windows project was still having trouble getting off the ground. Programmer after programmer tried to make it work, yet the software still didn't have the quality it needed—or at least the quality that would satisfy Gates, who wanted nothing less than "the Mac on the PC." Finally, Neal Konzen, a 20-year-old programmer who had been deeply involved with Microsoft's Macintosh applications, rewrote Windows from the ground up. Using the Macintosh data structures and programming form, he created exactly what Gates was looking for—a PC version of the Mac. Konzen's version even included small Mac-like applications, such as a paint program, a clock, and a puzzle.

Steve Jobs got a look at Windows late in 1984 when Gates demonstrated Excel to him for the first time, and he went ballistic. He thought that Excel would be a great application for the Mac, but Windows—this primitive graphical interface overlay for DOS—was clearly the Mac in PC clothing. He accused Gates of breaching their confidentiality agreements, and worse: theft. Gates listened, unintimidated, as Jobs blustered and yelled. He ignored the threats, knowing it would all blow over. Besides, Gates knew Apple needed Excel if it was going to make any headway in a business community that so far had not responded to its offbeat image.

Jobs, however, had no intention of succumbing to Gates' maneuverings. He was determined to do something to stop Microsoft. Around this time Apple hired a new intellectual property attorney, Irving Rappaport, a veteran of the minicomputer and videogame industries. His job was to make sure no one stole Apple's crown jewels.

The issue, after all, was survival. At the time the Macintosh was selling only a few thousand machines a week not even close to the 20,000 a week Apple needed to break even. To complicate matters, internal problems shook the company. In the spring of 1985 Jobs was ousted as head of the Macintosh division at Apple, following a political battle with John Sculley. Yet even after an executive meeting attended by 75 of Apple's top managers, during which Sculley publicly dressed down Jobs, Jobs had the wherewithal to ask Rappaport what had become of the "Windows problem?" Jobs was prepared to fight Microsoft, insisting he would never have given it a license had he known it would eventually undermine the Mac.

Gates wisely realized he needed a clear license agreement between the two companies, and this was the time to get it, especially with Jobs on his way out. Gates suggested in a letter to Sculley, now in solitary, albeit shaky, control, that Apple license its operating system and hardware to various other hardware makers. Creating a bigger market for Apple machines, he said, would be good for all of them. Unbeknownst to Gates, however, Sculley had already rejected an internal proposal that would have extended the Mac's influence into the PC universe. The proposal called for creating a MAC-to-PC board, that could turn an IBM PC into a Macintosh clone. But Apple was concerned that it would eat into its lucrative margins and so decided against it. If Apple wasn't going to coopt the PC with a Mac clone, it certainly wasn't going to license its hardware to other manufacturers. Sculley ignored Gates' letter.

Still Gates wouldn't let up: He wanted Sculley to offer some guarantee that Apple wouldn't cause trouble for Windows when it was released that fall. Without the guarantee, he threatened, he would pull all his Macintosh applications off the market, and stop working on future Macintosh products. Sculley polled his executive staff and was told to stand up to Gates. The consensus was that Gates was bluffing. Because the Mac accounted for a third of Microsoft's revenues, it was too valuable to abandon.

Sculley called Gates to tell him that, from Apple's point of view, there were indeed legal problems with Windows. Gates flew off the handle at first, but then later that night Gates and Microsoft attorney Bill Neukom flew down to Cupertino for a private dinner with Sculley and Al Eisentstat, Apple's general counsel. Rappaport, a proponent of the stand-up-to-Gates approach, was notably absent. The following morning Sculley breezily told Rappaport that everything had been taken care of: Apple had agreed to give Microsoft a license for version 1.0 of Windows, insisting it wasn't very good anyway, and so couldn't be much of a threat. In return, Microsoft had guaranteed to make Excel proprietary to the Mac for at least a year, and to create another, better, version of Microsoft Word for the Mac as well.

Rappaport was astounded. Apparently, Gates had manipulated and maneuvered until Sculley had acquiesced. His capitulation came only one day after promising to take an aggressive stance. Rappaport tried to salvage the situation by drafting a tightly restrictive agreement that limited Microsoft to marketing only version 1.0, which had to include Apple's copyright on the Windows start-up screen. At this, Gates erupted again. His next move was to convince Eisenstat to remove Rappaport from the project, saying he found the attorney "too aggressive."

The agreement that was finally signed was much more beneficial to Microsoft. No public display of the Apple copyright was required, and Microsoft was free to market "present and future software programs" based on version 1.0 as well. Gates had even managed to slip in language that allowed Microsoft to license the Windows version of the Mac interface to third parties for use in their software programs. This freed Microsoft to unleash Apple's carefully created software to the rest of the computer industry at will.

In short, Apple had been completely bamboozled by the kid from Seattle. In exchange for his capitulation, Sculley only got a commitment for Microsoft not to release Excel for Windows until October of 1986, which was less than one-year grace period. And as it turned out, Microsoft didn't finish the PC version of Excel until the fall of 1987, a year later than the agreement specified, so Apple got nothing for giving up its copyright to the interface.

Could Apple have protected itself better? Rappaport, then the company's intellectual property attorney, thinks so. The struggle with

Microsoft was "based on look-and-feel, the visual appearance of a work. This was definitely protected by law, and is called a visual copyright," he later explained. Software, however, was a new confusing subject for the law; it crossed booklike copyright with patentlike function issues. Clearly, copying the actual code that made a piece of software do something was a copyright infringement. But if different software code performed the same function as another product, did that constitute infringement, too? In the case of the IBM PC clones, it appeared that it was not.

No one had yet tested the issue in operating systems, because Kildall and his crew at Digital Research declined to sue Microsoft over DOS. Now Gates made the argument that Apple didn't own the visual appearance or the way its operating system worked, since Xerox had pioneered graphical interfaces to begin with.

Patenting the Apple interface, and then trying to extract licensing fees for derivative work based on it, opened up a whole new area of intellectual property law that wouldn't be clarified for years. In 1993, in a case brought by Lotus Development against Borland International involving 1-2-3 and its competitor QuattroPro, the courts ruled that mimicking a prior software program's features was illegal even if the underlying programming code was completely different. On that basis, Apple might have won had it pursued a lawsuit against Microsoft.

By putting Microsoft on notice that Apple considered Windows to be an infringement from the start, actions brought later, when Windows had finally become viable, would have carried much more weight in the courts. Letting it go to version 1.0 was a major mistake on Sculley's and Eisenstadt's part.

In October 1985, as the final details of the Apple contract were being resolved, Gates celebrated his 30th birthday. The party was held in a local roller rink, to which the guest of honor came dressed as Jay Gatsby. The next day, he told his board of directors that he was going to make a public offering. For several years, Microsoft had been distributing stock to its staff under an employee stock ownership plan (ESOP), but Gates had been resisting the move to become publicly traded. Money wasn't the issue to either Gates or Allen, who both had plenty by now. Rather, Microsoft was on the brink of introducing Windows, so it seemed an auspicious time to make the move. Over the next few months, the company would seek underwriters, eventually settling on Goldman Sachs and Alex Brown. The stock began trading on the NASDAQ market on March 12, 1986, priced at $21 a share. That day Gates had a paper net worth of $311 million on his 45 percent stake in Microsoft. His salary at the time was $122,000 a year. A key group of programmers also became wealthy, as did anyone who was smart enough to buy the stock. Today, 100 shares of that initial offering, priced at $2100 then, are worth $560,000.

Windows 1.0 was introduced at the November COMDEX convention of 1985 to great fanfare, despite the fact that the company held the record for the worst delivery schedule in the software industry: two years. Along with all the product hype, Microsoft trumpeted its licensing deal with Apple that cleared Windows from any possible legal action. At its launch, the highly touted interface, remarkably, had only one program—a graphics program called Micrographix. Microsoft's own programs—Word, Excel, File, and Chart—wouldn't be ready for at least a year.

The lack of software made Windows a dud initially. It didn't help that Windows was just plain ugly. Instead of using the overlapping metaphor for its windows that Apple had perfected, Microsoft had adopted a tiled look. This divided the screen and displayed every window in evenly sized sectors making it hard for users to focus. In addition, the mouse never worked smoothly with the IBM PC because it had to be plugged into an add-on board; it wasn't integrated into the software, like Apple's mouse was. But most detrimental was that the IBM PC computers in 1986 were still built around 16-bit 80286 microprocessors, which simply didn't have the power to manipulate the millions of pixels required for a visually-oriented computer display. (The Macintosh used Motorola's 32-bit 68000, and could better handle screen graphics.)

Gates wasn't too worried about Windows' shortcomings just then. He had another iron in the fire, a venture he thought would spell the future of the company and industry. It was called OS/2 and it was IBM's next-generation operating system. In mid-1985 IBM had no choice but to strike a deal with Microsoft to work on its new operating system; much as it wanted to avoid it. IBM had tried to find another company to work with, but there was really no alternative. The IBM staff had grown to dislike the arrogant Microsoft programmers, and now they were forced to work with them. The bad memories of getting Microsoft to improve DOS back in 1983 and its interminable delays were still fresh in their minds. If that wasn't bad enough, by 1985 the PC clones had taken a serious chunk out of IBM's market share, and though Microsoft had been IBM's software partner, it had turned around and sold its product to the compatibles makers. To the traditional IBMers, this was tantamount to an arms merchant supplying both sides in the war.

The OS/2 agreement was hammered out between IBM's Bill Lowe and Microsoft's Steve Ballmer and Bill Gates, and was called the Joint Development Agreement, or JDA. It specified which firm would deliver which pieces of the operating system that would be built around one key technical concept: the so-called "protected" mode, which meant that the computer would survive the crash of a particular software program and be able to "multitask," or run several programs simultaneously. These capabilities were crucial to the mainframe-oriented IBM crew if its PCs were to survive on the market. To date, the PC, and most of Microsoft's applications, were subject to crashing and rebooting; an error could fry a program and destroy data. The only solution was to restart the machine. This was due in part to the hardware, which was short on memory, but also was the result of Microsoft's cavalier attitude toward testing. Getting a program up and running was always more important than fine-tuning it. And because of the economics of networks, Microsoft could get away with delivering software with bugs, then charge for the upgrades it developed to fix them. This practice made the PC software industry different from all others. Would Maytag's customers accept an upgrade to its washing machines to get clothes "really" clean? In no other market was this absence of quality control acceptable.

At IBM, where customer satisfaction was truly company policy, this kind of approach was unconscionable. OS/2 was intended to bring big computing dependability to the world of the small computer. At first, Gates argued vociferously for Windows as the interface for this new operating system. But IBM wanted to use a TopView-oriented interface, a product in keeping with its Systems Administrative Architecture, SAA. (TopView enabled several programs—or sessions—to run on-screen at once.) SAA was a companywide foundation for consistent programs and operating environments. "Consistently bad," the wags at Microsoft said. Worse, IBM had altered its XTt generation PC—called the PS/2—in such a way as to obsolete all of the existing add-on boards that had made the PC industry so vibrant, by enabling users to customize the base PC for thousands of purposes. Still, the decision was IBM's to make. So even though Microsoft was sure that IBM was pursuing a seriously flawed strategy, it quietly went down the garden path with its still much bigger partner, making money, attempting to do what IBM wanted, but never fully committing to the project. Microsoft had no intention of backing out of the deal. The original partnership with IBM had been spectacularly successful, so no matter how misguided Microsoft believed OS/2 to be, Microsoft was poised to become even more profitable. Meanwhile, Gates continued to develop Windows.

The OS/2 project quickly devolved into chaos, a victim of too many ideas, too many features, and too many meetings. Making matters worse, IBM also insisted on using an outdated microprocessor, the 80286, which Gates called "brain damaged." IBM, dogged by its long lead times and bureaucratic management stayed committed to the older processor. Gates argued with IBM about it, but to no avail.

The upshot was that COMPAQ stole the lead when it released a new generation of computers based on the new microprocessor. Gates, always ready to play every angle, offered to supply COMPAQ with a new and enhanced version of DOS for the new microprocessors, along with version 2.0 of Windows. Simultaneously, Microsoft dutifully played along with IBM's ambitions for OS/2.

OS/2 seemed doomed on all fronts. Another blow came from the changing marketplace. OS/2 required significant quantities of memory to run—even ponderously. A year before, Intel had gotten out of the memory business, so by late in 1987, when OS/2 was first released, memory prices had skyrocketed. In essence, IBM was asking its customers not only to buy new hardware, the PS/2, but also to install several thousand dollars in memory. Not surprisingly, the project languished while sales of Microsoft-powered DOS machines, sold only by IBM's competitors, soared. Nevertheless, most of the industry believed IBM would eventually work out the bugs on the OS/2, and triumph in the marketplace.

By the end of 1987, Microsoft had finally topped Lotus sales at about $350 million, with income of $72 million. DOS was the company's cash cow, accounting for more than 50 percent of revenues, the Macintosh applications were a strong second, led by Excel and Word. Bringing up the rear was the PC applications business, where Excel was starting to make headway as Lotus continued to be unable to get viable upgrades out the door. The weakest link was Windows; of the 500,000 copies distributed, most had been given away, in contrast to more than 20 million PCs with DOS.

Windows was starting to look like a dead end. Only Gates himself remained determined to make it succeed. Ballmer was putting all of his effort into making the relationship with IBM work, and he argued long and hard for developing Excel, only for the OS/2. Gates maintained that IBM was so misguided that Microsoft needed Windows as a hedge. As usual, he persevered. So, in the fall of 1987, when Excel was ready to be released for the PC, it came with a new version of Windows, 2.0, which was some improvement over the initial effort. It sported overlapping windows, like the Macintosh, but it was still a clunker, generating nothing but raspberries from analysts and consultants, who in the main chose to stay with DOS and wait for OS/2 to mature.

But Windows 2.0 had something its older sibling did not: a GUI. Hewlett-Packard, the venerable Silicon Valley company, had been testing the graphical user interface waters. In 1986, its reps had approached Apple, in hopes of licensing the Macintosh interface for its own version of a GUI. Because Apple refused, the HP people went to Microsoft, where they found a warmer reception. Late in 1987, HP released New Wave, a graphical user interface overlay that worked on top of Windows 2.0. Though still ugly and barely useable when outfitted with Windows 2.0, the IBM PC with New Wave behaved remarkably like the Macintosh.

Apple, especially Irv Rappaport, the company's dogged intellectual property attorney was quick to react. New Wave, he felt, was a clear violation of Apple's rights. And when he talked to the folks at HP, they indicated that they had developed New Wave under what they understood to be a license from Microsoft, with direct input from the Bellevue troops.

The Mac at the time was experiencing a rebirth, and was starting to sell to businesses on the basis of the Excel spreadsheet program in addition to a new concept called desktop publishing. All this was featured on the newly introduced Mac II, an expandable, top-of-the-line machine. This resurgence gave Apple's president, John Sculley, the confidence to stand up to Gates. Disagreeing on the interpretation of the original license, Apple claimed it covered only version 1.0; Microsoft of course said it went further. Apple filed suit on St. Patrick's Day 1988. Gates, who was informed when reporters started calling him for comment, exploded. The lawsuit would drag on for years, and wear out two judges. Originally hinging on the interface—the software's look and feel—it became a contest of wills over more than 100 "points of similarity," each of which was taken out of context and analyzed separately. Ultimately, the court decided a half dozen could be litigated. Again Gates triumphed. The agreement that Sculley had signed for Windows 1.0 came back to haunt him. The court ruled that Apple had licensed the interface and couldn't change its mind later.

The ultimate victory, however, could not change the fact that 1988 was one of Microsoft's worst years. The relationship with IBM was abysmal as a result of the conflicts over OS/2. Its word processing program, Word, was still a distant second to WordPerfect. Microsoft was struggling on every front. Only the nearly ten-year-old operating system DOS kept the company's revenues viable. But Microsoft knew it couldn't count on DOS forever, not in the ever-changing computer market place.

At this point Ballmer became determined to make OS/2 a success. He and Gates traversed the country talking it up, promising that future versions of the operating system would be great. (Privately Gates would admit that it had problems.) All the while, Microsoft continued to improve Windows, and to create better versions of all the key company software programs for it, as well as for DOS throughout 1989.

While Gates and Ballmer, were out supporting IBM and OS/2, Big Blue made two key mistakes: first, it announced it would start selling a version of UNIX, in effect competing with OS/2 for the departmental and networking computing business. The company also agreed to license a new operating system from Gates' nemesis Steve Jobs, who after being ousted from Apple, had designed a stylish and functionally advanced computer at his new company called NeXT. The new machine was visually appealing but incompatible with everything else on the market.

Gates was dumbfounded; what was IBM doing? The answer was, hedging its bets. Few could deny that OS/2 was starting to look like a loser. This was not news to Microsoft, but now IBM was having doubts too.

Gates, who lived by the adage "the best defense is a good offense," turned his attention to the next version of Windows. His intention was to win over all DOS users. And he didn't care if he had to fight for the right to do so in the courts. If he lost, he figured, Microsoft would appeal; if he won, Microsoft would also be ready with versions of its programs ready to work under Windows. The third version of Windows was finally a legitimate competitor to Apple's now six-year-old interface, though still not quite as elegant.

As part of the push, Gates had hired an executive who was able to get applications out the door in a timely fashion. Ironically Mike Maples had come from IBM ("one of the only decent managers we ever met there," Steve Ballmer would say), and had whipped the applications group into shape. It was clear to Gates that a combination of a new graphically oriented operating system overlay for DOS, Windows 3.0, and new and improved applications designed specifically to take advantage of the new features of Windows 3.0, would give the company the ammunition it needed to capture dominant market share in the various key applications sectors. He was well aware that all his major competitors were still hung up on DOS applications and OS/2, which, both IBM and Microsoft were still touting publicly as the next-generation OS. Of course, he would have to make his move surreptitiously, while paying lip service to Microsoft's commitment to OS/2 and IBM.

It wouldn't be quite as easy as he hoped, however, because IBM assigned a new manager to try and unravel the OS/2 mess. Jim Cannavino was a tough, street-smart manager who immediately was at odds with Gates. Coming from the mainframe world, Cannavino was a proponent of "the more code the better" approach to programming, whereas Gates, coming from the "less is more" world of PC software, believed success came from tighter, smaller code. While they argued, Gates was setting in motion plans to roll out the new Windows—to, essentially, do an end run around OS/2 and its clunky Presentation Manager interface.

But Cannavino was no fool. Industry scuttlebutt and comments from Gates himself made Cannavino suspect that Gates was planning a coup. So Cannavino made a preemptive strike of his own. IBM floated the idea of a Presentation Manager "lite" to provide a consistent interface for DOS. Gates reacted as expected. The idea of IBM driving the market into the waiting arms of OS/2 was more than he could bear. In a month of non-stop negotiating, Gates derailed the new IBM project. In a marathon month of meetings at IBM, Gates appeared to achieve rapprochement with IBM. Presentation Manager would be the strategic project of the future, with Windows the alternative for low-power customers. It was a hard-fought battle; and when the news was released, it appeared that IBM had stopped Windows. But in fact, Gates had killed the consumer version of Presentation Manager, leaving the field open for Windows.

At the Fall 1989 COMDEX show, IBM and Microsoft announced a new "spirit of cooperation" claiming that OS/2 was the one true operating system for the future. On the surface, the relationship was patched up; the reality was another story. No doubt about it, Gates had outmaneuvered his partners once more. The PM Lite project was dead and Windows had survived. A few months later, as Microsoft was gearing up to invest more than $10 million to promote Windows 3.0, Gates admitted that the company was dragging its feet on fixing the myriad bugs in OS/2, and was instead betting the farm on Windows. Shortly thereafter, the companies starting talking divorce.

In May 1990, Windows 3.0 was released, and it started a tidal wave of success for Microsoft. That year the company's revenues rose to $1.5 billion, more than Lotus and Novell combined. The third time was the charm for Windows. Finally, this version of Windows worked smoothly. Furthermore, computer hardware was powerful enough now to handle a graphical user interface, and memory prices had plummeted. Most PC users were ready to adopt a graphical user interface. It had taken six years, but the graphical user interface revolution finally caught on in the PC compatible market.

By the fall of that year, "it was war" as Steve Ballmer said, between Microsoft and IBM. All the energy that Microsoft had expended keeping the IBM relationship alive now went into destroying it. A "divorce" decree was drawn up, and each company went its own way. As was becoming the pattern, Microsoft had won. Along the way, Microsoft had been paid millions of dollars in programming fees under the Joint Development Agreement with IBM. Now it received all the revenues from Windows, in addition to royalties from every copy of OS/2—whether it was running on an IBM machine or a clone.

And as far as the Windows campaign was concerned, Gates had made all the right moves: Priced at under $100 a copy (OS/2 cost $500), the marketplace voted with its wallet. Microsoft made it seem imperative for the world's PC owners—by 1991, there were 60 million of them—to upgrade to Windows. And of course, these users would have to also own the new programs that took full advantage of the added power of the operating system. It was a masterful one-two punch, made even more potent by the failure of the competition to be ready with Windows products. Borland, WordPerfect, and Lotus, all scrambled to catch the wave. But they were too late. By 1996 Microsoft enjoyed an 80 percent share of the productivity software market—on top of 100 percent of the DOS and Windows operating system business.

Gates had outfoxed two more experienced executives. Microsoft did the same in the applications arena. Getting all its competitors to commit to OS/2, then introducing a powerful version of Windows with—surprise!—a group of applications available and ready to go from Microsoft was a masterful move. By using its knowledge of Windows to cobble together its own programs, the Windows Office Suite completely decimated the competition. Having the DOS, and now Windows, operating system royalties to cushion any financial troubles, Microsoft could match competitors' price cuts dollar for dollar with minimal pain, and continue to pour money into applications program R & D. When the break came with IBM, Microsoft drove the much bigger company into the ground with marketing gusto. IBM was never able to counter the prevailing view that OS/2 was a disaster, and that Windows was the next stage in the personal computer revolution.

Of course, America is supposed to be the country of the aggressive entrepreneur, but once Windows smashed OS/2 and took over the market, the press and the industry started to whine about Gates and Microsoft's aggressive tactics. It was as if they had all forgotten that this was exactly what business was all about. Bill Gates played the game as hardball. He wanted to win more than everyone else. The key difference between Gates and everyone else was wealth. He was born to it. When Microsoft went public, and he became fabulously wealthy, it didn't change him. But it changed everyone else. The limos, and the big houses, and the toys and the trophy wives corrupted and weakened all his competitors. They could have fought him tooth and nail, but they didn't. They all played for money, and when they got it, they no longer played to win at all costs. Gates played for the joy of the game. And he kept playing.

He was lucky, certainly. He had the good fortune to land a monopoly for the operating system of the IBM PC. But no one stopped Apple from creating its own operating system for the PC. No one stopped Lotus from bringing together its control of spreadsheets with networking to create a viable alternative. No one stopped IBM from creating its own next generation operating system. Gates was lucky to have competitors at Lotus, and Ashton Tate and Borland and Novell and Word-Perfect, who were happy to make their stock option money and build nice mid-sized businesses, without the wherewithal, drive or skills to create software empires. He was lucky that his competitors ignored evidence of OS/2's fatal flaws, kept milking the DOS cash cow, and stayed away from Windows too long. He was lucky to have a partner in IBM that first of all, handed him the store on the deal for the original DOS, then later tried to create software by committee for a machine that was the ultimate expression of individuality.

Gates had been there at the start of the personal computer software movement, and he knew this field inside out. He was also driven, by a competitive fire so strong it prompted the phrase "You've been Gates'd" meaning out-maneuvered. Sometimes he took it too far—in one memorable case Microsoft was sanctioned and paid dearly ($40 million plus) for stealing a data compression scheme from a much smaller rival. But he was always a risk taker, a guy willing to work just this side of the law and always willing to up the ante. That became spectacularly clear for all to see when he took on the Internet, and decided to give away the company's browser in order to keep any other company—even a small one like Netscape—from establishing a beachhead in that field.

But even Microsoft has an Achilles heel. As the hardware and the technology matures, it will be content that counts. Only time will tell whether Gates, the master manipulator, will be willing and able to unleash the creative forces within his dominion that will keep him on top in the free-for-all of the Internet. But before that question is answered, Gates must face a foe that has succeeded in knocking off their stride other great American entrepreneurs: the U.S. Government.

When Microsoft set off to conquer the Internet—not just with tools and enabling applications, like web page design software, but also with content and commerce sites for things like airline tickets and used cars—every business in the world felt threatened. With the PC and

Windows a de facto monopoly in the market, people had to buy Microsoft products to have a place in the digital universe. Now that the company also supplied tools to every business that emerged as a viable online enterprise it seemed unfair to compete on both fronts. The result was a groundswell of dissatisfaction first from its Internet competitors, then the antitrust arm of the Department of Justice, and finally the customers themselves. As IBM had found twenty years before, running a company under the scrutiny of government regulators was a powerful distraction. Microsoft had created the modern day PC software industry. Gates, who for years had stayed firmly focused on programming languages, operating systems, and software applications, now seemed determined to chase the consumer retail market on the Internet. With revenues from operating systems paying the way, Microsoft had the luxury to do so.

The irony in the explosion of the Internet was that it was Microsoft's creation of a unified, widespread, graphically oriented computing market that allowed the Internet to flourish. As the Internet started to take hold, millions of PC and Windows users wanted to find a way to communicate easily, and graphically, in a way that was similar to the PC desktops they had grown accustomed to using. However, as it developed, the Internet created a whole new world based on standards that had nothing to do with Microsoft. In that world, Windows could become irrelevant. It was that fear that drove Gates to make the entire company Internet-conscious in the fall of 1995. It is a clear sign of Bill Gates' peculiar genius that he was able to throw Microsoft into the fight for financial marketshare with such force, that within three years, the competition and the U.S. Government would be attempting to stop him by using the courts. By 1998 his personal fortune was worth more than $60 billion. Microsoft's earnings and revenues kept rising, driving up the stock market, and he was beset on all sides. The software entrepreneur who had built the greatest software company in history, was in the fight of his life. And in this one, the rules of the marketplace were much less important than the court of public opinion. There, aggressiveness and ruthlessness and perseverance were not seen as the greatest of attributes. But they were exactly what made Bill Gates, and Microsoft, a grand success. This might not be the set of traits we would choose for a best friend, but is there any doubt that this is the kind of company most would like to invest in?

Watching Bill Gates testifying in 1998, before a Senate subcommittee bent on excoriating him, was like seeing a bemused Jay Gatsby wondering just what he had done wrong. He had run his business superbly, rapaciously perhaps, had bested all serious competition in the PC's core software businesses, and yet he was being censured and ostracized.

His reaction was equally predictable: Fight.

Bill Gates against the federal government.

Who has met their match?

Craig McCaw, cellular phone pioneer, who sold his business
to AT&T for $12 billion in 1994.

CHAPTER 10

>─────◆─────<

Airwaves
MCI & Cell Phones

In the 1980s the finest telephone system in the world was the one linking the 50 United States. Thirty years earlier, 75 percent of the nation's 43 million phone lines were party lines. By 1970 there were 120 million private phone lines, in 90 percent of the nation's households, an astonishing feat of technological disbursement. Long-distance calls were still a relatively pricey option for many Americans, however, even though a call from San Francisco to New York had fallen from $2.50 a minute in 1952 to $1.35 a minute in 1970.

Americans traveling abroad found that European systems were unreliable; their line quality was dicey, and service was hardly universal, even while it was exorbitantly expensive. In most Asian countries outside of Japan in the 1980s telephone service was poor, and in China it was virtually non-existent. The American Bell System—better known as Ma Bell—was without question the greatest regulated industrial enterprise of its time and the largest corporation in the world in terms of assets, $135 billion strong in 1981. A combination of monopolies of both long-distance and local telephone service, the company served 60 million miles of telephone wire and generated $17 billion in revenues. Ma Bell's monopoly was essentially free to set rates that suited its purposes. To win this power, the Bell System managers made a quid pro quo pact with the government, specifying that business services would underwrite low-cost "universal" home service to every corner of the United States. This universal service was a massive undertaking, one that in the government's opinion justified a monopoly structure. By the early 1970s the monthly cost of the line was about $25 according to Ma Bell; but residential customers were only paying an average of $9 a month, and most local calls *were included in that price. Business customers were paying three times that, an average of $30 a month with every call metered, and the rest of the shortfall was cross-subsidized by high long distance charges. It made sense when all the money ended up in the same phone company's pocket.*

This was the status quo until the early 1980s, when a handful of entrepreneurs fought enormous odds, deep pockets, governmental regulators, the will of the Bell System management and even the American populace to generate something that was completely foreign to Ma Bell: competition.

❖   ❖   ❖

SOMEWHERE IN THE MILES between Chicago and St. Louis, the future of the telephone industry in the United States started to take shape about 1962. Originally, the idea of providing an alternate communications network didn't seem particularly revolutionary to John Goeken, a dealer for GE's mobile radio division and sometime private pilot and aviation electronics technician. From his small repair and electronics business at the Joliet Airport in Illinois, Goeken spent hours flying the route between St. Louis and Chicago. Joliet was 30 miles southwest of Chicago, right along the main highway, Interstate 55, that stretched through the middle of the state before meeting the Mississippi River in St Louis, Missouri. Following the highway was the easiest way to chart his flight in either direction, so his route paralleled that of the trucks barreling back and forth between Chicago and St. Louis.

As he flew over the fields of Illinois soybeans, Goeken had plenty of time to think, and he started wondering why the two-way GE radios he sold couldn't be used to create a dispatch service that would enable the delivery trucks making the 300-mile trip to stay in touch with their base stations. (At the time, two-way radios worked only within the limits of a single transmission tower.) Perhaps, Goeken thought, he could form a network of transmitters and towers, and thus extend the range of the two-way radios.

Goeken himself maintained a transmitter in Springfield, the state capital, to provide local service. But he was imagining something more ambitious. Each two-way transmitter had a range of about 30 miles and used a particular segment of the radio spectrum reserved for dispatch services. Coincidentally, the Bell System and a few corporations had started to use microwave frequencies to transmit telecommunications traffic over longer distances. These "micro," or very short, waves were an outgrowth of research in radar, and had a very directional orientation. A small microwave dish, mounted high up a mast, could be tuned to another dish 20 miles away, and they could transmit to each other as long as the terrain was flat enough to allow a line-of-sight connection.

Microwave systems had first been installed in the 1950s, to serve as the data communications links for the first national air defense system—the SAGE computer network built by IBM for the U.S. government. In 1959, the FCC allowed the construction of private microwave networks, as there was plenty of frequency spectrum in the microwave band—above 890 megahertz—to accommodate both the needs of the common carriers and businesses that needed to transmit data as well. Common carriers were businesses working in regulated industries like trucking or shipping or telecommunications that agreed to carry a specified type of traffic in goods from anyone, in return for being able to use U.S. Government–owned highways or airwave frequencies. As computers started to reach into the fabric of American business during the 1950s and 60s, letting them communicate with each other and enabling employees to get data from computers in distant places became an increasingly important business opportunity. Microwave networks had significant advantages for companies with big data communication needs—especially since once installed these systems were essentially free of per line and hourly access charges. AT&T had started using microwaves in the 1960s to transmit voice traffic over 20-mile distances, but the field was very much in its infancy.

Goeken was a self-taught engineer, with a particular interest in aircraft electronics. He studied the esoteric field of microwave transmission in trade magazines and decided there was no particular magic to it. And certainly getting the equipment he needed would be no problem, because companies like Motorola, GE, and Lenkurt were starting to sell microwave transmitters and receivers and he was already buying from them for his aircraft electronics business. From his birdseye vantage point, he imagined a series of transmitter/receivers linked across the flat Illinois farmland to form a communications network for the truckers.

He planned to set up a series of 10 or 11 towers across the fields along the interstate—paying the farmers who owned the fields a token fee for the privilege—to relay voice traffic. A private two-way radio communications link would be installed on each tower to connect anyone using a two-way radio within range of the towers to the microwave network. The radio–based voice traffic would be transferred to the microwave network, then sent to Goeken's operators, who would subsequently route the call to the appropriate dispatch company office. And, if he played his cards right, he figured he could sell the mobile service to the big-city dealers of two-way radios at either end of the route, who could then resell it to trucking companies whose drivers frequented the Chicago–St. Louis route.

But before his plan got off the ground, Goeken ran into obstacles in the form of the United States government and AT&T. To proceed with his plan, he would first have to get a license from the FCC. His timing wasn't bad, although he didn't realize it at the time; by the early 1960s, a few licenses had been granted to companies like Lockheed and Boeing for setting up private microwave communications links. But those systems were designed for internal employee communication and data traffic only. No one had proposed creating a private telephone network that would be available to any customer.

In fact, the Bell System had expressly been fighting such encroachment on its turf for years. In 1949, the Department of Justice had started an antitrust investigation into the relationship between Western Electric and the Bell System, which many thought to be a little too "cozy." All the equipment used on the Bell System's telephone network was supplied by Western Electric, and the arrangement smacked of an illegal monopoly. By the middle of the 1950s in two important court cases, the FCC allowed interconnection between an outside firm and the Bell phone system. In one, the Jordaphone case, telephone-answering devices were allowed to be attached as long as the Bell System was protected from harm. For years Bell engineers claimed that other manufacturers' gear could send spikes of voltage that would destroy central switching gear, or burn up customers' houses, or even bring the whole telephone calling grid of the United States to its knees. It was the kind of scare tactic that a big monopolist could play, and because of Ma Bell's size, it was given far more credence than it deserved. In the other case, the Hush-A-

Phone company, which made "collars" that fit around the mouthpiece of a phone to reduce ambient noise, was allowed to sell its product over the strenuous objections of Ma Bell.

The Bell antitrust case was settled in 1956 by government negotiators who allowed the phone company to maintain its monopoly, over protests from the antitrust mavens at the Department of Justice. The reason? National security: The Bell System managed all crucial communications links for the U.S. government. AT&T, the publicly traded umbrella corporation of the Bell System, was allowed to keep control of Western Electric, though it did have to make some concessions. The most significant was that it was specifically prohibited from entering any business other than common-carrier telephone transmission, and it could only build computers for its own use. The phone company was free to provide data communications services, but not to build the computers that generated the data to be communicated. The idea was to keep the phone system out of the computer business in return for maintaining its monopoly on common-carrier telecommunications.

Initially, AT&T and Ma Bell were happy with the deal, because data communications were only a fraction of the giant's revenues until well into the 1960s. In fact, at the beginning of the decade, less than 1.5 percent of the company's $8-billion revenues came from data; by 1968, that figure had grown, but it still accounted for less than 10 percent of the company's $15 billion sales. Shut out of the computer arena, Bell stayed focused on voice communication.

But as the computer business grew explosively, led by IBM in mainframes and the development of time-sharing at General Electric, AT&T couldn't keep up with demand, so the FCC had to allow others to encroach on its data communications turf. Time-sharing, the dividing up of computational cycles of a single big computer among many distant users working at terminals, was all the rage in the early 1960s. This new field made data communications crucial, and whereas Ma Bell was slow to offer dedicated data services, a number of businesses led by IBM petitioned the FCC to allow them to build private networks of their own to handle the traffic. AT&T grudgingly accepted the competition because voice telephony was booming.

Mobile telephony was another area where the slow-to-innovate Bell System dragged its feet. Goeken, on the other hand, was quick off the mark. With the backing of a handful of small-town Joliet investors, he filed an application with the FCC in 1963 to install a private microwave network and sell the service to trucking companies. He was sure his extended two-way radio scheme would work technologically; but he wasn't prepared for the regulatory morass that would tie up his proposal. It was six years before he got his license from the FCC.

From the FCC's perspective, an alternative telephone system between Chicago and St. Louis should have been a good thing. Early on the commission had gone on record as a champion of smaller businesses that wanted to use the nation's airwaves for innovative purposes. But there was no precedent for implementing such support. Prior to Goeken, no one had applied for a license to install a public telephone system, one that circumvented the tarriffed lines of AT&T and Illinois Bell. Goeken was a pioneer in this effort. In December 1963, he flew to Washington, DC, hired an attorney with communications industry connections, and filed his application. He and his partners named their venture Microwave Communications Inc., or MCI.

When Goeken's application was opened for public comment in the mid-1960s, all hell broke loose. AT&T filed a series of objections to granting the license, claiming that Goeken's cost figures were completely absurd. Microwave Communications Inc. was proposing to build microwave towers for about $1,000 apiece, which broke down to: $200 for a Sears & Roebuck prefab shed, $700 for an antenna, another $100 for the tower structure, and some miscellaneous hardware. AT&T, on the other hand, always bought and graded the land on which it erected its towers, built massive sheds that included full bathroom facilities, and surrounded the structures with high chain-link fencing. Minimum cost? $100,000.

AT&T also questioned Goeken's technical competency to run the network, claiming that the high-school-educated, self-taught engineer would make mistakes and interfere with crucial communications services. The AT&T scientists claimed there were technical difficulties— the maximum range of the antennae, for example, was less than Goeken's estimate. On and on the criticism went, effectively stalling the application in various parts of the FCC bureaucracy for years. Goeken patiently addressed the objections. During those years, he made innumerable trips to Washington, D.C., and became a fixture at the FCC offices, where he befriended staffers, who took to the unprepossessing Midwestern entrepreneur.

It was David versus Goliath. AT&T might have had powerful connections at the top of the agency, but John Goeken had made friends with people working in the guts of the operation. Through them, a number of confidential documents made their way into his hands; the Committee for Small Business let him delay payment of the $1,200 filing fee (Goeken was strapped for cash at the time); likewise, his attorney agreed to defer payments. The angels were on Goeken's side, and his quest took on the spirit of a mission. He would not be intimidated by the high-powered lawyers and experts AT&T threw at him. When, at one point, AT&T claimed his towers were too far apart at 26 miles, Goeken pulled out AT&T maps showing it had towers as far as 36 miles apart.

Finally, in 1967, the FCC scheduled formal hearings on Goeken's application. By that time he was broke, living on credit cards, and trying to avoid creditors. In early 1968, Goeken finally got the license. It cost $100,000 all told, with filing fees, deferred payments to his lawyers, weeks of nights spent in cheap Washington D.C. motels, the airline tickets, and whatever meals he couldn't scrounge from friends and acquaintances.

The same year, another feisty entrepreneur, Tom Carter, cracked AT&T's stranglehold on the mobile phone business with his Carterfone, a mobile radiophone that interconnected with the regular phone network to place local and long distance telephone calls. The phone giant fought the intrusion because Western Electric didn't make the mobile radiophone; it claimed that the Carterfone would permanently damage the integrity of the voice network. Carter proved that this was not the case, thereby invading Western Electric phone-gear monopoly. Carter's victory would ultimately help Goeken expand his dream: Not only would he be able to offer dispatch connections, but he would be able to give two-way customers a way to make phone calls directly from their trucks as they cruised down the highway.

Once he had his license, Goeken had only won a small part of the battle. Now he had to raise the money to actually build the network. Even his years of experience fighting the FCC and AT&T didn't help in this effort. His team of small town investors called everyone they could find, asked for leads, tried to steer someone, anyone, with deeper pockets towards their partner. But nothing came through. He was utterly broke in 1968 when he was introduced to a New York financier who had already made several fortunes in the stock market. Bill McGowan was a savvy Pennsylvanian who was 35 when he met Goeken. He had graduated from Harvard Business school, worked for a couple of powerful Hollywood producers (Mike Todd and George Skouras), taken a couple of companies public, was financially comfortable, and was making good money as a business consultant telling other companies what to do.

McGowan had partnered with Wall Street insider, Ed Cowett, author of the "Blue Sky Laws" in an investment company. (Adopted by the SEC in the 1950s, and enacted on a state-by-state basis, these regulations were designed to warn investors when a company offering had about as much value as "a patch of blue sky." They were the precursors of the warnings that accompany many high-tech and biotech stock prospectuses today. Essentially, Blue Sky Laws enabled highly speculative companies to offer shares to the public for the first time.) In 1959 McGowan was introduced to Cowett and they formed a business— COMAC—to invest in small innovative electronics companies making intercoms and cordless shavers. Together, they did well with their public offerings, until Cowett got involved with an international financial con game, a securities-based pyramid scheme known as Investors Overseas Services (IOS). After the IOS empire collapsed, voluminous litigation resulted, and McGowan ended up on the hook for $100,000. It signaled the end of the partnership.

By the late 1960s McGowan began searching for something new. To clear his mind, he took a leisurely trip around the world, reading voraciously and pondering his future. When he returned to America, a Chicago lawyer he knew suggested McGowan meet with a business group who needed help raising money. He told McGowan the group had an interesting proposition: They wanted to build an independent two-way mobile phone system between Chicago and St. Louis, and already had a government license to set it up.

At the meeting, Goeken took an immediate dislike to McGowan and his high-powered persona. An A-type personality, McGowan chain-smoked, worked incredibly long days, and drank gallons of coffee to keep him going. When the smooth financier asked how much money he needed, Goeken told him $35,000, the exact amount of his outstanding debt. McGowan ridiculed him, asking what they would then grow the business with. Goeken may have been put off, but McGowan was fascinated by the project. This was something he could get excited about. He imagined going head to head with AT&T, one of the largest companies in the United States. He researched the situation, and found that many computer companies were looking for reliable alternative data circuits, and that other companies were already starting to talk about setting up their own networks similar to Goeken's. This was sounding better and better to McGowan, and the dispatch radio part seemed less valuable than an alternative long distance network.

McGowan even had a vision for how to expand Goeken's kernel of a business plan. He would develop local versions of the St. Louis-to-Chicago microwave run for 16 other key routes across the United States. This meant getting 16 licenses, however, which would require lots of regulatory work. Goeken was still dubious about McGowan, a go-getter who was now raring to take on the company. One of the investors, Tom Hermes, convinced the rest of them that the New York City businessman was just what they needed. Eventually Goeken went along, but he never fully trusted the new partner, and McGowan, sensing it, left the original Chicago-to-St. Louis leg in the hands of Goeken. But the business consultant quickly forged ahead with plans to build a series of other microwave links. With its head start (its one license), McGowan knew it could be operational before anyone else. MCI could then cobble the 16 city-to-city microwave telecommunications traffic links together, to form an alternate telecommunications channel that could serve much of the country. It would then use a local connection, called a point-of-presence, in every city so that calls could be made at local rates. AT&T's long distance rates were set artificially high to cover subsidized local service. MCI could take advantage of owning its own microwave network and low local phone rates, to price calls far below Ma Bell. By charging less than AT&T and offering special data options, MCI could cream off Ma Bell's best customers.

Picturing how it could work, McGowan quickly laid out a new MCI business structure for the systems necessary to build a nationwide phone network: Instead of a series of limited partnerships with rights to portions of the network—which had been Goeken's model for the original Chicago–St. Louis run—he launched a national corporation that would build and own the entire network. The new venture was split in quarters: McGowan, Goeken, investors, and the company itself (which retained 25% for stock options and future offerings of equity) all held equal stakes, but McGowan could count on the support of the original investor group, and that put him in power. What a difference having a businessman made. By the fall of 1968, MCI had raised $5 million and, with only 10 employees, was rushing to install its micro-wave network across the most densely populated sections of the United States. Soon its list of customers included Continental Can, Grey-hound, and Kraftco. But a year later the company was still waiting for the final go-ahead from the FCC to set up microwave networks in var-ious parts of the country.

When it came in May 1970, it also cleared the way for several other enterprises to enter the telecommunications business. The largest was the Southern Pacific Railroad, which planned to use its train-track right-of-ways to start a microwave and fiber-optical cable telecommunications network. To do so, it hooked up with the only other big autonomous telephone company in the United States, General Telephone and Elec-tronics, or GTE. This became the modern-day Sprint. Their primary market target was the lucrative 24-hour leased data line business. Because leased lines still comprised only 2 to 4 percent of AT&T's rev-enues by 1970, the FCC ruled that it would have minimal impact on the Bell System.

The FCC was wrong. Data would eventually engulf voice service, and propel all of the growth in the telecommunications market. At the time, though, it actually looked like a great opportunity for the Bell Sys-tem. In 1969, a *Forbes* article entitled "A Whole New Market," exam-ined the burgeoning business:

> Ma Bell has never been a glamour girl. Rather, for decades she has been a hard-working, slightly overweight, graying lady with a near-monopoly on U.S. telephone service. Hardly the kind of company one would asso-ciate with a windfall. Yet American Telephone and Telegraph, to give Ma Bell her proper name, is on the receiving end of a windfall that will give her a lot more sex appeal.
>
> The windfall is data communications—people talking to machines and machines talking to other machines. The explosive growth of data communications makes it predictably certain that by 1975 half of

AT&T's traffic will be data. True, most of that will move during reduced-rate periods. But by 1980 half of AT&T's revenues will be from data transmission. It is, in effect, a whole new business destined to be bigger than the company's original business of voice communications.

It wasn't just the leased lines for computers either, another telecommunications revolution was also in the making. By the early 1960s, both the U.S. and Russian military had perfected the art of launching orbital satellites. The military implications were obvious, but these satellites also could be used in voice and data transmission for commercial purposes. A government agency—Communications Satellite Corporation (Comsat)—was formed to manage the U.S. effort for this alternate use. By the end of the decade, AT&T had joined forces with the agency and was planning a series of satellite launches to create an extraterrestrial communications network. At first it seemed that only a company the size of AT&T could manage such a gigantic effort. Then IBM decided to enter the arena. Big Blue established a new division, Satellite Business Services, to provide high-quality long-distance circuits for data transmission. AT&T invested heavily to keep up. But in no time, another seemingly safe haven for Ma Bell was flooded with competitors.

By 1972, MCI had achieved the breakeven point, when it leased 300 of its initial 1,800 circuits to charter customers. The circuit is the basis of all traditional telephony—when a call is made from one phone number to another a "circuit" is opened up between the two phones that remains intact until the call is terminated. To meet the equipment demand, it was feverishly installing towers and transmission systems; to meet the financial demand, MCI went public. In June of that year MCI was offered at $10 a share, and raised $33 million. (Goeken's secretary, who had once accepted shares of the company in lieu of salary when cash was short, was happy to learn they were suddenly worth $20,000.) Anticipating unlimited expansion, the company hired salespeople to call on the major accounts. MCI offered private, dedicated line—the equivalent of leased-line, or permanently open phone circuits connecting two points—services for time-sharing and data communication, and foreign exchange privileges. (These are local phone numbers that allow a business to offer local telephone numbers for customers but which are geographically distant.)

In the face of MCI's remarkable growth, however, AT&T remained intransigent when it came to negotiating the connections to its local phone network. (As part of the FCC rulings that gave MCI the licenses, AT&T was required to provide local connections at reasonable prices.) AT&T Chairman John deButts would not budge. A lifelong AT&Ter and a confrontational man, he, along with his handpicked successor, Charles Brown, and AT&T management, devised a series of delaying tactics. John deButts had begun his climb up the AT&T ladder when he drafted a mission statement in 1949 defending an integrated AT&T as the best way to serve the nation's telephone consumers. It was subsequently used as a central pillar in the company's defense during the 1950s' antitrust proceedings. In 20 years, his opinions hadn't changed. He was dubbed Pope John for his unswerving faith in the doctrine of an unchallenged AT&T. He was a staunch defender of the status quo.

In May 1972, a group of Bell System executives gathered for a secret strategy session at Key Largo, Florida. The main item on the agenda: How to stop MCI. The tape-recorded notes from this meeting would later be "discovered" during the antitrust allegations that first MCI, then the Department of Justice, brought against AT&T beginning in 1974. Among the many damaging statements recorded was the following: "Shouldn't we act now rather than wait until they have a going business, which regulators might not let us dislodge?" said one participant. "You bastards are not going to take away my business," said another. And finally, the company's soon-to-be chief executive, Charles Brown, warned of "a large amount of revenue [being] vulnerable," and suggested that the Bell System should "choke off" MCI.

At the same time MCI was negotiating with the Bell System for local connections, it was privately sending documents and records to the Justice Department to back their accusations that the phone giant was again engaging in antitrust behavior. Not surprisingly, negotiations between the two companies broke down. As a result, though MCI had lots of salespeople, they couldn't get phone lines to connect with. Circuits would suddenly shut down, stranding MCI's customers. To reach MCI's network, users first had to dial a special number, then enter another string of numbers that included a billing code and the number they were calling. Even if they made it through that maze, the line might mysteriously go dead. Needless to say, this caused chaos and a loss of confidence in MCI. The company's momentum, as well as its status on Wall Street, started to suffer. Its credit began to run out, and some of the banks that had loaned MCI $192 million started to get nervous.

By 1974 MCI was nearly broke. The marketing division continued to drive hard for business, but the company couldn't install the fancy services it promised. Its top executives thought perhaps their best opportunity lay in a bulk long-distance service MCI was calling ExecuNet. This dial-up alternative service was geared to small and midsized companies. It was similar to AT&T's WATS (Wide Area Telephone) service for major customers. WATS worked by using a specialized switching box to route every call over the cheapest path, be it a private line, or the public network. The service was very successful for Ma Bell, but then MCI had figured out how to accomplish the same thing using its own networks and a piece of telephone equipment called a WATSBox. And because MCI owned its own lines, in many cases, it could offer the service at far lower costs than AT&T. Companies with heavy-volume voice traffic, especially those situated along one of the corridors where MCI had a microwave network already in place jumped at the cheaper alternative. MCI's customers soon included duPont, Sperry Rand, and American Airlines (which had recently developed the SABRE airline reservation system and needed as much telecommunications capacity as it could buy). By the middle of the 1970s, MCI's average rate was 81 cents per month per circuit mile, 10 percent lower than AT&T's regulated 89 cents.

But this business was hardly enough to sustain MCI. The microwave company wouldn't survive unless AT&T agreed to connect MCI to the local phone network in sufficient amounts to support the number of lines the company *could* sell. It was AT&T's stranglehold on MCI. The sticking points for AT&T revolved around four specific areas of MCI's business: foreign exchange connections that enabled local calls to be made from outside the local calling range; leased extensions, which connected MCI terminal points to nearby communities (today called points-of-presence); "through" connections that linked a specialized common carrier like MCI to another; and interconnections to corporate communication networks, where Bell companies provided the interoffice switching on its premises. In short, AT&T wanted to shut off the lines, or working connections, and without them, MCI had no business. Negotiations were brutal. Of course lawyers got involved. AT&T wanted to triple the tariffs, or access charges, levied for connections to the local phone network. A bill was introduced by a congressman from Wyoming, Teno Roncalio, to make an anti-trust exception for AT&T. Essentially, this would have decreed that a monopoly phone system was best for the USA and would have legislated the maintenance of the status quo. It was beaten back after a nasty battle between populists and monopolists in the U.S. Congress.

AT&T finally ran out of appeals on the issue in January 1974, when a judge in Philadelphia denied all appeals and confirmed that AT&T had to provide MCI connections equal to those provided to its own long-distance arm, AT&T Long Lines. Though AT&T began to provide interconnections to MCI, it was not giving up nor giving in. In 1974 *Forbes* ran a story that explained the unique challenges facing then-chairman deButts, and how he was dealing with them.

Why should AT&T worry about competition? Who else's telephones *could* its customers use? The answer is that decisions by the Federal Communications Commission over the past six years now allow other companies to nibble at AT&T's previously protected business.

The challenges come in three separate areas: First, there's phone equipment itself. Bell now rents switchboards—made by wholly owned Western Electric—for around $1000 a month, not counting the individual phones that are connected to them. Non-Bell companies—chiefly General Dynamics' Stromberg-Carlson and International Telephone and Telegraph's Automatic Electric—did an estimated $200 million worth of this business last year. Their slice has been growing since 1968 when the FCC's CarterPhone decision gave outsiders a crack at the attachment market. But that $200 million is just crumbs; AT&T still has the pie. Equipment rental yields about $4 billion a year, one-sixth of AT&T's total revenues.

A similar situation exists with private-lines communications services between, say, a plant in Kansas and the home office in Chicago. This market is $1 billion annually now, but it is projected to hit $8 billion by 1980. AT&T has more than the lion's share but MCI Communications, its 2-year-old competitor with revenues of only $15 million, is making waves. It has just won an important legal test, and now MCI customers can make long-distance calls for less than regular AT&T rates.

Finally, there's the pie in the sky—satellite communications. In addition to the AT&T-Comsat proposal, the FCC approved five *other* domestic satellite systems. . . .

If you think all this is peanuts compared to AT&T's $23.5 billion annual revenues, deButts doesn't agree. In most cases, he explains, money AT&T loses to competition isn't accompanied by an equivalent drop in Bell's costs "Our plant and carrying charges are still there," says deButts, "and if we lose $100 million in revenues right off the top, that's a $50 million after-tax impact on the bottom line—almost 10 cents a share. [deButts] isn't taking the challenge sitting down.

The MCI that was fighting AT&T for the right to build a nationwide phone company wasn't the one John Goeken had dreamed of all those years ago while flying over the central Illinois heartland. He had just wanted to run a small microwave link between the two cities. In 1974, he abruptly resigned from the company. After MCI's public offering, his stake had been reduced to 10 percent, but that was then worth more than $3.5 million ($113 million in 1998). Tired of struggles over the years, but still a dreamer, he launched a new telecommunications enterprise. Called Airfone, it would consume him for years, as he went up against not only the FCC and AT&T, but also the Federal Aviation Administration for the right to install telephones on commercial jetliners. Eventually, he would succeed. He never had anything much to do with MCI again.

In April 1974 MCI officially filed an antitrust suit against AT&T. Six months later, the Justice Department followed suit. AT&T had dragged its feet too long. (These lawsuits would prove to be the basis for an order that ten years later broke up the long-distance business of AT&T.) MCI won its case in 1980; the company was awarded actual damages of $600 million. As a punishment, it was given three times that, $1.8 billion for antitrust violations—subsequently reduced to $113 million on appeal in 1985. Dollars aside, the most important part of the trial was the publicity that the action generated for the little company. A benefit of playing David to the Bell System's Goliath was that MCI became a nationally known company. Sales grew steadily, if not spectacularly, from about $17 million in 1976 (earnings $1.3 million) to nearly $62 million (earnings $7 million) by 1979. By then the long-distance market was $12 billion a year and growing at 15 percent a year, so there was plenty of room to grow.

That is exactly what MCI did as soon as its antitrust case was over, and AT&T was out of excuses for not providing interconnections. Finally free, in 1980 MCI actively pursued both residential and commercial customers. By the end of 1981, MCI's revenues had nearly tripled, to $140 million; its stock peaked at 55 while sales kept expanding, and by 1983, the company had revenues of more than $1 billion. Residential service in particular proved a smash hit for MCI, partly as a result of smart marketing that featured free calling on Christmas, and partly thanks to television advertising that portrayed it as an underdog.

The telecommunications picture was further altered when, after interminable delays, on January 8, 1982, the Justice Department announced a settlement of its case against AT&T. It was a powerful one-two punch that would shift the balance of telecommunications power in this country forever. The reason for the settlement was plain: AT&T had realized during the trial that the judge, hearing the case in lieu of a jury, was very skeptical about the company's case. Assuming they were going to lose, AT&T management opted to cut the best deal it could.

Called the Modified Final Judgment, the agreement was entered on August 24, 1982 by U.S. Judge Harold Greene, an activist who previously had been one of the drafters of the 1964 Civil Rights Act. To date, Greene continues to act as the overseer of the AT&T empire. The agreement essentially split up Ma Bell; AT&T was free to sell long-distance services of all kinds, but local telephone connections and services would be managed by newly-formed and publicly-traded regional Bell operating companies (or RBOCs). Most advantageous for AT&T, was that the agreement rescinded the 1956 consent decrees' restrictions on allowing it to finally compete in the computer business. Local phone companies would be split off as seven regional companies, as would Western Electric, AT&T's manufacturing company. The agreement rendered AT&T primarily a long-distance network services company, competing directly with the MCIs and Sprints of the world.

Early in 1983, in order to build financial muscle to flesh out its networks, MCI raised $1 billion in convertible bonds from Drexel Burnham Lambert. Called "junk bonds," these risky but high-yield investments paid 9½ percent interest, and included warrants for stock. MCI was finally in the big leagues. With this war chest, MCI was going to be able to expand its networks faster and more widely.

The creation of seven companies out of the former Bell System turned out to be a boon for investors. In 1983, AT&T had assets of $165 billion, and one million employees; when broken up, AT&T kept $34 billion of these, splitting the rest ($131 billion) between the 7 new regional Bell operating companies. But 15 years later the combined market cap of the 8 companies was $390 billion, and the group's assets were valued at $233 billion. They were: Pacific Telesis, USWest, Southwestern Bell Corporation, Ameritech, Bell Atlantic, NYNEX, and Bell South. Several have joined forces since. However, while long-distance rates continued to plunge, and more competitive telecommunications firms entered the marketplace, local rates stayed the same. Like the company from which they were created, the so-called Baby Bells fought to keep competitors out of local phone service. It wouldn't be until the Internet started to become viable in the 1990s with its ability to carry voice phone calls along with data, that the regional companies made any grudging attempt to offer competitively-priced local access. Even when forced into it by the Telecommunications Act of 1996, the local Bell companies still dragged their heels. The Act was meant to open up local competition by letting the local RBOCs sell long distance service to their customers only once they could show that they had allowed competitors access to the local customers in their regions. However, several years later there was still little action in the local market, and the phone companies were starting to find ways around the restrictions by offering long distance service over that new and emerging technology: voice over the Internet.

In the summer of 1986, MCI's stock plunged to $6 a share, as a result of the breakup of AT&T. MCI no longer had much of a defensible advantage to investors. The new RBOCs looked like better bets in the new deregulated world because they retained lucrative monopolies on local calling. The "last mile" became the key to providing enhanced telecommunications services because the cost of rewiring every home in a region was prohibitively expensive. Aggregators and competitors might install big fiber-optic cables to carry traffic between cities, but unless they could actually get those services to the individual business or home, they were stymied. The RBOCs controlled that gateway and were in no hurry to give it up. Furthermore, many AT&T investors had grown accustomed to the dividends that the Bell System had been paying for years, and the new RBOCs were structured to continue to do so.

So although it had slain the dragon, MCI ended up in the most competitive part of the telecommunications business. Many investors now believed MCI was facing even tougher competition against a newly unrestricted AT&T. And, ironically, MCI was paying the price for a move made more than a decade earlier. In the 1970s, the FCC mandated connection charges for MCI and its cohorts that were 70 percent lower than AT&T's claimed costs. This gave MCI an enormous economic advantage when it came to pricing. But after divestiture, the FCC allowed the RBOCs to charge what they claimed were "market rates" for the connections to local phone networks. By 1986 when all subsidies—the de facto effect of the complicated skein of pricing considerations that had been used when AT&T was a monopoly phone company—were to be phased out, MCI's long-distance cost advantage over AT&T fell to about 10 percent, from 40 percent only a few years earlier. Now AT&T paid the same price to the local phone company that MCI did for each long distance call that a customer made through its system. This was called the access charge, and by evening it out AT&T was able to drop prices to compete head-to-head with MCI and Sprint.

MCI suddenly looked small and insignificant. The next year, 1985, the first following the actual AT&T breakup which occurred on January 1, 1984, MCI's revenues flattened, and profits fell. In that year (1985) MCI booked $2.5 billion in revenues, less than 10 percent of AT&T's. By 1986, MCI posted losses of $448 million.

The problem was inertia. For two years following the divestiture of AT&T, consumers were free to select any long-distance carrier. During that period, AT&T retained nearly 75 percent of the households in the United States; MCI signed up only some 15 percent. Losses mounted as the company rushed to complete its nationwide microwave network, 15 years after it had started building it and spent heavily to convince customers to switch from old comfortable Ma Bell. Technical problems continued to bedevil the network, and customers were starting to lose patience with MCI's excuses.

But all was not lost. In the fall of 1983, MCI had introduced an electronic mail service, called MCI Mail. Though it didn't catch on—it was too hard to use, and not enough of the country was computerized yet—it did give the company a foothold in data traffic, enabling it to start to build a fully digital network specially for computer communications. This was the direction to which MCI turned. By 1985, half MCI's revenues were from the consumer sector, but the company was working to fix that. This was the least lucrative part of the market. To succeed, MCI had to deliver a full set of business telecommunications services and expand its capability to sign up major corporate customers. To do that, it sold 16 percent of the company to IBM, still considered the leading brand name in American business.

It didn't work. The following year, MCI posted massive losses, forcing it to lay off 2,400 of its 16,000-person workforce. And when things couldn't seem to get any worse, they did. In 1987, right after his 58th birthday, McGowan's bad habits caught up with him. He had a heart attack. And after a heart transplant operation he left for nine months to recuperate.

AT&T, in contrast, roared ahead, offering prices that were close to MCI's via strong marketing campaigns. To add insult to injury, MCI's other competitor, Sprint, finished its own fiber-optic cable network and was able to demonstrate much higher-quality service than MCI. Soon Sprint's share of the long-distance business had risen to 8 percent, nipping at the heels of MCI's 10 percent. But AT&T still had the lead.

It wasn't until McGowan returned to the helm that MCI started to hum again. By 1988, it was profitable once more; and in 1989, it earned $558 million on revenues of $6.5 billion—although this still represented only 12 percent of the long-distance market in the United States. AT&T was still in control with over 70 percent of the market. But MCI's fortune continued to improve. In the early 1980s, it had cost the firm about $1,000 per mile to build its network; but thanks to advances in digital switching and the higher capacities of newer equipment, that price had plummeted to the equivalent of $1 per mile by 1990. This meant that operating margins shot up, hitting the high teens by 1991. Cash flow, negative in 1987, reached $1 billion by 1990. The stock roared back to

$36 per share, and MCI used the new value to acquire overseas network components by buying assets from RCA and Western Union.

By the 1990's MCI was a part of the American telecommunications landscape. Though AT&T remained much larger, eventually reaching $50 billion in revenues by the end of the decade, MCI continued to grow, reporting $20 billion in sales. Then in 1998, MCI was acquired by another pioneer telecom pioneer, Bernard Ebbers of Worldcom. Worldcom was a competitive long-distance carrier formed in the wake of the AT&T breakup. Its business was buying capacity at wholesale from long distance carriers, then reselling it to business customers. MCI's management had fallen asleep at the switch, believing that voice and traditional business data traffic was the future. Ebbers, eyes wide open, had seen the coming popularity of the Internet and had already acquired several of the largest Internet service providers (companies that sold Internet services to businesses and individual consumers). Combining with MCI made great sense to shareholders.

As data communications and telephone calls started travelling over increasingly sophisticated network equipment, MCI's new ownership led it directly into the new world of the Internet. McGowan died of a heart attack in 1992, but no doubt he would have agreed with the new direction. After all, this was a man who had challenged the most powerful company in America and tackled it to the mat. Dominating the Internet would have been a challenge Bill McGowan could have relished.

Long distance telephone service was only one of the telecommunications technologies that exploded in the 1970s and 80s. For all of MCI's aggressiveness and innovation in the 1980s, there was another major telecommunications business in which it didn't take part—wireless technologies. Ironically, the concept had been at the core of John Goeken's original business plan for the company. MCI's focus on long-distance business turned it away from the opportunity in wireless telephony. Part of its reluctance came from the FCC's rules, which made the RBOCs dominant in the field. (From the start each received one of two licenses in every metro region of the country.) Furthermore, building a cellular network was a staggeringly expensive proposition; and besides MCI already had its hands full trying to extend its microwave system.

Cellular telephony was an outgrowth of the 1970s' two-way dispatch radios, like those that Goeken originally sold. In a two-way radio communications model, a single transmission and reception tower handled all the calls in a region. That limited the available channels in a metropolitan area to a few hundred. In a cellular configuration, the same geographical territory could be carved up into small "cells," each of which had its own tower. The cell structure enabled many more calls to be handled simultaneously; the phones required less power, making them truly portable, unlike their two-way predecessors. With the advent of computerized switching (around 1980), callers could even pass from one cell to another, and their calls would be handed off as they moved.

When cellular technology became viable in the early 1980s, the FCC decided that the RBOC should be given a growth opportunity since they had been locked out of long distance and had been forced under terms of the Modified Final Judgement to stay in the barely profitable local telephone market. The FCC's rules for awarding cellular licenses, established in 1981, decreed that every metropolitan sector of the United States would be granted two licenses: one to a competitive bidder, the other reserved for the incumbent "wireline" local telephone operator. There wasn't much objection to this decision—the systems were very expensive to implement, and most telecommunications companies had little interest because this was an unproven technology. In the initial round of bidding, many of the metro areas were awarded to a sole bidder.

The absence of competition set the stage for an entrepreneur who could take cellular telephony and turn it into a viable business. McCaw, a billionaire entrepreneur from Seattle, frequented the same posh social stratum as Bill Gates. He had even attended the same school—Lakeside. As a kid, McCaw and his family were served dinner by butlers in their 28-room mansion. His dad, Elroy McCaw, was a radio station entrepreneur and cable TV system operator, an early airwaves wildcatter drilling for profits. In 1953, Elroy bought a major New York City radio station, WINS, from Bing Crosby for $450,000. He already had interests in eight other radio stations in several states, but the WINS acquisition put him in the big leagues.

Elroy began his career as an FCC radio engineer. Before the Second World War, he started a radio station in Centralia, Washington—KELA.

After the War Elroy and his wife, Marion (who kept the books), started building a chain of small radio stations, using KELA as collateral. Elroy was a good talker, a classic small-time wheeler-dealer. He knew bankers everywhere. His modus operandi was simple: leverage himself to the hilt to buy a distressed station; once acquired, quickly pare down expenses to the bone and raise operating cash flow. This system took care of servicing the debt and left a little over besides. He would repeat this process over and over.

Later, he combined KELA with a local cable TV operation when that market was established in the early 1950s. It was nothing like the cable networks of today. Initially, anyone with a big antenna could pick up signals from television stations in major cities, then route them along cables strung on telephone poles, and sell the high-quality reception to consumers who had invested in new-fangled TV sets, but who couldn't pick up much of anything but snow. It was a wild and unregulated business that attracted a broad cross-section of American entrepreneurs.

Elroy had a feel for the radio business. It was the twilight of the radio era when he bought WINS. Thanks to his ear for talent and a pair of outrageous DJs, he built it into the biggest radio station in the country. In 1969, he sold it to Westinghouse for $10 million. It was his 18-year-old son Craig who was given the check to deposit at Centralia Bank.

A few months later, Elroy had a heart attack and died; Craig found the body. Despite his father's $10 million payday, Craig McCaw found his father's estate to be a complex mess. Essentially, he was bankrupt. There were interests in 54 separate businesses, and a $2.5 million insurance settlement, and it took eight years to unravel it all. Luckily, before Elroy had died, he had transferred a single cable TV franchise (a successor to the original KELA operation) to a trust for his four sons. It was safe from creditors during the long probate.

Called Twin City Cablevision when the boys inherited it, the cable TV enterprise served a community of about 12,000 in Centralia, Washington, with a staff of 10, and had 4,000 homes wired up. Generating some $8,000 a month in gross income, it was barely breaking even. Nevertheless, when a buyout offer was made by the Seattle Times newspaper group, Craig, the second eldest, convinced his brothers to forgo the $180,000 each would have received in order to hold onto the business. It was the beginning of a tradition of the family standing united, which continues to this day.

After his father's death, 19-year-old Craig McCaw wanted to quit Stanford, where he was a sophomore, to take over day-to-day operations at Twin City. His mother intervened, and convinced him to finish college first. Already he preferred wheeling and dealing in business. In his sophomore year, he attempted to take over Stanford's vending machines to improve the quality and range of choices. When that didn't succeed, he began to run Twin Cities Cablevision out of his dorm room; and by the time he graduated, he had already determined his business strategy: growth by acquisitions. He knew from an economics courses that the rule was expand or die. He could only succeed in business by achieving economies of scale.

Out of school in 1972, McCaw bought the cable system serving nearby Winlock, Washington, for $50,000—29 percent down and eight years to repay the balance, financed at 8 percent. He raised the cash by borrowing against the equity in Twin Cities Cablevision. It was the start of a long run of acquisitions that were leveraged entirely with that one cable TV franchise. His father would have been proud.

A new era was beginning in the cable television business, and Craig McCaw was perfectly positioned to take advantage of it. The days of the small cable system operator (usually a local TV repairman or ham radio enthusiast who had cobbled together a cable operation with wires and an antenna) were over. Home Box Office, HBO, took off in the 1970s by delivering premium services over satellite to individual cable operators, who then sold premium subscriptions to customers. To compete, local entrepreneurs had to invest and expand their equipment, and usually they were strapped for cash. McCaw, in contrast, had the muscle, and with it he set out to buy cable operations all over the Pacific Northwest. His technique mimicked his father's: buy a system, reduce its operating costs, increase marketing to entice more customers, then use the resultant cash flow and equity to finance the next deal.

He went on a buying frenzy. McCaw bought cable systems from a drunk in a Fairbanks bar, from dentists, from a beauty salon owner, an ambulance driver, and a deep-sea diver in Oregon. He paid $700,000 to somebody named the Fat Man who watched porno movies in his office during the negotiations. He paid $3 million in cash to an Oregon man who lived deep in the woods in a mobile home. McCaw worked fast: He flew in, made an offer higher than the operator expected, crunched numbers, and worked the deal all night. The next morning he put a contract in front of a surprised small-town operator. "What will it take to get you to sign right now?" became the famous McCaw query. Timing was crucial. The advent of popular, premium cable services like HBO and Showtime meant cable operators could grow revenues, but only if they were well enough organized to keep investing. Not many mom-and-pop shops were.

As more Americans wired their homes for cable and signed up for premium services, banks started to regard the business as legitimate and were willing to offer loans based on four or five times cash flow. McCaw and his team (now including his two younger brothers) knew how to squeeze every last penny out of operating costs and make the numbers look better—a lesson. They coddled their customers, improving customer service in order to "make our signal look better," although they rarely spent much to improve the technical capabilities. McCaw was a master at running big central telemarketing operations that aggressively sold premium channels, while he played off the various premium services against one another to drive the best possible bargain. After a McCaw takeover, 50 percent improvements in operating cash flow were common; every dollar of improvement provided more against which he could borrow for the next acquisition.

Soon, however, he became bored with the cable TV business. By 1981, the group had some $5 million in revenues—although not a lot of income—and McCaw began to feel constrained. It didn't help that buying cable franchises was getting much more expensive, because most of the small operations had been snapped up; the big market segments had been acquired by John Malone of TCI and a handful of other well-heeled national players. Furthermore, the cable TV business soon became a regulatory sinkhole as its monopolies on local areas came under attack by politicians of all stripes. McCaw, 30 years old in 1981, and with 30,000 subscribers in Washington and Alaska, sold 45 percent ownership of the company to Affiliated Publications (owners of the *Boston Globe*) for $12 million.

In 1980, McCaw and the vice-chairman of Affiliated Publications, Wayne Perry, started looking into a new group of telephone frequencies known as cellular. (It was Perry, a communications lawyer, who had first brought the cellular phone idea to McCaw's attention in the late 1970s.) The FCC had started testing the technology in 1977, and by 1983 it was ready to auction licenses for the country's 306 Metropolitan Statistical Areas (MSAs) and 429 Rural Statistical Areas (RSAs).

The business opportunities of the technology were clear: it held out the promise of cheap wireless telephony service all over the country. But the network still had to be expanded and proven to work with the tens of thousands—even hundreds of thousands, of subscribers it would need to be economically viable. It was at this point that the FCC ruled that two licenses would be sold in each region, one for the local telephone monopoly, the other available to an outsider. From 1983 to 1987, McCaw spent approximately $3.5 million of family money to buy six of the top 30 MSAs in the country, including Seattle. Pricing was based on population; the average price per "pop" was $4.50 (a "pop" was a member of the adult population living in the region). To value the licenses, McCaw used AT&T's 1981 projections for cellular phone penetration which turned out to be ridiculously low figures. AT&T estimated total cellular penetration in the United States would top 1 million by the year 2000; by 1993, there were already more than 10 million subscribers. Nonetheless he determined that each pop was worth $80. His bankers, friends from his cable TV days, agreed with McCaw's math and not only continued to fund the acquisitions, they agreed to accept the licenses as collateral for the loans. In this way, McCaw's became a self-financing business, and the McCaw team bought and traded for significant city licenses, including sections of San Francisco, Pittsburgh, Minneapolis, and Denver. And they did so on the cheap. Everything was leveraged; all of it was financed.

Now they had to build the cellular network and like MCI, McCaw needed a lot of money to buy and install the equipment to deliver the service. Over the next three years, financed by a pair of well-heeled partners, which put up about $100 million, and a consortium of banks that bought junk bonds floated by Michael Milken, McCaw raised $1.3 billion and went on a buying spree. It was reminiscent of his cable acquisitions, McCaw purchased cellular licenses from anyone he could find. Using the skills he had honed during the company's cable TV days, McCaw executives criss-crossed the country. Two notable beneficiaries were the First Couple, Bill and Hillary Clinton. McCaw bought out their $5,000 investment in a portion of the Arkansas license for $48,000—in the mid 1980s.

By 1986, pops were going for about $20 each—still far below the value of $80 McCaw had determined five years earlier. MCI, then down on its luck, sold its cellular and paging businesses, Airsignal, to McCaw Cellular for $122 million. McCaw immediately sold the paging division for $75 million, and kept MCI's cellular licenses, which represented 7 million pops for $47 million—less than $7 each. It was a brilliant buy. In contrast, in the same period, Southwestern Bell purchased Metromedia's cellular licenses at $40 a pop, and Pacific Bell paid between $25 and $30 per pop in California.

Following this flurry of activity, even the indefatigable McCaw was worn out. In 1987, he took a sabbatical and sailed the Caribbean. By the time he came back, he had decided on his next move. He sold all his cable TV holdings to Jack Kent Cooke for $775 million, then took McCaw Cellular public. In the IPO, the company raised $309 million; add another $600 million in junk bond debt—high yielding bonds that were risky when analyzed by the hard assets that secured them. Looking at it another way, if junk bonds were secured by the rapidly rising value of cellular franchises, they were still speculative, but not so foolish. By 1988 McCaw had acquired 127 additional cell phone franchises, covering a total population of 47 million people. He was still paying only $25 per pop, and he was far ahead of anyone else in stitching together a nationwide cellular phone network.

These acquisitions became even more valuable as the new Baby Bells, loosed by AT&T's deregulations, became desperate to buy the unregulated cell phone licenses in territories outside their home markets. McCaw knew that by aggressively buying pops, even at unheard of prices, he would always have a ready secondary market with the RBOCs should he need cash. While at the start he was able to buy the licenses at cut-rate prices, by the end of the 1980s others had realized what was going on and prices rose. But McCaw was not put off. Selling to the other big players became his safety hatch, to justify the frenzy of acquisitions. It was a lesson his father had taught him many years before: always have a way out of any deal. Feeling secure, he continued to spend. By 1989 the company had more than $1 billion in debt, and was losing more than $300 million a year, but it didn't stop him. Even as prices began to escalate wildly, he bought. He went up against Bell South which had made an offer for Mobile Communications of America's licenses of $710 million or $85 a pop. McCaw lost because he didn't have the kind of deep financial pockets the RBOCs could draw on. A lesser gambler might have grown cautious, but McCaw if anything, became more determined. His response to the defeat was to sell 22 percent of McCaw Cellular to British Telecom, which had just floated a public offering and was flush with cash. The $1.5 billion it brought gave him the cash he needed to feed his passion. With the help of TCI's John Malone, whom McCaw had brought onto the McCaw Cellular board, he went for broke.

The vehicle was a startling bid for Lin Broadcasting, the New York–based independent that was second only to McCaw in number of pops. By the time the dust settled, in 1989, and the prize was finally his, McCaw had paid $3.4 billion for 50.1 percent ownership in 25 million pops. The final cost? A staggering $350 a pop. His reason for paying so much? Location, location, location. Lin's franchises encompassed important market segments of Los Angeles, New York, Philadelphia, Houston, and Dallas. With these, combined with his own holdings, McCaw was ready to launch a nationwide cellular network. McCaw had over $2.3 billion in debt, and was in a precarious position financially, but he was in so far that the banks and his primary junk bond holders didn't dare pull the plug.

The groundwork for the network had already been laid. In 1985, before he bought MCI's licenses, McCaw had struck a 100 percent financing deal with AT&T for telephone switching equipment, giving him favorable customer pricing and reliable gear. No one had paid much attention to this deal at the time except to wonder why he had made it. By 1990 McCaw Cellular was on a tear to build cellular towers to cover its territory. By ensuring that all McCaw switching equipment was compatible with AT&T's, McCaw was able to use AT&T's long distance services to offer his customers a nationwide roaming service as soon as he had acquired the licenses to do so. The RBOCs had no reason to do so as aggressively as McCaw—they weren't betting the entire future of their businesses on creating a massive cellular network, in many ways they were simply hedging their bets to ensure that cellular never replaced their crucial local franchises. McCaw was also able to engineer enhancements like voice mailboxes and call waiting, and could amortize equipment costs over many systems by having a consistent hardware platform.

It was a masterful move, targeted directly at the early adapters of cell phones: mobile executives. At the same time McCaw went after the residential market, offering nationwide calling via his own network. Marketing expenses, however, skyrocketed with the effort, which ultimately failed. The cellular market suddenly went flat during the mini-recession of 1990–1992. McCaw fell on hard times, weighed down by debt and a sluggish cell phone market. The company's stock was hammered down to the 20s in 1991, half of what it had been when British Telecom came in. Luckily, McCaw settled a dispute with Pacific Bell and was awarded half of the San Francisco franchise, one of the last franchises he needed for his national coverage footprint.

In late 1992, McCaw was talking to AT&T about a deal, acknowledging the fact that the business had changed from one of acquiring franchises and building the network to running an ongoing business. This was not McCaw's forte, but AT&T certainly knew how to do it. McCaw sold 33 percent of McCaw Cellular to AT&T for $3.8 billion. To seal the deal, McCaw had to relinquish control. Ultimately, AT&T bought out the McCaw family and McCaw Cellular for $11.5 billion. The family members split about $2.6 billion in the end.

Since selling out to AT&T, Craig McCaw has started several new ventures. One in partnership with Bill Gates, is a satellite system called Teledesic. The plan is to launch more than 400 stationary satellites over the next few years to enable communications both with the Earth and between the satellites. The goal is to build an Internet in space, and offer high-speed digital services to any place on Earth. Is it a more farfetched idea than cellular telephony was in 1980?

In the 1970s and 1980s, MCI and McCaw Cellular completely changed the face of telephone communications worldwide. They opened the market to hundreds of new companies at the same time the computer network and data industries exploded. Together they and other entrepreneurs were a powerful force for economic expansion: lower prices for consumers, coupled with more business opportunities expanded the market in many directions that would have been unthinkable before they each succeeded.

But the only constant in the digital world is change. For all the impact of MCI and McCaw Cellular, their day may be over. Today, neither is a stand-alone company. The promise of Internet telephony and the phenomenal growth of the World Wide Web may be their undoing. The irony is, of course, that the Internet could never have become popularized without the AT&T monopoly in the 1950s and 60s. The universal availability of telephone service was the bedrock upon which the Internet was built. In that world a whole new ethos and cast of characters are taking center stage.

Sandy Lerner and Leonard Bosack, the founders of Cisco Systems, in 1992.

CHAPTER 11

>──◆──<

Webs

Networks & the Internet

While the twentieth century has been marked by rapid changes in the technology business, nothing matches the speed with which the Internet has become a significant force in many lives. Books, cars, airline tickets, all of these can now be ordered easily over the Internet; five years ago it was unheard of. This online bazaar has developed along with a vast outpouring of personal creativity and information that is found in billions of Web pages, all of which can be quickly pulled up from any Internet browser. And the phenomenon is only just beginning.

It is the true dawn of the Information Age. In less than 15 years, networking has moved from an obscure technology launched by a group of personal computer wizards, to the single most powerful communications force of the twentieth century. As packets of data zip around corporations and the larger World Wide Web, information has overtaken voice communications as the most important traffic in the telecommunications world. This explosion of interest in the egalitarian world of data communications has unleashed billions of dollars in shareholder value and generated a new and wide-open playing field for entrepreneurs of all stripes.

For years the technology of networking was developed in a series of federally funded projects that created the standards that fuel today's local area networks (LANs) and the Internet. Unlike every other great business enterprise of the digital age, networking started with a government-ordained standard, and grew up because of the government's leadership role in it. At first the project was classified. Then, when it was unleashed to the public domain, it quickly became a chaotic business, characterized by lots of small technically advanced companies that brought it to the *desktop PC as that business mushroomed in the 1980s. But the fledgling industry didn't really take off until one company, financed by a single venture capital firm, took the networking technology and made a success of it in the marketplace. That company was Cisco Systems, and in ten years it grew from $60 million to $8 billion, on the back of the latest great natural monopoly of the digital age: the data router. Today, better than 80 percent of the equipment that powers the Internet is supplied by Cisco.*

However, the gear that underlies the Internet, and most corporate networks (or intranets) is only the enabling technology. The real excitement of the Internet is in the tools that give users access to all that information, search engines like Yahoo, browser companies like Netscape, and online services like America Online. These are the companies pointing the way to a new world where all the rules have changed, where a young entrepreneur with a new idea can set up a Web site and start doing business with the realistic expectation that anyone in the world can reach the business with a single click. This stands all traditional business models on their ears. It also promises to set an accelerating pace of new business formation at a pace never before seen.

It is far too early to say which new businesses, or business models, will survive. But one thing is perfectly clear: The Internet and World Wide Web are only in their infancy. The potential they hold for unlocking the entrepreneurial spirit in the world is limitless.

✿   ✿   ✿

THE ROOTS OF NETWORKING lie back in the early 1960s, in an obscure U.S. government research project. At the time, the United States had various troops posted all over the globe, and the U.S. military needed a command and control network to effectively keep in touch with all of its far flung assets: soldiers. Such a network required money, lots of money, and most of it was to come from new taxes that funded a series of government programs. One of these programs came to be known as the Advanced Research Projects Agency, or ARPA. The government had set it up after the Russians launched Sputnik in the late 1950s, to avoid being surprised the way America had been surprised by the Soviet entry into space.

ARPA was not a typical government operation. It was designed to be very fast-moving and freewheeling, with little red tape. One of its internal groups was the Information Processing Techniques Office, or IPTO. This was a behavioral sciences division funded to do research in computer graphics, network communications, supercomputing, and advanced educational machines. At the time computers were generally locked into big sealed rooms, and could only be run by a priesthood of data processing monks who carefully fed punch cards into the huge machines and read results hours later. But a loose confederation of scientists in the think-tanks and labs that ringed Boston and San Francisco Bay were starting to investigate a different approach to computing.

Bob Taylor was one of them. He believed in Camelot. He had come to Washington along with the Kennedy Administration and took up the challenge when the country's youngest president exhorted Americans to "Ask not what your country can do for you. Ask what you can do for your country!" Taylor had a degree in experimental psychology from the University of Texas. Straight out of college in 1957 he went to work for Martin Marietta in Orlando, Florida, where he was assigned to develop a computer system to run the Pershing missile, a mobile rocket that could be fired from a portable launch pad. His job is to help create the human interface. In this way he became interested in interactive computing as a way of making it easier for soldier-operators to control the missiles they ran. In the course of his work he made contact with some folks at the National Aeronautics and Space Agency (NASA), over on the other side of the Florida peninsula at Cape Canaveral. Eventually he wrote a research proposal for NASA that dealt with humanizing computer systems. NASA agreed to fund it, but only if Taylor would come and join them. He took the offer and went to Washington in early 1961. There he became NASA's representative to a small research project hosted by the Stanford Research Institute. The project's goal was to develop better ways for human beings to interact with computers, and it was run by a solitary researcher, a visionary whose ideas resonated with Taylor: Douglas Engelbart. Among other things, Engelbart proposed using a "mouse"—a block of wood with wheels on its underside—to act as a screen-pointing device for computers. This was exactly the kind of thing that Taylor wanted: an easier way for NASA operators to work with a computer.

Sometime in 1962 Taylor attended a meeting with representatives from most of the advanced projects at IPTO. The head of the IPTO group at the time was a Harvard-trained psycho-acoustician, J.R. "Lick" Licklider. Acoustics is the science of sound production, transmission, and reception. In the 1940s, experimental psychology grew in importance in the United States, and the perception of sounds became an important subject, spawning the field of psycho (logical) acoustics. During the Second World War, Licklider conducted seminal experimental work in the field of noise cancellation, helping to create aircraft earphones for crew members working in the noisy propeller planes of the 1940s.

As a result of this work, Licklider had been one of the first psychologists allowed to work with Whirlwind, the huge and pioneering interactive computer built at MIT in the late 1940's which was at the heart of America's first integrated air traffic and defense network. At that time, Licklider was affiliated with Bolt Beranek Newman (BBN), a technology research group in Cambridge. By the end of the 1950s, at BBN, Licklider had been given an individual computer terminal in his office—something almost unheard of in those days. His terminal was hooked up to an early Digital Equipment Corporation (DEC) computer, and configured as if it were his own "personal" computer. A handful of terminals all "shared" the powerful computer's processing power. This was essentially the first "time-sharing" system. Licklider explored the relationship a person might be able to have with a computer if it were a constant companion during working hours. His explorations yielded a series of academic papers that laid out key ideas for the "man-machine interface", or how a person might work with a computer. This would later come to be called the graphical user interface, or GUI.

Lick was hired to be head of IPTO in 1961 and was charged with bringing to the organization the best and brightest in information-processing research. At the 1962 gathering in Washington which Bob Taylor attended, Licklider let it be known just how serious ARPA was when it came to funding information technologies projects. He announced that his budget for the year was in the $20 million range. The rest of the group stared at each other in disbelief. This was nearly ten times the combined budgets for all the projects represented there. At the meeting Licklider also demonstrated some of the concepts that the nation's most advanced computerists were working on. These included remarkable on-screen graphics, light pens, easy-to-use interfaces, and understandable commands that had English names to them. Lick's vision was that a computer did not have to be a mysterious behemoth whose power could be parceled out only to those with the right credentials. He saw computing as a force that should be available to everyone, as widely available as electric power, as easily accessible as plugging into a wall socket.

Licklider's ideas were similar to some of those proposed by Taylor's research project leader, Douglas Engelbart. But Engelbart's ideas for "augmenting knowledge" were less formed, and slightly abstruse, hard to follow. (They were also far ahead of their time, incorporating a concept that would eventually come to be called "hypertext," with links between information that far pre-dated today's Internet.) In contrast, Licklider was talking about specifics that everyone in the room could grasp. Engelbart might have been a visionary and inventor, but Licklider was the person who could articulate the dream.

Lick was considered something of an academic Pied Piper. He traveled the country constantly, seeking out new and intriguing work wherever he could find it. When he found promising projects, he would usually be able to get them some IPTO grant money to help them grow. Among his collection of small speculative ventures, he had one pet project: time-sharing. The idea for it had emerged at General Electric in the late 1950s, when the company's early foray into computer work spawned a product that would have enormous impact over the years: the modem (an acronym for MOdulator-DEModulator). This device could convert data from a computer into sounds that could pass over telephone wires (MOdulate them), and then convert those sounds back to data (DEModulate them). Modems thus enabled computers at different locations to share data—that is, to communicate with each other via telephone lines.

While big mainframe computers were proliferating in the late 1950s and early 1960s, a group of BBN researchers started thinking about how they might share an expensive computing machine with more than one user at a time. They had learned that most of the time these big computers were idle. Even while processing a stack of punch cards, the circuitry inside the gargantuan machine was hardly exercised at all. So, they thought, why not share the computer's processing power among a number of users?

Once the time-sharing concept had been developed and later proven, some members of the BBN team convinced the heads of MIT to let them experiment with a mainframe on that campus. The university was then facing a crisis, as its thousands of engineering students inundated the campus computer rooms with their boxes of punch card programs. By 1960, students often had to wait an average of a week to get the results of their programs. Time-sharing looked like a godsend for MIT, and the BBN proposal was quickly approved. Licklider brought in extra funding for the project, and by 1962, a giant IBM mainframe had been reworked to allow a dozen terminals—television-like monitors with keyboards—to be attached to the device. This was called the CTSS, or Computer Time Sharing System.

As sensible as time-sharing seemed to be, however, most of the computing establishment was dead set against it because it threatened to reduce the number of computers sold. IBM in particular wanted nothing to do with it, and even forced MIT to dismantle its early system. Big Blue saw revenues in leasing more and more dedicated machines, not in rewiring their machines so more and more users could connect to the same number of mainframes. Where was the profit in this? As a result, the corporation erected formidable barriers. In the early 1960s, IBM was nothing to trifle with: the company boasted $1.4 billion in annual revenues and was already selling 60 percent of all the computers used in the world. The giant company dismissed the people pushing interactive computers, calling them rebels.

On the other hand, GE, which had started the movement into data communications with modems, saw the concept as a big opportunity. Together with Licklider's IPTO, GE and MIT then financed an ambitious effort to make time-sharing into a viable commercial field. Called Project MAC (which stood for both Multiple Access Computing, and Machine Aided Cognition, depending on who was doing the talking) the hardware was developed quickly, and soon MIT students were able to work directly on separate terminals that were wired to a central GE mainframe. But the operating system software proved to be more troublesome. Called MULTICS (Multiplexed Information and Computing System) this project was assigned to a group of MIT researchers working in the fledgling, but highly touted, field of artificial intelligence (AF), which was supposed to make a computer "think" like a human brain. MIT funded an endless stream of graduate students and a series of academic projects to develop AI, and along the way create the new operating system, but they never panned out (although the concept became the media's darling for many years). The operating system these intellectuals created never made it out of the experimental stage.

But in the early 1960s, time-sharing made sense, at least from a user's perspective. It allowed someone to actually sit at a terminal and work directly with the machine, even if it meant waiting a turn while the mainframe computer worked its way through other people's requests.

It was about as close to individual, desktop computing as anyone had yet come.

A strange new world soon came into existence. The computing culture at MIT produced an insular coterie of programmers who called themselves "hackers" (based on the Model Railway Club's slang that referred to a brilliant wiring solution as a "hack"). These hardware aficionados were obsessed with computers. They exhibited the same "hard-core" personality traits that would later be exemplified by the likes of Bill Gates, Steve Wozniak, and a host of other driven, antisocial computer enthusiasts. Money from the MULTICS project financed these MIT hackers. They spent endless hours working on the operating system software, often staying up all night to create outrageous programs.

One of the hackers created the first computer game, called Space-Wars, in which several players could compete in an electronic science fiction world. It was the first instance of a group of networked users all working on the same program, operating at the same moment. Another hacker wrote a program that could calculate the fastest route to each and every one of the subway stops in New York City. Another created a series of chess games in which the computer defeated one of the biggest critics of artificial intelligence—and thus silenced him.

The hackers programmed in front of adoring acolytes during the wee hours of the morning. And they broke all the rules. Their attitude was that all doors were meant to be opened, all passwords were designed to be revealed, all restrictions were established to be overcome. For the first half of the 1960s, they freewheeled through the MIT computer community, all the time writing code and programming on whatever machines they could get time. Along the way, they denigrated mainframe systems, and refused to annotate or document their code. They effectively created the first counterculture of programmers. Most of all, they grew accustomed to two things: personal, private direct interaction with computers; and networking. One of the first "hacks" the boys at MIT accomplished was a method for leaving messages for each other on the computers. Since they all worked odd hours, they needed an efficient way to let each other know what they had done. This was the genesis of e-mail. This wasn't the only programming stunt that yielded real value. The hackers started a revolution with practical, accessible, useful computer applications. Eventually a number of them started companies that would make them very wealthy. The first great computer game company—InfoCom—was started by several of these hackers. VisiCalc, the first spreadsheet program for personal computers, was programmed by Bob Frankston, who had long been an MIT hacker. Danny Hillis, another alumnus, created a new breed of super computers, called parallel processing machines, at Thinking Machines Inc. Seminal work in speech processing was done by another graduate who worked his way through grad school on the Project MAC payroll. Ivan Sutherland, a computer graphics pioneer, produced one of the first computer paint, or sketch, programs while he was working on Project MAC; he called it Sketchpad, and it effectively provided primitives for drawing onscreen on a computer. It also led him to cofound one of the most influential computer graphics companies in the world: Evans and Sutherland.

In the early 1960s, MIT-style time-sharing caught on with customers, despite IBM's early efforts to fight it. In part, this popularity was due to the number of computers in use. Honeywell led the market with a series of IBM-compatible mainframe computers that could be used for time-sharing. At the same time, IBM found itself under pressure from leasing companies that bought its mainframes, then leased them to customers for less than IBM did. All of this, along with a maturing commercial computing business after 15 years, produced a spectacular rise in the number of mainframes in use. By the end of the decade there were some 30,000 big computers at work around the world, and time-sharing made sense as a way to extract as much value as possible from the million-dollar machines.

Meanwhile, the IPTO folks, heavily influenced by the hackers and the MIT culture, started thinking more and more about networking. Connecting the various terminals at a given site quickly led to the notion of connecting systems between distant sites in a time-sharing environment. The military applications for this concept were obvious. In 1966, Bob Taylor, by then head of IPTO, started wondering why his staff couldn't share messages and information on the various IPTO projects through some kind of electronic mail system. Taylor recalls his thought process: "In the Pentagon, where IPTO was headquartered, I got on one terminal and I could have a set of electronic mail conversations with a group of people around MIT; then I got on another terminal and I could have electronic mail communications with the people in Santa Monica. But these two groups couldn't talk to each other. That seemed patently absurd.

"There had to be a way to send messages between systems. I convinced the head of ARPA at that point—Charlie Hertzfeld—that we had to do this. He did more than say yes. He took a million dollars away from one of his other programs to give it to us."

Taylor still had two problems: First, he needed gateways, a way to ship data back and forth; second, he needed a manager to make it all work. "I knew just who I wanted as the program manager, but he wouldn't come: Larry Roberts." Roberts was a top researcher at the Lincoln Lab, an MIT research facility located at a secluded Air Force base about 30 miles north of Boston. It was closely allied to nearby MITRE, a top-secret missile and defense research facility. Roberts was a scientist, and that was just who Taylor needed to build what would be called the ARPANET. (The network had begun in J. R. Licklider's fertile imagination as the Intergalactic Network, a loose confederation of people to whom he sent memos. It soon evolved, transmuted by Taylor, to the ARPANET.) Taylor leaned on Roberts' boss, and Roberts took the job.

In approaching his task, Roberts started out with an idea created by a Rand Corporation researcher, Paul Baran. In 1956, Baran had postulated an electronic concept called *packets*. In his formulation, packets were blocks of data, collections of binary bits, arranged in such a way that other machines could read a "header," identifier text, at the start of the packet and figure out what to do with the rest of the data included. The header specified a number of key items, such as the size and type of the data, the sender's address, the recipient's address, and the like. In Baran's estimation these packets of data could then be broadcast around a network. That was as far as Baran took the packet concept, because what he was really doing was trying to design a network that could theoretically withstand a nuclear attack. He thought a highly interconnected mesh of connections, with many redundant interconnections between each node (essentially, every point would broadcast packets out to every other location on the network, and read every packet broadcast by others), was the only way the government could be sure of having at least some communications capability in the aftermath of a full-scale atomic war. But his ideas had been rejected at AT&T, where his theoretical work indicated that the nation's long-distance network, with its big concentrated cable routes, would fail in the same war game scenario. Ma Bell refused to believe him, wouldn't let him have access to its long-haul telecommunications maps, and essentially buried the idea of a completely democratic packet network like it. The ideas lay dormant until Taylor and Roberts resurrected them in 1966.

This pair was creating something no one had ever seen before: a communications channel that could link millions of computer terminals all over the world, nearly free of charge. It started as a way for half a dozen research facilities around the country, all linked via voice phone lines, to share mail and messages. It all seemed promising, but there was a lot more Taylor and Roberts had to do to make it work. At first, packets were broadcast by their author, then passed along electronically throughout a network; only the receiver could actually open the packet. Every other receiver on the network could see the packet but wouldn't open it, and simply send it on to the addressee. The scheme needed a way to let all the different computer systems at the various ARPA sites access packets simultaneously—and read each other's mail, no matter how different their underlying computer systems. The answer? A shared format that allowed each site to translate the messages. The format came to be called a protocol, the precursor to Internet Protocol or IP.

The protocol they adopted was the predecessor to what eventually became the Transmission Control Protocol/Internet Protocol (TCP/IP), which today dominates most data traffic traveling throughout the world. In 1967, it didn't exist; it had to be built from scratch. And there was a bigger problem: There were very few standards in the computer industry then. Every computer system was different. One system, the computers at the Stanford Research Institute, which were being used by far-thinking computer scientist, Douglas Engelbart, included an "X-Y Pointing Device" that would later be called the "mouse." Others, such as UCLA and the University of Utah, modified existing mainframe computers. And many organizations had multiple systems in use on their campuses.

A few months into the project, Taylor despaired of ever figuring out how to get different computers to share information. The answer was the router. A router is a simple and powerful device that directs packets of data around a network. The idea for it was first suggested in 1965 by the same man who had designed several of the most advanced non-IBM machines during the previous ten years: Wes Clark. While most of the academic computerists involved with IPTO were pushing the time-sharing model, Clark, widely considered the most brilliant computer designer of his generation, had been moving in a completely different direction. Wes Clark had created some of the logic and architecture—the essential operating blueprint of a big computer, expressed in an electronic circuit design—of the SAGE, successor to the Whirlwind. From there, Clark had gone on to create the first two transistorized computers at MIT's Lincoln Labs: the TX-0 and TX-2. These were virtual blueprints for DEC's first commercial computers, the PDP series. Having done all that, Clark went off on a radical tangent. In 1961, while still at Lincoln Labs, he set out to create a computer so simple that buyers could assemble it themselves: a kind of kit computer. The only group he could interest was a band of psychobiologists, who wanted to be able to collect real-time experimental data on animals and humans.

Clark called his kit machine the LINC; and it was the successor to the first transistor machines he built. Since the machine incorporated every bit of transistor and logic-circuit knowledge that Clark had, it was very efficient and very inexpensive. Around 1961, when Bob Taylor was getting to Washington, Wes Clark was trying to solve the design limit that he had set himself for the LINC, Laboratory Instrument Computer. It couldn't cost more than $25,000. At the time the "cheapest" computers were sold by DEC, and they cost $80,000 each. Clark's LINC had several innovations: a kind of mouse—four knobs that allowed a pointer to be moved over the screen; keys that stayed depressed until a process was completed, and then they popped back up; 1,000 bits, 1K, of core memory.

Here was a machine that could be built by a group of biologists, nonengineers, in a lab. Although it didn't have a microprocessor—because the device wouldn't be invented for another ten years—it was in almost all other respects, the first personal computer. All of the participating biologists were given their computers for free funded by Lincoln Labs, MIT, and grants from the National Institute of Health (NIH). In order to get the computer, the psychologists and biologists had to show up at a seminar held at MIT in the summer of 1963 where they built their own machines. There was no shortage of scientists who wanted their own LINC, including John Lilly, who would become famous for his work with dolphins. He wanted to use the LINC to facilitate the communication between man and dolphins.

In the end, though, the LINC project never really succeeded. Clark had trouble securing funding, and by the mid-1960s, he had moved from MIT to Washington University in St. Louis. He continued to refine the project, but time-sharing was creating the big buzz then. Clark's objective was exactly the opposite: He was trying to put a powerful computer into an individual's hands. There were few believers. Nonetheless he was a member of the IPTO crowd, and was regularly invited to conferences where advanced computing ideas were discussed.

At one such meeting in 1967, the topic of conversation was about making Taylor and Roberts' idea of a computer network work. As the debate wore on, Clark suddenly realized that these computer scientists had it all wrong: They were trying to make each "host" (or mainframe) computer at the various sites talk to every other computer system. The simpler solution was to design a new computer which would do two things: first, pass data around the new ARPA network to other similar computers located at each participating thinktank or university; and translate that data, when it was addressed for people at its site, into the format for the computers that were used there. Clark's suggestion: use the basics of his cheap LINC computer to intercept all network traffic, route it, and pass it along.

It didn't take the project leaders long to realize that the router was the perfect solution. The official name adopted for it was the interface message processor, or IMP. Putting one of these at every location in the network solved the problem of incompatibilities between computer systems; every computer would translate its data into the common language IMP format, and the IMPs would talk to each other, passing data back and forth over the network. In this way, the big computer systems at each site, which were called "nodes" in the developing language of networking, wouldn't have to be modified. All that was left to figure out was a way to convert data from a particular computer system into the IMP format, and vice versa.

Roberts and Taylor decided to use Clark's ideas, but not the LINC itself, which had not been designed to handle packet data. Instead, the pair enlisted a team of computer scientists at BBN, who built the IMPs on a Honeywell minicomputer base that was specially modified to handle message traffic. A number of these refrigerator-sized machines were built throughout the 1970s, almost all at BBN, and they weren't cheap—the base contract bid was for $1,000,000, covering the cost of the first four machines.

Clark's computing legacy was the IMP, or router idea, which made the ARPANET possible in the early days. Today, every router that carries traffic around a local area or wide area network owes its existence to him. And the original concept of separating message traffic from the computing systems then enabled the egalitarian, peer-to-peer Internet to grow exponentially later on.

In the early days it was hard to get others to join the network. Resistance existed both inside the government, and among the defense contractors who had high enough security clearance to be asked to join. It was hard for many people to see what the value of a big data network like this might be. Wasn't the mail good enough for sending documents? Why invest in all the gear, wiring, and terminals required to let staff type messages to each other when it was much easier to simply pick up the phone, or drop a memo in the mail. And the most important communications company in the world continued to resist the idea of an alternative network, especially a "packet-based" one that had its genesis in the ideas of a few egghead scientists who had the audacity to question whether the phone network would survive a nuclear holocaust. Taylor and Roberts went to Bell Labs for instance, in 1967, and tried to interest its management in packet networking, asking the AT&T subsidiary to be a technical node for them. The AT&T group refused to get involved; they didn't think it would work.

But Taylor wouldn't be set off course. He was convinced that interactive computing, through networking, was worthwhile. To further his cause, he decreed that all recipients of IPTO and ARPA funding had to join the network. As he predicted, the more he and his colleagues used the system, the more convinced they became that it was an astonishingly powerful communications tool. Electronic mail proliferated on the system as several researchers created ad hoc programs to allow messages to be sent to anyone else on the network. Soon it came to be called E-mail, and the name stuck. Newsgroups, which were electronic bulletin boards, also flourished. Anyone could post a new idea or the results of an experiment on the newsgroup for every member of the group to read and comment on.

The government continued to fund IPTO-related projects into the 1990s. Between 1960 and 1990, the capital invested to create the Internet's backbone—the network of routers that trafficked data around the country—totaled $2 billion in U.S. government funds. The system was perfected throughout the 1970s, but it remained a network chiefly of *academic* and government agencies, with thousands of simple text–based messages passing back and forth daily, and a handful of newsgroups being sustained by like-minded scientists. As yet, there was no commercial content on it. In the early 1980s, the U.S. government decided to declassify the system.

By then Bob Taylor had left IPTO. Frustrated by the bureaucracy, the secrecy, and the lack of commercial prospects, he headed for Xerox's Palo Alto Research Center (PARC) in 1971. This would prove to be a very important move, because he brought with him deep knowledge of packet data networking from the ARPANET project. When Taylor arrived at PARC he had an audacious vision: He would assemble the best computer scientists in the world there, and they would create an entirely new computer system that put all the power of a computer at each user's desk. Each computer would then be linked in a networked environment where users could share information and cooperate in their work. It was a vision for the office of the future, perfect for Xerox.

The first person to see the value in Taylor's vision was a colleague and software expert named Butler Lampson. At PARC Lampson and a hardware specialist named Chuck Thacker agreed that Taylor had the right idea. But to devise practical, individual computers, each with the power of an entire time-sharing system, they would have to reduce the cost of those systems, which ranged up from $250,000 apiece. The trio decided to build their own machine from the ground up, using as many integrated circuits as possible. In this way they could reduce their costs by using more hardware to address some of the new and complicated problems they were tackling—things like high-resolution, user-friendly screen displays and graphically oriented programs.

They called their new computer the Alto. From the beginning, it was intended to be one in a series of powerful individual machines, linked together in a network that used the same packet networking scheme that had been devised for the ARPANET. In 1972, Lampson was the first to use the phrase "personal computer." In a memo that fall he wrote: "If our theories about the utility of cheap, powerful personal computers are correct, we should be able to demonstrate them convincingly on Alto. If they are wrong, we can find out why."

Six months later, the first Alto was complete. It used a mouse as an input device, and had what was called a "bitmapped display," meaning that each dot, or pixel, on screen could be controlled individually. It displayed images in crisp black-and-white. (The first image it showed was Cookie Monster from *Sesame Street*.) Best of all, the computer cost about $20,000, almost one-tenth the price of the cheapest comparable time-sharing system.

Without a doubt, the development of the Alto was astonishing and it took Butler Lampson into uncharted waters. It was 1973, and as the primary system architect, he had a computer that offered unprecedented capabilities. At its heart the machine offered enough horsepower—residing in numerous integrated circuits and system boards—to control every dot onscreen individually. This required a lot of the new semiconductor memory chips that Intel and Texas Instruments were selling, simply to hold the screen's image. Then there were a number of computing circuits—all of these were created in circuit boards, because the first microprocessors from Intel and Texas Instruments were still far too rudimentary for the sophistication of this new computer. Essentially the guys at Xerox had created a custom-built minicomputer, with special-purpose graphics and input devices. Now the question became, How could he use all that power? Very early, Lampson adopted an idea that Doug Engelbart had shown in a rudimentary demonstration in 1969: overlapping windows, each containing its own information. As Lampson added more and more windows on his screen, he realized that he needed a way to manage them. Thus was born the concept of the icon, a miniature image of a particular window that would allow him to work on another window, yet have instantaneous access to the other reduced window if need be.

The method of input was another essential innovation of the Alto's working operating system. Using both the mouse and the keyboard, the user could control a cursor that could be moved anywhere on the screen. Various combinations of the mouse buttons performed different tasks, but these combinations were consistent through all the various applications. Menu buttons were generally displayed on-screen, and users could click on them to initiate commands. Scroll bars were arranged atop and alongside the windows onscreen, and allowed either sequential movement through a document (or along an image), or the ability to jump to another region. This had never been achieved with such sophistication before.

Another critical element Lampson mastered was the matter of "views": how to display information effectively. With the advent of the bitmapped complex screen, he was able to create a feature called "what you see is what you get," or WYSIWYG. This meant that a document looked exactly the same on-screen as it would when it was printed; no arcane formatting codes were visible. Furthermore, he experimented with different views, taking a graphic image, for instance, and presenting two different portions of it on-screen at once.

There was also the matter of integration, that is, providing a consistent user interface that made it possible for data in various applications to be merged. This was especially complicated when combining pictures with text, but Lampson knew the graphic elements of the system were critical to its success. He assigned a group of engineers to build a number of tools that could draw directly on-screen, and manipulate the pixels so that graphics would be reproduced accurately on the Alto. Lampson drove himself and his team hard, creating not only the operating system but also all of the key applications that ran on the machine. The result was an astonishing feat of intellectual creativity and sheer hard work.

Taken all together, the Alto represented a remarkably advanced computer system for the early 1970s. Unfortunately, Lampson's team had bet on the wrong technology horse. The hardware they had built was all based on integrated circuits, but by the mid-1970s, cheaper microprocessors had burst onto the scene. No matter what they did, the PARC group could never get the Alto's price below $20,000. And Xerox's marketing department didn't appreciate the machine. It sold the Alto only as part of a larger set of computers for a single workgroup. That essentially made the machine a $150,000 sale, taking it right out of the small business market.

But PARC was still awash in plenty of cash from Xerox's near-monopoly on copiers. Budgets rose year by year. The researchers at PARC generally thought of themselves as an academic research facility, not a consumer operation. Executives back at Xerox corporate headquarters in Stamford, Connecticut, rarely thought about the engineers in California at all, as they didn't see them as crucial to the company's business. In fact, over the years, numerous breakthroughs at PARC wound up falling between the cracks at the big company; there was simply no one who could figure out how to turn the academic advances into viable commercial products. Thacker and Lampson continued to build Altos. Eventually there were more than 100 of these machines around the PARC offices, but precious few sold outside the company. A few years later, a more business savvy PARC employee tried to market a less expensive version, called the Star. It failed to make a dent in the market too. But the Alto had profound impact on the industry: it was the graphically oriented machine that inspired both Steve Jobs and Bill Gates.

Later, Lampson and Thacker would design a series of dedicated computers, the first of what we now call "servers." These computers gave the hardware more power by offloading some of the more computationally intensive tasks and directing them to dedicated devices. One such device was a print server that fed pages to a laser printer. The laser printer, too, was designed, engineered and built by another Xerox genius, Gary Starkweather, who, along with Ron Rider, another Xerox PARC colleague, and Butler Lampson, created typeface-quality lettering—the predecessor to laser typesetting.

In order to have anything worth printing, Lampson needed an electronic text editor that worked within the realm of a graphical user interface and display. So he also came up with the first text editor that displayed words exactly the way they would eventually print. This was called Bravo, and it was co-designed by Charles Simonyi (now a chief software designer at Microsoft). This product became the basis for Microsoft's Word later.

Despite its failure as an individual "desktop" system, the Alto was a cutting-edge achievement. By mid-1975 it was a complete computing system of individual machines, all linked into networks with file servers (where files were stored) and all able to generate laser printer-quality output. The PARC computerists had moved the state of the art ahead by years. They had anticipated much of the direction of computing for the next decade.

There was only one problem: the guys who ran Xerox still couldn't figure out how to sell it. But the rest of the industry clearly recognized the value of the work. Companies like Adobe grew out of products created at PARC. The entire laser-printing industry was based on its work. The graphical user interfaces that Microsoft and Apple would battle over had been created inside Xerox PARC. All of these breakthroughs were important, and alone they would have made the research facility famous. But the innovation that really put Xerox PARC on the map was the creation and first implementation of a networking system for personal computers. This was the network scheme that the Alto machines had been built around. Called Ethernet networking, this system would eventually create the office of the future—but not for Xerox.

Local area networks—LANs—are simple networks of PCs. Often oriented around workgroups, or clusters of cubicles, they enable computers to exchange sets of files stored on a central server and to share expensive devices like printers or scanners. PARC's seminal work, thanks to Taylor's ideas and experience with the ARPANET, provided for simple, inexpensive, and heterogeneous networks of interconnected personal computers. Networks became increasingly important in many American businesses during the mid-1980s. In the process, this created the first great company of the data networking age: Cisco Systems. Its key product was the first real router—a commercial product with that name, and designed to manage the transmission of data packets out to other locations on an interconnected data network—based on the ARPANET's IMP. It quickly became a huge business, but Xerox missed out on all of it.

When Taylor left IPTO back in 1971, Larry Roberts was left to carry on. By the early 1970s, there were some thirty nodes on the nationwide ARPANET network. Throughout that decade this net remained classified; access was granted only to institutions that were doing work for the Department of Defense. It was assumed that every site was secure. After all, if an institution had the rights to get on this Defense Department network, it already had security clearance and could certainly afford to get the gear to make the connections. But this also meant that the network had almost no internal security features. Incorporating these features would become a major issue when the architecture was finally made available for public use.

A bit earlier, in 1969, the same ideas about packet-data networks were being used to power a network being developed in Hawaii. The University of Hawaii had a unique problem: its campuses were located on several islands. In the early 1970s, AT&T had the monopoly on telephone traffic, and rates were exorbitant for calls between the islands. A handful of engineering professors wanted to send data back and forth between seven campus locations scattered among the islands. AT&T phone calls were very expensive and the cash strapped university needed a cheaper method of communicating. One of the university's professors created a system called AlohaNet. It used custom hardware to convert computer data into packets and relied on old taxi radios, radio transmitters, and receivers to move the packets around. The idea was to broadcast packets of data out onto the airwaves, instead of sending them over wires. The network receivers on other islands were tuned to the same frequency and so could pick up the signals. If the packet was addressed to a specific machine, it would be captured only on that machine; other network addresses ignored it. This was essentially the packet data concept applied to radio, and it resulted in a working inter-island network. It also supplied the impetus for the computer networking scheme that was developed at Xerox's PARC a few years later. One of the key developers at PARC, Robert Metcalfe, had written his Ph.D. dissertation on the AlohaNet system. At Xerox, he helped create a similar but improved system, which was rejiggered to operate over coaxial wire (and eventually over regular telephone wire). This became the Ethernet networking scheme that is in common use today.

By 1973 the ARPANET was starting to encounter serious problems. The original architecture had been built before there was any real knowledge of the kind of challenges that could be encountered in a big network like this. Now that there were lots of nodes, and thousands of users, some early decisions proved to be the wrong ones. But reconfiguring such a system was no simple task. By 1974, a group of key ARPANET contractors at Stanford and UCLA had set to work on a new design for the network. But because there was no commercial urgency to the project, it wasn't finished until 1980. The protocol they created, the Transmission Control Protocol (TCP), was key to the redesign. Because it could run on any operating system, it allowed disparate computers to join the network. The three key authors of this protocol were Steve Crocker, Bob Kahn, and Vinton Cerf. By the late 1970s, all of them were working at UCLA, and the protocol had gone through numerous rewrites. Finally, in 1981, the ARPANET officially switched over to TCP. This was the birth of the Internet. Gradually, control of the network passed from ARPA, which was a research organization, first to the Defense Communications Agency (an arm of the Pentagon), then finally to the National Science Foundation. In the process, by the early 1980s, the classified ARPANET system gave way to a widespread primarily academic (although there were a few defense contractors involved as well) network of interconnected sites that anyone with a router could join. The name became the Internet.

The introduction of TCP and the related Internet Protocol (IP), was of crucial importance. The widespread adoption of TCP/IP opened up the possibility of "internetworking," combining a number of networks. In essence, TCP provided a standard way for any two machines to share network traffic, while IP provided a way for packets to be addressed and delivered. Again, routers played a key role. Packets were broadcast and passed through routers on the inter-connected network until they reached their destination.

All of this was in place by the early 1980s. And it might have remained a strictly academic vehicle, used to communicate research, if it weren't for a romance between two computer science students. The married couple, Sandy Lerner and Leonard Bosack, were graduate students at Stanford University in 1984. They were assigned to manage the computer labs that housed the dozens of computer terminals used by the university's science and engineering students. The two worked long hours in separate buildings and became frustrated that they couldn't send messages back and forth via computer. The reason: Stanford had dozens of small computer networks, but each of them was isolated from the others.

As Lerner and Bosack pondered the dilemma, they thought perhaps they could rework the idea behind the IMPs for local use. At that time data traffic from different segments of the Stanford campus was passed up to the Internet—to reach another part of the campus it would then be broadcast across the net and received at the "IMP" machine for that other sector. The pair of computer graduate students thought this was crazy, and they set about creating a way for local data traffic to be passed around on campus, before it was sent out to the Internet. Instead of using $100,000 specialty IMP routers, where all traffic was handed off to the Internet, why not design a small local router, whose job was to manage data traffic among various small local networks? In this way, messages with local—i.e. Stanford—addresses would stay on the campus Ethernet wires; messages that had Internet addresses would be routed out to the Internet at large.

Because they were at a school with a strong engineering tradition and a lot of computing power, Lerner and Bosack were given room to try out their ideas. In 1984, after tinkering for a while, they perfected their design and started a company called Cisco Systems to build simple, small routers. By the mid-1980s, PCs were appearing all over the place, especially on desktops in companies. Once this started happening, it wasn't long before business users needed to wire up those desktop machines to share information or printers, or exchange e-mail. Apple, with its Macintosh line, was early into the fray, offering a built-in, low-capacity networking feature called AppleTalk. The price was right (the feature was free), and it worked. However, as that company did with almost everything, it invented its own proprietary system, and so it wasn't compatible with any IBM computers or clones. It also proved too slow for commercial purposes.

At the same time, Xerox's Ethernet scheme was being used only for sending messages and packets of data around a local company. Groups of desktop machines could be equipped with Ethernet cards, then be plugged into a "hub"—devices that linked a local workgroup of users, all of whom shared the same networking branch. Each hub was then connected to others like it, and all shared a common wire for interconnections. As packet traffic was broadcast out onto the network, it was sent throughout all the hubs attached together in a common segment, and packets of data addressed to a specific machine would automatically end up there.

This worked fine as long as all the traffic stayed on one segment of the network with a bunch of interconnected hubs. To connect different segments, however, another device called a "bridge" was developed. These devices indiscriminately pass all data traffic that appears on either side of its connections, acting like a bridge between network sectors and allowing packets that were broadcast on one section to reach other sectors as well. This extends the reach of the network, but it also vastly increases the amount of data traffic scurrying around the wires. As networking started to catch on, corporate networks started generating vast amounts of network traffic.

Unfortunately bridges were quickly overwhelmed. Cisco's routers on the other hand, designed in a continuum that started with the LINC and the IMP, not only maintained lists of addresses to which to send their data, but were also smart enough to inspect the packets and route them to the right place. The router accepted packets of data from any computer system using TCP/IP, examined the destination in the header of the packet, then routed it appropriately. When a router recognized the address on an incoming packet as belonging to the local network, it captured it and held it there; otherwise it let packets flow through. Local traffic never had to go out to the rest of the network, so congestion was markedly relieved. As long as the routers kept updating each other on the addresses they could find, it didn't matter where each was located in the network.

By the mid-1980s this capability to interconnect lots of different computer systems, which was at the core of Lerner's and Bosack's original idea, was crucially important. In most businesses, there were not only lots of legacy mainframe and minicomputer systems, but also a variety of personal computers—from Apples to PC-compatibles—as well as various higher-powered workstations for engineers and technical professionals. Trying to get older and newer machines, Apples and PCs to directly communicate with each other was a nightmare. But by having all the computers use TCP/IP as their language of data packets, and handing the traffic off to a series of interconnected routers that all exchanged router tables with each other, the difficulty of networking was neatly solved.

As the IBM PC started to gather momentum in the late 1980s, networking became an important force. And Cisco had the right idea at the right time. As more and more traffic started moving across corporate nets, and more and disparate corporate sites were linked together in those nets, the need for routers grew. Cisco's founders had originally created their device by coupling a microprocessor with a fairly sophisticated set of software that could inspect, rout, and manage every packet. In 1987 the company was still rather small—it had only ten employees and reported sales that were under $5 million. Worse, a new pair of companies in Boston, Synoptics and Wellfleet, were better financed and offered more sophisticated routers. After all, the router idea was based on the original BBN IMP machines, and there was no great secret to it. The hard work was in creating the software that managed address tables—locations of every other router reachable on the network—that could direct packets of data accordingly.

In response, Cisco's founders, Lerner and Bosack, started making the rounds of the venture capital community in northern California. They were smart enough to know that it would require a major infusion of money to take the company to the next level. Not only did their routers have to be upgraded so they could handle more data traffic, but the company needed to hire a sophisticated sales force that could sell to corporate managers. That same year, they took a $2.5 million investment from Sequoia Associates, a venture capital firm headed by Don Valentine. Valentine had been the marketing director at National Semiconductor, and had worked for a while at Fairchild as well. For years he had been kicking himself for missing out on Apple when he had the chance to invest in the company early on. Instead, he let his former employee, Mike Markkula, provide the seed capital (and go on to become a multimillionaire).

Cisco Systems struck Valentine as the company that could ride the networking revolution, if only its founders would let him guide the business. With his $2.5 million investment (which was the only venture money Cisco would ever take), Valentine became chairman of the board and started to push the founders into taking a more professional tack with the company. Neither Lerner nor Bosack had ever worked outside of academia, and they lacked the competitive instinct that Valentine knew was essential to succeed in this increasingly competitive market. He sensed that TCP/IP would become the world standard and he understood the essential rule of network economics: as more corporate networks adopted TCP/IP and Ethernet-based systems for their networking, eventually no other scheme would be able to get a toehold even if it was better. Valentine wanted to spend heavily, and early enough, to create a business that could become the market leader as the networking imperative took hold.

However, the more he pushed for aggressive action, the more he found resistance from the co-founders. Finally, in 1988, he made a proposal: He would install his own colleague, John Morgridge, as president, and buy out the original partners. Sequoia offered $200 million to the founding pair to get them out of the way. Valentine was a straight shooter, a guy with a no-nonsense attitude. He hadn't liked Steve Jobs, and he felt the same way about Lerner and Bosack. The couple took the offer and walked away from Cisco, pocketing their money. She became a noted animal liberation financier and cosmetics company president. He started another computer start-up; this one aimed at speeding up computing.

Betting on TCP/IP allowed Cisco to explode in the early 1990s. As Valentine had predicted, TCP/IP was adopted as the de facto networking standard. With an enormous existing base of academic networks already using the TCP/IP protocols for their Internet traffic, along with a new generation of academic workstations (built around an engineering operating system called UNIX that had TCP/IP built into it), there was already a base of experienced users. With Ethernet based on the same packet data standards, corporate network buyers standardized on

TCP/IP and Ethernet protocols. The more the standard proliferated, the more gear the networking industry sold. At the core of the networking industry, the most profitable device was the router. And the company with the best and biggest routers was Cisco. In 1990 Cisco's revenues had grown consistently, to about $70 million. Nevertheless, the company, now with 250 employees, was still in a dogfight.

With the release of a new version, number 3.0, of Windows and IBM's failure to make OS/2 a viable alternative, the corporate marketplace went on an explosive expansion of networking capabilities. This version of Windows came with networking capabilities built into the operating system, so any computer running the operating system could join a network by adding an Ethernet interface card, setting some numbers, and plugging it into the proper cabling. That meant business for the suppliers of routers and hubs that made corporate networking possible. Under Morgridge Cisco had built an extremely effective national sales team. At the same time, the company developed a router operating system of software that made it particularly valuable for customers to standardize on Cisco gear. Starting in 1990, the company's revenues doubled every year, reaching $1.3 billion in sales and $323 million in income for 1994. While it was clearly one of the leaders in the corporate networking market, Cisco still had heavy competition in the form of 3Com and Bay (the latter formed by the merger of Synoptics and Wellfleet).

Then the Internet started to get popular, as a result of the development of the World Wide Web, which brought a standard, and elegant way for graphics and information to be shared over the formerly text-only network. Because of its roots in academic computing at Stanford, Cisco was poised and ready to take advantage. Since the Internet was entirely run on TCP/IP packets, Ethernet networking gear was naturally the way it would be built out. At its heart, the Internet is simply a worldwide collection of very large routers, all of which talk the same language and can pass messages back and forth. A long-distance message might pass from small local routers, through bigger ones at a university or internet service provider, through still larger ones at a network gateway hosted at one of several big sites around the country, then back through the reverse of that process down to an individual address behind another router on the other side of the globe. The need for all these routers was very good for Cisco Systems. The $200 million stake bought by Valentine and Sequoia was worth $6 billion by 1995. John Morgridge, Valentine's hand-picked president, ended up with 1.5 percent of the company, or ten million shares, worth nearly $1 billion dollars by the middle of the 1990s. In 1997, Cisco boasted $7 billion in sales on $1.3 billion in income. Best of all, even while it was slugging it out with competitors for the corporate data networking business, it held onto 80 percent market share in the equipment used to run the Internet. This leadership position gave Cisco a major advantage as the Internet continued to double in size every few months, and the future of all voice and data communications traffic looked likely to pass over the Internet in some form.

While corporate networks were using routers to let their various divisions and locations send e-mail and communicate with branch offices, an entirely new group of users were being introduced to the world of data communications via modems. Most PCs supported modems, devices that allowed a computer to use regular phone lines to send and receive data. Consequently, starting in the early 1980s a number of companies tried to make a business of offering a series of services that could be accessed from a computer equipped with a modem. These were called online services and were the predecessor to the World Wide Web.

Proprietary online services—access to collections of information, tips, news, mail, software, games and so forth—were packaged together in a single consumer-friendly software "package." As long as a computer had a modem and could run the software, these services were reachable. MCI made a stab at providing widespread e-mail service for all computer users, led by Vinton Cerf, one of the key developers of the TCP/IP standards. But the system—MCI Mail—had an interface that only a computer enthusiast could understand, with a series of arcane text-based commands. CompuServe, owned by H&R Block, claimed it was the first public consumer online service. But its product promised much more than it could deliver over the slow modems of the time. CompuServe created a business, but it appealed primarily to hard-core technicians, with its many computer forums that offered plenty of shareware to download.

The breakthrough for online services came from one of the only businesses to succeed based on a Macintosh platform: America Online (AOL). The company was originally part of an internal Apple project to launch an Apple-specific online service, with a lively attitude and graphics to match. But when Apple changed direction and abandoned the branded online services business, it released the interface that had been created in that process. This was an early, primitive version of today's AOL start-up screens, and at the time, it was much better than anything else available on Windows.

Apple sold the rights to the visually oriented online service back to the company that had hosted the service: Quantum Computer Services. This business was run by a smart young man who had grown up in Hawaii, Steve Case. Case and his older brother, Daniel, had started a number of small ventures during their teenage years, ranging from a limeade stand to selling magazines. As soon as he graduated from Williams College in 1981, Case continued on the entrepreneurial track. A chance meeting with the founder of one of the first online videogame companies—The Source—gave him the idea of providing online services for the fledgling PC or videogame markets. The company made deals with Atari, Commodore and Coleco (all consumer electronics, videogame, and computer makers of the mid 1980s), and then won the big prize: Apple. Case struck a deal to manage Apple's online services, and his company, Quantum, was in the black.

When Apple backed out, Case quickly gave AOL a Mac-influenced look for its Windows version. When Windows sales skyrocketed in the early 1990s, Case took advantage of the opportunity to grow market share online. AOL released a graphical Windows version of its software ahead of CompuServe. That head start, aided by smart and aggressive marketing, as well as Case's willingness to continually upgrade, made AOL the clear winner in online services. It certainly helped that in the period—1990 to 1995—the number of PC-class machines sold in the United States went up rapidly, rising from 10 million to 100 million by 1995. Almost all of them came with modems. America Online's number of subscribers followed suit, and soon outdistanced CompuServe, which had been the first to break the one-million mark in the late 1980s. By 1997, AOL claimed 15 million subscribers—AOL would eventually buy out Compuserve as well. By 1997 its revenues were $2 billion, with a market capitalization of $13 billion. Coincidentally, that same year Apple, which had opted out of the online business, reported sales of $6 billion and a market cap of $4 billion, which was shrinking.

However, even 15 million subscribers were nothing compared to the universe that the Internet could potentially reach. The promise was that anywhere there was a phone line, there could be a router or a modem with a connection to the Internet. AOL and CompuServe were following a model that required them to give users their software—with its graphics, components, and connection engines. But on the Internet, no special software was needed. This lack of barriers to entry allowed it to take off so rapidly.

The online services had prepared the market for the revolution that was about to occur with the growth of the Internet. By 1990, the Internet had long outgrown its Department of Defense parentage. Control had passed to a series of task forces and standards bodies that decreed what changes would be made. The Domain Name Service (DNS) took over the registration of domain names that came to define online communities, or destinations, in the Internet world. The elegance and simplicity of the protocols, and the fundamental network design that allowed anyone to join as long as they agreed to pass traffic along transparently, made it grow broadly in the worldwide academic and governmental spheres—though it was still far from any commercial applications.

One of the key nodes on the worldwide network as it was then was in Geneva, Switzerland, at the headquarters for the *Conseil Européen pour la Recherche Nucleaire,* or the European Lab for Particle Physics, known as CERN. With 9,000 affiliated physicists, it was also one of the largest individual members of the Internet community, and it was facing a problem: How could these top scientists share notes and research papers, photographs, graphics, and annotation links to other papers internally and externally without it costing a fortune? The answer would come at the hands of a programmer named Tim Berners-Lee, who could not have known that his program would become the door through which the rest of the world would enter the Internet. It would be called the World Wide Web.

In 1979, Berners-Lee wrote a primitive program, when he was a grad student at CERN. His idea was to create a web of interlinked and interconnected electronic documents. At that time, it was very hard to do and he abandoned the effort. In 1990, however, the now 35-year-old Berners-Lee thought it might not be so far-fetched. Furthermore, he thought it could be done on a new computer that he had just seen, one that seemed to have the proper mix of hardware and software to display information visually. It was Steve Jobs' newest computer: the NeXT.

The stylish, all-black machine ran a version of UNIX, the operating system that most of the Internet universe used then, which incorporated TCP/IP. The cube was never a commercial success although it was popular in academia. It took Berners-Lee a couple of months to rewrite his original program for the new computer. What he created was a "browser" supported by a handful of web "pages" that he could jump to. It was the first version of the World Wide Web. Berners-Lee coined that name himself, and he usually shortened it to WWW. While Berners-Lee created the framework for the system to work, it was left to others to actually implement the code that lies at the heart of it today. This is built around a set of codes that defined what attributes a particular area of the screen would display. Called HTML, for HyperText Markup Language, these codes specified the style of any object on a web page. The page was accessible to anyone with access to the address of the HTTP, or HyperText Terminal Program, machine that served it up.

By using a simple language of "tags" that modified the way a block or line of text was displayed onscreen, then combining them onto a "page," and bundling the text in a stripped-down version with the "page," Berners-Lee had produced a way to create relatively sophisticated displays without having to make them very large. This meant that they could be sent over the Internet and opened at any connected machine, in a reasonable time period. The result was the appearance of local interactivity, even though the viewer might be thousands of miles away from the computer where the first page was stored. And that page, in turn, might be thousands of miles away from a page it offered a link to.

A link describes clicking on an area of one page then jumping the viewer to another page. This ability to dynamically link information provided by thousands of Internet users, and to create combinations of millions of different pages on the fly, is a big part of what makes the World Wide Web so popular and powerful. None of these details would matter to the user, who was surfing from one page to another. On his machine, the pages would display within a "browser" window. A link would simply be a different colored word, or a graphic. And because all of it was based on a set of shared layout standards, it would look the same to every viewer.

Berners-Lee was a purist, and he had no use for graphics. In his view, they cluttered up the clean line of intellectual discourse. So while his ideas were interesting, they remained a tiny element in the still-small Internet community.

Starting in about 1992, the people at CERN started distributing copies of Berners-Lee's program and inviting some of their friends across the Internet to try it out. The first web page was *http://info .cern.ch.* Slowly, people began trying the new program. But this was a time when only students, academic researchers, and technicians used the Internet. Though powerful, it was very difficult to use.

But the elegance and power of what Berners-Lee's accomplishment wasn't lost on a small coterie of computer science students around the world. By 1992, several other browser programs had been written, and there was growing interest in Berners-Lee fledgling web. Browsers weren't very complex pieces of software anyway; they were seen as a kind of library card for the digital age. The simple browser would let a user grab a web page and look at it. And the web pages themselves were quite primitive: lots of text, no graphics. Up to then the only online graphics had been delivered by online services, such as AOL. To achieve that level of graphics on the Internet, though, meant using software provided by the online services themselves (which contained the pictures), and forced the user to work within the structure and constraints of the online service's system.

In November 1992, one of the professional staff members at the National Center for Supercomputer Applications (NCSA) at the University of Illinois in Champaign saw some literature on the WWW, and he became intrigued. Dave Thompson used another Internet search tool—Archie, which was popular then—to look into the World Wide Web and he downloaded several of the free browsers offered on the CERN site. He thought that the system might be just what the NCSA needed to let its thousands of computer scientists share information and research easily and effectively. He showed it to his boss, who was also intrigued, and also to a young minimum-wage hacker who was working in a basement office at the center. His name was Marc Andreessen.

Andreessen was a big, bright kid from Wisconsin. He had grown up in a tiny farm town where his father was a seed salesman. At the University of Illinois he majored in computer science, but he was having a few problems getting along with his boss at the NCSA, Pei Wei. She didn't think he was a very good programmer, and worse, he had a nasty habit of trying to take credit for much of the work others on his team did on PolyView, a graphics program. Andreessen freely admitted that he didn't want to be a programmer—he wanted to be a team leader, a motivator, and even a businessman. But Andreessen did have the hacker's ethic: he was willing to completely subsume himself in a project, to stay awake for days on end to get something done. Just days after seeing Thompson's demonstration of the CERN browsers, Andreessen had hacked a rough version of his own.

In truth Andreessen wasn't much of a programmer. His software was often buggy and clunky. He did, however, have one advantage over most of his fellow hackers in the basement: He was powerfully persuasive, and so he was able to convince one of the most gifted members of the team, Eric Bina, to help him. Bina was known as a kamikaze programmer, a madman who would work on a project for 48 or 72 hours straight. Better yet, he was considered a software superstar, capable of elegant feats of programming. Six weeks later the two had created a smooth new product. They named it Mosaic.

In creating Mosaic, Bina had taken on the two biggest problems with the rudimentary browsers that were available at the time, and solved them both. At its heart what he created was an interface—a way for a human being to work with the material he found over the Internet, and to do so in a way that was natural and comfortable. First, he was able to make the product work smoothly and easily by hiding the complicated and cryptic commands under the "skirts" of Mosaic. Bina's new browser was simple and logical, and it worked the way an unsophisticated user would expect: point at things, click on them with the mouse buttons, and watch what happens. Second, he figured out a way to integrate graphics with text in the display window. Previously, Berners-Lee had included the capability to display graphics in his browsers, but he had hidden them under icons. In Mosaic, graphics were automatically displayed as long as the originals, residing on the web page itself, were stored in a graphics format that was compatible with the viewer's machine.

It was combining the simple interface with the capability to display graphics automatically that separated Mosaic from other browser programs. While several of the other programmers around the world were struggling to make images and text interact easily, Bina accomplished the task in just six weeks. Suddenly a web page could look like a magazine page more than a computer display. NCSA—which owned the product since its own employees created it on company time—distributed Mosaic freely to the Internet community. By the spring of 1993, it was available for download, and within months more than a million copies had been distributed over the Internet. It started a small explosion of usability for the previously hard-to-use Internet. But it still had limited impact. After all, this was an academic movement, with little in the way of promotion behind it, and having a million downloads was very different from having millions of web pages. Until the WWW could boast millions of users actually posting things on it, in a format that all the others could access, it was going to remain a small and interesting experiment, no more.

In December 1993 Marc Andreessen graduated from the University of Illinois and headed to California to take a job with a firm looking to create a secure method for buying and selling things over the Internet. In the years since the old ARPAnet had been handed off to the NSF, it had slowly started to change from a purely academic network, to a kind of public data universe. Well into the 1990s, working with it required a dedicated computer science orientation, because its navigation and management tools were decidedly unintuitive, but as the PC revolution gained momentum there were more and more people who had the skills to use it. As a result, it had now developed a number of forums and special interest groups, and some of the more advanced users were starting to think that it might have the capability to create an economic force. This was especially popular among software companies, who thought that the world of software distribution could be turned on its ear by distributing programs over the Internet. Still, this was a long way from being a mass medium. The browser that Andreessen had helped to create was getting around, and various people were looking at it. One of them was John Markoff of the *New York Times*, who early in 1994 wrote a glowing story about the fascinating possibilities of Mosaic. Not long after the story ran, Andreessen received an e-mail from Jim Clark, a former Stanford business professor who had started Silicon Graphics, a company that specialized in high-priced workstations for engineers and movie special-effects creators. Clark had just been forced out of the company he co-founded, and was searching for something to do. Because Silicon Graphics' machines used a variant of the UNIX operating system, which was the software system of choice for most of the academic computers linked to the Internet, Clark had deep connections with the Internet community. Over the next several weeks Clark talked with Andreessen about whether Mosaic could be used as software for interactive television. But, the more they talked about the possibilities inherent in the WWW, the more the two started thinking that perhaps there was a business producing a commercial version of the Mosaic browser.

The company they started in April 1994 was called Mosaic Communi-cations, and the idea behind it was to improve the Mosaic browser. Clark owned the lion's share of the firm, but Andreessen got 20 percent for his role in bringing over a number of the basement hackers from NCSA, especially Bina, over to the company. The University of Illinois objected to the use of the software that had been developed on its time and with its money, and sued the founders of the new company. The parties eventu-ally settled. In 1994 the company was renamed Netscape.

Jim Clark had a sterling reputation among venture capitalists. Silicon Graphics had been a success story in the late 1980s and early 1990s—rising to sales of over a billion by 1992. Clark was tall and blonde, and good-looking, and he liked to hobnob with the power elite of Silicon Valley. Better yet, he had a bit of Hollywood glamour about him, since his previous company's design machines were used at places like Pixar (creators of animated digital movies), and film director George Lucas' Industrial Light & Magic, famous for special-effects wizardry. As a result, Netscape was handsomely funded and able to launch a massive public relations campaign. It was built around the fiction of Marc Andreessen as the wunderkind of the World Wide Web, the boy-man who had made the Internet accessible with his browser. Because the NCSA was still giving away its version of the browser, Netscape had to find a different way to generate revenue. They decided to give away the browser as well and then sell more advanced software for servers and companies that wanted to use the principles of the Web to provide information to employees, customers, or the public.

Netscape benefited from a remarkable combination of luck and tim-ing. By late 1994, enough people had started to use some kind of browser that a buzz was building about the Internet. The standards-based soft-ware system that Berners-Lee had created was simple enough to allow many computer-literate users to create Web pages. No longer limited by the rules and formats imposed by an online service such as America Online, the new Internet environment became a free-for-all where only skill, smarts and imagination made the difference. Suddenly, with almost no economic incentive, Web pages started to proliferate. Every interest was represented. Every hobby, passion, or perversion soon had its corner of the web. With the explosion of material available in the format, Web use exploded as well. By the end of 1994, Netscape had become the hot media story of the new phenomenon of the Web, and Andreessen was its star. Internet usage shot up, and like every other digital–age success story, the more people who started to use it, the more valuable it became.

Netscape's decision to give away its software, while it generated no revenues, propelled the Internet into a new dimension. Netscape's was a classic digital-age approach: Give away your product in hopes that enough people will start to use it so you can create a viable business later by selling related products. By August 1995 the company had its initial public offering of stock—barely 16 months after the company had been formed, and long before it made any money. After the offering, Jim Clark was worth $565 million, Marc Andreessen, $100 million. It was a long way from Wisconsin for the 25-year-old.

However, if anything, the Netscape story might prove to be the ultimate cautionary tale of Silicon Valley. Marc Andreessen may have $100 million in stock, but he has never written a single line of programming code since he joined the firm. No one works for him. His job is to advise the technicians who run the company on the Internet, and to answer his e-mail. This is the kind of job that used to be called a sinecure. He was at the right spot at the right time, and he parlayed it into a personal fortune that is breathtaking in its dimension.

Things might have continued to go well for Netscape if not for Bill Gates. A few months after the Netscape IPO, Gates started to realize that another force was sneaking up on Windows that could have dire consequences on his company's control of the desktop computing world. In short, a browser-based world might make Windows irrelevant. Users in the near future could conduct all their daily business through a browser window, accessing both programs and information over the Internet.

Gates turned Microsoft on a dime and in a message dated on December 7, 1995 (not, inconsequentially, Pearl Harbor Day in the U.S.) pushed the company toward the Internet. Most of the new efforts were based on work that the company had already done on its unsuccessful online service: MSN (Microsoft Network). Within a year, Microsoft would offer its own version of the Netscape browser, and would also give it away for free. All of the company's massive suite of programs were to be Internet-enhanced. Microsoft launched a series of Internet-based content and commerce projects that disrupted the cozy world of the Internet, but also telegraphed how important a force it was about to become.

It would also mark the beginning of the slide for Netscape. While the company continued to sell its corporate software, its browser lost market share to Microsoft. On the other hand, in selling big computer system software for servers—machines that "serve up" web pages and information to browsers anywhere on the World Wide Web—it proved much harder for Netscape to make headway. Big companies, who started to think of a web presence as essential for modern business, were loathe to bet their businesses on a shooting star of a company. By 1997, Netscape had started to lay off employees, and was trying desperately to enlist the one ally that could help create a safe haven from Microsoft's aggressive tactics: The U.S. Government. Netscape succeeded. In May 1998, the Department of Justice and 22 states sued Microsoft for antitrust violations. The charge: using its dominance of the Windows market to force resellers of its operating system to include only the Microsoft browser.

Netscape, whose business was based on a single idea, was on the ropes. The company had certainly helped to launch the Internet explosion, but then it had lost its way. Netscape had nothing that it owned uniquely, nothing that couldn't be copied, and nothing that it had invented.

A dramatic contrast is Cisco, a company that did create products, then defended them, and aggressively acquired new companies that could extend its reach as the networking market matured. As the networking phenomenon continues, with data networks carrying voice and video too, Cisco continues to profit from it.

Companies like Yahoo! and Excite are expanding the Internet bringing features like free e-mail, search capabilities, online games, and news directly to the user. Netscape achieved none of that. Its failure to create lasting value, its ability to float a huge stock offering without owning any underlying technology or innovative edge, might be a lesson to future entrepreneurs. Investor frenzy is a predictable part of every thriving new marketplace. Maybe that's a sign that the digital age is finally coming of age.

Or maybe it is a demonstration of just how unprecedented the Internet world is. The Internet generation isn't scared of technological knowledge. Computer and network know-how has reached far enough out into society at large that it has unleashed an outpouring of entrepreneurial activity. There are lots of potential Mark Andreessens. In the past two years there have been more than 65 Internet-related IPOs. The combined market value? Nearly $90 billion. It isn't just the inventors and entrepreneurs who are taking part in this mad rush to the Web. Investors, individual investors, are now savvy enough to support companies that could never have found money in the public markets ten years ago. An online bookseller like Amazon.Com can come from nowhere, go public, and make its founder worth over $300 million as it becomes one of the country's largest book distributors within a couple of years. All thanks to the Internet. Two graduate students can brainstorm an idea, develop a search engine that acts like a Yellow Pages for the Web, get venture capital funding, and go public as Yahoo!, each worth hundreds of millions of dollars before their 30th birthdays.

And this is just the beginning. The true promise of the Internet is that it can break down barriers for smart entrepreneurs all over the globe. Certainly it is a phenomenon that began in the United States, a country where universal telephone service ensured that an egalitarian Internet-style network could emerge. It was nurtured by investors who had spent enough time in the personal computer revolution to feel confident backing the newer Internet movement, investors willing to take big risks.

But most of all, the Internet in all its glory and tawdriness, owes its exuberance and vigor to the spirit of entrepreneurs of all ages who can see a new, wide open, and limitless vista before them. The Internet is the new frontier. And the only limits to the Internet are those of the human imagination, and the personal will of new entrepreneurs to create business successes. If the experience of the past ten years—or even the fifty years of the digital age—is anything to go by, there's no shortage of either of those things in this world. If anything, the supply of both is increasing.

Blame the Internet. Hail the Internet.

Blame the computer. Hail the computer.

This book was created from three primary sources: interviews with many of the principal characters over the last fifteen years; contemporary magazine and newspaper accounts; and books written about the digital phenomenon.

The business story of the Computer Age is not recorded in any one place. It is a living evolving story that has been primarily captured in the business magazines, like *Forbes* and *Business Week*, and a national newspaper, The *Wall Street Journal.* Trade magazines have been primarily technical, and hometown papers, local TV and network news were late to start covering business, let alone technology. Unfortunately, indexing schemes for pre-1980s publications are spotty at best, and the text is rarely available online. Nonetheless, back issues of *Forbes* from the 1950s and 60s provide a very intriguing picture of IBM, the electronics industry, and telecommunications.

The most cohesive source of data are the series of business books that have been published over the past fifty years looking into various companies and characters of the digital revolution. Many of the books are out of print, and it is hard to verify much of their data. As always, many are self-serving, and present the victor's view of things. However, there are a handful of books worth searching out for further data on the people and events covered in these pages.

CHAPTER 1 ❦ PIONEERS & PIRATES
The story of Atanasoff is contained in the special collections department at Iowa State University in Ames, Iowa. There an enormous collection of material—letters, news clippings, patent applications, legal testi-

mony—is on file, and the university now also maintains a working model of the original ABC machine, built faithfully to the original design. The inventor's son—John Atanasoff Jr.—is a businessman in Boulder, Colorado and provided some insight into the events, although he was too young to remember the pivotal years.

There are two books about the man. Clark Mollenhoff's *Atanasoff: Forgotten Father of the Computer* (Iowa State University, 1988) is an adoring recitation of the story, written with some verve. The other, *The First Electronic Computer: the Atanasoff Story* (University of Michigan Press, 1988) was written by two mathematicians who worked closely with Mauchly and Eckert on the ENIAC project: Alice and Arthur Burks. Although dry, this book comes to the conclusion that Atanasoff was the true inventor of the modern computer. Another book that is an excellent pictorial and textual source for the early history of computing (although only through the 1950s) is *A Computer Perspective: Background to the Computer Age* by Charles Eames (Harvard University Press, 1973). However, while it is full of nineteenth and early twentieth century machines, it was written before Atanasoff's reputation was resurrected after the Sperry Rand v. Honeywell lawsuit of the early 1970s, and omits him.

There remains much controversy over the issue, as can be found in the pages of an obscure academic journal, *The Annals of Computer History*. There John Mauchly, and since his death, his widow Kathleen Mauchly, wrote a number of letters over the years trying to put straight the record according to them. These and various rebuttals provide some invaluable insight into the events. The best account of the business story that led to Remington Rand is available in Nancy Stern's *From ENIAC to UNIVAC: An Appraisal of the Eckert-Mauchly Computers* (Digital Press, 1981). Most of the material on James Rand came from *Forbes* magazine.

CHAPTER 2 ❦ BIG BLUE
The remarkable tale of the playboy son of IBM who led the company to glory is told in wonderful detail in Thomas Watson's *Father, Son & Co.: My Life at IBM and Beyond* (Bantam, 1990). Filling that out were two other books that provided a more nuts-and-bolts perspective: *Building IBM: Shaping an Industry and Its Technology* by Emerson Pugh (MIT

Press, 1995); and Robert Sobel's pioneering business work, *IBM: Colossus in Transition* (Times Books, 1981). Katharine Fishman's *The Computer Establishment* (Harper & Row, 1981) offers some insight into the giant company IBM had become by the 1960s. Most of the numbers come from *Forbes* stories about first, the office equipment business, then data processing.

CHAPTER 3 ❧ QUANTUM LEAP

The story behind the development of the transistor has yet to be told in any detail. The best archive on the early development of the product is at Bell Labs. Stanford University, where William Shockley ended his career as a professor, has his papers in its special collections holdings. Texas Instruments also has extensive materials, and a bevy of research librarians eager to help. There have been few books on the subject. The best popular account is *Microcosm* by George Gilder (Simon & Schuster, 1989), although T. R. Reid's *The Chip* (Simon & Schuster, 1984) has great color as well. The best book looking at the business history of the early electronics age is *Revolution in Miniature* by Ernest Braun and Stuart Macdonald (Cambridge University Press, 1978). For the science behind the breakthrough and some of the personal drama, *Crystal Fire* by Michael Riordan and Lillian Hoddeson (W. W. Norton, 1997) focuses on the development of the transistor. Charles Weiner's *How the Transistor Emerged* (American Institute of Physics, 1973) does a fairly good job of making something as paradoxical as the behavior of electrons understandable. Once again, most of the numbers and economic citations come from the pages of the magazine.

CHAPTER 4 ❧ BITS

With this chapter principal characters are still alive. The material in large part comes from interviews with Jay Forrester, Wes Clark, and Douglas Engelbart. The only book that looks at Project Whirlwind is by Kent Redmond, *Project Whirlwind: The History of a Pioneer Computer* (Digital Press, 1980). The best source for information on early transistorized computers, and many of the early experimental systems is *A History of Personal Workstations, a Compilation* edited by Adele Goldberg (ACM Press, 1988). This last book includes material on Engelbart. There is only one book worth reading on the rise of Digital Equipment

Corporation: Glenn Rifkin and George Harrar's *The Ultimate Entrepreneur: The Story of Ken Olsen and Digital Equipment Company* (Chicago Contemporary Books, 1988). One other book is a good source for the early computing milieu: *Hackers: Heroes of the Computer Revolution* by Steven Levy (Doubleday, 1984).

CHAPTER 5 ❦ CHIPS

Some of this material is covered in books mentioned in Chapter Three. Again, interviews with Federico Faggin, Gilbert Hyatt, and Ted Hoff make up some of the material. That material, combined with several older interviews with Bob Noyce, as well as more contemporary sessions with Andy Grove, as well as a number of key current and former Intel lieutenants, forms the central core of the chapter. The seminal resource for material about Bob Noyce is a magazine article that Tom Wolfe wrote about him in a 1983 issue of *Esquire*. One of the company principals has written several books; the best is *Only the Paranoid Survive* by Andrew Grove (Doubleday, 1996). A book by Michael Malone entitled *The Big Score* (Doubleday, 1985) looks at the wild world of Silicon Valley in the 1960s. A more recent book, *Inside Intel: Andy Grove and the Rise of the World's Most Powerful Chip Company* by Tim Jackson (Dutton, 1997), does not deliver much of an inside view but is valuable for some historical color. It is also flawed by a dependence on Intel's "official" view of the events surrounding the development of the microprocessor—a self-perpetuating, self-serving, inaccurate myth that is swallowed unthinkingly by almost everyone who has ever written about the company. Most of the numbers come from a string of *Forbes* articles that started to cover the brand new field as it emerged.

CHAPTER 6 ❦ MECHANICS

Several days spent with Ed Roberts provided most of the material for the story of MITS—several of his contemporaries like Bob Marsh and Les Solomon filled in the details. There are two books which cover the early days of the personal computer industry: *Fire in the Valley: The Making of the Personal Computer* by Paul Freiberger and Michael Swaine (Osborne/McGraw Hill, 1984); and the aforementioned *Hackers*. The story of Bill Millard, IMSAI, and ComputerLand is recounted in Jonathon Littman's *Once Upon a Time in ComputerLand: the Amazing Billion-Dollar Tale of Bill Millard* (Simon & Schuster, 1990).

CHAPTER 7 ❧ WIREHEADS

It would be impossible to list the number of interviews that make up the research for this chapter. These include sessions with Steve Jobs, Stephen Wozniak, Dan Fylstra, Dan Bricklin, and almost every member of the group at Apple that created the Macintosh and Lisa computers. The Apple story has attracted a number of writers, including the author of this book. *Steve Jobs: The Journey Is the Reward* by Jeffrey Young (Scott Foresman, 1987) was the source for much of the biographical material on Jobs and Wozniak. Two other books worth reading are: Michael Moritz's *The Little Kingdom: The Private Story of Apple Computer* (W. Morrow, 1984) which recounts the Apple story before the Macintosh; and *West of Eden: The End of Innocence at Apple Computer* (Viking, 1989). There were a number of stories about Apple in the pages of *Forbes*, starting in the late 1970s. Most of the economic numbers come from the pages of the magazine.

CHAPTER 8 ❧ PCs

Many interviews with team members of the original IBM PC group contributed to this chapter. Among named participants, Lew Eggebrecht, Don Estridge, and Gary Kildall all discussed their roles with the author at different times over the years, but there were dozens of others who shared their memories. The best book about the thinking inside IBM during the crucial early 1980s is *Computer Wars: How the West Can Win in a Post-IBM World* by Charles Ferguson and Charles Morris (Times Books, 1993). There are two widely cited books about the phenomenon of the PC, but both have some flaws: Paul Carroll's *Big Blues: The Unmaking of IBM* (Crown Publishers, 1994) and *Blue Magic: The People, Power, and Politics Behind the IBM Personal Computer* by James Chopsky and Ted Leonsis (Facts on File, 1988). Someday a history of this fascinating moment in American corporate history will be written. Not surprisingly, there are a number of articles in *Forbes* about IBM during this period, and many of the statistics are drawn from that source material.

CHAPTER 9 ❧ HARD CORE

Interviews with Bill Gates and Steve Ballmer, as well as many other Microsoft employees and people involved in the personal computer industry from all companies and points of view, provided material in the chapter. Irv Rappaport, Apple's intellectual property attorney at several key points in the narrative, provided invaluable insight into how Gates outmaneuvered John Sculley. One Microsoft competitor—Philippe Kahn, formerly of Borland—provided enormous insights into the business of software in the late 1980s and early 1990s, but over the years I've interviewed just about every key executive, including Jim Manzi of Lotus and Ray Noorda of Novell as well. As befits the world's wealthiest person, there have been several books written about Bill Gates. The best are all written by Seattle area journalists. Steven Manes and Paul Andrews wrote the most comprehensive biography of the man, *Gates: How Microsoft's Mogul Reinvented an Industry and Made Himself the Richest Man in America* (Doubleday, 1993) but the book ends with the drive for Windows dominance in the early 1990s. The most readable pair of books are: *Hard Drive: Bill Gates and the Making of the Microsoft Empire* by James Wallace and Jim Erickson (J. Wiley, 1992); and *Over Drive: Bill Gates and the Race to Control Cyberspace* by James Wallace (J. Wiley, 1997).

CHAPTER 10 ❦ AIRWAVES

Literally dozens of interviews make up the bulk of the material in this chapter. In 1984 I covered the break-up of AT&T, and during that period talked with numerous Bell system and MCI employees, including both Charles Brown of AT&T and Bill McGowan at MCI. In addition, a story on airplane telephony led to an interview with Jack Goeken. The portrait of Craig McCaw and the story of the rise of the cellular phone industry has been drawn from a series of articles in *Forbes* over the years. The creation of this industry, and its high-stakes milieu, was of particular interest to readers for many years. While there are no books on McCaw and the cellular industry, there are a number about the break-up of AT&T and the rise of MCI. The best book about MCI is *On The Line* by Larry Kahaner (Warner Books, 1986) which recounts the history of the company through the AT&T divestiture, and presents a vivid picture of the personalities involved. On the other hand, there are many books on AT&T and its break-up. None of them seem to be able to dig beneath the surface of the voluminous legal record to capture a sense of what the giant company meant to the American cultural and social landscape both before, and after, the break-up. There were numerous articles on telecommunication in *Forbes* over the years, and most of the economic data presented in the chapter comes from the pages of the magazine. Another source that proved particularly helpful for statistics is *After Divestiture: What the AT&T Settlement Means for Business and Residential Telephone Service* by Samuel Simon (Knowledge Industry Publications, 1985).

CHAPTER 11 ❧ WEBS
This chapter is primarily comprised of material from interviews with principals. People interviewed include: Bob Taylor, Larry Roberts, Butler Lampson, Chuck Thacker, Bob Metcalfe, Don Valentine, Steve Case, Ray Noorda, and countless employees of both Netscape and Microsoft. The only book specifically about Xerox is *Fumbling the Future: How Xerox Invented, Then Ignored, the First Personal Computer* by Douglas Smith and Robert Alexander (W. Morrow, 1988). For technical background on the development of the Alto workstations, the aforementioned *A History of Personal Workstations*, a compilation edited by Adele Goldberg (ACM Press, 1988) remains the best single reference source. In recent years a number of books have appeared that purport to tell the story of the Internet. Most are flawed by selective memory on the part of participants. The best single source for determining what really happened is a book of interviews with key players called *The Soul of the Internet: Net Gods, Netizens and the Wiring of the World* by Neil Randall (International Thomson Computer Press, 1997). Another book worth reading is *Where Wizards Stay Up Late: The Origins of the Internet* by Katie Hafner and Matthew Lyon (Simon & Schuster, 1996).

ACKNOWLEDGMENTS

Entrepreneurs and inventors are equally necessary to create high technology businesses—but there are many more inventors than great entrepreneurs. This book was my attempt to write a business history of the digital age that was focused more on the business heroes, and less on the technology gurus, although the two are utterly intertwined in every business covered.

From the start to the finish, much of the book was the work of John Wiley & Sons' team of editors, principally Renana Meyers, Henning Gutmann, and Jeanne Glasser. They provided invaluable insight, feedback, and direction. Katie Calhoun of Forbes Inc. pushed the book, then cajoled, shoved, shaped, and sweated the project as it was evolving. Her partner on the business side at Forbes was Barbara Strauch, who took care of contracts and negotiations, while my agent Ginger Barber held my hand and kept me at work. Research help, from the Forbes archives and many other sources, was provided by Anne Mintz and her staff of skilled librarians at the Forbes Library. The Forbes statistics department under Steve Kichen converted dollar figures into 1998 numbers. David Churbuck of the *Forbes Digital Tool* web site put up with my absence during several crucial stretches of time; so did Bill Baldwin and Eric Nee at *Forbes* magazine. As the draft was completed Michael Noer, a longtime *Forbes* editor, did an extensive edit that made many of the hidden themes explicit, identified missing and critical stories that needed to be woven into the tale, and simplified and streamlined the business threads of the book.

Finally, my wife Janey, and our three children—Alyssa, Fiona, and Alistair—put up with me while I wrote it. To them all, I owe a deep debt of gratitude.

INDEX